EXPLORING Business
FOR THE 21ST CENTURY

Authors

Michael E. Liepner

Jane G.N. Magnan

Alan Wasserman

McGraw-Hill Ryerson

Toronto   Montreal   Burr Ridge, IL   Dubuque, IA   Madison, WI   New York
San Francisco   St. Louis   Bangkok   Bogotá   Caracas   Kuala Lumpur
Lisbon   London   Madrid   Mexico City   Milan   New Delhi
Santiago   Seoul   Singapore   Sydney   Taipei

COPIES OF THIS BOOK
MAY BE OBTAINED BY
CONTACTING:

McGraw-Hill Ryerson Ltd.

E-MAIL:
orders@mcgrawhill.ca

TOLL FREE FAX:
1-800-463-5885

TOLL FREE CALL:
1-800-565-5758

OR BY MAILING YOUR
ORDER TO:
McGraw-Hill Ryerson Order
Department,
300 Water Street, Whitby,
Ontario, L1N 9B6.

Please quote the ISBN and
title when placing your
order.

McGraw-Hill
Ryerson Limited
A Subsidiary of The McGraw·Hill Companies

Exploring Business for the 21st Century

ISBN 0-07-089158-3

http://www.mcgrawhill.ca

1 2 3 4 5 6 7 8 9 0 TRI 0 9 8 7 6 5 4 3 2 1

Printed and bound in Canada

Care has been taken to trace ownership of copyright material contained in
this text. The publishers will gladly take any information that will enable
them to rectify any reference or credit in subsequent printings.

National Library of Canadian Cataloguing in Publication Data

Liepner, Michael, 1938-
    Exploring business for the 21st century
2nd ed.
Previously published under title: Exploring business: a global perspective.
Includes index.
ISBN 0-07-089158-3

    1. Canada—Economic conditions—1991- . 2. Business.
I. Magnan, Jane G. N. II. Title. III. Title: Exploring business,
a global perspective.

HF5351.L54 2001   330   C2001-900822-8

Publisher: Patty Pappas
Project Manager: Maryrose O'Neill
Developmental Editors: Krysia Lear, Denyse O'Leary, Judith O'Leary,
Jessica Pegis, Rochelle Redford
Supervising Editors: Cathy Deak, Crystal Shortt
Copy Editors: Ann Keys, Krysia Lear
Permissions Editor: Maria DeCambra, Linda Tanaka
Production Co-ordinator: Sue Penny
Editorial Assistants: Joanne Murray, Erin Parton
Interior Design: Dave Murphy/ArtPlus Ltd.
Page Layout: ArtPlus Ltd.
Illustrations: Donna Guilfoyle, Jeremy Kessler/ArtPlus Ltd., Steve Schulman
Researcher: Yvonne Reindel

Reviewers

Lennox Borel
OISE, University of Toronto

Brian Childs
York District School Board

Adrian Della Mora
Toronto Catholic District School
Board

David De Santis
Halton Catholic District School
Board

Deborah Evans
Lakehead District Public School
Board

Laura Gini-Newman
Toronto Catholic District School
Board

Jeff Goodall
Grand Erie District School Board

Ruth Hernder
Niagara District School Board

Michael Kake
Peel District School Board

Judi Kleffman
Limestone District School Board

Sandra A. Motta
Toronto Catholic District School
Board

Zenobia Omarali
Toronto District School Board

Betty Tamas
Halton District School Board

Table of Contents

A Tour of Your Textbook

Welcome to *Exploring Business for the 21st Century*. This textbook provides you with a firm foundation in the world of business, helping you to understand the concepts, functions, and skills that you will need to meet the challenges of business in the 21st century. You will investigate the role and impact of business, the way business is conducted, and the effect of entrepreneurship and globalization on business. You will also have the opportunity to learn about how to handle your own personal finances.

← Cover

The cover illustrates the central idea of this text and the course—that business is an exciting and integral part of your world today and tomorrow.

Unit Opener →

- **Meeting the Expectations:** The overall expectations indicate the goals of the unit. They are tied directly to the curriculum and outline the content of the chapters to follow.
- **Mini Table of Contents:** The titles of the chapters in the unit are listed here and provide you with the large picture of the unit.
- **Photos and figures** from the unit highlight the focus of the chapters in the unit in a visual way.
- An **Overview** helps to put the entire unit into perspective within the larger course.

← Chapter Opener

- **Specific Expectations** clearly indicate the goals of the chapter.
- The **Key Terms** are shown in the chapter in bold and defined in the text where they appear, and in the glossary at the end of the book.
- The **introductory paragraph** invites you into the subjects of the chapter and clearly indicates what you will be studying in the chapter.

A Tour of Your Textbook

Designed and written to make the world of business understandable
and exciting for today's young people.

Each chapter opens with a **Business Profile** feature that will help you focus on the topics to be covered in the chapter and will present you with a model of best business practices.

Student Book Features:

All the major features in *Exploring Business for the 21st Century* will help you understand the main curriculum objectives of the chapters. These features are integrated into the subject matter and focus of the chapters, and will include activities to help you use your understanding in practical ways.

Issues Affecting Business deal with technology, ethics and social responsibility, or environmental concerns. This feature will also help you extend and amplify the major expectations on which each chapter focuses.

Connecting Business with . . . will offer you examples of business as it connects with the art, sports, home, crafts, your community, cartoon, invention, demographics, ecotourism and more. You will see business situations that reflect the concepts in the expectations for the chapter.

A Tour of Your Textbook

Career Connects will offer some ideas on how the business topics in the chapter may connect with your future careers in business.

Web Connects in the margin of chapters will offer brief notes on Internet links to Web sites that are connected to the topic of the chapter section. At the McGraw-Hill Ryerson site, you'll get some further direction on what to look for and how to use the resources of the largest library on earth.

Skills Appendix margin references will direct you to the Skill Helpers section at the back of the book. You'll have guidelines and checklists to help you solve problems, make decisions, analyse media, give an oral presentation, write a report, build a persuasive argument, and more.

Check Your Understanding activities will offer you a range of activities broken down into the categories of the Ontario Achievement Chart—knowledge/understanding, thinking/inquiry, communication, and application activities after the major sections of each chapter.

Biz Bites appear as margin notes throughout the book—interesting facts, statistics, and quotations that give you something to think about as you go through the chapter.

A Tour of Your Textbook

Figures and visuals include photographs, diagrams, charts, line drawings, text tables, screen catches, and comic strips and political cartoons, all of which have captions to help you integrate the visuals with the text contents.

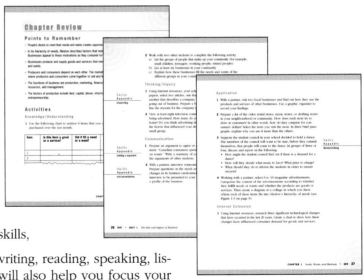

Chapter Review

Points to Remember will help you recall the main concepts and subjects dealt with in the chapter you have just finished.

End of Chapter activities are designed to reinforce your skills and knowledge.

Knowledge/Understanding activities help you focus on your knowledge of facts, terms, principles, and concepts covered in the chapter.

Thinking/Inquiry activities will ask you to draw on your critical and creative thinking skills,

Communication activities will draw on your writing, reading, speaking, listening, viewing, and representing skills. They will also help you focus your attention and your communication on your purpose and your audience.

Application activities will help you draw your knowledge together as you apply the understanding of concepts and skills from the chapter in activities that will help you connect and use technology to make connections between your world and the world of business.

The Role and Impact of Business

Overall Expectations

By the end of this unit, you will

- demonstrate an understanding of how businesses respond to needs, wants, and demand

- compare types of businesses

- evaluate the impact of business on your community

Did you know that business could not survive without you?

In this unit, you will examine the relationship of business to your own life, and the impact of business on your community.

In Chapter 1, you will learn about your own needs and wants, and about the way that businesses promote the right products and services to consumers just like you. You will learn how business works – what business does and how it runs, how it finds customers, and how it creates products or services.

Next, you will examine the types of businesses people can own. There are lots of ways to be "in business," depending on your personality, financial resources, the time you have to run a business, and your willingness to assume risk. Chapter 2 outlines some of the pros and cons of the main types of business ownership. In this chapter, you will also examine emerging business opportunities that are being shaped by forces such as technology.

Business affects not just you, but your whole community. In Chapter 3, you will examine how business shapes many aspects of your community life. The types of jobs being offered in your community and the number of people who are employed will have a dramatic impact on your community's quality of life. Business also creates lots of social and environmental issues for you and your neighbours. This chapter examines some of these issues.

Business is a vital part of your life. After examining this unit, you will understand why.

1 Needs, Wants, and Business

Specific Expectations

After studying this chapter, you will be able to

- **describe the concept of demand and the conditions that give rise to demand**

- **explain how needs, wants, and demand create opportunities for business**

- **compare the ways in which different companies address similar consumer needs and wants**

What role does business play in your life? You certainly need and want the goods and services that business offers. And businesses need you to buy what they produce and offer. Business and consumers depend on each other. But what is business and how does it work? What factors does a business person have to consider to be successful? How do businesses find markets where they can sell their products and services? How do they convince consumers to buy their products? In this chapter, you will examine how business works and how consumers' needs and wants create opportunities for business. You will also be introduced to the functions of business.

Business and Simone

Simone's clock radio goes off for the third time at 7:30 on a Monday morning. Now she has to get up. She looks outside and sees that it has snowed overnight. After she showers, Simone dresses warmly, thankful that she's got those great new boots and warm sweater. Then she goes down to the kitchen and has breakfast. Nothing fancy, just the usual: orange juice, a banana, her favourite cereal, and milk, lots of fresh cold milk. Next she checks her backpack for books, computer disk, her English report, and lunch.

Simone walks to the corner to wait for the school bus which will probably be late—yet again—because of the snow. As she walks, she thinks about the busy day ahead: she has to hand in an English report (it's a good thing that her Mom bought a new printer cartridge), work on an Internet research project with her business team, and get to a dentist appointment after school.

Simone reminds herself that when she gets back home, she has to shovel Mrs. Ruffino's walk and driveway. Mrs. Ruffino is alone now and she is 82 years old. Many of Simone's neighbours are older people who were very enthusiastic when Simone and her friend, Amy, started a small lawn-mowing business during the summer. Their business grew when a few of the neighbours asked Simone and Amy to keep their walks and driveways shovelled during the winter.

How does Simone's story relate to business? Let's take a closer look!

Figure 1-1 Business supplies many of your needs and wants. Think about how you interact with business every day. How is business affecting your life right now?

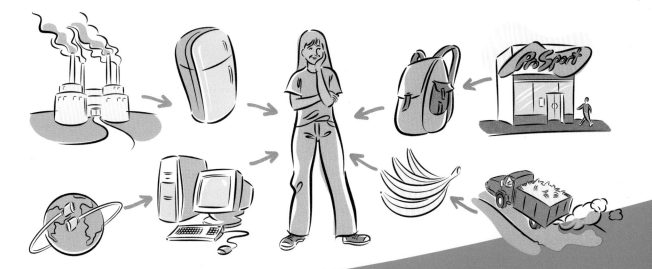

Needs and Wants

As Simone got ready for school, she was motivated to satisfy a number of needs and wants. **Needs** are the things you must have in order to stay alive: warmth in winter, clean water and air, food, shelter, and medical care. **Wants** are the extras; you don't need them to survive but they make life more pleasant. Your wants might include your favourite brand of cereal, the latest videos, lunch out with friends, a new soccer ball or concert tickets. People's wants are often shaped by their stage in life, their culture, and their personality. For example, Simone's new sweater will not only keep her warm, but it is also a popular brand. That's why she wanted that particular sweater.

What does all of this have to do with business? Businesses exist to earn money for themselves by providing for your needs and wants. As a consumer, you play a critical role in the business environment. A **consumer** is a person or business that buys and uses food, clothing, or anything grown, made, or provided by producers. Simone was able to satisfy most of her needs and wants because of businesses.

- The heat for her family's townhouse came from a natural gas company that supplies fuel for the furnace. The energy that runs the printer and the refrigerator comes from an electricity generating company.

- Simone's new boots came from a store in the local mall, and her favourite sweater from an online catalogue on the Internet.

- The breakfast cereal came from a grocery store, the bananas came by truck from Mexico, and the oranges by train from Florida.

- Simone's milk is kept cold in a refrigerator manufactured by a Canadian appliance company and bought from a Canadian department store.

- The computer printer was made by a manufacturer in Japan, and the printer cartridges came from a company in Quebec.

- Simone's business team at school can research using Web sites because an Internet provider supplies the school with access over phone lines. The Web sites her team visits were created by Web designers, who are likely to be self-employed.

- Even her dentist is in business. He and his sister formed a partnership to provide dental services to Simone's community.

- Simone runs a small home-based business. She and Amy mow lawns in the summer and shovel snow in winter.

Can you find any other links to business in Simone's story? How has business satisfied your needs and wants today?

Community Needs and Wants

Your community also has needs and wants. Someone has to provide transportation so that grocery items get into your local supermarket on time and without spoiling. Garbage and recycling have to be taken care of. Communication tools—on the Internet, television, radio, newspapers and magazines—have to be developed, upgraded, and maintained.

National and international communities also have needs and wants that business fulfills. You can fly from Newfoundland to British Columbia in Canada, or from Canada to anywhere in the world. And you can do this because some businesses manufacture airplanes, others operate the airlines, and still other companies provide the fuel for planes and maintain the airports.

Figure 1-2 This advertisement shows one way that businesses influence your choices as consumers by appealing to your needs and wants. How might this advertisement influence a car buyer to buy a Saturn rather than some other car?

Consumer Needs and Wants

There are as many varieties of needs and wants as there are types of human experience. Almost everything that makes you different from the person next to you on the bus is reflected in your needs and wants. For example, because you attend school, you need a strong backpack to carry books and equipment. And you probably want a backpack that looks great, possibly with a recognizable brand name. On the other hand, the 35-year-old woman sitting next to you on the bus may be concerned about her need for a place to live. If she wants to buy her own home, she will likely be more interested in saving money for a down payment than in more clothes or accessories. Many factors influence consumers' wants and needs—stage of life, interests, tastes, priorities, abilities, family responsibilities, trends, and fads.

Web Connect

www.school.mcgrawhill.ca/resources/
View some advertisements from the past to see which consumer needs and wants marketers focused on. How have times changed? Or have they changed?

Consumer Trends and Fads

Both trends and fads influence consumer needs and wants. A **trend** is a general direction in society that may last for a long time. Trends have a major impact on consumer buying habits and on business. For example, the trend towards women entering the workforce has been growing for a number of years. Because of this trend, consumers have demanded convenience foods, extended shopping and banking hours, more versatile household appliances, and more at-home services. Some businesses have become very successful by responding to these consumer needs and wants.

On the other hand, a **fad** is a craze that people take up quickly and then drop just as quickly. Hula hoops were once a fad, so were pet rocks. When you were young, you may have desperately wanted Pokémon stickers or the latest brand of action figures. Consumers don't have a long-term commitment to fads, so they can be very risky for business to get involved in.

Businesses usually prefer to invest in trends rather than fads. The trend is the safer and more predictable investment. It is more likely to indicate new ways for business to successfully satisfy consumer needs and wants.

Biz.Bites

It's not always easy to distinguish a trend from a fad. In the 1920s, David Sarnoff, who became the head of RCA, tried to convince people that the radio was a new technology that consumers would want. He was told, "The wireless music box has no imaginable commercial value. Who would pay for a message sent to nobody in particular?"

Abraham Maslow and Personal Motivation

Abraham Maslow, a psychologist who studied human behaviour, suggested a theory of human motivation which many people believe is valid. Maslow explored the different causes for human actions. He used the word "needs" for these motivations, even those that seem like wants.

Maslow said that humans are motivated to satisfy their needs according to a hierarchy. A hierarchy shows the ranking of higher and lower orders in a system. Maslow used his hierarchy to illustrate how people are motivated to satisfy their most basic physical and safety needs first. Once those needs are filled, Maslow said, people will be motivated by their higher needs for love, esteem, and, finally, self-actualization. Late in his life, Maslow said that the self-actualization motivation included the need to know and explore, the need to find beauty, the need to reach your own potential, and to help other people develop theirs.

But people who have no food or who are in danger during a war are not likely to be very concerned about their esteem or self-actualization needs. Once they eat reasonably well and feel safe, people become interested in satisfying their higher needs. They have the mental, emotional, and physical strength to do so.

Maslow's theory has been very useful to business people, especially advertisers and marketers. Think about advertisements you've seen during the last few days. How many of these appeal to your motivation to have love, acceptance, and esteem?

5 **Self-actualization Needs**
The need to fulfil ourselves

4 **Esteem Needs**
The need to be respected by others

3 **Social Needs**
The need to feel that we are accepted by others

2 **Safety Needs**
The need to be protected from physical danger

1 **Physical Needs**
The basic needs for survival

Figure 1-3 People first need to have water, food, clothing, shelter and safety. Then they can think about filling their social, esteem and self-actualization needs.

Competing for Customers

Focus on what motivates you, as a consumer, to buy certain goods and services rather than others. Why do you choose what you do? What are you really looking for when you buy one brand of blue jeans rather than another? Why is there a greater demand for some brands or products than for others?

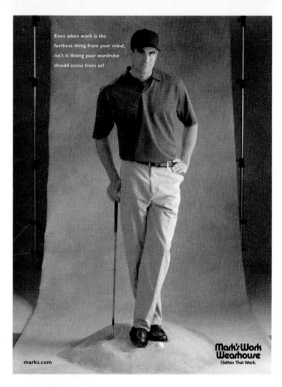

Businesses compete for your consumer dollars. Each business is trying to satisfy the needs and wants of the consumers who buy a particular type of product. Each manufacturer of blue jeans wants you to buy its brand. Each seller of blue jeans wants you to buy the popular brand at its store. Businesses may present their brand as being the best quality or as having the best price. But whether they are selling a chocolate bar or a cellular phone, businesses often advertise their products as filling your social, esteem, or self-actualization needs.

Take the case of cellular phones. The three or four major providers are competing for the group of people who might buy and use cellular phones. The providers decided that there are enough people who will buy this product to make it worth competing for these consumer dollars. The companies provide similar services, but they have to differentiate their product to consumers. One company might compete by offering a better price, another by offering a new design with slightly different features from the others, and another by presenting their product as satisfying your social or esteem needs.

Figure 1-4 Which of Maslow's needs is this advertisement using to sell products? Which group of consumers does the ad target? Why do you think the advertisers chose this focus to motivate consumers to buy their products?

Check Your Understanding

Knowledge/Understanding

1 Work with a partner to list as many items as you can recall buying over the last week. Give yourselves five minutes. Then write down, for each item, whether it satisfied a need or a want. If some items satisfied both, note that too.

2 Using Figure 1-1 (on page 5) as a model, create a mind map showing how local businesses respond to your needs and wants in a typical day.

Thinking/Inquiry

3 Write a list of needs and wants that create opportunities for business. Explain how businesses in your community satisfy three of those needs and wants.

Then list needs and wants that could create new business opportunities in your community.

Communication

4 Create a 30-second radio commercial in which you use an appeal to social and esteem needs to sell your new brand of sports clothes.

Application

5 Look again at Figure 1-2 (on page 7) and then at Figure 1-3 (on page 9). How have the creators of the Saturn advertisement used Maslow's theory of human motivation to compete against other car manufacturers? Explain whether you think this is an effective use of Maslow's principles.

Skills
Appendix
analysing media

What is Business?

What is **business**? The short answer is that business is the production and sale of goods or services to consumers. A business can be as small as the vendor selling jewellery on the corner of a busy intersection or as large as Bombardier, or Bell Canada, or the CBC (Canadian Broadcasting Corporation).

Business is a major and influential part of Canadian society. As you saw in Simone's story, everyone is involved in the business world to some extent. We all make, buy, sell, or exchange goods and services. We need and want what business provides. Usually, the relationship between business and the consumer works more or less to the satisfaction of both parties.

The business world has always revolved around two interest groups: producers and consumers. **Producers** make goods or provide services, and consumers buy and use them. Any item or product that you can purchase, possess, and use is a **good**. The binder for your school notes, the computer on which you prepare your schoolwork, the roll of steel used to make your family's car, the video you rented last weekend, and the banana you ate for breakfast are all goods. **Services**, on the other hand, are not physical objects. They are acts—helpful acts—performed in exchange for pay. A haircut, a shoe repair, and a consultation with your dentist are examples of services. Some businesses provide both goods and services. A computer store that sells computers and repairs them provides a good (the computer) and a service (the repair).

Biz.Bites

In the 1960s, consumer goods and services were very different from those available today. There were no computers, no Internet, no recyclable pop cans. Telephones were attached to the wall, not carried around. And you couldn't get a video game. They hadn't been invented yet.

Earlier in this chapter you read about the business decisions that Simone and her family make every day. They decide which goods and services will satisfy their needs and wants.

Professional buyers also make decisions about needs and wants. The difference is that they make decisions about which goods and services will satisfy the needs and wants of their business, especially the customers.

Almost everything you buy has been chosen by a professional buyer. For example, sporting goods buyers choose the equipment for sporting goods stores or departments. They select the brands of hockey skates and running shoes that will sell best in the store.

As well as knowing what customers want, buyers must know manufacturers' and suppliers' strengths and weaknesses. One company may make good summer T-shirts but make poor quality sweaters for winter.

What kind of skills do professional buyers need to have? If you were a professional buyer, what would your tasks be? What skills would you need in order to be successful in your career?

- To find out what customers wanted, you would have to research current trends and look at sales reports. You would need to know which products your customers want. This would require good investigative and analytical skills.

- You would need to be able to calculate how much you could pay the manufacturer and how much you could charge your customers. Your store's profit is based on the difference between your costs and the store's revenue. So, you would need good math skills.

- You would need to be able to make decisions quickly—sometimes while talking with your supplier.

- You would also need to be able to negotiate the best price from your supplier. For that you'd need to have strong oral communication skills.

- Being flexible will help you make adjustments in your thinking. While you want the best possible price, you'd also have to be able to understand your supplier's point of view about the cost of products or service.

- You'd need to be able to weigh the costs and benefits of each buying decision. You'd need to be able to think your choices through carefully before making any decision.

ACTIVITIES

1 List the skills that would help you succeed as a professional buyer. Suggest two more skills that were not mentioned in this feature.

2 With a partner, role play a negotiation for buying a supply of basketballs for your sporting goods store. One of you plays the professional buyer and the other plays the supplier. Work to avoid conflict as each of you tries to get the best deal for your business. Remember each of you needs the other. A supplier without a buyer is as bad off as a buyer without a supplier.

For Better or for Worse

© UPS Reprinted by Permission

Figure 1-5 What advantages does a business gain by offering its customers more than one good or service?

Interdependence

Interdependence in a business setting means that consumers and producers depend on each other. Consumers need producers to manufacture and supply goods and services. Producers need consumers to buy the goods and services they manufacture and offer.

To do well, businesses must constantly stay in touch with consumers, monitoring their needs, wants, and demands. Paying attention to consumers can mean the difference between success and failure. In the 1970s, the North American automobile industry learned this lesson the hard way. It did not change the size or fuel efficiency of its cars at a time when oil prices rose steeply. So consumers bought smaller and cheaper-to-run foreign cars, which caused serious problems for the North American automobile industry.

On the other hand, a week after Loblaws introduced its Green line of products in 1989, the company had sold $5 million worth of phosphate-free laundry detergents, biodegradable diapers, bathroom tissue made from recycled paper, and unbleached coffee filters. Loblaws had successfully responded to consumers' demand for environmentally friendly products.

Many businesses also depend on each other. For example, a jeans manufacturer makes clothes but must buy, or consume, the materials that go into making the clothes: denim, zippers, and thread. The manufacturer also needs to buy the equipment to run its factory and offices: sewing machines, telephones, photocopiers, and desks. Most businesses are both producers and consumers.

Biz.Bites

During 2000, Canadians spent more of their disposable incomes on goods and services than they had in 1999. The following list shows the percentage increase in consumer spending for each province.

Province	Increase (%)
NF	5.1%
PEI	6.4%
NS	5.4%
NB	5.0%
QC	4.9%
ON	6.3%
MB	4.6%
SK	5.1%
AB	7.5%
BC	5.3%
YT	5.3%
NT	6.1%
NU	5.3%

Statistics Canada 010409

Producers and Consumers

The producers of the goods that satisfy our needs and wants are divided into two groups, manufacturers and suppliers. A **manufacturer** is the company or business that produces the goods. A supplier provides the consumer with the good or service. For example, a furniture manufacturer produces couches, and a furniture store supplies them to consumers.

Goods that consumers purchase directly to satisfy their needs and wants are called *consumer goods*. The consumer who purchases a good for his or her personal use is called an *end* or *ultimate consumer*. Goods that businesses purchase from producers are called *business-to-business goods*, and the consumer, which in this case is a business, is called a *business-to-business consumer*.

If you bought a loaf of bread to eat, you would be the ultimate consumer of that bread. However, if a restaurant bought bread from the same bakery to make sandwiches to sell to its customers, the restaurant would be a business-to-business consumer. The customer who buys the sandwich from the restaurant is the ultimate consumer.

Figure 1-6 Grocery stores provide a market where many businesses compete to fill consumers' needs and wants.

What is a Market?

A **market** exists wherever buyers (consumers) and sellers (producers) come together to do business, the buyers with money to exchange for the goods or services offered by the sellers. All the places you shop for goods and services are markets. Whether you take a trip to buy clothes or order a book over the Internet, you are visiting a market. Markets exist for any good or service—clothing, banking services, Internet connections, NHL hockey tickets, automobiles, housing—that has a price that consumers are willing to pay.

Markets can be divided further into two major groups: the consumer market and the business-to-business, or industrial, market. The *consumer market* is made up of all the individuals or households who want goods and services for personal consumption or use. The *business-to-business market* is made up of all the individuals and organizations that produce, sell, rent, or supply goods and services to other businesses. The cash registers in your grocery store, delivery vans, the farm tractors are all sold in the business-to-business market.

Your local grocery store is one consumer market where people who want to buy food can connect with a business that wants to sell it. The grocery store may be owned by one person or be part of a large chain of stores owned by a corporation.

Grocery stores let growers and manufacturers get their products to you, something that would be difficult for them to do on their own. How would the Fijian pineapple grower or the Moroccan clementine orange grower ever be able to get his or her fruit to you? The grocery store lets the suppliers offer goods for sale. You, as the buyer, have the benefit of seeing a wide variety of foods and grocery products so you can compare them and decide what you want.

Web Connect

www.school.mcgrawhill.ca/resources/
Visit two of the marketing boards that help Canadian farmers sell their products. How do these organizations focus on meeting consumer needs and wants? How do they help their members sell their products?

Demand

Demand represents the consumer side of the market. Consumer demand for a product is directly related to price. Generally speaking, consumers are willing to buy more of a good or service when the price is low. When compact disc players were first introduced into the market, they were fairly expensive and consumer demand was limited. However, as the price decreased, consumer demand increased.

As you saw in the example of Loblaws' Green line products, consumers' demands go beyond price considerations. Today many consumers insist that companies be socially responsible. These consumers do not want to buy products from companies whose manufacturing processes hurt animals or pollute the air, water, or land. Some businesses realize the business opportunities in such demands. For example, The Body Shop has a number of programs and products that support its claim that its business is ecologically sustainable.

Figure 1-7 Many consumers who buy from The Body Shop agree with the company's stand against testing cosmetics on animals.

Consumer demand for a good or service is affected by several other factors. Supply and demand, and the factors that affect them, will be discussed further in Chapter 5.

Check Your Understanding

Knowledge/Understanding

1 List two examples of businesses in your community for each of the following categories: (a) only provide services, (b) provide goods and services, and (c) are business-to-business consumers. Explain how your choices fit their categories.

2 Explain in your own words how producers and consumers are interdependent.

Thinking/Inquiry

3 Describe a situation where the following goods could be classified as both a consumer and a business-to-business good: tomatoes, wood, flour, paper, cleaning supplies, and desks.

Communication

4 Use a graphic organizer to show your response to the following questions:
- Which of the goods and services that you have used in the last three days were produced in your local community?
- Which of these goods and services came from outside your community?
- Could any of those that come from outside be made locally?
- What would be the effect of this change on your community?

Application

5 Consider one problem in your community that might create a business opportunity. Why do you think no one has started a business to solve that problem?

Skills
Appendix

problem solving

Connecting Business with *The Market*

Women Drive the Automobile Market

The experience of buying a new car can be an exciting one. However, the huge selection of makes, models and features can make buying a car difficult and confusing. The Ford Motor Company did research that told them that women are especially anxious and concerned about the car-buying process.

Bobbie Gaunt, who was then the general sales manager at Lincoln-Mercury, was the highest-ranking woman in Ford's marketing and sales operations worldwide. Today she is president and chief executive officer of Ford Motor Company of Canada. She believes in research and in listening to what consumers say. "My work in research and in marketing and sales has been, and is, dedicated to finding out what our customers want in their preferred product and throughout their ownership experience, and then working to make it happen!"

Gaunt knows that women influence 80 to 85 percent of all car-buying decisions. Market research also shows that more women are buying cars and spending more time in them than men do.

Women's priorities in looking for a car include affordability, reliability, performance, security, versatility, quality, and safety. If they have children at home, they are interested in built-in safety features and storage. Women tend to carefully research new cars—they are highly informed consumers.

Figure 1-8 Women's influence in the car market is a trend that manufacturers watch carefully.

They put more emphasis than men on opinions from colleagues, family, and friends.

Many changes are taking place at Lincoln-Mercury to meet its goal of helping women feel more comfortable with the buying process. "It makes a lot of sense to let our customers lead the way," says Gaunt. She believes that the "people, who actually drive the cars [and] often spend hours and hours on the road each day, know what they want. We are working on designs that answer their needs."

Sources: Adapted from Peebles, Tanya, "A Woman's Attitude: How It Affects an Automaker," *Contemporary Women's Issues Collection*, Feb. 1, 1995, vol. 7, pp. 14-16.

ACTIVITIES

1 Explain how the marketing of Ford automobiles will help women fulfill their wants.
2 Discuss how the changes that Ford is proposing might affect the consumer demand for their automobiles.
3 Create a concept web to show how Ford's marketing activities could create new business opportunities for the company.

Functions of Business

Although we come into contact with business regularly, we often do not think about what goes on behind the scenes. Consider Simone and Amy, whom you met in the Business Profile that opens this chapter. They are thinking about expanding their lawn-cutting service. What should they consider?

First, they will have to be aware of the competition, and the prices that others in the same business charge. Then, they will have to decide how to promote their business. Otherwise, how will anybody know it exists? Simone and Amy might have to obtain financing in order to buy the equipment that they need. This would involve a certain amount of risk because they would have to pay back the money. They will also have to decide which tasks each of them will perform and how much money they would like to make. In addition, many factors will be beyond their control. For example, what will Simone and Amy do if it is a rainy summer?

These are some of the many questions that a person operating a business needs to consider and answer. These considerations are functions of business and can be organized into five categories: production, marketing, finance, human resources, and management.

Production

One basic function of any business is producing goods and services. **Production** is the process of converting a business's resources into goods and services. In the case of the lawn-cutting business, Simone and Amy take their labour, tools, equipment, and money, and convert them into the serv-

Figure 1-9 Automation in automobile manufacturing plants has made production faster and cheaper for business owners but has replaced many employees.

ice of lawn care. Naturally, the factors involved in this process vary with different types of businesses. A bicycle manufacturer requires larger amounts of money, more specialized machinery and equipment, and much larger premises than a dry-cleaning service.

Factors of Production

A closer look at the production process reveals that it involves a number of factors, or elements. These factors are commonly called the **factors of production** and include land, capital, labour, information, and entrepreneurship. When **land** is defined as a factor of production, it refers to the natural resources used to produce goods and services (for example, wood for a furniture maker or aluminum for a bicycle-manufacturer).

Capital is the money used to start a business and to keep it running. Capital includes the value of machinery and equipment required to produce goods and services.

Labour is the human element and includes all mental and physical work that people put into producing goods and services. In the last century, technology allowed businesses to change the ways that labour was used. For example, the Ford Motor Company invented the assembly line that helped it produce more cars. This allowed Ford to sell its cars at a lower price, which made it possible for the workers to afford the cars they helped produce, which created greater demand.

Another factor is **information**. Using computers and other technologies, businesses track information about their operations, customers, and competitors. Managing information is especially important for the companies plants and offices around the world.

The final factor is **entrepreneurship**, the activity of people who bring together all the factors of production to start a business. Entrepreneurship includes having the skills and determination to start and operate a business and to accept the calculated risks involved. Entrepreneurship is discussed more fully in Unit 4.

Figure 1-10 These five factors are part of the production process.

Land   Capital   Labour   Information   Entrepreneurship

The entrepreneur must stay in tune with the changing needs, wants, and demands of the consumer in order to identify possible business opportunities. For example, the demands of overworked consumers and of an aging population gave one company, Grocerygateway.com, the idea to offer online grocery shopping and home delivery (see Figure 1-11).

Can you count the grocery bags you've carried in life?

(Probably not. But you can count on us to make sure you never have to carry another.)

grocerygal

Now delivering 7 days a week

grocerygateway.com
You grocery shop online.
We deliver. Now this is progress.

grocerygateway.com

Figure 1-11 How does this advertisement appeal to consumers' needs and wants? Who would be most likely to use Gateway's services?

Marketing

When we hear the term marketing, we tend to think of advertising, but marketing includes much more. **Marketing** can be defined as all the business activities used to plan, price, promote, and distribute goods or services to satisfy consumer needs and wants. Marketing may involve making contact with consumers to find out what they want. This process is referred to as market research. For example, through market research, Simone and Amy may discover that their customers want to have their lawns watered while they are on holiday.

Market research helps businesses reduce the risk of providing goods or services that the consumer does not want. The marketing function of a business can be very costly and requires careful planning to get the best results. Marketing is discussed in detail in Chapter 7.

Finance

All businesses need to keep accurate records of the money coming in and going out. They need to know who owes money to the business, to whom it owes money, how money is spent, and whether there is enough money in the bank to pay the bills. Managing money is referred to as **finance**. Large businesses usually have accounting departments, which are responsible for managing the business funds. In small businesses, the owner usually takes on the financial responsibilities. Regardless of size, all businesses must keep accurate financial records in order to know whether they are making a profit. Business accounting and finance are discussed in detail in Chapter 8 and personal finance in Unit 3.

Human Resources

Human resources are the people aspect of a business—in other words, the owners, managers, and employees. Businesses depend on their employees and do better if they understand how to hire and keep good employees. Large businesses provide a wide range of benefits as well as pay, in order to attract and keep enthusiastic and committed employees. For example, many businesses provide dental plans, life insurance, and pension plans for employees. Some businesses offer free trips to salespeople if they meet certain sales quotas. Other businesses provide memberships in recreational clubs to keep morale high. A small business may have to depend on good relationships to keep employees.

A human resources department is usually responsible for
- determining the requirements of each type of job in the company
- recruiting and interviewing new employees
- selecting the right person for the job
- training and developing employees
- assessing their performance
- deciding on employee wages and benefits

Human resources are discussed in detail in Chapter 6.

Management

Management can be defined as the planning, organizing, and controlling of all business activities. Managers have to set short- and long-term goals and organize the employees and other resources so the goals of the business can be achieved. Managers must be able to communicate clearly and effectively because their job requires a great deal of interaction with many types of people. Managers have to possess

Web Connect

www.school.mcgrawhill.ca/resources/
Visit a virtual factory to find out how one business uses the factors of production to manufacture its products. Take a walk around the factory, visit it's different departments, and see the production process.

leadership qualities and be able to motivate employees. The effective management of a business can often mean the difference between its success and failure. Management is discussed in detail in Chapter 6.

Check Your Understanding

Knowledge/Understanding

1 List and explain, in your own words, the five functions of business.
2 Select two businesses in your community and compare them in terms of how they use land, capital, labour, technology, and entrepreneurship.

Thinking/Inquiry

3 Write a paragraph explaining how a business could use the factors of production to fill consumers' needs and wants. Why would a wise use of these factors improve a business's chances of success?

Communication

4 Write a brief article explaining three ways that automation has caused changes in the labour needs of one manufacturing business.

Skills
Appendix

working in groups

Application

5 In a small group, discuss how the five functions of business—production, marketing, finance, human resources, and management—would affect the activities of a student painting business.

Once there were two young entrepreneurs who threw the music industry into turmoil. Michael Robertson of MP3.com and Shawn Fanning of Napster were in their teens when they started businesses that allowed consumers to download music—free of charge—from Web sites on the Internet. They saw the demand and figured out how to satisfy it.

The music on CDs has to be converted to a different format to become a computer file. Before Robertson and Fanning invented their conversion programs, downloading music files was long, slow, and usually unsuccessful. Robertson and Fanning used new technologies to speed up file conversion and to allow almost unlimited copying of music files. These two men thought they had simply seized a business opportunity.

But the music didn't actually belong to Napster or to MP3.com, and that's where the trouble started.

The music companies who produced the CDs claimed that MP3.com and Napster were infringing on their copyright. Copyright is the right to make copies of someone else's creative work. The law gives authors, designers, and artists the exclusive right to print, publish, perform, film, or record original literary, artistic, or musical material. Although the music companies were not the artists, they held the copyrights because they had made copyright agreements with the writers and the artists who performed it. This right is important because owners get paid each time someone uses their work.

How had these two innovative companies infringed copyright? MP3.com allowed people to download their own CDs to a locker on its Web site. A copy was then made from MP3.com's database of CDs and deposited into the user's online locker. All that people needed to do to hear their own music was to log onto MP3.com's

Figure 1-12 By seizing a business opportunity and by inventing new technologies Shawn Fanning and Michael Robertson have changed the music industry.

Web site from any Internet-connected device. And many, many people did just that. But, inside the lockers at their Web site, MP3.com also had a database of some 80 000 CDs. That's where the courts found that the company broke the law. Since Universal Music held copyright to the music on the CDs, it claimed that MP3.com had no legal right to have Universal's music on its Web site. The U.S. courts agreed with Universal.

Eventually, MP3.com was ordered by the U.S. courts to pay $53.4 million to Universal Music Group for infringing its music copyrights.

Napster took a different approach. Its software allowed users to quickly find music files on the Internet and download them to their own computer. Many of these files were of copyrighted music. Napster was sued by major record companies for giving millions of people free access to music that it didn't own. Napster argued that it was not breaking copyright because people who used its software were only copying music for personal, noncommercial use, an activity that Napster argued was permitted by the law.

In February 2001, the U.S. courts ordered Napster to stop allowing users to trade copyrighted music files on its Web site. Since then, Napster has fought to stay online, trying to set up deals with music companies to offer its users a subscription service. Meanwhile, MP3.com has managed to set up licensing agreements with Warner Music and BMG, but it is now being sued by another music company.

Other business people have also been affected by Napster and MP3.com's activities. Songwriters and recording artists, who are often independent business people, are worried. What happens to their rights and royalties when their music is distributed online? Music store owners are also worried. What will happen to their retail businesses if more and more consumers get their music online instead of buying it from stores?

While the two young entrepreneurs continue their legal struggles, the music distribution environment has changed. By 2001, an estimated 40 million people downloaded music from Napster

Summers © Tribune Media Services

Figure 1-13 How does this editorial cartoon relate to the issue of business ethics? What stereotypes does it use to get its point across?

and MP3.com. The music industry recognized that the market for online music distribution existed, and they made deals with other online providers who will charge users subscription fees to download music.

ACTIVITIES

1 Summarize the conflict between Napster and MP3.com and the large recording companies. How, and why, did it start? How was it resolved?

2 Why are questions of copyright such a problem when it comes to the Internet? What is it about the medium that throws the whole idea of copyright into doubt?

3 What do you think should have happened to Napster and MP3.com? Prepare an argument for or against free music services. Be sure to have evidence to back up your argument.

4 Work with a partner to research the current state of copyright issues and music online. Create a timeline to demonstrate what has happened regarding these issues since the date when this book was published. (Check McGraw-Hill Ryerson's copyright page in the front of this book for the publication date.)

Chapter Review

Points to Remember

- People's desire to meet their needs and wants creates opportunities for business.

- In his hierarchy of needs, Maslow describes factors that motivate people. Businesses appeal to these motivations as they compete for consumers.

- Businesses produce and supply goods and services that meet people's needs and wants.

- Producers and consumers depend on each other. The market is any place where producers and consumers come together to sell and buy.

- The functions of business are production, marketing, finance, human resources, and management.

- The factors of production include land, capital, labour, information, and entrepreneurship.

Activities

Knowledge/Understanding

1 Use the following chart to analyse 6 items that you or your family purchased over the last month.

Item	Is this item a good or a service?	Did it fill a need or a want?	Was it purchased from a manu- facturer or a supplier?
1.			
2.			

2 Work with two other students to complete the following activity.

a) List the groups of people that make up your community (for example, small children, teenagers, working people, retired people).

b) List at least six businesses in your community

c) Explain how these businesses fill the needs and wants of the different groups in your community.

Thinking/Inquiry

Skills
Appendix
researching

1 Using Internet resources, your school resource centre, and daily newspapers, select two articles, one that describes a successful company and another that describes a company that is having difficulties or is close to going out of business. Prepare a brief summary of each article and outline the reasons for the company's success or failure.

2 View at least eight television commercials. Record the goods or services being advertised. How many do you or your family use or have in your home? Do you think advertising influenced you to buy them? Analyse the factors that influenced your decision and explain your analysis to a small group.

Communication

Skills
Appendix
building an argument

1 Prepare an argument to agree or disagree with the following statement: "Canadian consumers spend most of their money on needs not on wants." Write a summary of your argument and compare it with the arguments of other students.

Skills
Appendix
oral presentations

2 With a partner, interview someone in a business in your community. Prepare questions on the needs and wants the business fills and on the changes in its business environment. Prepare an oral summary of the interview to be presented to your classmates. Open your summary with a profile of the business.

Application

1 With a partner, visit two local businesses and find out how they use the products and services of other businesses. Use a graphic organizer to record your findings.

2 Prepare a list of the video rental stores, music stores, or clothing stores in your neighbourhood or community. How does each store try to draw in customers? In other words, how do they compete for consumers' dollars? Select the store you visit the most. In three brief paragraphs, explain why you use it more than the others.

3 Suppose the student council in your school decided to hold a dance. The members of the council will want to be sure, before they commit themselves, that people will come to the dance. In groups of three or four, discuss and report on the following:

Skills
Appendix

decision-making

   • How might the student council find out if there is a demand for a dance?
   • How will they decide what music to have? What price to charge?
   • What should they do to inform the students in order to ensure success?

4 Working with a partner, select 6 to 10 magazine advertisements. Categorize the content of the advertisements according to whether they fulfill needs or wants and whether the products are goods or services. Then create a diagram or a collage in which you show where each of these items fits into Maslow's hierarchy of needs (see Figure 1-3 on page 9).

Internet Extension

1 Using Internet resources, research three significant technological changes that have occurred in the last 20 years. Create a chart to show how these changes have influenced consumer demand for goods and services.

2 Types of Business

Specific Expectations

After studying this chapter, you will be able to

• **compare the features of sole proprietorships, partnerships, corporations (public, private, and Crown), and co-operatives**

• **explain why a person or group of people may choose to establish one type of business rather than another**

• **identify the types of businesses and business sectors that have experienced the greatest growth in recent years**

Once people decide to go into business, they need to choose a type of business to own. Should it be a sole proprietorship? A partnership? A corporation? A co-operative? Or perhaps a franchise? By examining the advantages and disadvantages of each type, you will understand why different people choose one type and avoid others.

Recent developments in the business environment have caused many businesses to change direction. New technologies have been created. Global business has increased. The number of small businesses, especially in the service sector, has grown. And business people have become more aware of their responsibility to society and to the natural environment.

Clearnet

In 1985, a small Pickering, Ontario, company was helping businesses send messages by two-way radio. Its name was Clearnet. The company sold airtime to businesses that used dispatch radios: taxis, couriers, and emergency service vehicles. Bob Simmonds, who ran the private company, had graduated from the University of Toronto's engineering science program. He came from a family of entrepreneurs. His long-range goal was to create a wireless network that would allow Canadians to use cellular phones to communicate across the country. In 1987, Bob hired George Cope to be president, and Bob became the chairman.

Clearnet developed new technologies to reach its goals. It would use a broadcast bandwidth called radio spectrum, which is the channel over which cellular phones operate. The federal government wanted to encourage innovation in the use of this bandwidth. So, Industry Canada licensed radio spectrum to companies that had enough subscribers to warrant the licenses. The process is similar to that of radio stations getting licenses for their broadcast bandwidth.

Clearnet had enough foresight to license as much radio spectrum as it could, at a time when others weren't paying much attention to it. The company kept developing its technology. Clearnet formed partnerships with other companies—Motorola Canada Ltd. and Nextel Communications—so that it could use their innovations as well as its own.

Then, in 1994, Clearnet announced that it was going to build its own digital wireless network over the next three years. What a challenge! At the time there was almost no market for cellular phones. Clearnet was also going to compete with some very large and powerful companies—Rogers Cantel Mobile Communications Inc. and BCE Mobile Communications Inc.—in developing the new industry of wireless communications. Bob Simmonds and George Cope took the risk

Figure 2-1 Bob Simmonds and George Cope (who are standing at the back of this group) used their imagination and knowledge of technology to build Clearnet into a highly successful Canadian business.

Figure 2-2 Clearnet's engaging marketing campaigns have made sure that Canadians don't forget about the company and the services it offers consumers.

Send and receive wireless email.

TELUS mobility

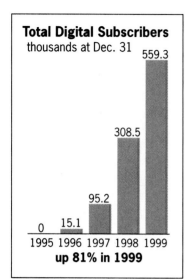

Total Digital Subscribers
thousands at Dec. 31

559.3

308.5

95.2

0   15.1

1995 1996 1997 1998 1999
up 81% in 1999

Figure 2-3 The growth in Clearnet's cellphone subscribers from 1995 to 2000 has been astonishing. What are some of the reasons for this growth?

because they believed that someday Canadians would want to communicate with each other using the convenience of wireless technologies.

The investment in technology and development was larger than the private company could handle, so Clearnet decided to become a public company. In October 1994, it raised $112 million by selling its first stock offering. Clearnet hired more engineers and other employees to develop the new network.

By 1999, the Canadian wireless industry was adding subscribers by the million. Approximately 22.5 percent of the Canadian population used cell phones. Clearnet also offered new products, which expanded the market beyond conventional voice service and moved it into digital technology. New applications allowed customers to use their mobile phones to get access to the Internet. According to George Cope, "the future is the wireless Internet." In January 2000, he said, "In a few years there will be more mobile phones with Web browsers than there will be personal computers."

On August 21, 2000, Clearnet, the small private company that grew into a major public Canadian corporation, announced that it was being sold to Telus Corp. for $6.6 billion. The combined companies made Telus the largest telecommunications company in Canada. And what happened to Bob Simmonds and George Cope? George Cope became the president and CEO of Telus, and Bob Simmonds kept a financial interest in Telus and will no doubt go on to develop new far-sighted technologies for our future.

As you work your way through this chapter on types of business ownership and change, keep Bob Simmonds, George Cope, and Clearnet in mind. How does Clearnet embody the growth and the changes happening in the Canadian business environment? How does it represent the current trends in Canadian business? How did its owners and managers take advantage of those trends?

Types of Business Ownership

Deciding which type of business ownership you want to establish needs serious thought. If you are a sole proprietor, you would own the business. That has it advantages, but it also has some disadvantages. In a partnership, you would share both ownership and responsibility. On the other hand, perhaps you should form a corporation, or join a co-operative, or buy a franchise. Each of these types of businesses has its benefits and its risks, as you will see in Figure 2-4.

Over time, the form of business ownership you use can change, as it did for Clearnet. A small private business may grow to become a large public corporation as it expands its manufacturing plants or service operations. Or a sole proprietor may be the only owner and employee but decide that incorporating is a good choice. Or someone who starts a business as a sole proprietor may decide that he or she needs a partner as the business expands. The partner may bring in money to invest in expanding the business, or may be an expert in a particular skill that is important to the business.

Sole Proprietorship

A **sole proprietorship** is a business owned and operated by one person. The owner is responsible for all operations of the business and assumes all the risks.

More than one million sole proprietorships exist in Canada, which means that this is the most common form of business in the country. Many of the businesses that provide you and your family with services are sole proprietorships—the car repair centre, your favourite restaurant, the accountant your parents use to help them prepare their income tax, and the salon where you get your hair cut.

Advantages of a Sole Proprietorship

Two of the main advantages of being a sole proprietor are that you keep all the profits and can make all the decisions. If you like being your own boss and would take pride in owning your own business, you might want to become a sole proprietor.

As a sole proprietor, you can quickly take a new direction when you see a business opportunity. In a partnership or larger corporation, it may take a long time and many meetings before the business can change course. And, by the time a decision is made, your business opportunity may be lost.

Biz.Bites

The sole proprietors in your community may be
- architects
- artists
- authors
- baby-sitters
- carpenters
- computer specialists
- construction consultants
- digital designers
- ecotourism guides
- engineers
- environmental consultants
- farmers
- gardeners
- industrial designers
- inventors
- photographers
- researchers
- song-writers
- Web designers

Types of Business Ownership

Type of Business Ownership	Some Advantages	Some Disadvantages
Sole proprietorship	• Owner makes all decisions and is his or her own boss. • Owner keeps all the profits. • All financial information can be kept secret. • This type of business is easy to start or close.	• Owner has responsibility for all debts. • Costs and time commitment can be high. • Funding can be difficult to obtain. • Owner is responsible for all aspects of the business. • Owner doesn't have fringe benefits.
Partnership	• Partners co-own the business. • They share responsibilities. • They may have greater financial resources than a sole proprietor. • They share business losses. • They share time commitment.	• Partners have unlimited personal liability for all the other partners. • They may have conflicts. • Profits are shared. • Partnerships are more difficult to close down than sole proprietorships.
Public Corporation	• The owners are shareholders. They have limited liability for the debts of the corporation and share the profits. • Usually shareholders do not operate the company. They hire employees to do so. • Corporations can usually raise funds more easily than sole proprietors or partners. • Corporations usually have a lower tax rate than private owners. • A corporation can continue to exist after the death of its owners.	• Corporations have more complicated structures than sole proprietorships or partnerships. • Employees who are not owners may not be committed to the business. • Corporations must publish annual reports, which could give away important secrets to competitors. • The value of company shares can change depending on changes in the stock market.
Cooperative	• Members own and control the business. • Members share the start-up costs and the running of the business. • They share the financial risk. • Members may pay less for goods and services and get more for those they sell.	• Because each member only has one vote, members may not want to invest money for expansion. • Because of the number of members, making decisions can be difficult. • Members can have conflicts.
Franchise	• Franchisees buy a business with a good reputation. • Franchisors supply training and financial knowledge. • Franchisors usually provide packaging, advertising, and equipment to the franchisee.	• Franchises can be expensive to buy. • Franchisees may have to follow a lot of rules laid down by the franchisors. • If a franchisor's business fails, so will the franchisee's business.

Figure 2-4 As you read the descriptions of these types of business in the following pages, think about which type suits you best. Why would you choose to start up one type of business rather than another?

In a sole proprietorship, all financial information can be kept confidential. Keeping some aspects of the business confidential can be important for success. For example, an Internet Web designer may not want competitors to know how much money she is making on a popular new service she is offering to her clients.

Sole proprietorships are also easy to start up and close down. They can be straightforward to organize and have low start-up costs. The increasing acceptance of businesses that operate from home-based offices has added to the appeal of starting a sole proprietorship.

Disadvantages of a Sole Proprietorship

While the independence of sole proprietorship may be very appealing, it has its downside. As a sole proprietor, you really are on your own. The owner and the business are legally the same thing. So, you are responsible for paying all the debts, or liabilities, of the business. This responsibility is called **unlimited liability**. If your business debts are greater than the profits, you will have to pay the debts from your personal income or the sale of your assets. A sole proprietor who gets into too much debt runs the risk of losing his or her home, car, and savings.

You have to know yourself well before you try a sole proprietorship. You need to be able to face such risks and challenges.

Sole proprietors may also find it difficult to obtain funding to expand, or even to cover everyday expenses. And your everyday costs can be high. You may need to buy equipment and supplies and pay for advertising, rent, and utilities. Borrowing money from the banks may be difficult because they usually require collateral when lending money. *Collateral* is

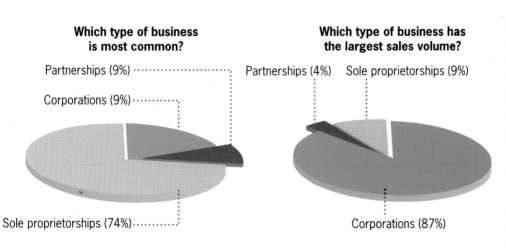

Which type of business is most common?

Partnerships (9%)

Corporations (9%)

Sole proprietorships (74%)

Which type of business has the largest sales volume?

Partnerships (4%)   Sole proprietorships (9%)

Corporations (87%)

Figure 2-5
Sole proprietorships are the most common form of business ownership in Canada (74%), but they only have 9% of the sales volume. Compare these two pie charts. What conclusions could you draw about the relative sales and profits of sole proprietorships and corporations?

security that a borrower offers against a loan, such as property pledged as guarantee for repayment of the loan.

As a sole proprietor you are responsible for all aspects of operating a business: production, sales, marketing, and accounting. However, you might not have the expertise to make the best business decisions in each area. You may produce wonderful Web sites in your Web design business. You may have all the creative and technical skills you need, but may have few accounting skills. If you want your business to succeed, you will either need to hire an accountant or take the time to learn the skills to manage money.

In addition, the time commitment can sometimes be great. Ask the owner of a convenience store how many hours a day he or she works. Many sole proprietors work 12 hours a day, 7 days a week, and rarely take a vacation. In addition, sole proprietors do not have the fringe benefits that employees of large corporations enjoy: insurance, vacation pay, and a set number of hours to work per week.

Figure 2-6 Brian Basset, who creates the Adam@Home comic strip, runs his small business from home. So he knows that solving problems as a sole proprietor sometimes requires very quick thinking.

Adam @ Home

Copyright © 2001 Universal Press Syndicate

Partnership

A **partnership** is a form of business organization in which two or more people own and operate the business together.

Partnerships are more complex to set up than sole proprietorships. Since more than one person is involved, the partnership must be created by either a verbal or written agreement. It is best to have an experienced lawyer draft a written partnership agreement. If there are any disputes in the future, the terms will be upheld in court.

Whenever two or more people form a business, they need to consider—and agree on—many issues, including

- how much time and money each partner will put into the business
- how the profits will be shared
- who will make decisions about different aspects of the business
- who will manage the employees
- how the partnership might be ended

All partners must sign the partnership agreement which includes

- the name and location of the business
- its purpose
- the amount of the partners' investment
- the way that the profits and losses are to be divided
- the duties and responsibilities of each partner
- the procedures for ending the partnership

Figure 2-7 Many professionals—lawyers, accountants, dentists, and doctors—have found it more profitable to form partnerships than to be sole proprietors.

Advantages of a Partnership

As with sole proprietorships, partnerships are relatively inexpensive to set up and may be relatively easy to organize. The start-up costs often involve only lawyers' and government registration fees, which could add up to approximately $1000.

Usually, but not always, all the partners provide the financial resources to start the business, rent an office, buy necessary equipment, hire employees, and pay for marketing. If more financing is needed, partners can often borrow more easily from a bank than sole proprietors can because the partners can combine their personal assets for collateral.

If you have a partner, you can share the responsibilities of running your business. Each partner brings his or her own expertise, knowledge, and skills. You may be better at keeping track of costs and finances, and your partner may be better at communicating with clients. Together, you can provide better management and operation than if each of you ran a sole proprietorship. Sharing responsibilities reduces the risk of business failure. And, if the business is not doing well, you and your partner share the debt according to your partnership agreement. Partners have another advantage over sole proprietors. They can take a vacation or a sick day because their partner can manage alone for awhile.

Disadvantages of a Partnership

Partners who take an active role in operating the business have unlimited liability for the debts of the business. Even if two partners are sharing profits 50-50, each is 100 percent liable for any debts of the business. So, in a partnership, your financial risk is similar to that of a sole proprietorship. Your personal assets—home, car, and personal savings accounts—may have to be used to pay off your business debts.

If the business is successful, you and your partner share the profits of the business according to the terms of your partnership agreement. This is the case even if you feel that you are contributing more than your partner.

Conflicts can arise in partnerships. For example, if you have put up more money to start the business, but your partner spends more hours per week working in the business, you may each start to believe you should get more of the profits than the other person.

Probably conflicts are the most common problems faced by partners. You and your partner may disagree about how much money to spend or how much risk is acceptable. You may also have very different ideas about ethics. Many partnerships are dissolved because partners are unable to resolve differences. And it can be difficult to end a partnership unless you have clearly stated the terms in your partnership agreement.

Web Connect

www.school.mcgrawhill.ca/resources/
How do you start up a sole proprietorship or a partnership? What are the most important factors to consider? And how do you stay on the path towards success? Human Resources Canada offers some useful guidelines.

Corporation

A **corporation** is a legal entity that exists independently of its owners, who are called shareholders. Inco, Bombardier, and Nortel Networks are owned by thousands of people, and each of these huge companies is a separate legal entity. According to Industry Canada, "a corporation has the same rights and obligations under Canadian law as a natural person." A corporation can acquire money and other assets, or it can go into debt, just like a person can. A corporation can even be found guilty of committing a crime.

Corporations may be very complex in nature, as you can see in Figure 2-9. **Shareholders**, the people who buy shares in a company, are all part owners of the company. These shareholders elect the *board of directors*, who direct the overall affairs of the corporation and who hire the *officers*. These officers (for example, the president of the corporation) decide the objectives for the company and hire the *managers*. Managers, in turn, supervise the employees.

Corporations are classified as private corporations, public corporations, Crown corporations, or non-profit corporations.

- A **private corporation** can have up to 50 shareholders. Its shares are not offered to the public. A single person who incorporates may have only one shareholder: him- or herself. Although private corporations are usually small, they do not have to be. Until recently, the Eatons department store chain, which is now owned by Sears Canada, was a private corporation.

- A **public corporation** does not have restrictions on its number of shareholders. Its shares can be sold to the general public. These shares are bought and sold (traded) on stock exchanges, such as the Toronto Stock Exchange and the Vancouver Stock Exchange. (The stock market will be discussed in more detail in Chapter 11.) Canadian public corporations include McGraw-Hill Ryerson Ltd., Inco, and Magna International Inc.

- **Crown corporations** are owned by federal, provincial, or municipal governments. The function of Crown corporations is usually to provide a special service to the public. Some examples of Crown corporations are the Bank of Canada, the Royal Canadian Mint, Canada Post, and the Canadian Broadcasting Corp. (CBC).

Figure 2-8 Inco became a corporation in 1916 when it began mining nickel, copper and other metals in Ontario's Sudbury Basin. Today Inco supplies about 24% of the world's demand for nickel, and its products are used in everything from the kitchen sink to computers.

Owners/shareholders (elect board of directors)

Board of directors (hire officers)

Officers (set corporate objective and select managers)

Managers (supervise employees)

Employees

Figure 2-9 This diagram illustrates the structure of a large public corporation. Why would a corporation like Bombardier or Telus Corporation need such a complex structure to keep it running smoothly?

Figure 2-10 The Royal Canadian Mint is a Crown corporation that has one shareholder—the Canadian government. The Mint employs some of Canada's most highly-skilled metal designers.

- **Non-profit corporations** are not organized to make a profit. Their purpose is to undertake fundraising, to do research, or to lobby for a particular cause in order to help people. The United Way and Children with Diabetes are non-profit corporations, as are many hospitals, religious organizations, museums, and athletic and artistic organizations.

A corporation is brought into existence by drawing up and filing with the proper government agency a document called the *articles of incorporation*. Most people need a lawyer and accountant to help them write this document.

Like Clearnet, corporations can begin small and grow to be very large. In a small corporation, a director of the corporation may also be the manager, but in large corporations managers and directors may operate separately and may even come into conflict.

Corporate Expansion

During the 1900s and early 2000s, a number of large corporations joined to expand their markets, to increase productivity, and especially to become more competitive in global markets.

Some companies grew because of mergers and others through acquisitions. A *merger* occurs when two companies unite to form one company. For example, in 1998, Loblaws and Provigo of Quebec merged to form one very large supermarket chain. An *acquisition* occurs when one company buys another company. When Telus acquired Clearnet in August 2000, Telus became the largest telecommunications company in Canada at that time.

Advantages of a Corporation

One of the main advantages for those who share ownership in a corporation is that they are only liable for the company's debts to the extent of their financial involvement. This is called **limited liability**. This means if you, as a shareholder, invest $5000 in a corporation and the corporation fails, you will lose your $5000 but no other money or possessions. Even if a corporation owes money, you are not liable for its debts. On the other hand, the corporation itself does not have limited liability, so the corporation can lose everything it owns.

A corporation usually has more financial resources than sole proprietorships or partnerships because of the money shareholders invest in it. For example, Clearnet's first sale of shares gave the company $12 million to expand and develop new technology. Corporations use their financial resources to grow. They can build more manufacturing plants, buy more materials, and hire more employees. In addition, if a corporation needs a loan, it has more assets to use as security. The banks know that the corporation's products, buildings, and equipment can be sold to pay back the loan.

Figure 2-11 Nortel Networks is a large Canadian corporation in the Internet and communications technology field. At the end of 2000, shareholders had $28 760 million dollars (U.S.) invested in Nortel.

Corporations also pay tax at a different rate than that of private individuals. This tax rate difference is one of the reasons why a sole proprietor might incorporate. If your tax rate as an sole proprietor is 40 or 50 percent of your year's earnings, and your tax rate as a corporation would be approximately 23 percent, you might think seriously about incorporating. However, you have to be careful. Tax regulations are complex, especially for corporations, and an error in judgment can be costly.

Finally, a corporation has a life apart from its owners. It is a legal entity. The death or retirement of a shareholder does not mean the end of the corporation. Ownership is easily transferable, unlike a sole proprietorship or a partnership.

Disadvantages of a Corporation

A corporation has a more complicated structure than a sole proprietorship. Usually a lawyer and an accountant are needed not only to start up a corporation, but also to keep it running smoothly. Because of government regulations, more reporting is required of a corporation than of a sole proprietorship or a partnership. Also, a corporation must be registered in every province in which it does business, and the registering process can be time-consuming and expensive. Closing down a corporation can also be more complex and expensive than closing a sole proprietorship or a partnership.

In sole proprietorships and partnerships, the owners usually run the company and work for it. In a small corporation, the shareholders may also work in the business. But in a large corporation, the business is managed by employees who may or may not also be shareholders. Employees

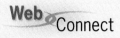

Web Connect

www.school.mcgrawhill.ca/resources/
Most public corporations now publish their annual reports on the Internet. Review the contents of one large corporation's annual reports to see whether or not you would like to become a shareholder.

may not have the same level of commitment to the business as the owners of a sole proprietorship or a partnership.

In addition, public corporations are legally required to publish an *annual report* outlining their financial position. This financial information could benefit competitors. If your profits increased greatly because one of the products sold much more than your other products, your competitors might decide to develop something similar.

Finally, although selling stock can provide a public corporation with financial resources, changes in the stock market can drastically change the value of the stock and the corporation. If the value of a share drops from $100 to $25, the corporation will have less money to work with and have more difficulty borrowing money from the banks.

Co-operatives

Co-operatives, also called co-ops, are businesses owned and operated by a group of people with a strong common interest. The start-up costs are shared among the members of the co-operative. Members own and control the business and make all business decisions.

As you can see in Figure 2-12, there are different types of co-ops. Many farmers belong to producer co-ops. The members bring crops to a central location to sell them. The co-op is able to monitor the supply of the crop and control its sale and price. The farmers do not compete against each other or undercut each other's prices.

Co-ops also allow the farmers to combine to buy equipment and seeds at reduced costs, and to share expertise. Saskatchewan Wheat Pool is a well-known Canadian co-op that markets and sells wheat and wheat products within our country and around the world.

In consumer co-ops, consumers join together to operate a business that provides them with goods and services. They divide profits among the members in proportion to the amount of business that each member does with the co-op. This system encourages members to do as much business as possible with the co-op.

Credit Unions, such as the Kenora District Credit Union in Kenora, Ontario, are financial co-ops. Credit unions and *caisses populaires*, (a popular financial institution in Québec) are something like banks, except that the profits are distributed annually to their members.

Figure 2-12 Co-op Atlantic is a wholesale co-operative that offers agricultural, food, groceries, real estate, and even petroleum products and services to 170 co-ops and their 226 000 members. How might smaller co-ops benefit from the services offered by Co-op Atlantic?

Advantages of a Co-operative

As a member of a co-op, you help run the business and share in financial decisions. Members are able to call on each others' different skills to run the business. Because of this shared ownership, the level of risk is less than it would be for a sole proprietor or a partner. Your liability would be limited to the amount of your share in the capital of the co-op.

Because each member gets only one vote on issues that affect business operations, no one person or group of people can dominate. (In a public corporation, shareholders have votes according to the number of shares that they own.) The people who own the most shares control the company. In co-ops the profits are divided so that members who do a high volume of business with the co-op receive more of the profits.

Co-ops offer their members favourable prices because they buy goods in large quantities, which usually gets them a discount on the cost price. If you were a sole proprietor and needed new computer equipment, you would need to search for the best price at various retail businesses. In a co-op, you would likely pay a better price for the equipment because the co-op buys in bulk.

Figure 2-13

Mountain Equipment Co-op offers, at its Web site, news and listings of events that members are likely to be interested in. Its members are very concerned about social and environmental responsibility.

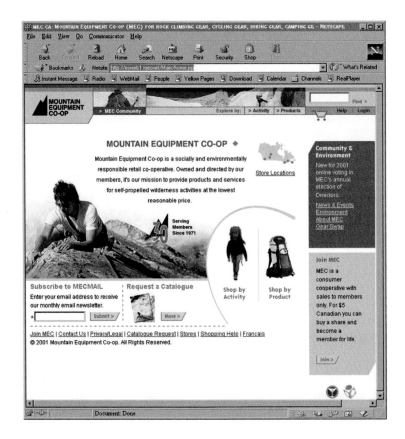

Co-ops also control the sale and price of goods produced by members. This helps members get the best price. Some types of co-operatives even help members run their own businesses more efficiently by offering training and expert help.

Disadvantages of a Co-operative

Most co-ops have difficulty raising additional funds to expand their business. Members may not want to invest more money. After all, they have only the same amount of control over the business as someone who has invested much less. Having only one vote can be an advantage and a disadvantage.

Decision-making can be difficult because of the number of people involved. Think about your own experience with large groups. What happens when your whole class has to decide on an issue? Isn't it usually harder to get everyone to agree than when you work with a small group? And aren't you less likely to make your vote count in a large group?

Another disadvantage of a co-operative is that the commitment of the members may vary. Some may have more money at stake or take the business more seriously than others. This can cause resentment or hostility among members.

Franchise

Web Connect
www.school.mcgrawhill.ca/resources/
Did you know there are co-ops everywhere in Canada, including the Arctic? Or that there are co-ops for health care, housing, community development, insurance, and funeral arrangements? Find out more about co-ops and the services they offer their members.

Franchising is one of the fastest-growing forms of business ownership. A *franchisor* sells to another person (the *franchisee*) the rights to use the business name and to sell a product or service in a given territory. Franchises are available in many different business sectors. You can buy one in anything from advertising and marketing to computer sales, fast food, funeral homes, campgrounds, and wine making.

A **franchise agreement** is the written contract between the franchise seller and buyer. Franchise agreements generally permit the franchisee to use the franchisor's name, products, and packaging. The franchisor will usually specify how the franchise is to be operated, what products are to be sold, how the advertising is to be done, and so on.

Cara Operations Ltd. is a large franchise organization operating in Canada. Cara owns and franchises Harvey's, Swiss Chalet, Second Cup, Kelsey's, Outback Steakhouse, Montana's Cookhouse Saloon, and Cara (airline catering).

In Canada, franchises employ more than one million people directly, provide many more jobs indirectly, and generate annual sales of $100 billion. The most common categories of franchise units are fast-food restaurants and automotive products and services.

Advantages of a Franchise

Franchisees can buy a business with a proven track record and a nationally recognized name. For example, if you buy a McDonald's franchise, you know that people will recognize the name of your business. You know there will likely be a market for your product.

Franchisees have personal ownership of their business, just like sole proprietors or partners. In addition, the franchisor has ironed out many business problems and agrees to share training, management, and financing expertise with the franchisee. If the business involves a complex production process, this can be a big advantage.

Biz.Bites

On average, a new franchise is opened, somewhere in the world, every two hours every day of the year.

One important way in which the franchisor helps the franchisee is in finding a suitable location. The franchisor also provides all the packaging, advertising, and equipment. Finally, the franchisor usually agrees not to open another operation nearby.

Disadvantages of a Franchise

Among the risks facing people who become franchisees is the expense. Franchises can be expensive to buy. A person buying a McDonald's franchise has to have at least $300 000 on hand. The franchisee is also required to pay an ongoing operating fee (or royalty) to the franchisor as well as to buy products only from the franchisor. This reduces the franchisee's profits.

Owning a franchise may be similar to owning your own business but it is not quite the same. Some franchisors have many rules and regulations, and as a franchisee you may have little say in how the day-to-day operations are run. In addition, unlike a sole proprietorship or a partnership, franchisees depend on the success of the franchisor. If the franchisor fails, then your business will fail.

Figure 2-14 Yogen Früz, whose franchisees sell frozen yogurt products, began in 1986 with a single outlet in Toronto. The store was so successful that the owners decided to sell franchises. The first franchise operation opened in London, Ontario, in 1987.

Check Your Understanding

Knowledge/Understanding

1 The name of a business often indicates its ownership. Collect the names of eight businesses in your community and challenge your fellow students to identify the form of ownership from their names.

2 Define, in your own words, each of the types of business ownership discussed in this section of Chapter 2. Then explain the risks that someone in each type of business would face. Finally, name three examples of each type of business ownership in your community.

Thinking/Inquiry

3 Review the advantages of becoming a member of a co-operative. Which of these advantages would be most important to you? Compare the reasons for your choice with those of your classmates. Why do different people have different views on this subject?

4 Darach McGee meets Andrea Retteghy, a university classmate. After discussing old times, Darach and Andrea discover that they are both interested in opening a business that would provide a disc jockey service. They are each prepared to invest $4000 in this new venture. Write a brief report answering the following questions. Explain the reasons for your answers.

    a) Would it be to their advantage to form a partnership or to each form a sole proprietorship offering the same service?

    b) What are the factors they should consider before they decide?

Skills
Appendix

writing reports

Communication

5 Working with a partner, select a business that you would both be interested in starting up. Then brainstorm some of the issues you would need to resolve to start and run this type of business. Decide whether it would be better for you to own this business as partners, sole proprietors, or a corporation. Report your decision—and the reasons for your decision—in a brief oral presentation for your classmates.

Skills
Appendix

oral presentations

Application

6 Select a partner and create a role-play in which one of you is considering starting a new business and the other is offering advice. Each of you should consider the type of business, the risks in starting the business, and the resources and skills needed to succeed.

Skills
Appendix

decision-making

Connecting Business with *Home*

Kitchen Table Tycoons

About 14 years ago, lawyer Doug Chalke sat behind his desk in a Vancouver office tower and decided he'd much rather be at home. Chalke did not want to quit his family law practice. He was just tired of "going to the office."

Today, Doug and his wife, Angie, work out of their home, offering mediation counselling primarily to couples going through divorce. They say they have one of the busiest practices in Canada, and would never work in a conventional office again.

Thousands of other Canadians have discovered the same satisfaction. The 1996 census found that 474 000 Canadians were self-employed and working from home. "It is growing," says Douglas Gray, a Vancouver lawyer who has written a guide to running a small business from a home office. "You tend to find this kind of business evolving after people are laid off from their jobs, or when they get severance packages, or if they have houses that are paid off and they are financially secure." David Baxter of the Vancouver-based Urban Futures Institute adds that people who work at home often have a specialized skill that doesn't require a formal office.

Working from home is not as easy as it seems. The Chalkes had to turn their living room—and later their carport—into an office. People in a home office also have to remember to dress appropriately if their clients come.

However, the financial advantages of working at home can be significant. If your main place of business is your home and you set aside a room for the business, you can save on income taxes. Revenue Canada lets you deduct a portion of the cost of running a home from your gross income.

Figure 2-15 Working from home can be a challenge when the sun is shining and the lawn needs mowing, or when the kitchen sink is full of dishes that need to be washed.

The cost of office furniture and equipment can also be deducted. The lower your income, the less taxes you have to pay.

Source: Adapted from Jennifer Hunter, "Kitchen-table Tycoons," The *Maclean's Guide to Personal Finance*, January 1, 1999, page 87.

ACTIVITIES

1 Describe some of the advantages and disadvantages of starting a home-based business.
2 Why might some people who start home-based businesses choose to incorporate?
3 Why are a growing number of Canadians starting home-based businesses?

Growth in Canadian Business

The business environment constantly changes. To survive, people in business must be prepared to take advantage of the opportunities that change offers. As you saw in the Business Profile, Clearnet recognized the business opportunities in a wireless network long before most Canadians had any idea of how popular cellphones would become.

What changes have helped Canadian businesses to grow? There have been many in recent years, but these few stand out.

- advances in technologies, especially in information technologies
- an increase in global business connections
- the growth of the small business and service sectors
- a greater emphasis on the natural environment
- a focus on business ethics and social responsibility

Changing Technology

Over the last 150 years, technology has changed at an increasingly rapid rate. During the 1800s, uses for electricity were discovered. Railways, steel-making, automobiles, and machinery for agriculture and industry were developed. During the 1900s, new technologies gave us refrigeration, airplanes, plastics, motion pictures, satellites, atomic energy, and computers. All of these changes have affected business.

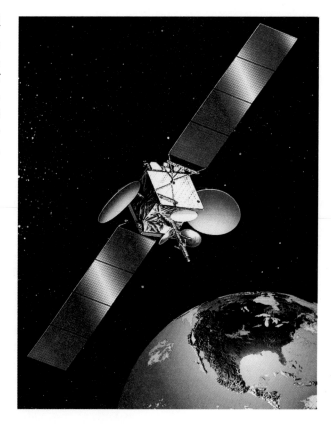

Figure 2-16 Telespace Ltd., which is a Canadian company started in 1980, is one of the leading satellite communications consulting companies in the world. Telespace has helped the governments of Canada, Brazil, Thailand, Norway, and Israel set up communications satellite programs.

**TechnologyTimeline:
1900 – 2000**

1902 Air conditioning

1903 Airplane

1908 Model T Ford

1914 Panama Canal

1920 KDKA, the first
regular commercial
radio station

1926 Liquid-fueled rocket

1927 Television

1929 Commercial
frozen food

1938 Nylon

1939 Prototype of first
digital computer

1942 Atomic reaction

1945 Atomic bomb

1947 Polaroid camera

1948 Electric guitar

1951 UNIVAC 1
(first commercial
computer)

1953 Heart-lung machine

1957 Polio vaccine

1958 Space satellites
(Sputnik and
Explorer I)

1965 Minicomputer

1969 Moon landing

1972 First video game

1974 Barcode on products

1980 Video camera

1981 Space shuttle

1982 Artificial heart

Recent changes have been so great that the phenomenon is called the *technological revolution.* New technologies change the way businesses produce, buy, and sell goods and services, the way they communicate with each other, and the way they obtain financial and other resources.

Technological advances in communications and computers have contributed to other trends and affected millions of jobs and the way millions of people work.

The Information Age

Competition among businesses is very fierce. And one of the things that gives companies a competitive edge is information. For this reason, governments all over the world are developing information systems to help businesses in their countries compete. Telespace Ltd. (see Figure 2-16) helps many countries set up their satellite telephone systems.

Today, information technologies, such as laptop and palm-held computers and cellular phones, give employees fast access to information. This information can help a business operate efficiently and quickly.

For example, at Federal Express, employees use information technologies to find our where parcels are and when they will arrive at their destination. Customers can track the movement of their shipments over FedEx's Web site. Couriers use handheld computers to record the movement of parcels and envelopes. Federal Express has one of the world's largest computer and telecommunications networks. The company even has its own air network of Boeing 727s to deliver its customers' parcels.

Thanks to the Internet, businesses can search the world to find the best quality and price for production materials and other resources. Financing to expand a business may come from New York or from Tokyo. Production arrangements may be made with a company in Brazil or in China. And as for customers? They may live anywhere on the planet.

Increased Globalization

Canadians have been doing business with other countries since Europeans settled along the east coast in the 1600s to fish for cod and send their catches back to Europe. Canadian companies no longer just send their natural resources to Europe and buy manufactured goods from European businesses.

In the twenty-first century, Canadian businesses produce, market, finance, and manage globally: from Asia to South America, from Europe to the Persian Gulf. Businesses from other countries also operate in Canada. Toyota and Honda are two Japanese companies that produce automobiles in Canada. The information age and communication technology have reduced the impact of the geographic barriers. Doing business internationally is called **globalization**. Globalization gives Canadian businesses, such as Magna, Nortel Networks, and Bombardier, the chance to increase their profits.

Magna International, a large Canadian manufacturer of automobile parts, is a global company. It employs more than 59 000 people in 198 manufacturing and research and development facilities in Canada, the United States, Brazil, Poland, Germany, Turkey, the Czech Republic, Italy, Japan, Korea, and India. Magna designs, engineers and manufactures exterior and interior vehicle systems, using the latest technology and components from different countries.

Globalization has also increased competition for markets. Because more businesses try to get the same customers and because of advances in technology, businesses have had to become more efficient. Governments have also recognized the pressure of this increased competition and have established trading blocs. Such blocs encourage trade between member countries. Free-trade blocs are discussed in detail later, in Chapter 17.

Growth of Small Business

Over the last 20 years, many Canadians have started small businesses. With every passing year, another record is set in the number of new small businesses that are registered in Canada.

A **small business** is one that is independently operated, not dominant in its field, and meets certain size limits in terms of employees and annual sales. In all sectors other than manufacturing, a small business is defined as one that has fewer than 50 employees. In the manufacturing sector, a small business is one that has fewer than 100 employees.

Many of these small businesses were started by entrepreneurs, people who saw a need or market trend, most often in the service sector, and tried to fill it. Small business owners tend to develop a close relationship with their customers, find out what they want, and try to serve them better than their competitors.

TechnologyTimeline
(continued)

1990 Hubble Telescope

1990 Human genome project

1990 The Internet's World Wide Web

1993 Pentium microprocessor

1995 DVD (digital versatile disc)

1997 Sojourner images from Mars

1997 Cloning of Dolly the sheep

Figure 2-17 Use your imagination to extend this timeline into the future. What technologies do you expect will be developed during the next 10 years? How will they change business?

Biz.Bites
- Of the 150 000 new businesses started each year, most are small businesses.
- About one million small businesses exist in our country, and another one million people are self-employed.
- Almost half of all Canadians are either self-employed or work for companies with fewer than 100 employees.

For example, Connie Parsons's goal (see Figure 2-18) is to provide the highest quality dance education to her students, to make them feel confident about their dance skills, and to deliver a very high standard of service. As a small business owner, she knows that she will attract and keep customers by satisfying their existing needs and anticipating their future needs.

Small businesses have also taken advantage of the trends towards computer technology and globalization. The technology of the Internet has allowed Canadian entrepreneurs to start small businesses in communities as remote as Davis Inlet in Labrador and Pelly Bay in Nunavut.

Figure 2-18 Connie Parsons won the Young Entrepreneurs Award for Newfoundland from the Business Development Bank of Canada in October 2000. She runs her successful small business—the Connie Parsons School of Dance—in St John's, Newfoundland. Connie teaches ballet, tap, jazz, modern stage, and ballroom dance. Her plans include opening more studios and a dancewear store.

Home-based Small Businesses

Many new and part-time small businesses are being operated from homes. Home-based businesses are considered the fastest growing form of small business. Some factors contributing to this trend are
- the growth of information technologies
- the growth of service businesses
- the disappearance of many traditional jobs
- people wanting to be their own boss or to change their lifestyle
- the appeal to women who have found their careers blocked because of sexual discrimination

As you read in Connecting Business with Home, people have many different reasons for establishing home-based businesses.

Many small, home-based businesses, have only one employee, the owner. People who are experts in fields such as business operations or computer programs may become consultants. Others, like writers, work from home because they work better alone. They can do projects for large companies because technology allows them to send projects to clients and get comments back using the Internet. Dressmakers and tailors have worked out of their homes for years to reduce their operating expenses.

Biz.Bites

The latest estimates are that 50% of self-employed Canadians—about 9% of the total Canadian workforce—work from their homes.

Career Connect ❯ *Speaking for Yourself* ················

Being able to talk comfortably and clearly is especially important if you are a small business owner. You need to be able to get your point across if you are going to convince your customer to buy your goods or services.

Business people need good oral communication skills to

- make presentations. To get a loan, for example, you need to convince a loan officer that you are a good business risk. To promote your business, you might talk to a group of business people at a meeting of the local chamber of commerce.

- negotiate an agreement. If you can clearly explain the reasons for a delay, your customers are less likely to be upset with your service.

- talk to strangers. If you can respond with a quick description, when someone asks what you do, you might end up with a new customer or supplier.

- leave clear voice mail messages for prospective clients. If you don't state your name, phone number, and the reason for your call, you aren't likely to get a return call.

Talking is only effective if your listener receives the same message you tried to send. How can you make your communications clear?

You may be surprised to learn that the language you use is only one aspect of good communications. Tone and body language also play an important part in getting your message across.

- Language includes the words we use and the way we put them together. If you get a job at Sam the Record Man, you'll need to use "business-like" language. When you greet a customer, you would say "May I help you?" rather than "What ya' want?"

- Tone is the sound and quality of your voice. Business people make a strong impact if they sound confident. If you asked a sales associate at a sports store whether a skateboard had smooth action, and he said "Sure" in a hesitant way, how would you feel? Would you buy that board?

- Body language includes the messages you send through your gestures and physical actions. If another student makes a class presentation and doesn't look at anyone, how do you and your classmates feel?

ACTIVITIES

1 With a partner, prepare two scripts for the following scenes. Practice with each other. The second script should communicate better than the first. Next, role-play one scene to a small group. Afterwards ask for comments on language, tone, and body language.

- A prospective employee applies for a job to a store manager. In the first script, the applicant is nervous. In the second script, the applicant is more confident.

- A student asks a teacher, who doesn't like to give extensions, for an extension on a project. First, the student uses unclear language to present his or her reasons. The second time the language is clear.

- A student, who has a reputation as a clown, tries to convince a vice-principle that he or she should make the announcement for a fundraiser at an assembly. First, the student's body language does not back up what she or he is saying. The second time it does.

Growth of the Service Sector

The most significant growth of small businesses in Canada has been in the service sector. As you learned in Chapter 1, service businesses provide a service to customers. These services involve a wide range of jobs: travel agents, consultants editors, store clerks, hazardous waste collectors, lawyers, doctors, and communications specialists.

One reason for this growth is that Canadians have more money and less time than they had 50 years ago. People are willing to pay others to care for their children, to prepare and serve their food, to do their accounts, or even to wrap presents for them.

The success of the Molly Maid franchise happened largely because people are willing to pay others to clean their homes. The company markets its services by advertising that they give their customers more time to do all the other things they need or want to do.

Another reason for the service sector's growth is that fewer manufacturing jobs are available to Canadians. Technological advances in robotics and automation means fewer people are needed to run manufacturing plants. Between 1960 and 1999, the percentage of the total workforce in manufacturing fell from 30 percent to 15 percent.

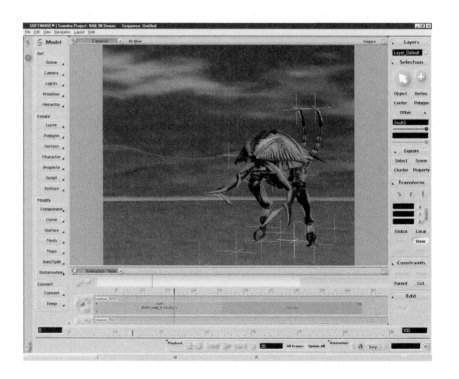

Figure 2-19

Softimage Inc., a Canadian company specializing in computer graphics, provides software products and services to the motion picture industry. This screen shot shows a stage in the development of the dinosaur animation for *Jurassic Park*.

Some large companies rely more on outside service businesses than they did in the past. And the trend is likely to continue, especially in the areas of computer programming, communications, telecommunications, and financial planning. In addition, because Canada has an aging population, services that are critical to the elderly, such as health care, are likely to be more in demand.

Growing Concern for the Environment

Worldwide concern for the environment has had a significant impact on the way businesses are run. Among the concerns are

- the depletion of the ozone layer. Many scientists associate this with global warming and the burning of certain kinds of fuels.

- toxic waste in our water systems. The seriousness of such waste was brought home to people in Ontario in the summer of 2000 by the tragedy in the town of Walkerton. At least six people died and hundreds more became seriously ill from drinking contaminated water.

- huge amounts of waste and garbage. Industrialized countries produce waste from toxic gases, chemicals, disposable products, and overpackaging.

Figure 2-20 In order to eliminate the danger of POPs to Canadian Inuit peoples, governments and businesses from around the world need to agree to reduce industrial pollutants. Why does this problem need an international solution?

The extent of the dangers of industrial pollution is illustrated by the problem of persistent organic pollutants (POPs) in the Canadian Inuit community. Because of global climate patterns, POPs (which are used in pesticides, insecticides, and industrial applications), travel from tropical and temperate climates through the atmosphere to the Arctic. In the Arctic, these toxic chemicals move through the food chain to the Inuit. According to Chuck Birchall of the Canadian Arctic Resources Committee, "Many Inuit have levels of POPs in their bodies well in excess of the 'level of concern' defined by Health Canada."

Web Connect

www.school.mcgrawhill.ca/resources
The Canadian Arctic Resources Committee continues to work to clean up the Canadian Arctic environment. Find out more about this organization and its concerns. What is the current status of POPs in the Arctic?

In 1999, the federal government passed the new *Canadian Environmental Protection Act*, which focuses on "pollution prevention and the protection of the environment and human health in order to contribute to sustainable development." Sustainable economic development meets the needs of the present without endangering the environment for future generations. Canadian businesses are required to follow the provisions in this act and to incorporate environmentally responsible policies in their normal operations.

Business Opportunities

The growing concern for the environment has provided entrepreneurs with business opportunities. As we are encouraged to reduce, reuse, and recycle, many businesses are rethinking how to dispose of their garbage and to reduce the amount they produce. Today, service stations, trucking companies, and car dealerships pay significant fees to dispose of used motor oil. Environmental consultants work with many companies, advising them on how to safely dispose of toxic waste products.

Two Canadian companies are working on innovative solutions to deal with the pollution from our use of cars and trucks. Ballard Fuel Cells of Vancouver is working with the automotive industry to develop clean, efficient, and reliable fuel cell engines to replace the internal combustion engine. For more information on Ballard Fuel Cells, see chapter 3. Westport Innovations Inc., also of Vancouver, is developing natural gas engines that will reduce pollution and costs for the trucking industry.

Business Ethics and Social Responsibility

Closely connected to environmental concerns is the growing emphasis on ethics and social responsibility in business. **Ethics** are standards of conduct that society believes people should follow. Businesses, like individuals, must follow ethical standards and be socially responsible towards their employees, their immediate community, and the wider global community. **Social responsibility** is the duty to care for others whose actions can be affected in a damaging way. More consumers and workers are demanding that businesses show a genuine commitment to employees and communities.

Consumers exercise their power by supporting companies that practice ethical and socially responsible behaviour and by not supporting those companies that do not follow ethical standards.

Figure 2-21 The Westray coal mine explosion in May 1992, killed 26 miners in Plymouth, Nova Scotia. These men are part of the rescue team. This tragedy shows the complexity of business decisions. The venture was risky, but economic concerns in an area of high unemployment were allowed to outweigh safety concerns —with tragic consequences.

A major force for change during the last 100 years has been the labour movement. Unions and the labour movement have addressed serious issues: dangerous working conditions, lack of pensions or compensation for injured workers, child labour, low pay, and long hours.

A company's ethics and values are part of its corporate culture and its code of behaviour. Corporate culture has an impact on the company's goals and policies and how it implements them. The culture also determines how the company treats its employees and customers.

Some goals of socially responsible businesses and citizens are

- to end discrimination of women and minorities in terms of hiring, promotion, salaries, and firing

- to halt the production and sale of weapons and land mines.

- to practice sustainable development and not to allow short-term economic considerations to replace longer-term, more socially responsible considerations (see Figure 2-21)

- to end white-collar crime (usually thefts by employees), which has become more complicated in the age of Internet finance

- to ensure that the Canadian marketplace remains fair and competitive by outlawing price fixing and bid rigging (secret agreements among competitors to control prices)

- to eliminate from the global market place dangerous drugs produced by pharmaceutical companies

Knowledge/Understanding

1 Match up the chapter topics on growth in Canadian business in Column 1 with the examples in Column 2 and explain why you have chosen your matches.

Growth in Canadian Business	Examples
1. the use of technology in manufacturing	a. a caterer who specializes in weddings
2. home-based business	b. a health and safety poster campaign in the workplace
3. concern for the environment	c. a virtual online shopping mall
4. the use of information technology	d. an automotive assembly line
5. business ethics and social responsibility	e. a freelance write
6. the service sector	f. a convenience store
7. small business	g. a local newspaper that uses only recycled paper

2 Explain, in a paragraph, how either technology advances or globalization have created opportunities for Canadian business. Exchange your paragraph with a partner and offer each other suggestions on how your explanations could be improved. Then revise your paragraph.

Thinking/Inquiry

3 Prepare a collage in response to the following questions:
   a) How has consumer demand for greater environmental and social responsibility influenced business in your community?
   b) What affect has this demand had on business growth?

Communication

4 Listen to a radio or television news reports on a business issue related to one of the changes discussed in business in this section. Use a decision-making organizer to show a possible solution to the problem.

Application

5 Write a short illustrated report on how one company shows social responsibility towards its employees. Use your illustrations as evidence to support your opinion.

Skills
Appendix

decision-making

Skills
Appendix

writing reports

While you may not recognize Steve Jobs' name, you will certainly be familiar with what he is famous for. He and his partner, Steve Wozniak, revolutionized the world of personal computers, making them easier to use by developing the mouse, icons, and pop-up menus. The two Steves got Apple Computers Inc. off the ground. Steve Jobs was in charge of the advertising, marketing, and product design. Steve Wozniak was the hardware designer. He had the technical and engineering expertise. They wanted to build a user-friendly computer that anyone could use for any purpose.

They both had the ability to understand people's wants and needs in a computer, so they created the first computer with a graphical user-friendly interface that was very easy to operate. Icons, for example, allowed users to click on a tiny symbol to open a program or file. Before that, users had to type in directions using codes and patterns that were tricky to remember.

Their friendship began at Hewlett Packard when Jobs was 13 and Wozniak was 18. Jobs was still in high school when HP hired him. Later they designed video games for Atari, a computer software company.

Eight years after working at Hewlett Packard, they joined forces using Steve Jobs' garage to build the personal computer that changed computing. They called it Apple, after Steve Jobs' favourite fruit. To fund their project, both men had to sell prized possessions. Jobs sold his Volkswagen, and Wozniak sold his scientific calculator.

In 1976, Apple was the first personal computer to be mass produced. With their first sale of 50 Apple computers at $666 each, Apple Computers Inc. was born. Apple brought com-

Figure 2-22 While he was still in high school, Steve Jobs attended Hewlett-Packard seminars on technology. This led to his being offered a summer job at HP—at the age of 13!

puters into people's homes. Before that time, the computer had been a tool that only governments and large businesses could afford. In 1977, Jobs and Wozniak created Apple II and gave it a sleek plastic covering and the Apple logo—the apple with a bite taken out of it. The Apple II was a more general-purpose computer. It was compact and simple to use. Apple II was created for a new market—school children.

When IBM began developing and manufacturing personal computers, it quickly passed Apple Computers in sales because its operating system was the industry's standard. The IBM computers were not compatible with Apple and its products.

To compete with IBM, Steve Jobs hired John Sculley from Pepsi Cola. In 1983, Sculley became Apple Computers' president. In 1984, Apple created the Macintosh computer. Where Apple II was geared towards home and small business

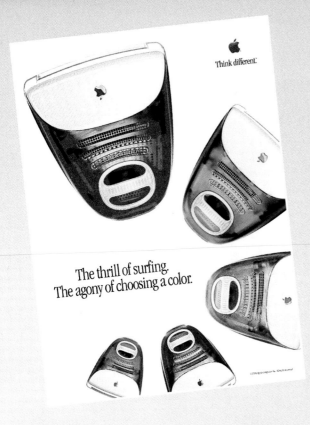

Think different.

The thrill of surfing.
The agony of choosing a color.

Figure 2-23 The sleek, colourful design of Apple computers has helped the company market its product as "the coolest-looking computer on the planet."

computer use, Macintosh was geared towards the medium and large business needs of the corporate workforce. The strengths of the Macintosh lay in its user friendliness, flexibility, and adaptability for carrying out creative work. Macintosh quickly became the favourite computer for graphic designers.

However, the creation of Apple II had a down side. Jobs and Wozniak began to have problems in their partnership because they had different ideas on setting a fair price for the computer. Jobs wanted to increase the price in order to make more money, while Wozniak strongly disagreed.

Another problem arose between the two of them with the creation of Macintosh because Jobs' concept of the Macintosh took priority over Wozniak's Apple II. In 1985, Wozniak left Apple Computers because of the conflict and opposition within management.

Steve Jobs ended up leaving the company shortly after that because of problems with the man he had hired to be the company's president, John Sculley. Their differences in personality grew. John Sculley felt that Steve Jobs was creating problems for the company. Eventually Steve Jobs felt that he had been robbed of his power within the company, began to doubt his future in the company, and resigned.

After leaving Apple, Steve Jobs experienced success and failure. His failure was in trying to build a company called NeTX Inc. His success was in purchasing PIXAR in 1986 from Lucasfilm Ltd. Steve Jobs incorporated it as an independent company, and it has produced some very successful digital movies such as *A Bug's Life*, *Toy Story* and *Toy Story 2*. In 1996, three years after John Sculley resigned, Steve Jobs returned to Apple Computer. He remains a major force in the computer technology industry. He proudly carries the titles of CEO of Apple Computers Inc. and CEO of PIXAR.

ACTIVITIES

1 Why did Steve Jobs and Steve Wozniak form a partnership?

2 What were the short- and long-term consequences of the conflicts between Jobs and Wozniak and between Jobs and Sculley?

3 How does the advertisement in Figure 2-23 appeal to consumers? What target audience is it aimed at?

Chapter Review

Points to Remember

- A sole proprietorship is owned and operated by one person who is solely responsible for all aspects of the business.

- Partnerships are owned by two or more people who share responsibility for the business.

- A corporation is a legal entity that is separate from its shareholders. Shareholders have limited liability for a corporation's debts.

- A co-operative is owned and controlled by its members who share the responsibility and benefits of the business.

- Franchises have the right to use the franchisor's business name, products, and packaging.

- To be successful today, businesses must adapt to changes in technology, information management, and globalization.

- The rate of self-employment and small business growth in Canada continues to increase. Many small businesses are home-based.

- The service sector is expanding as people hire others to do work for them.

- Consumers are insisting that businesses behave in an environmentally and socially responsible manner.

Activities

Knowledge/Understanding

1 Name one sole proprietorship, partnership, corporation, co-operative, and franchise. Explain why you think the decision was made for the specific type of ownership in each case. What benefits do the business owners and consumers gain from each type of ownership?

2 Tell a brief story that illustrates how a Canadian business person has taken advantage of the growing trend towards either home-based or service businesses to create a successful small business. Use the elements of a story—plot, characterization, mood, dialogue, and setting— to keep your listeners interested in your story.

3 Suggest three ways that a small Canadian corporation might be affected by the combined forces of globalization and environmental protection. Explain the reasons for your choices.

Thinking/Inquiry

Skills
Appendix

researching

1 Using Internet, media, and library resources, research a co-op and report your finding on the following: the history and evolution of the business, the way that people become members of the co-op, the mission and values of the co-op, the commitment that the co-op has made to social and environmental responsibility, and the reasons why this business has or has not enjoyed success.

2 Sean owns and operates a successful business selling carpet-cleaning machines. Sean is an expert salesman, and his business is doing well. He earns $250 000 in profits annually. He wants to expand his business by providing more services to his customers, but he also wants to spend more time with his young family. Al is an expert mechanic, who owns a business that provides maintenance and repairs to carpet-cleaning machines. Al's business has been suffering. He has only managed to earn $35 000 profit annually. He can no longer make a healthy profit in his repairs business because the cost of carpet-cleaning machines has been decreasing. Many carpet cleaners are replacing their machines rather than having them repaired. Al is also an expert carpet cleaner and makes a profit selling carpet-cleaning courses to people who want to start a carpet-cleaning businesses.

Skills
Appendix

critical thinking

   a) Identify the benefits and drawbacks of Al and Sean forming a business partnership.

   b) If you were to provide advice to Al and Sean, what would you suggest they consider in their partnership agreement?

Communication

Skills
Appendix

oral presentations, writing reports

1 Work with your classmates to create a list of the franchise businesses in your community. Continue to work together to develop a business letter that you will use to request a franchise kit from some of the franchisors on your list.

   a) In small groups, examine the franchise kits and develop an oral presentation from the perspective of the franchisor. Your classmates will act as potential franchisees. Your presentation should include information on the cost of the franchise, including royalties; the training and support provided by the franchisor; the obligations that the franchisee has to the franchisor; the advantages and disadvantages of owning the franchise; the franchisor's marketing and advertising programs; and the potential earnings of the franchise.

b) As you listen to the presentations of other groups, write questions you need to ask in order to evaluate each franchise opportunity.

c) After all the presentations have been made, identify the franchise that you would be most likely to purchase. Write a brief report explaining the reasons for your choice.

2 Debate the issues around the following statement: "Technology creates jobs and business opportunities." For the purpose of this debate, focus your attention on jobs and business opportunities in Canada.

Skills
Appendix
building an argument

3 Investigate the Westray mining disaster (see Figure 2-21) and explain how both government and business failed to protect the interests of the Westray mine workers. Prepare a three-minute radio report or a multimedia presentation on the causes of the tragedy.

Application

1 As a class, brainstorm ideas for starting your own summer business. Then work with a partner to select one summer business that you two might start together. Develop a partnership agreement for your business. What areas did you and your partner find easy to agree upon? What areas did you find it difficult to agree upon?

2 Write a newspaper story about how you became a successful business owner. Describe how your business evolved through at least two types of business ownership. Include in your story information about your background and about how the company started and how it achieved success. Your newspaper article should answer the questions who, what, where, when, why, and how. It should also have a headline and an illustration.

Skills
Appendix
working in groups

Internet Extension

1 Use Internet resources to research the business and careers of the future. Which businesses and careers will likely experience growth in the future? What type of education and training will be required?

3

The Impact of Business on the Community

KEY TERMS

economy

standard of living

gross domestic product (GDP)

per capital

quality of life

expenses

profit

revenue

employment

income

unemployment

employability skills

labour movement

health and safety program

equal oportunity

Specific Expectations

After studying this chapter, you will be able to

- describe how business can generate wealth, jobs, and incomes, and how they influence the standard of living

- distinguish the various ways in which business activity can affect the quality of life

- investigate issues in your community that have been created or affected by business

- analyze the impact that business activity has on the changes occurring in your community

Imagine your life without business—without shopping malls, movie theatres, or banks. Business has a large impact on both your standard of living and your quality of life because it affects your family's income and that of other members of your community. Some people acquire wealth from owning businesses. Others earn income through employment. How much income you earn is affected by a number of factors which we will discuss in this chapter. Business also has an obligation to provide safe, healthy, and fair workplaces for employees and to be a responsible member of the community. Sometimes, though, conflicts can arise between business interests and those of the members of a community.

Canadian Tire

Canadian Tire employees judged their company to be the best Canadian company to work for, according to a February 2000 survey commissioned by *The Globe and Mail's Report on Business* (ROB) magazine.

Brian Toda, the Hewitt Associates consultant who headed up the Best Company to Work For project, says employees based their judgment on more than just salaries. They had to feel valued. According to Toda, the best companies create "a sense in an organization that when people come in to work at that company, it is worth a day of their life each day." While salary and other financial benefits are important, it's a company's attitude towards its employees that makes the difference.

Why did Canadian Tire get such a positive reaction from its employees? What benefits does it offer employees and local communities?

Cliff Hacking, who works for Canadian Tire, wasn't surprised that the company was so highly rated by its employees. He joined the company because it had such a good reputation in business and in the community. "It's the kind of organization that treats people extremely well," he says. "It's fair and it's reasonable and the rules are well stated. You can understand what you need to do to be successful."

Canadian Tire's corporate policies contribute to its employees' high degree of satisfaction. The company provides a safe and healthy work environment. It regularly reviews health and safety policies, procedures, and programs, and educates employees about the issues. The company also invests in outside education for employees. When Cliff Hacking decided to take his Master of Business Administration at the University of Western Ontario, Canadian Tire paid the full $52 000 cost of the program.

Employees are rewarded for doing a good job. The "Wall of Winners" at head office is filled with photos of employees who have offered exceptional customer service. Employees earn performance bonuses. In addition, since the company started in 1922, employees have had a profit-sharing plan through which they can financially benefit from the success of their company. ➤

Figure 3-1 Canadian Tire believes in rewarding its employees for jobs well done and in recognizing their contributions to the company and to their communities.

Figure 3-2 Canadian Tire employees responded to the 1998 ice storm by providing food, clothing, and essential goods to those affected by the disaster. How would this kind of activity contribute to the well-being of both the communities and the employees?

Canadian Tire is recognized as environmentally responsible. It's stores serve as collection sites for products containing hazardous materials, such as car batteries and nickel cadmium batteries. In most provinces, Canadian Tire has depots for collecting used motor oil, another hazardous product. The company reduces waste by reusing packaging materials.

The organization is a corporate sponsor of Pollution Probe and of a number of community cleanup efforts. It supports an annual earth week and an environment, health, and safety month. Its retail stores give grants to environmental projects run by local non-profit organizations, such as high-school cleanup and public awareness campaigns in Nova Scotia and construction of part of the TransCanada Trail near Sudbury, Ontario.

Through its Foundation for Families, Canadian Tire provides "a helping hand to families in crisis by ensuring (that their) basic needs are met." On an ongoing basis, the Foundation supports lunch programs for school children, and soup kitchens and hostels for the homeless. When people in eastern Ontario and Quebec were left without power during the ice storm in 1998, the company and its stores delivered 65 emergency tractor trailer shipments to affected communities. And when there were no more Canadian Tire trucks available, employees drove shipments of supplies in their own vehicles.

As you read this chapter think about how a business can contribute to the quality of life of its employees and its community. How do company policies and practices affect a community? On a more personal level: What kind of employment environment do you think would be worth "a day of your life each day"?

The Impact of Business on the Canadian Economy

The economy of Canada is made up of contributions from business, labour, and the government. Within this economic community, some people own property and businesses. These business owners take the financial and social risks of starting businesses, and keep the wealth they gain from the profits of their successful businesses. Other people work for businesses as employees, providing the labour and the human resources that businesses need. Employees earn money with which to buy the goods and services produced by business.

Business owners, employees, and the community are very interdependent. Take a close look at Figure 3-3.

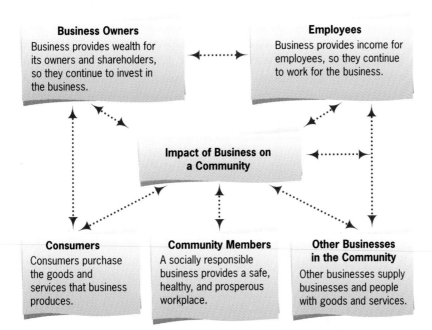

Business Owners
Business provides wealth for its owners and shareholders, so they continue to invest in the business.

Employees
Business provides income for employees, so they continue to work for the business.

Impact of Business on a Community

Consumers
Consumers purchase the goods and services that business produces.

Community Members
A socially responsible business provides a safe, healthy, and prosperous workplace.

Other Businesses in the Community
Other businesses supply businesses and people with goods and services.

Figure 3-3 A successful, socially responsible business affects the members of a community in positive ways. What would be the effect on the community if such a business closed down?

Figure 3-4 In Atlantic Canada, the loss of the cod-fishing industry has caused hardship for the whole community. Those affected include fishers and their families, fish-processing plant owners and employees, and local businesses that depend on the fishing industry.

Canadian governments at all levels also participate in the economy. They get their revenue from the taxes that businesses and individuals pay. Businesses in Canada pay between 25 percent and 40 percent of their profits to the federal and provincial governments in the form of income taxes. Businesses also pay municipal property taxes.

Governments regulate business though laws that deal with issues such as environmental protection and minimum wages for employees. They also take on the function of business through government-owned enterprises that meet the needs of citizens.

Not-for-profit organizations also contribute to the economy because they too act like businesses by hiring employees and by purchasing, providing, and, in some cases, selling goods and services. These agencies get their income from businesses and individuals and through government grants.

When a country has a strong economy, its people can meet nearly all their needs and many of their wants. The impact of a good economy is often measured in a country's standard of living and the quality of life its people enjoy.

Standard of Living

A country's **standard of living** refers to the number of goods and services that the members of that country enjoy. The more money a country has, the higher is its standard of living. In general, the citizens of industrial countries—like Canada and the United States—have a higher standard of living than the citizens of developing countries.

One measure that is used to compare the standards of living of different countries is **gross domestic product** or **GDP**. GDP is the annual total value of final market goods produced and services provided in a country. GDP is often calculated **per capita**, which is the total GDP divided by the number of people in a country or region. By comparing the GDP of a number of different countries (see Figure 3-5), you will get some idea of how different Canada's standard of living is from much of the rest of the world.

Businesses contribute to the standard of living of communities in a number of ways.

- They provide profits and wealth for business owners.
- They pay income to employees.
- They support other businesses which in turn provide wealth to their owners and income to their employees.

In Canada, people with low or no income can receive help from governments, not-for-profit agencies, and religious organizations.

Comparison of Annual GDP Per Capita in Different Countries

Country	GDP
Argentina	$9070
Brazil	$4930
Canada	$20 082
China	$745
Ethiopia	$104
France	$23 843
India	$402
Ireland	$20 603
Kenya	$356
Mexico	$4265
Russia	$3028
South Africa	$3331
United States	$28 789

Source: United Nations, InfoNation, CyberSchoolbus, 1997 figures.

Figure 3-5 Compare the annual GDP in this selection of countries. Which countries have the highest and the lowest standards of living? How would these differences affect the lives of the people living in these countries?

Quality of Life

Quality of life includes peoples' material standard of living, but it also includes a number of social and environmental factors. According to the United Nations, the quality of life indicators of a country include

- the life expectancy of its citizens
- the illiteracy rate
- the amount of money spent on education
- its communications facilities (telephone, newspapers, television)
- its population density
- its infant mortality rate

Web Connect

www.school.mcgrawhill.ca/resources/
Visit the United Nations InfoNation Web site to find statistics on the countries listed in Figure 3-5. What is likely to be the quality of life of people in the different countries?

Businesses contribute to the quality of life of Canadians. Hospitals, education, roads, and social programs are all funded by business and personal tax money. Tax money is also used to attract businesses to communities and municipalities through loans and grants. Arts groups also benefit, which aids employment and enhances quality of life. Governments provide grants to arts organizations and businesses give them significant gifts and some act as sponsors.

There is growing pressure on businesses to contribute in other ways to the quality of life and well-being of their communities. To meet their responsibilities to society, companies like Canadian Tire consider the interests and concerns of many groups. Responsible businesses make sure that they provide a healthy and safe working environment for their employees and a safe environment for the community. They also have hiring and employment practises that treat everyone fairly, including minorities, women, older workers, and those who are physically challenged.

Figure 3-6 Maritime Life takes employee quality of life, satisfaction, and participation very seriously. The company offers employee benefits such as daycare, fitness centres, and bonuses. It is also firmly committed to co-operative education, a commitment that earned the company an Employer Recognition Award from Dalhousie University.

Check Your Understanding

Knowledge/Understanding

1 In your own words, describe how a successful business can have a positive impact on the people who live in the community it serves.
2 What is the difference between standard of living and quality of life? What effect does standard of living have on quality of life?

Thinking/Inquiry

3 Create a bar chart of the statistics in Figure 3-5 (on page 70). Then write a caption for your chart in which you draw a conclusion about the quality of life in the different countries.

Communication

4 Create a concept web to show how one business contributes to the standard of living in your community. How does this business create wealth, jobs, and income for business owners, employees, other businesses, and the people in your community.

5 In the Business Profile for this chapter, you saw how Canadian Tire demonstrated its commitment to its employees and to the communities served by its retail stores. Write a newspaper article about another company that has demonstrated its commitment towards its employees and its community.

Wealth, Income, and Employment

Ownership and Profits

Business profits are necessary to keep the Canadian economy healthy. They provide wealth for business owners and shareholders and an incentive for them to start, expand, and maintain businesses. Profits can also provide increased income and job security for employees.

A business earns a profit when it has money left over after paying all its **expenses**: wages to employees, the cost of supplies, taxes, and payments on loans. **Profit** is the amount by which the **revenue** of a business exceeds its expenses. **Revenue** is the money that a business receives from the sale of goods and services.

Canada's Most Profitable Companies in 2000

Company	Profit ($000)	Number of Employees
BCE Inc. (Dec.00)	$4 851 000	75 000
Royal Bank (Oct.00)	$2 274 000	49 232
Canadian Imperial Bank of Commerce (Oct.00)	$2 060 000	44 215
Bank of Nova Scotia (Oct.00)	$1 926 000	40 946
Bank of Montreal (Oct.00)	$1 857 000	33 200
Bell Canada (Dec.00)	$1 453 000	45 073
ManuLife Financial (Dec.00)	$1 075 000	28 000
Toronto Dominion Bank (Oct.00)	$1 025 000	44 798
Bombardier Inc. (Jan.01)	$975 400	58 000
Alcan Aluminum (Dec.00)	$618 000	53 000

Figure 3-7 Some of Canada's most profitable companies also have the highest number of employees. How do these company profits contribute to Canadians' wealth and income?

Missions that Match

Business is learning that partnering with charities means gaining customers as well as giving to the community. It's a win-win situation for both the business and the charity. The business gets to help the charity continue to do its good work, and the business is viewed by consumers as a good corporate citizen.

More and more charities are offering companies an opportunity to work together with a cause that is a match with the company's corporate mission.

For example, coffee retailer Second Cup has successfully partnered with Foster Parents Plan of Canada. Second Cup wanted to support people in the developing countries where their coffee is grown, and Foster Parents Plan already had a program of community building in place in those countries. Today, Foster Parents Plan receives financial support through Second Cup's in-store fundraising promotions. Franchisees and customers donated more than $200 000 over the last two years. Foster Parents Plan also provides information about issues faced by developing countries to franchisees and staff through Second Cup's internal training programs.

Helping companies create a "feel good" experience for their customers is one way that charities are winning companies over. The Juvenile Diabetes Foundation Canada recognized that it was targeting an audience that Shoppers Drug Mart really cared about: people with diabetes. In 1994, the Foundation approached Shoppers to sponsor its annual charity walk. As part of the partnership, Shoppers customers are invited to show their support of diabetes research (and over 800 000 did in 2000) by contributing a loonie in exchange for the opportunity to sign their names on colorful paper shoes which are plastered on store walls and windows.

Figure 3-8 These two Second Cup employees visit with children in one of the African regions where the coffee sold in their store is grown.

Establishing corporate alliances is a strategy that many charities have adopted. They invest time and energy learning what companies want. They are also becoming more creative about how they can partner with businesses. By working together, businesses and charities make our society a better place for everyone.

Source: Adapted, with permission, from "Picking a Philanthropic Partner," *Marketing Magazine*, Sept. 7, 1998, vol. 103, page 16.

ACTIVITIES

1 Explain how business partnerships with charities can improve the quality of life for Canadians and people in developing countries.
2 Identify three companies and three charities in your community that would make a good partnership together. Explain your choices.
3 Identify a local community need that a business could help sponsor. Write a business letter encouraging the company to support your idea.

Profit can act as a regulator by ensuring that high quality goods and services are provided at prices that appeal to consumers. A business is more likely to earn a profit when it is run efficiently, which means that costs and expenses are kept as low as possible without affecting the quality of its goods or services. If the quality drops, then so will the sales and then the profits.

A profitable business needs to be run effectively. An effective, successful business meets the needs and wants of consumers and responds to consumer demand. A business that is not serving consumers will not be effective and will eventually stop earning profits.

A profitable business also needs to be able to expand and develop new products. Once a business is established, its owners need to be sure that it will grow and remain successful. Since a business will not be competitive in the future if it is not expanding and developing, it needs to use some of its profits to pay for new development. The research and development that goes into new products can be very expensive. However, the wise investment of some of a business's profits today will benefit owners, employees, and consumers in the future.

When the profits of a large company suddenly fall, the change can affect a country's economy. For example, after Nortel Networks reported lower than expected profits in the first quarter of 2001, its stock value dropped steeply, and it laid off thousands of workers in Canada and around the world. The fall in stock price of this reputable company also made people nervous about investing their wealth in new technology companies.

Employment

A strong business environment usually means most of the people in a community who want to work, are working. To have a strong economy, countries and communities need a high rate of employment.

Most Canadians earn money by working for a company or organization. Fortunately, business needs employees so it provides jobs. They can range from entry-level to senior executive positions.

The lowest paying jobs generally require few skills or require skills that many people have. The highest paying jobs generally require sophisticated or hard-to-find skills, and acceptance of difficult conditions, such as high rise construction, or danger, such as working on an oil rig in the Atlantic Ocean.

Figure 3-9 PCL, Canada's largest general contractor, was judged by its employees to be one of the best companies to work for in Canada. The company, which has been in business since 1906, is 100 percent owned by its employee shareholders. What difference do you think it would make if, as an employee, you shared the ownership of the company you worked for?

A combination of factors attracts people to jobs: location, a match of company requirements and a person's skills and aptitude, salary and benefits, and the opportunity to contribute to the organization or to society.

Jobs and the Economy

The state of the Canadian and global economies can also affect the creation of new jobs. When the economy is healthy, businesses tend to employ more workers and create more jobs. They employ more people so that they can produce more goods and services and take advantage of new business opportunities. When the economy is unhealthy, employment and job creation decrease. This makes it difficult for young people to get jobs.

When a large number of businesses have problems being profitable, the impact affects communities. During the early 1990s, the Canadian economy was in a recession. Consumers bought fewer goods and services. Businesses didn't produce as much, and they laid off employees. You will learn more about recession in Chapter 5.

From 1990 to 1996, the total workforce in Canada remained in the 13 600 000 to 13 700 000 range. Few new jobs were created, and so it was difficult for young people to get jobs. However, once the economy picked up during 1998 and 1999, the workforce numbers increased. Between April 1998 and April 1999, 371 900 new jobs were created.

Unemployment

To be classified as **unemployed**, Canadians have to be out of work and actively looking for work. Economic recessions are an important cause of unemployment. The factors of technology and globalization have a more complex relationship with employment. They can contribute to both employment and to unemployment, depending on the circumstances. For a company like Clearnet, advances in technology increased the need for employees. But for the Atlantic fishing industry, advances in technology led to a drastic decrease in the need for employees on fishing boats, in fish-processing plants, and in the many businesses that depended on the fishing industry.

A 1999 report called *Taking On Youth Employment—Canada's Business Venture For The New Millennium* (issued for the Corporate Council on Youth in the Economy) stated that young people suffered the most from the 1990s recession and have never fully recovered. The report indicated that, while total unemployment has declined, the percentage of unemployed young people remained unchanged. Young people often fill part-time, short-term positions, which are usually low paying, with few benefits or career opportunities.

The report went on to say that business and government had to find solutions to the many obstacles to employment that young people face. Otherwise, youth unemployment will have an enormous impact on Canada's economic future. As Anne Cira, a member of the Corporate Council said, "This is a wake-up call for corporate Canada. Tackling youth unemployment is not just a matter of social responsibility nor philanthropic contribution. The cost of ignoring this crisis will have enormous long-term impact on our country's future prosperity and productivity. It's pay now or later."

Level of Income

Your level of **income**, or the money you earn, affects your standard of living and quality of life. If you earn an adequate income, you will be able to satisfy your needs and wants, and likely will be able to solve the economic challenges that you face.

Figure 3-10 When people have a decent income, they are more likely to contribute to the charities that serve their communities.

Your level of income also makes an impact on your community. If your income supplies your needs and wants, then you will be able to support the businesses and charities in your community. These organizations, in turn, will create more products and provide services that help to improve the quality of life for the members of your community. People with a decent income are able to contribute money to help people in need.

As your level of income improves, you will also pay higher income taxes to federal and provincial governments. As you saw earlier in this chapter, governments use tax revenue to provide health and community services.

Factors Affecting Level of Income

Since your level of income has such a direct effect on your standard of living and quality of life, you need to know which factors decide income level. Among the most important are education, skills, and the conditions in the job market when you look for employment.

Education

Education, training, and lifelong learning are very important to businesses and their employees. Both your employment and job satisfaction will depend, to a large extent, on your level and type of education, and on your ability to continue to learn and to adapt to change. The business profile on Canadian Tire that opened this chapter shows how one successful company focuses on continued training and education for employees.

Percentage of Workforce Unemployed in 1999	
Average for total workforce	8.3%
Age bracket 25 or over	7.0%
Age bracket 15-24	15.0%
High-school drop-outs	14.7%
High-school graduates	8.3%
Technical/college graduates	6.6%
University graduates	4.3%

Figure 3-11

Education is a key factor in obtaining employment. In general terms, the more education you have the more likely you are to be employed.

Without education, as Figure 3-11 demonstrates, you run a greater risk of being unemployed.

In today's and tomorrow's business world,

- For 80 percent of jobs, workers will require at least a high school diploma.
- Workers who do not have a high-school diploma can expect to be unemployed for about 35 percent of their lives. It will also be hard for them to move up to better-paying jobs.
- Of the 80 percent of jobs requiring a high-school diploma, 50 percent will require an additional five years of education and/or training.
- In the areas of business with the fastest growth (for example, businesses related to Internet Web technologies), 90 percent of jobs will require college, university, or other educational training.

Employability Skills

According to the Conference Board of Canada (see Career Connect on page 80), you need to develop employability skills, not just at a paid job but in everything you do: at school and in volunteer work, sports, and clubs. **Employability skills** are the skills that employers are most concerned about. They are the critical skills that you must have to succeed in business whether you become a sole proprietor, a partner, or an employee. Many of the skills you learn everyday can be transferred to your work activities. A transferable skill is one that can be transferred from one situation to another.

For example, the teamwork that you practice on a soccer or hockey team will help you understand how workplace teams operate. Think of what would happen on a sports team if members didn't work together. What would be your chance of success if players were not willing to pass the soccer ball or hockey puck to other players?

Knowing which skills employers are looking for is important. Businesses pay more to employees who have the skills that they need. For example, today there is a need for educated and skilled workers in the software development industry. Some of the most creative and skilled of these workers are young people who developed their understanding of software and computers, not just through education, but also through their own curiosity about how such programs and systems work.

Market Conditions

Changes in market conditions cause changes in businesses' need for employees and in the wages businesses pay. As you saw in Chapter 2, changes such as globalization, advances in technology, and the growth of small businesses, especially in the service sector, have opened up new avenues of employment opportunities.

A major shift in the source of jobs occurred in the late twentieth century when the demand for services grew. The service industry covers fields such as marketing, accounting and auditing, finance, management consulting, telecommunications, and transportation as well as businesses related to computers. More high-paying jobs exist in service businesses than in manufacturing.

Employability Skills 2000+

The Conference Board of Canada knows the skills that employers are looking for because it is made up of business leaders, educators, and government representatives. The Board created Employability Skills 2000+ because teachers and students wanted to have a clear outline of the skills that Canadian employers are looking for. You will need these fundamental, personal-management, and teamwork skills to enter the workforce. And, after you are in the workplace, you will need to continue to practise and develop these skills to stay employed and to improve your income level.

Fundamental Skills

The skills needed as a base for further development.

You will be better prepared to progress in the world of work when you can:

Communicate

- Read and understand information presented in a variety of forms (e.g., words, graphs, charts, diagrams)
- Write and speak so others pay attention and understand
- Listen and ask questions to understand and appreciate the points of view of others
- Share information using a range of information and communications technologies (e.g., voice, e-mail, and computers)
- Use relevant scientific, technological and mathematical knowledge and skills to explain or clarify ideas

Manage Information

- Locate, gather and organize information using appropriate technology and information systems
- Access, analyze and apply knowledge and skills from various disciplines (e.g., the arts, languages, science, technology, mathematics, social sciences and the humanities)

Personal Management Skills

The personal skills, attitudes and behaviours that drive one's potential for growth.

You will be able to offer yourself greater possibilities for achievement when you can:

Demonstrate Positive Attitudes & Behaviours:

- Feel good about yourself and be confident
- Deal with people, problems and situations with honesty, integrity and personal ethics
- Recognize your own and other people's good efforts
- Take care of your personal health
- Show interest, initiative and effort

Be Responsible

- Set goals and priorities, balancing work and personal life
- Plan and manage time, money and other resources to achieve goals
- Assess, weigh and manage risk
- Be accountable for your actions and the actions of your group
- Be socially responsible and contribute to your community

Teamwork Skills

The skills and abilities needed to contribute productively.

You will be better prepared to add value to the outcomes of a task, project or team when you can:

Work with Others

- Understand and work within the dynamics of a group
- Ensure that a team's purpose and objectives are clear
- Be flexible: respect, be open to and supportive of the thoughts, opinions and contributions of others in a group
- Recognize and respect people's diversity, individual differences and perspectives
- Accept and provide feedback in a constructive and considerate manner
- Contribute to a team by sharing information and expertise
- Lead or support when appropriate, motivating a group for high performance
- Understand the role of conflict in a group to reach solutions
- Manage and resolve conflict when appropriate

Fundamental Skills
(continued)

Use Numbers
- Decide what needs to be measured or calculated
- Observe and record data using appropriate methods, tools and technology
- Make estimates and verify calculations

Think & Solve Problems
- Assess situations and identify problems
- Seek different points of view and evaluate them based on facts
- Recognize the human, interpersonal, technical, scientific and mathematical dimensions of a problem
- Identify the root cause of a problem
- Be creative and innovative in exploring possible solutions
- Readily use science, technology and mathematics as ways to think, gain and share knowledge, solve problems and make decisions
- Evaluate solutions to make recommendations or decisions
- Implement solutions
- Check to see if a solution works, and act on opportunities for improvement

Personal Management Skills
(continued)

Be Adaptable
- Work independently or as part of a team
- Carry out multiple tasks or projects
- Be innovative and resourceful: identify and suggest alternative ways to achieve goals and get the job done
- Be open and respond constructively to change
- Learn from your mistakes and accept feedback
- Cope with uncertainty

Learn Continuously
- Be willing to continuously learn and grow
- Assess personal strengths and areas for development
- Set your own learning goals
- Identify and access learning sources and opportunities
- Plan for and achieve your learning goals

Work Safely
- Be aware of personal and group health and safety practices and procedures, and act in accordance with these

Teamwork Skills
(continued)

Participate in Projects & Tasks
- Plan, design or carry out a project or task from start to finish with well defined objectives and outcomes
- Develop a plan, seek feedback, test, revise and implement
- Work to agreed quality standards and specifications
- Select and use appropriate tools and technology for a task or project
- Adapt to changing requirements and information
- Continuously monitor the success of a project or task and identify ways to improve

www.school.mcgrawhill.ca/resources/
The Conference Board of Canada offers many suggestions that will help you identify and develop your employability skills. Review their recommendations for developing skills at home, at school, in the workplace, and in the community.

ACTIVITIES

1. Brainstorm ways in which you already use some of these skills in your daily life.
2. How could feedback from others help you develop your employability skills?
3. Problem-solving is one of the most important skills in today's workplace. In small teams, create a chart to show how you could practice your problem-solving skills at home, at school, at work, and in your community.

There's no telling how far you can go with Talvest's complete family of funds. With mutual, segregated, index, 100% RSP-eligible and labour-sponsored funds, Talvest has all the tools you need to build and protect your wealth.

For more information, contact your financial advisor, call us at 1-800-268-8258 or visit our web site at www.talvest.com.

Life's long. Be ready.

The road ahead is all mine.

TALVEST
Mutual Funds

Other market conditions also have an effect on employment. For example, if you live in a region of Canada where the economy is depressed, there may be few job opportunities because businesses in the region are not doing well. On the other hand, discoveries of new resources can attract businesses and new residents to once remote or poor regions. Following positive exploration results, new mining companies are seeking diamonds in the Northwest Territories. Companies that prepare uncut gems for sale have brought in highly skilled Middle Eastern workers to train local residents. Companies that supply equipment and services to mines will locate nearby and attract employees.

People's changing needs and wants also affect business activity. As the baby boomers, who were born after World War II, move into their 60s, 70s, and 80s, there will be employment opportunities in businesses that serve this growing segment of the Canadian population. Which businesses might benefit from this change in demographics? Some examples are health-care, travel and tourism, and financial businesses.

Figure 3-12

Talvest Mutual Funds knows that retired Canadians form a growing market for their services.

Skills
Appendix

critical thinking

Check Your Understanding

Knowledge/Understanding

1 How do business profits generate wealth for business owners and shareholders?
2 How will your level of education affect your chances for future employment?
3 Why should you research market conditions when deciding on your career?

Thinking/Inquiry

4 What did Anne Cira mean when she said, "It's pay now or pay later" (page 73)? Discuss this quotation in small groups. Then, write a paragraph explaining how high unemployment among young people would affect Canadian society as a whole.

Communication

5 Working in a small team, investigate current factors that affect unemployment in one region of Canada. Watch television news reports for a few days and decide on one issue that interests all the members of your team. Research the issue using online and print sources. Then prepare a summary report and present it as a televised news report on the situation.

Application

6 Review the Conference Board of Canada employability skills (pages 76–77). Select one skill that you would most like to develop further. How could you work on developing this skill in your daily life—at home, at school, and in your leisure activities? Create a graphic organizer to show some ways that you could develop this skill.

Skills
Appendix

analysing media

The Workplace Community

Businesses contribute to the quality of life of their employees in a number of ways. A responsible business will make sure that the workplace is safe and healthy for its employees. It will also provide equal opportunity for all of its employees. Because these issues are very important in our society. Canadians have insisted that the provincial and federal governments create laws to ensure healthy and safe working environments where all people are treated equally.

Contribution of the Labour Movement

The Canadian **labour movement** is responsible for much of the federal and provincial legislation protecting workers' health, safety, and rights. Throughout the 1900s, unions fought for improvements to members' standard of living and quality of life: pensions, safe working conditions, health insurance, a living wage, maternity rights for women, and the workers' right to organize. As unions gained these rights, other Canadians insisted that governments pass laws giving the rights to everyone.

Biz.Bites

In 2000, approximately 3.7 million Canadians belonged to labour unions or federations. According to Statistics Canada, during 1999, the average hourly earnings of unionized workers were higher than those of non-unionized workers.

During the early 1990s, many union members lost their jobs because of the recession and global competition. At that time, job security and retraining became union issues. As business owners and managers reduced the number of employees, unions fought back. Algoma Steel Corporation, the steel industry and the unions arranged for the retraining of thousands of laid-off steelworkers in new careers. Some workers learned new trades while others trained to become nurses and teachers.

Safety in the Workplace

Figure 3-13 This historic photo by Lewis Wickes Hine shows a worker on the Empire State Building which was built in 1930-1931. Hine believed that he could use photos to persuade authorities to enact better labour laws. How might this photo have helped him achieve his goal?

On November 18, 1994, Sean Kells was pouring a chemical product containing toluene, a hazardous chemical, from a drum. The drum exploded and Sean received third-degree burns to 90 percent of his body. It was his third day on the job.

Sean was rushed to hospital, but died the next day. He was 19.

The drum containing the hazardous toluene wasn't marked. Sean hadn't received any training and he didn't know his health and safety rights and responsibilities. Since Sean's death, his family has been active, trying to increase health and safety awareness for young people. It can't bring Sean back, but they hope they can help prevent other deaths and injuries among young workers.

This true story from the Young Worker Awareness Web site illustrates the need for safety in the workplace. A good **health and safety program** for employees is preventative, and includes training for workers, regular inspections by professionals in the health and safety field, and a process for reacting swiftly to accidents and injuries. Employees should also be encouraged to approach their supervisor, a health and safety official, or human resources personnel if they have a health and safety concern.

Figure 3-14

On November 15, 2000, scaffolding on the Detroit Windsor Bridge broke. These two workers, who hung 36 metres over the icy Detroit River for 45 minutes, were saved by the safety harnesses that they had attached to the bridge.

- Prevention: It is employers' responsibility to create an environment that ensures workers' safety and health and to prevent accidents and environmental factors that cause illness. The Occupational Health and Safety Act of Ontario specifies regulations that businesses must follow. All dangerous or hazardous materials or situations are to be clearly marked, and Material Safety Data Sheets (MSDS) are to be available for all hazardous products. These MSDS need to describe the hazards of a product, it safe use, and the steps to take in case of an emergency.

- Inspection: Businesses must do regular inspections to ensure that all health and safety regulations are being followed, that the workplace is safe, and that employees are properly trained.

- Training: Employees, should be trained to use safely any hazardous materials or machinery they will work with. They should be trained for emergency situations, for use of dangerous materials in general—receive Workplace Hazardous Materials Information System (WHMIS) training—and have specific training for their workplace.

- Reaction: Employees should report any injury to a supervisor and have the injury attended to immediately. Injuries also need to be reported to the Workplace Safety and Insurance Board (WSIB).

Biz.Bites

Some work environments have been found to contain toxic mould. In January 2001, the York Region District School Board found toxic mould in a dozen portables at a Markham school. The problem was so severe that the portables had to be destroyed.

Web Connect

www.school.mcgrawhill.ca/resources
For suggestions on how to stay safe in the workplace, visit the Young Worker Awareness site. While you're at the site, see how well you do on the Safety IQ Test.

Health in the Workplace

Many employers recognize that the healthier their employees are, the more productive they will be. After all, employees spend almost two-thirds of their waking hours at work. In a healthy environment, employees work more efficiently and take less time off.

As a result, many companies are providing

- better lighting and less noise
- more ergonomically sound office equipment (equipment that has a shape and size that reduces strain on users)
- more nutritious cafeteria food
- exercise programs
- access to occupational health nurses, nutritionists, massage therapists, and similar professionals who regularly visit the company

Stress can be a major health problem as business becomes more competitive and employees struggle to balance work and home responsibilities. Stress can make people sick. Successful employers pay attention to workloads, redistributing them when a difficult deadline looms. They also keep lines of communication open, so that employees can discuss their concerns about job insecurities, the demands of their jobs, and other workplace stresses.

Figure 3-15 Keith Kocho, who runs ExtendMedia Inc., takes his dogs to work and has found that their presence helps relieve employee stress.

Equal Opportunity

The Canadian Charter of Rights and Freedoms says,

Every individual is equal before and under the law and has the right to the equal protection and equal benefit of the law without discrimination and, in particular, without discrimination based on race, national or ethnic origin, colour, religion, sex, age or mental or physical disability.

To protect Canadians from unfair treatment or discrimination, the federal and provincial governments have created laws to provide **equal opportunities** in the workplace.

The Ontario Human Rights Code states that every person has a right to freedom from discrimination in employment. This includes the promotion of equality in advertisements for jobs, as well as in application forms and job interviews.

The Canadian Employment Equity Act of 1995 states that "no person shall be denied employment opportunities or benefits for reasons unrelated to ability." The Act goes so far as to say that some people who have been discriminated against in the past—persons with physical disabilities, women, members of minority groups and Aboriginal people—may need special treatment to gain equal opportunities in the workplace

Employees who feel that they have been discriminated against can contact the Human Rights Commission. It has been set up to hear and investigate complaints. If the employee has evidence that the discrimination has caused damages, he or she can request and obtain compensation.

While these statements about equality sound hopeful, they are not always easy to put into effect. Ironically, it took 15 years and both decisions from the Federal Court of Canada and a Canadian Human Rights Tribunal before the federal government agreed, in 1999, to pay up to $5 billion in back pay to about 200 000 federal public service workers. The back pay was ordered to bring the salaries of female federal government employees up to the level of their male counterparts.

Figure 3-16

Janet Mahoney-Rose reads through pay-equity related papers in October 1999. She had joined the public service as a secretary in 1958 and figured she would receive $30 000 to $35 000 in back pay from the federal government.

Knowledge/Understanding

1 How has the labour movement contributed to better working conditions for Canadians?

2 Explain, in your own words, the four elements of a good health and safety program.

Thinking/Inquiry

3 How can employers ensure the health of their employees? Role-play a scenario where an employee representative presents employee health concerns to his or her supervisor.

Communication

4 Prepare a panel discussion on the benefits companies gain by offering equal opportunities to all employees. Also consider how the community at large benefits from equal opportunity.

Application

5 As a class, decide on one current safety or health issue that is related to business and that is being talked about in the news media. Discuss the following questions: What problems does this issue reflect? What has caused these problems? What has been done to resolve the problems? What solutions would you recommend?

Skills
Appendix

oral presentations

Skills
Appendix

working in groups

Business and Community Challenges

Sometimes business interests conflict with other community interests. The Issues Affecting Business feature at the end of this section describes how conflict over a potential waste site created a deep divide in the local community. When such conflicts arise, both sides need to try to negotiate a solution. Finding one isn't always easy though.

For example, what happens if you are unemployed and could get a job at the new manufacturing plant proposed in your community? What if your friends and neighbours don't want the plant because it would be built on wetlands? You and your children enjoy seeing the wildlife, but you need the job. Considering both sides of the issue, would you vote for or against the construction of the manufacturing plant.

Environmental Concerns

As you saw in Chapter 2, protection of the environment has become a high priority. When manufacturing by-products containate the environments, pollution results. Misuse of land, water, and air resources, ozone depletion, and greenhouse gas emissions have also caused problems.

Pollution control and protection of the environment are the responsibilities of the individual, business, and the government. A socially responsible business takes action to reduce or eliminate operations that pollute. The government has an obligation to pass laws to ensure the environment is protected. These laws often include heavy fines for businesses that ignore or neglect their responsibilities.

Ballard Fuel Cells

Some companies are focussed entirely on finding solutions for pollution. Automobile companies have been talking about environmentally friendly cars for many years. However, Ballard Fuel Cells of Vancouver has gone well beyond the talking stage. The company, whose motto is "Power to Change the World," has developed environmentally clean fuel cells to run cars and buses and to generate electricity. These fuel cells don't depend on gas and oil products, so they don't pollute the atmosphere or contribute to global warming. Ballard cells run on hydrogen and oxygen. The only by-products are heat and pure water vapour (see Figure 3-17).

Figure 3-17 When the first Ballard fuel-cell buses were introduced in Vancouver, British Columbia's Transportation Minister Joy MacPhail drank a toast—using water vapour from the bus exhaust!

Ballard works in partnership with DaimlerChrysler AG and Ford Motor Co. to make the expensive fuel cell affordable. The company also has orders from Honda and Nissan to supply fuel cells and support services to develop environmentally friendly cars. The car companies and Ballard hope to begin manufacturing cars using the fuel cells by 2004. BC Transit in Vancouver already has test fuel-cell buses in service.

Figure 3-18 How do natural spaces like this one contribute to the quality of life of people living in the surrounding community?

Land Use

Should land in our communities be used for farms, factories, roads, garbage dumps, shopping malls, and/or green belts? Who should decide how land is used? These are some of the difficult issues communities face.

Members of a community sometimes face conflicting needs and wants regarding land use. After all, a community needs employment, so some land has to be given to businesses. Homes are needed for the people who work in the businesses. Roads are needed so people can get to and from work. Shopping malls are needed to provide the goods and services that satisfy the community's needs and wants. Yet land is also needed for growing food, recreation, and wildlife habitats.

Sometimes, business decisions have a devastating affect on a community. The garbage accumulated by households and businesses creates a major environmental problem, and many steps have been taken to reduce the amount generated. We have recycling programs for paper, plastic and glass, but we still need garbage dumps.

An Olympic Bid

Even an Olympic bid can create concerns. With Toronto as a contender for the Olympic games in 2008, the town of Markham proposed building a $13.3 million aquatic centre. This centre would provide the community with jobs, generate additional income, and have a positive impact on the community.

On the other hand, depending on the location of the centre, the impact could be negative for some residents. Some homes may be expropriated. Expropriation is a legal process whereby the government can claim a property because it is judged to be essential to the general welfare of the community. The landowner receives a price based on fair market price but is forced to move. At the very least, congested roadways and additional parking could be a problem for citizens of Markham who live near the sports facility.

Traffic

The transportation services needed for business also create problems. When automobiles became affordable, people enjoyed more convenient, quicker travel over longer distances. Canadians also began to suffer from rush hours, pollution, delays because of road maintenance, and the dangers of moving hazardous materials.

Building a highway to move goods and people faster can cause hardships for a community. If the new highway bypasses the community travellers will no longer frequent local restaurants and gas stations.

When companies have trouble getting goods from their plants to buyers, they often move to locations that are more accessible. Many companies that once located in downtown Toronto to be near the railways, the major mode of transportation, are now in less expensive surrounding regions. They also choose a site that is more accessible to highways, such as the 401, so they can ship goods east to Montreal, south through Buffalo, New York, or west to the U.S., through Windsor.

Figure 3-19 Many people face this kind of rush-hour traffic problem as they travel to and from work each day. Can you and your fellow students come up with any possible solutions to this annoying problem?

The Interdependence of Businesses

Changes in the business environment of a community can also cause short- or long-term problems for other businesses. The opening or closing of a business can cause losses for others.

In 1999, the Eaton family announced that it was closing many of its stores. Most of these stores were in shopping centres. Many Eatons' employees lost their jobs. This proved very stressful for the people, families, and communities involved.

Smaller businesses located near those stores also suffered because consumers stopped coming. This also happened at Fairview Mall in Toronto, when two major businesses shut down, Loblaw's grocery store in 2000 and the Cineplex Odeon movie theatres early in 2001.

For a number of years, Future Shop, which sells computers, home audio equipment, and appliances, has been a successful consumer electronics business in Canada. Then an American company, Best Buy Co., announced that it would open up between 40 and 60 stores in Canada, starting with Ontario in the fall of 2001. Best Buy owns more than 360 stores in the U.S. and is a very aggressive retailer. The company is likely to offer consumers lower prices than Future Shop. This may result in fierce competition. While this will benefit the consumer in the short-term—because of lower prices—the move may damage the business community in the long-term if it seriously hurts Future Shop's business.

Check Your Understanding

Knowledge/Understanding

1 What environmental problem is Ballard Fuel Cells trying to resolve? Why is it important to solve this problem?

2 How might decisions about land use cause conflicts in a community?

Thinking/Inquiry

3 Discuss how land is used in your community. Estimate how much land is used for manufacturing and other businesses, for farming, roads, green areas, and shopping malls. If there are problems around the land use in your community, how would you resolve these problems?

Communication

4 Prepare an illustrated report to respond to the following questions. What have been the short- and long-term effects of retail business closings or openings in your community? What problems were created for other businesses by those openings or closings?

Application

5 Research one Canadian environmental problem that has been caused by business development. Prepare a brief oral report and present it to your classmates.

Skills
Appendix

writing reports

Skills
Appendix

oral presentations

In 1990, the saga of the Adams Mine began. The iron ore mine near Kirkland Lake, Ontario, closed in March putting 350 miners out of work. Notre Development Corporation, a North Bay company, bought the mine and wanted to turn the site into a garbage dump. The saga ended 10 years later when a proposed deal to ship Toronto's garbage to the abandoned mine went sour. In the intervening years, the Adams Mine was a focal point for business, community, and environmental interests. Was any one interest right or wrong? You be the judge.

When the mine closed, the residents of the three neighbouring municipalities—Kirkland Lake, Englehart, and Larder Lake—were anxious about the decline of the northern Ontario mining industry. The growing global economy and a drop in international gold prices had spurred this decline. Then the value of iron ore dropped. In all, seven mines closed. The rate of unemployment among the 10 000 residents of Kirkland Lake, the largest community in the area, rose considerably.

More than 300 kilometres away, the city of Toronto was running out of space to dump its garbage. Local landfills were almost full and those still operating were scheduled to close soon. What could Toronto do with the 1.7 million tonnes of waste per year it was producing? Only about 250 000 tonnes of it was getting recycled every year. The Adams Mine seemed like a perfect solution.

Initially, some people were positive about reusing giant mine pits as a dumpsite. The mayor of nearby Englehart said her community supported the project because it would save jobs. One Kirkland Lake businessman said: "My son, my daughter, my neighbour's son, my neighbour's daughter, they could all use the jobs that are going to be created." In 1990, Toronto selected Adams Mine as the "preferred site" for its garbage.

Figure 3-20 "I am here representing the Algonquin people, but I am also representing a broad-based coalition which includes Aboriginals, farmers, residents of Ontario and Quebec, English and French. Here we have an example of all residents of the watershed working together to protect the earth and to protect our future." Chief Carol McBride, Timiskaming First Nation.

Soon there was a deal between Toronto, councillors from Kirkland Lake, Englehart, and Larder Lake, and a consortium known as Rail Cycle North (RCN), to allow Toronto's garbage to be hauled to the abandoned mine. The partner companies in the consortium included Notre Development Corporation, Canadian Waste Services (which would manage the site), CN Rail and Ontario Northland (which would haul the garbage to the site), and Miller Waste Services (which would haul it within Toronto).

The deal said the Kirkland Lake region would be a "willing host" for Toronto's garbage. Toronto would pay about $50 per tonne to ship it. The Rail Cycle North deal was one of several bids Toronto received. It was also the lowest bid by far. But one year later, the Ontario government decided to examine the proposal more carefully. Was it truly safe and effective?

RCN maintained that it had a good system. It said that it had successfully handled the garbage of Seattle, Washington, since 1991. It planned a

Figure 3-21 Kirkland Lake is 598 kilometres from Toronto. If the Adams Mine site had been used for Toronto's garbage, what would have been some of the environmental problems that Toronto would have transferred to the region?

hydraulic containment system to prevent the dangerous leakage of toxins from garbage into the surrounding groundwater. Because ground-water flows inward and would push against the garbage, RCN said there would be little chance of toxins leaking outward. Water that collected in the pit would be treated with state of the art technology worth $8 million.

RCN projected staggering economic benefits to the area. It estimated that the landfill would generate $1 billion over a 20-year span. RCN planned to invest $40 million in the two-year start-up phase. Local communities could use the landfill at no charge and would receive more than $20 million in royalties. It was projected that the landfill would create 80 jobs. The value of wages and benefits was estimated by RCN at $6.3 million annually.

But many groups had unanswered questions. Farmers and other residents doubted that the RCN hydraulic containment system would work. It had only been tested on a computer model. In addition, the mine was to be lined with gravel instead of clay, which could allow toxins to leak through small holes. Some of Ontario's best farmland is situated at the tip of Lake Temiskaming, just downstream from the mine.

Temiskaming residents mounted a highly public campaign to have the landfill "dumped."

They protested regularly by blocking the railway tracks leading to the site. They presented their concerns to the Ontario government in 1998. The Temiskaming Municipal Association passed a resolution opposing the landfill.

The Algonquin people of the Temiskaming First Nation band located in nearby Notre-Dame-Du-Nord, Quebec, opposed the project. Chief Carol McBride said the band had "Aboriginal title to the Adams Mine site … so you might as well take the contract off the table." She also pointed out that the Algonquin people were concerned with the health and safety risks.

The Adams Mine Landfill received its Certificate of Approval from the Ontario Ministry of the Environment in April 1999. Opponents immediately called for the federal government to assess the safety of the mine.

The Adams Mine deal collapsed in October 2000 when RCN rejected a condition set by Toronto Council. The city wanted some protection against "unavoidable costs" should the system fail. RCN disagreed, wanting the city to pay such costs. Toronto went back to the drawing board to try to solve the problem of its growing garbage.

ACTIVITIES

1 Use a graphic organizer to trace the chain of cause and effect in this article. Where did the problems at Adams Mine begin? How did they lead to the situation at the end of the article?

2 Imagine what it would have been like to have been involved in this conflict. Do you think you could have found a solution? Hold a town hall meeting and try to work out a solution that will offer some benefit to each of the parties in the conflict.

3 Waste disposal has become a major problem for municipalities. What are some business opportunities that might arise from the need for a solution to this problem?

Chapter Review

Points to Remember

- The Canadian economy is made up of the contributions of business, labour, and the government.

- Business affects individuals, and communities, standard of living and quality of life.

- Profits help the economy grow and remain strong.

- Business environments and employment levels are closely connected.

- Economic recessions, technological change, and globalization can be causes of unemployment.

- Education, skills, and market conditions affect individuals' level of income and standard of living.

- Unions, employees, employers, and the government work to ensure safety in the workplace and fair labour practices.

- Environmental issues and businesses interpendence can cause problems for businesses and communities.

Activities

Knowledge/Understanding

1 Outline three possible negative impacts that business may have on a community.

2 Using the Adams Mine feature, prepare a chart showing the challenges this community faced as it tried to protect both local businesses and the natural environment. How did the business and community needs come into conflict?

3 Write a paragraph in which you explain how business owners, employees, and the community are interdependent.

Thinking/Inquiry

1 Working with two other students, brainstorm responses to the following questions: How does employee stress and illness affect the profit of a business? What is the cost, to a business, of employee sick days? What new businesses have started up as a result of employee stress?

Skills
Appendix

researching

2 Research one business issue that has had an effect on the quality of life in your community. Present the results of your research as a multimedia presentation, a role play of a town hall meeting, or a panel discussion.

3 Select a small business you might be interested in owning. Decide which of the Employability Skills 2000+ you would want your employees to have. Then write a classified newspaper advertisement for employees.

Communication

Skills
Appendix

critical thinking

1 Visit a local business, interview the owner, and write a summary of your interview. Focus your questions on whether the owner is satisfied with the return on the investment of time and money put into the business. What are the reasons for the owner's satisfaction or dissatisfaction?

2 Work with a partner to investigate the kinds of dangers young workers face in the workplace. Prepare a poster for a bulletin board on Young Worker Awareness.
   a) Select one of chemical, physical, biological or ergonomic hazards.
   b) Research the hazard and the steps that have been taken by industry and by governments in Canada to minimize its dangers.

Skills
Appendix

researching

   c) Be sure to include the steps that should be taken to prevent danger, to train employees, to inspect to ensure that all safety measures are in place, and to react quickly when an accident happens.
   d) Finally, draw up a safety checklist that would be useful for this particular hazard.

Application

1 Create a concept web in which you compare the impact of business on one high, one middle, and one lower income community or region of Canada. Select one of the topics discussed in this chapter as the focus of your concept web.

2 Jake is organizing a T-ball league for the neighbourhood children. The parents are interested, but the project will require money for uniforms, coaching, and refereeing. Jake agrees to approach local businesses to see if they would be interested in sponsoring a team.

   a) Outline what Jake should say when trying to convince the business people to give money to his organization in order to sponsor a team.

   b) Draft a letter that Jake might send to specific local businesses appealing for help.

   c) Exchange letter drafts with an editing partner and check to be sure that the letter is persuasive. Does the letter present convincing arguments? Does it clearly state the benefits to be gained by both the sponsoring business and by the community?

Skills
Appendix

building an argument

Internet Extension

1 Workplace safety is promoted in many media—posters, television commercials, newspaper advertisements, billboards, and Web sites. Some of these media campaigns are effective and others are not. Which medium do you think is most likely to have the desired effect on young workers? What kind of content will impress on young people the need for workplace safety?

2 Use E-Stat at Statistics Canada to compare the current employment situation in different provinces in Canada. How would these differences affect the standard of living and quality of life of Canadian living in those provinces?

UNIT

2

Conducting Business in a Competitive Marketplace and in the Changing Workplace

CHAPTER 4
Factors Affecting Business Success

CHAPTER 5
Market Conditions and Business Environments

CHAPTER 6
Human Resources and Management

CHAPTER 7
Marketing

CHAPTER 8
Accounting

Overall Expectations

By the end of this unit, you will

- analyse the major factors influencing the success of Canadian businesses

- explain how businesses are affected by variations in market conditions and environments for conducting business

- explain how current issues affect Canadian businesses

- explain the importance and role of human resources and management in business

- explain the role of marketing and accounting in business

When the factors of business success are discussed, you rarely hear much about "luck." That is because every business experiences good luck and bad luck. Therefore, the study of business focuses on the factors that, over time, are an asset to any business. You will learn about these factors in Chapter 4.

Businesses must compete within certain market conditions and business environments. You will learn in Chapter 5 about the role played by supply and demand, the stages of the business cycle, competition, and legislation to protect consumers. A key competitive advantage for a business is high morale among employees, so you will learn in Chapter 6 how business managers can help employees achieve their own goals, while making the business profitable. The role of the human resources department will be explored, as well as the rights and responsibilities of employees and employers.

You will learn in Chapter 7 how companies make marketing decisions. The best management, employees, products, or services in the world will not help a company if its message does not get out to the public through the critical function of marketing, which includes all forms of advertising.

But how does a business know if it is profitable or not? Did it make more money than it spent? The most important tool for determining whether a business is profitable is its accounting records. Chapter 8 will explain how the study of the key financial documents of a business provides information on its true value and profitability.

CHAPTER

4 Factors Affecting Business Success

KEY TERMS

e-business

intranet

extranet

market niche

demography

baby-boom generation

perseverance

front-line employees

quality control

product recall

ISO standards

Specific Expectations

After studying this chapter, you will be able to

- **identify various factors affecting business activity that have contributed to the success of Canadian companies and entrepreneurs**

- **compare levels of customer service and quality of goods and services among a variety of competing companies**

- **identify factors that influence employees' attitudes and the quality of their work**

Many different factors contribute to the success of any business. Businesses today have to be able to respond to change quickly, and they have to use the new information technologies–like the Internet–wisely. They need to understand demography and how it affects market demand so that they can satisfy consumers' needs and wants.

Successful business people know that they have to take risks, but not foolhardy risks. They need to have a vision and passion for what they do, and they need to have perseverance to get them through the rough times. More and more business people are working in teams to achieve their goals of providing quality products and customer service. Wise business people also know that they need to foster the kind of employee attitudes that bring about quality work.

Bombardier

Two visionaries enabled the Canadian company Bombardier Inc. to become a spectacular success: J. Armand Bombardier, who invented the snowmobile, and Laurent Beaudoin, who helped the company become a global business leader.

When Armand Bombardier started his small private company more than half a century ago, it manufactured his new invention, the snowmobile. Today, Bombardier has 79 000 employees in 23 countries and is a leading competitor for airplane and mass transit contracts all over the world. It has railway and subway cars in Disneyland, Montreal, New York, Asian countries, and the Chunnel, a tunnel under the English Channel connecting France and England. It has sold airplanes to companies around the world.

Why did Bombardier become so successful? How did a small local company become a global leader in each of the markets it entered? How was Bombardier able to respond so well to change in some of the most competitive global markets?

Back in 1922, in Valcourt, Quebec, when he was 15, Armand Bombardier built his first snowmobile, using an old sleigh, a propeller, and the motor from a Ford Model T automobile. He and his brother promptly smashed the new invention into a barn. But that didn't stop the young inventor. He continued to work on his plans for a snow car. He knew, long before others did, that such a vehicle would be useful during Canadian winters.

In 1942, Armand Bombardier started his company to manufacture tracked vehicles—snowmobiles—that could travel over the snow. During World War II, he diversified by developing wide-tracked troop carriers for the Canadian military. These vehicles could drive through snow, swamp, and deep mud. After the war, he again successfully diversified by introducing a wide-track, all-terrain Muskeg Tractor for construction work. By 1959, he was producing his first Ski-Doos. Armand Bombardier died in 1964, at the early age of 52.

Bombardier became a public company in 1969. By 1974, the high price of fuel had caused sales of Bombardier snowmobiles to fall by 70 percent. They were just too expensive for people to run. The company

Figure 4-1   The J. Armand Bombardier Foundation contributes 3% of the company's pretax dollars, $6 million in 1999, to national and regional organizations in education, health, culture, and social services.

Figure 4-2   Laurent Beaudoin began his career as a chartered accountant. How might this background have helped him bring Bombardier through its rough periods?

Figure 4-3 Bombardier has become one of Canada's leading exporters of business jets, regional aircraft, rail transportation equipment, and motorized recreational products. The company's headquarters remains in Montreal, even though it does business all over the world.

was in trouble. Laurent Beaudoin, the president of Bombardier, knew that the company would have to change if it was going to become successful again.

Beaudoin decided that Bombardier would become a leader in the transportation industry. He began by taking calculated risks on transportation companies that were in trouble. Over the next 20 years, Bombardier acquired four aircraft companies: Canadair in Montreal, Learjet in Kansas, Shorts in Northern Ireland, and de Havilland in Toronto. Because Beaudoin negotiated government support for these takeovers, he was also able to save local jobs.

Today, one of Bombardier's most successful products is the Canadair Regional Jet, which airlines in 14 countries have bought. This product fills a growing market niche for smaller regional jet planes. These aircraft allow smaller airlines to carry passengers to places that were considered out of the way a few years ago.

Bombardier continues to focus on product quality and customer service. It has to! Otherwise it could not succeed in its highly competitive markets where a single contract can be worth billions of dollars. By January 2001, the gross revenues of the company were $16.1 billion. As you read this chapter, keep these two visionaries—Armand Bombardier and Laurent Beaudoin—in mind.

Ask yourself, how vision, perseverance, and the ability to respond to technological and market change led to their success? Why can some business people spot market trends before their competitors do? How do commitments to quality and to customer service contribute to a company's success?

Qualities of a Successful Business

Some businesses, like Bombardier, become very successful. Other businesses do not do as well. What makes the difference? How do some businesses manage to make the right product or offer the right service, just when people want it?

One factor that improves chances of success is the ability to respond well to change. Change happens frequently in today's world. Competition for customers is fierce. If you don't adapt in order to meet your customers' demands, you can be sure that your competitors will.

You also have to know your target market well and find out everything about new opportunities and the new needs people will have. Then you have to focus on filling your market's needs and wants before your competitors do.

Responding to Change

At a time when technology changes quickly and when companies can easily operate around the world, businesses have to change or risk failure. As you saw in Chapter 2, the business environment in Canada and other industrialized nations is changing rapidly. To succeed, businesses have to respond quickly and effectively. Those companies that use the new technologies, especially the Internet and other communication technologies, and that take advantage of the global market will have a better chance of succeeding than those that do not.

Because of their size, small businesses are often able to respond to changing consumer demands more quickly than larger businesses. Small businesses are also likely to be in closer contact with their customers, so they know when their needs and wants change. This knowledge can give smaller companies a competitive advantage, at least in the short term.

However, some very large companies have also responded successfully to technological change. For example, today automated banking machines and

Figure 4-4 Both small and big business have to respond to the changing business environment. On its trains, VIA Rail Canada provides fully-equipped meeting facilities for small and medium-sized businesses. Why might this service convince business travellers to go by train rather than by airplaine?

Internet banking are available 24 hours a day. These technologies allow us to avoid long line-ups at Canadian banks. In the food industry, checking-out at large supermarkets became quicker in the 1970s when the food industry put universal bar codes on products and used scanners to collect information. Some supermarket chains, Dominion for example, are now experimenting with allowing customers to check themselves out.

E-Business

E-business, which is short-form for "electronic business," is business that is conducted over the Internet. E-business involves buying and selling as well as providing services and customer support. Both small and large businesses use the Internet to buy supplies and parts, to do research, to bid on proposals, and to work together. By using e-business, companies can work with business partners anywhere in the world.

Companies like Amazon.com and eBay have been able to use the Internet successfully. Some other companies, such as Lands' End (see page 114), have not been as successful in responding to this business change. As the failure of many e-businesses show, being quick to respond to change is not enough. Businesses also need to do research and develop a workable business plan to compete successfully in the e-business world.

More and more people are using the Internet to purchase everything from books (at Chapters' site) to computers (at Future Shop's site). However, some consumers are still concerned about the security issues of using their credit cards to purchase items over the Internet.

Intranets and Extranets

E-business also includes development of intranets and extranets, both of which are supposed to be secure networks that can be used only by those the company wants to let onto the network. However, some of these aren't all that secure. They have been quite spectacularly broken into by hackers who consider the word "secure" to be a challenge to their hacking skills.

An **intranet** is a network of computers that are connected within the company. As an employee, you can feel free to share company information without being overheard by people outside the company. An **extranet** allows businesses

Web Connect

www.school.mcgrawhill.ca/resources
Visit eBiz4Teens to find out more about ebusiness and to read some real-life success stories of teenagers who have become eBiz entrepreneurs.

to share information with selected suppliers or with other businesses. Extranets allow businesses to serve their business customers quickly and efficiently.

Shoppers Drug Mart has built its own satellite network which is owned and operated by the company itself. (See Figure 4-5.) David Parket, who administers the program, calls it a "lifeline to our stores." The stores get clearance for credit card and debit card transactions over their network. They use it to manage inventory, order supplies, and receive weekly marketing and operational information from their head office. Eventually, Shoppers intends to use the network to train employees through distance learning.

Competing for Sales on the Internet

In the battle for Internet sales, some companies have been very successful. Others have failed. In between these extremes are businesses that are building and adapting their online presence with greater or less success. For example, during the Christmas season of 2000, eToys Inc. expected to double its sales over the 1999 season. Instead, sales dropped and the company had to lay off 70 percent of its employees. Because it had spent so much to set up its Web site and distribution channels, the company didn't have much cash to fall back on when income dropped.

Figure 4-5 Dave Parket, of Shoppers Drug Mart, wants to use the company's network for distance learning for employees. How might this use of technology contribute to both employees' attitude towards Shoppers and to the quality of their work?

Retail Sales Problems

During the same 2000 Christmas season, Eatons (now owned by Sears), Hudson's Bay, and Canadian Tire ventured into the treacherous Internet waters to sell products at their web sites. How did these new e-tailers measure up?

According to Marina Strauss of the *Globe and Mail*, "there were flaws in the process at all three e-tailers." Customers had problems getting accurate information about products at the Web sites or even understanding some of the shipping and delivery instructions. Some orders arrived on time, but the wrong product had been sent. According to Ms Strauss, one of the main problems shoppers had was the lack of adequate customer service and accurate information when they called to correct an error in the shipment.

The Success of eBay

On the other hand, eBay has managed to successfully respond to the challenge of selling on the Internet by using an entirely different approach.

When Pierre Omidyar and Jeff Skoll started eBay in 1995, it was a small auction Web site that specialized in collectibles, like Beanie Babies. Since then, eBay has become a major force in Internet selling. eBay doesn't actually sell items; it serves as a site where sellers with things to sell can connect up with buyers who want to buy. One thing that Omidyar and Skoll did that many other start-up e-businesses don't do is hire a highly skilled business professional to run their company. They chose Meg Whitman, who had lots of experience as a consumers products executive.

eBay is still an auction site. But now it offers Sun Microsystems servers (for approximately $15 000), GM cars through eBay Motors, and even authentic Disney studio props such as Cruella De Vil's costumes from *102 Dalmations*.

Figure 4-6 How has eBay managed to establish itself as a successful e-business when so many others are either still struggling or have failed?

Filling a Market Niche

As a business person, you need to know where your best business opportunities are. You need to know to whom you want to sell your goods and services. You'll ask yourself: Do I want to try to sell in larger markets where there are many competitors and products? Or do I want to focus on a market niche?

A **market niche** is a small segment of the larger market. Some business owners look for these smaller, profitable markets and then design goods and services to serve them. Many small businesses focus on one particular market niche and try to position themselves as the specialist in that market. For example, a restaurant that specializes in chocolate desserts will not appeal to all consumers. But if the desserts are always delicious, then chocolate-dessert lovers will be regular customers.

In the computer field, users need many different components: printers, monitors, scanners, modems, and so on. Sometimes the big retailers and providers don't stock all of these components. Or, if they do, they can't readily help customers find the best item among the wide range of products available.

However, smaller companies, like Mark McLane's Printer Works (Figure 4-7), have seen a business opportunity in this computer component problem. They fill a market niche by knowing a great deal about the limited range of products they sell. Mark can offer his customers sound advice and good customer support, as well as the printers and scanners that they need.

Ani-Mat Inc., another small and specialized business, manages to address a market niche and help solve an environmental problem at the same time. The company recycles vehicle tires to create rubber mats which are designed for animal comfort. Dairy farmers, who are also in a very competitive market these days, find that these mats improve their animals' productivity. The fact that Ani-Mat has tripled its sales in three years shows that they have identified and are successfully serving a niche market.

Figure 4-7 Mark McLane has identified a market niche in his home province of PEI. Mark's company, Printer Works, specializes in the sale, service, and supplies of printing and imaging software. Since 1995, sales at the company have grown at the rate of 40 to 50 percent each year.

Understanding Demographics

Demography is the study of statistics relating to populations or communities. Demographers keep track of statistics relating to births, deaths, age, income levels, population movements, and so on. Studying demographic trends helps business people assess how population changes may affect the growth and development of the economy and business.

How do demographic statistics provide business opportunities? They give clues to the growth markets of the future. Creative and innovative entrepreneurs can spot the needs that will be created by these trends, and come up with ideas to fill those needs.

For example, if more people are moving into a geographic region than are moving out, a home builder may decide that it is a good place to build new homes. On the other hand, if a large proportion of the population is getting older, a business owner may decide to focus on products or services that the growing segment of the population will use.

Biz.Bites

Statistics Canada projects that by 2016 there will be more seniors than children in Canada. By 2016, seniors are expected to make up 20 percent of the population.

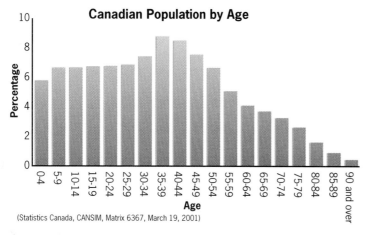

Canadian Population by Age

(Statistics Canada, CANSIM, Matrix 6367, March 19, 2001)

Figure 4-8 Where is the biggest bulge in this population bar graph? What kinds of markets would serve the demographic group represented by the bulge? How will this consumer group's needs and wants change over the next 20 years?

The highest concentration of the **baby boom generation**—people who were born between 1947 and 1966—is presently between the ages of 35 and 55. This group makes up about 30 percent of the total population, so it is a very large market for businesses. Baby boomers influence demand and the kinds of goods and services that businesses offer.

Approximately 12 percent of the population are now over the age of 65, and this segment will increase over the next decade. People are living longer than they did in the past because they are paying more attention to health, fitness, and proper nutrition. Advances in medicine are also helping people live longer (See Figure 4-8).

Demographics and Teenage Markets

Marketers study the demographics of your age group because, especially in North America, you and your friends are an important group of consumers. Many teenagers have money to spend. Marketers also believe that if they can attract you now, you will remain customers in the future. Think about your own needs and wants. What kinds of goods and services are you interested in? What businesses provide you with those goods and services?

One example of a product that is of interest to the teenage market is MP3 players. These players allow you to use new technologies to download and listen to music from the Internet or a computer network. There are two types of MP3 players: internal (SoundJam, MusicMatch) which stay in your computer, and external (Nomad and Rio) which you can carry around. A market exists for these players, especially the external ones. As you might expect, the main demographic group purchasing these players is teenagers and young adults.

The market for MP3 players didn't exist until a few years ago because the technologies to create them didn't exist. Once the technologies were developed, there was a market for such

Figure 4-9 Jones Juices targets the youth market with its unique soda flavours: Blue Bubblegum, Vanilla Cola, Pineapple Upside Down, and many more. The soda labels are created from photographs sent in by customers. You can even order cases with personalized labels.

players. Many companies, both large and small, leapt on the MP3 band-wagon. As you read in Chapter 1, Napster and MP3.com were two of the first businesses to take advantage of the new MP3 technologies.

Check Your Understanding

Knowledge/Understanding

1 What is e-business? Explain how a company could use e-business to gain a competitive advantage over other companies in the same industry.
2 How would demographics be useful if wanted to start a business?

Thinking/Inquiry

3 Write a paragraph in which you explain your answers to the following questions:
   - How and why did both Armand Bombardier and Laurent Beaudoin diversify Bombardier's product line?
   - How do their actions show that companies need to respond to change in order to be successful?

Communication

4 Discuss, in small groups, why companies advertising on the Internet might target teenagers and young adults. Consider advertisements for products that are in demand among you and your peers. Develop a Web page advertisment for a new product that would appeal to this target market.

Skills
Appendix

analysing media

Application

5 Create a timeline of changes in one successful business that you are familiar with. You could use a business in your community or you could select one from the Web Links index at the McGraw-Hill Ryerson Web site. Your timeline should show how responses to change, use of technology, and demographics have been factors in the business's success.

Skills
Appendix

critical thinking

Qualities of the Successful Business Person

For a business to be successful, the entrepreneurs who start it and the employees who continue to develop it and contribute to its success must have certain qualities. These qualities include risk-taking, vision and passion, perseverance, and the ability to work in a team. We'll have more to say about these qualities—as they relate to entrepreneurs—in Chapter 13.

Risk-taking

Successful business people see problems as opportunities. For some people, the bigger the problem they have to solve, the greater the satisfaction. This risk-taking should be calculated, of course, not foolhardy. You need to examine risks before you act. What are the possible advantages of taking this particular business risk? What might be the disadvantages? What do you stand to win or lose? How much will it cost if you lose? How much will you gain if you succeed?

It is important to remember that the road to success is often paved with failure. Sometimes avoiding failure means passing up success. The best business leaders understand that with risk comes the possibility of failure and that such failures can be used to the company's advantage.

An IBM engineer took a risk on a project and lost $1 million of the company's money. Tom Watson (the former president of IBM) called the engineer into his office. The engineer said to his president, "I guess you want my resignation?" Watson replied "Why? We have just spent over $1 million on your education." Watson knew that failure was an important element of success.

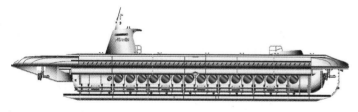

Figure 4-10 Vancouver's Dennis Hurd of Atlantis Submarines International, took a calculated risk when he launched the world's first passenger submarine, and then went on to develop the underwater sightseeing industry.

Atlantis Submarines

Dennis Hurd, of Atlantis Submarines International, thought that tourists in places like Hawaii, Guam, and Barbados would be interested in going under the surface of the sea. (See Figure 4-10.) He believed they would enjoy exploring the coral reefs and seeing exotic fish and old shipwrecks.

Hurd was right. By the year 2000, Atlantis Submarines had taken more than 6 million passengers on undersea adventures aboard its 28-, 48-, and 64-passenger submarines. Among these passengers were more than 40 000 local school children whose classes participated in the company's Living Classroom program. Hurd's fleet has grown to 14 submarines, and Atlantis Submarines had become a $20-million business.

Vision and Passion

Many business owners and entrepreneurs have a vision and are passionate about making that vision become a reality. Without such visions, many useful and exciting businesses and products that we enjoy today would not exist.

As you saw in the Business Profile that opened this chapter, Armand Bombardier had a dream that people might someday be able to travel safely through the snow in Canada. Laurent Beaudoin's plan for Armand Bombardier's company may have been different from the founder's, but it too was visionary. Because he could see where the transportation industry was going, Beaudoin diversified Bombardier into rail transportation and aircraft. Two different visions, but in each a passionate dedication to seeing those visions become reality.

The ability to recognize trends and market demands long before others is a characteristic of some of the most creative successful business people and their companies.

For example, when the two young engineers, William Hewlett and David Packard, started out as partners working in a garage, they had only their creativity and skills to go on. Their first product–the resistance capacity audio oscillator (HP 200A), an electronic instrument used to test sound equipment–may have been very new, but they found a buyer who needed and wanted it. Walt Disney used it in 1938 for his original version of the movie *Fantasia*.

Bob Simmonds and George Cope of Clearnet also had this vision and passion (see page 29). So did Steve Jobs and Steve Wozniak of Apple Computers (see page 57).

The Radar Ball

Today's young entrepreneurs also have this vision and passion. They are turning their creative ideas into products that consumers want. Dave

Biz.Bites

In 1899, Charles H. Duell, who was Commissioner of the U.S. Office of Patents for new inventions, wanted to close down the department. He believed that, "everything that can be invented has been invented."

Figure 4-11 Dave Zukatin plans to continue to invent sports equipment, perhaps a softball version of Radar Ball, or other baseball products for different age and skill levels.

Zakutin invented and developed a product that caused a "now why didn't I think of that" reaction in his industry. (See Figure 4-11.) Dave developed the Radar Ball, a baseball that measures the speed of pitches thrown by baseball players. Dave, whose company Zakutin Technologies is located in Waterloo, Ontario, is a 1996 mechanical engineering graduate.

Dave has partnered his business with Rawlings Sporting Goods Company, a large producer of baseball equipment. Most of the major league baseball clubs use the Radar Ball to train their pitchers.

Perseverance

Perseverance is the drive and determination you need to have if you want to turn your ideas into reality, to solve problems, and to achieve your goals. Successful business people must keep going because it is the only way they will overcome all the obstacles along the way to building a successful business.

Before he invented the light bulb, it is reported that Thomas Edison made several hundred experiments. After about 500 attempts, his assistant asked him, "Why do you persist in this folly? You have tried 500 times and you have failed 500 times." Edison was quick to respond, "Oh but I have not failed once. Now I know 500 ways of how not to make a light bulb."

Web Connect

www.school.mcgrawhill.ca/resources

Visit the Web site of the Business Development of Canada's Young Entrepreneur Awards and Mentor Program to read more business success stories about some of Canada's brightest young entrepreneurs.

Company's Coming

Perseverance has been an attribute of the Company's Coming Publishing Limited since Jean Paré started the company in 1981 in Vermilion, Alberta.

Jean Paré launched her small publishing company with her first *Company's Coming* cookbook. Jean, who was a successful caterer, marketed her book by travelling around Alberta, convincing store owners to sell her book. Her son, Grant Lovig, joined Jean in the company, and the pair persevered even though they were competing against some of the largest publishing houses in the world. By 2000, Company's Coming had sold 15 million cookbooks worldwide.

But Jean and Grant also knew where to stop. For years, they tried, unsuccessfully, to break into the U.S. market. In 1998, they decided that the return wasn't worth the effort and cost. In 10 years, the company had never earned a profit in the U.S. market. So they stopped trying to sell Company's Coming cookbooks there. However, they have been more successful selling Spanish editions in Mexico and Central America.

Teamwork

In many successful companies, people work in teams. Today, managers are less likely to tell people what to do and more likely to serve as a coach and member of a team of employees. Employees share decision-making with their supervisors and managers and have the power to put their decisions into action.

Teamwork skills are so important that the Conference Board of Canada lists them as one of the three main categories of employability skills that companies look for. (See pages 76-77) for a further breakdown of Conference Board teamwork skills.) Successful team members must be able to work with others in order to jointly and clearly establish the purpose for their project and then to follow through.

What skills does it take to function successfully in teams in business? Many are the same skills that you use to accomplish successful team or group assignments in school. Team members need to

- work together towards a common goal
- take responsibility for their share of the work
- communicate with each other frequently
- keep assessing their progress as they work towards their goal

When these teams work, they motivate employees and make them more productive and efficient in responding to customers' needs.

Figure 4-12 How does working in teams affect the quality of your work? What are some of the advantages and disadvantages of teamwork?

Teams at Boeing

When The Boeing Company redesigned its 747 airplane, it ran into a major production problem. The many parts that were supposed to fit together, didn't. It took many workers a long time to resolve the problems of the incompatible parts.

When Boeing was about to build its 777 airplane, the company decided that teams should build them. All the members shared their expertise and information with each other. The teams made their own decisions and even solved their own problems.

Boeing had a much easier time building the 777s than they did the redesigned 747s. When the huge planes were to be assembled, the components fit together to within thousandths of an inch. The teams has succeeded in working to all the quality standards and specifications required of them, adapting and learning as they went, and assuring the success of their huge project.

Figure 4-13

This Boeing 777 was built by teams of workers. Why would cooperation among team members be very important in building these huge airplanes?

Skills
Appendix
writing reports

Check Your Understanding

Knowledge/Understanding

1 List two characteristics of successful business people, and explain, in your own words, how they contribute to business success.
2 Write a paragraph explaining why perseverance is important in business today. Use current business stories to illustrate your main idea.

Thinking/Inquiry

3 What business skills do the business examples in this chapter demonstrate? Use the Conference Board of Canada Employability Skills chart on pages 76-77 to help you with this activity.

Communication

4 Think about a successful business person that you know personally or have heard about. Create a monologue, in role, in which you explain how vision and commitment have contributed to your success.

Skills
Appendix
giving oral presentations

5 Working in small teams, create a graphic organizer (concept web, mind map, or flow chart) to illustrate some of the challenges that the Boeing teams might have faced as they built their first 777. First, pool your knowledge about building and about how teams work. Then decide what would have been the greatest challenges faced by the Boeing teams.

Skills
Appendix

brainstorming

Competing for Customers

In today's business environment, a company will not continue to be successful unless it can provide its customers with a quality product and excellent service. There are simply too many competing products for consumers to choose from. Can you think of any market where there is only one good or service available? In a competitive business environment, customers buy from businesses according to the quality of their products and customer service.

Today, every business must decide who its target market is and then develop a strategy to sell to the consumers in that market. In 1908, when Henry Ford produced the Model T, he painted the one model in one colour—black. He reportedly said that the consumers could have any colour they wanted so long as it was black. But that situation didn't last long. Consumers began to demand other colours—and other models. Competitors entered the market, and the highly competitive automobile market was born.

Providing Customer Service

Successful businesses know that their customers are the most important people in their business equation. If a business doesn't take care of you quickly and efficiently, you'll find another that will. If customers don't come back, a company will have no business. By providing good customer service, a business can gain and keep an advantage over its competition.

This is one of the reasons why Canadian Tire uses as its slogan "To be the best at what our customers value most." Of course, what customers want most will change from one business to another, depending on the particular goods or services and on their reasons for buying that good or service.

Biz.Bites

Old customers are cheaper than new customers. Study after study shows that businesses spend 5 and even 10 times as much money to acquire new customers than to retain old ones.

Connecting Business with *Demographics*

FACES

For years, Canadian women of colour tried to find makeup that was suitable for them. Their choices were limited and the products that they did find were often very expensive. Most Canadian retailers considered these women's needs to be a small niche market that would not bring in enough revenue for them to bother with. Recently, though, the Canadian cosmetics industry has started to realize the business opportunity in providing women of colour with the products they've been requesting for years.

According to Statistics Canada, 11.5 percent of Toronto's population is of East and Southeast Asian descent, 7 percent is of South Asian descent and 5.5 percent has African or Caribbean roots. Only 40 percent has a British, French, or northern European background.

These multi-ethnic markets have simply become too large to ignore, says a representative of FACES, a Canadian chain of franchised cosmetics stores with 45 kiosks in malls across Canada. FACES checked out the market for their products carefully first. "We talked to a lot of women and asked them how they were served, and found that there was an over-all dissatisfaction with the availability of face makeup for them," Shelley says.

So, FACES decided to create a range of foundations, powders, and concealers to fill this market niche. The company offers a wide array of colours, for example, 200 shades of lipstick, 150 shades of nail enamel, and 125 shades of eye shadow. The FACES kiosks also sell skincare and bath products at affordable prices. All products are hypo-allergenic and none are tested on animals.

Because FACES franchised outlets are stand-alone boutiques that sell only FACES brand cosmetics, the

Figure 4-14 Why would not having to complete for shelf space be an advantage ro FACES franchisors?

company's products don't compete for shelf or makeup counter space as they would if they were sold in large retail stores. FACES franchisees own and operate their boutiques in high-traffic areas of shopping malls, after they receive training from the franchisor.

ACTIVITIES

1. What market conditions have conributed to FACES success?
2. What demographic trend in your community could provide an opportunity for a new business venture?
3. Work with a partner to create a comparison chart of the advantages and disadvantages of owning a FACES franchise.

Successful businesses recognize how important their front-line employees are. **Front-line employees** are those who take the orders from customers, help them find what they want, respond to complaints, and help solve problems. This need to provide a fast and efficient response to customers has caused some of the most successful companies to change their organizational structure and focus. To support the front-line workers, other departments also focus on customer service.

Employees are being given more power to take the initiative and make the decision that will keep the customer coming back to the company time and time again.

Customer Service at SkyDome

Companies that care about customer service put a lot of emphasis on how their employees treat their customers. For example, SkyDome, the entertainment and sports complex in Toronto, hires many part-time employees to work as ushers, ticket takers, elevator operators, and guest service representatives.

As far as SkyDome management is concerned, "During an event, other than the entertainment, our event staff are the most important people in the building." The company makes sure its service employees know how important they are. Employees are rewarded by receiving excellence awards on the spot (movie tickets, cash, CDs, concert tickets) or by receiving points that can be accumulated and cashed in for larger prizes (walkmans, TVs, microwaves).

What Customers Want

Finding out what customers want and then providing it for them is not always easy. How do you know what your customers want?

You need to talk with them, to try to get them to explain their problems rather than just going to a competitor to solve them. The best companies follow up to find out if their products and services are satisfactory, and if they are not, why not. If a customer has a problem, they try to fix it and not let it happen in the future. If you are a customer of a business with this attitude, aren't you likely to be loyal to the company?

Companies also need to decide which wants and needs they will focus on fulfilling. As you will learn in the marketing chapter, businesses target a group or a type of customer and focus on their specific needs and wants. Look back at the Saturn advertisement on page 7 in Chapter 1. What does this advertisement tell you about what Saturn has decided that its customers want? How has Saturn focused on these wants in the advertisement?

Fulfilling customers' wants can also get complicated. Sometimes the drive to satisfy customers in a fast-changing and very competitive marketplace can lead to disaster.

Lands' End

One problem with buying clothes on the Internet is knowing which size to order. In the fall of 2000 Lands' End Inc., a catalogue and Internet clothing retailer, thought it had found a unique solution to this problem. The company mounted a campaign to get people to use the virtual model facility at its Web site. The problem of ordering clothes without trying them on would be solved. Lands' End set up trailers in 14 North American cities where people could have an actual image made of their body. They could then access their images on the company's Web site whenever they wanted to buy clothes.

Figure 4-15 In a retail store, consumers can try on clothes to see which size fits them. In a virtual store on the Internet, cloths can't be tried on. Internet clothing retailers are experimenting with different ways to solve this problem.

Although it sounded like a good plan, the software program didn't work because it didn't give consumers an accurate clothing size. Sam Taylor, a vice-president at Lands' End, was asked why the program had been rushed to market before it was ready. He replied that the company had wanted to provide customers with a solution before the competition did. Lands' End was afraid that if it waited, "someone else would beat us to the punch." In the meantime, the faulty process brought the company a lot of bad press, including the article "Lands' End touts virtually useless cybertool" from which this story was taken.

Providing Quality Products

Controlling the quality of your company's products and services is another important factor in getting and keeping customers.

A product is of poor quality if it doesn't perform properly, wears out too soon, or breaks down. A company that ignores quality will quickly lose its reputation. Customers will stop buying from the company and go to the competition.

Quality control is achieved by developing a set of standards that are used to decide which products can be sold and which ones must be rejected. The emphasis is on producing quality products that satisfy customers's wants.

A large company may have its own quality control department. An industry and/or government agency may also set quality control standards, which are meant to protect consumers from defective or unsafe products.

Comparing the Quality of Products

The way the quality of particular products is defined also depends on what consumers demand from the product.

For example, if you were a considering buying an MP3 player, what quality issue would be the most important for you as you compared the different brands? Would you be concerned about the size of memory of the player, since memory size determines how much music you can take with you at one time? Or would you be more concerned with how long it took to download the music from your computer to your player? Or would ease of use be the quality issue for you? Perhaps it would be the quality of the sound? Price will also have an effect on how you view quality. How much are you able (or willing) to pay to get the highest quality product?

As you can see in the comparison chart in Figure 4-16, there are a number of product features that you'd want to consider before deciding which product to buy.

Product Recalls

A product may be recalled when it poses a hazard or health risk. **Recalls** are done to protect consumers and to correct any feature of quality control that has been missed in the manufacturing process. Companies can either recall products voluntarily, or they can be ordered to do

Web Connect

www.school.mcgrawhill.ca/resources
Visit Marketplace on the CBC or the Canadian Food Inspection Agency to see which products are currently being recalled and why they are being recalled.

Comparison of Some MP3 Players Features

MP3 Player	Price	Memory	Download time	Ease of use	Performance	Other features
Nomad Jukebox	$749.00	• stores music from over 100 CDs (a 6- gigibite hard drive)	• has fast transfer of files • can change standard CDs to MP3 files	• includes a good manual and quick-start guide • has a backlit, easy-to-read LCD panel	• is skip-free and has good audio technologies	• communicates with both Mac and Windows machines • can record in real time
RIO 600	$299.99	• can only record 30 minutes of music (has 32 3MB of memory)	• has fast transfer of files	• very easy to use and has an good manual • has an adjustable LCD light	• headphones are poor quality	• can be upgraded to 64MB (in the future) for $299.00
Audiovox MP1000	$299.00	• can only record 30 minutes of music (has 32 MB of memory)	• has slow transfer of files • has no USB connectivity	• has an LCD panel but the font size is too large and it isn't backlit	• some if its software is not compatible with current software	• very light, compact player. • can be upgraded to 64 64MB for $199.00

Figure 4-16 The prices of these players come from a StreetCents (CBC) show that aired in November, 1999. Compare the price and features of MP3 players on the market today with the prices and features in this chart. Why do you think that both the prices and the features have changed?

so by government agencies. These government agencies, such as the Canadian Food Inspection Agency, warn consumers of problems in products and notify them of recalls.

Some companies will replace the recalled product or refund the cost. Other companies will repair the product or offer consumers a kit or method to repair the product.

For example, in August 2000, Fisher Price Canada decided to recall its Lift'n Lock swings and Get Up & Go walkers. There had been reports that the small children who were using their products suffered minor injuries. Even though the Health Canada Product Safety Division did not order the recall, Fisher Price decided that there was a risk for children. So it issued a warning to parents to stop using the products and offered a repair kit that would make the products safe.

Firestone Tire Recall

On a much larger scale, also in August 2000, the Bridgestone/Firestone tire company recalled 6.5 million tires in the U.S. Consumers had complained that the treads on this particular brand of tire were separating and causing accidents. The tires were used by Ford on its popular Ford Explorer sport utility vehicles.

The problem created a serious safety hazard. The U.S. National Highway Traffic Safety Administration had reports of over 100 deaths and 500 injuries resulting from accidents involving Firestone tires. Bridgestone/Firestone was also sued by people who lost family members, or who were injured in these accidents themselves.

Figure 4-17 How might the Firestone tire recall affect consumers' belief in the quality of the company's products? What do you think will be the short- and long-term effects of the recall? How will the recall likely affect competitors in this market?

This tire recall was expected to cost Bridgestone/Firestone hundreds of millions of dollars. It also cost the company the loss of a great deal of consumer confidence.

Global Quality Standards

With people able to buy products from around the world, there was a need for global standards of quality and measurements. The **International Organization for Standardization (ISO)** is an organization that has been helping companies standardize quality and measurements since the end of World War II. Such standardization can be very important for Canadian companies.

For example, how can the Northern Ontario small-business owner who assembles computers be sure that the parts he has ordered from Japan, Mexico, the U.S., and Sweden will all be compatible? If all of the companies have put ISO standards into effect, the computer assembler will be able to depend on quality controls and standard measurements in the components.

Figure 4-18 An ISO International Standard helped standardize the format of credit cards, phone cards, and "smart" cards. Adhering to the standard, which defines such features as an optimal thickness (0.76 mm), means that the cards can be used worldwide. Why would this kind of standardization be important for today's business person?

You may have seen signs outside manufacturing companies that state that the company is ISO compliant. This means that the company has created and has documentation that will prove that it uses "guidelines to ensure that materials, products, processes, and services are fit for their purpose." ISO standards increase the quality, reliability, and effectiveness of the goods and services you depend on every day. International standards ensure that specifications for health, safety, and environmental protection are carried out.

For Canadian businesses that want to export to Europe, adhering to these standards is very important. The countries of the European Union require that any company that wants to do business with them must be certified by ISO standards.

Employee Attitudes and Work Quality

Ask business owners about their major concerns and you are likely to hear something about employees. One key to the success of a business is its ability to hire the most suitable employees for the job and to be able to motivate them to do their best. You will learn more about the importance of employees in Chapter 6. For this chapter, we'll look briefly at some factors that affect employees' attitudes towards the business they work for.

Many studies have found that satisfied employees tend to work harder, produce higher quality products, and stay longer with the employer they enjoy.

In general, the employees of small- and medium-sized businesses tend to be more satisfied with their workplaces than employees who work in big businesses or in the public sector. This is interesting because usually the salary in smaller workplaces is less than that in larger workplaces. Trust seems to be a very important factor, as is open communication between management and employees. The level of flexibility for meeting personal needs and the availability of opportunities for personal growth are also considered very important by employees.

Factors Affecting Employee Attitude

In the past, employees often had less independence than they have today. Managers tended to give specific instructions and expected the employees to carry out those instructions. Athough this is still the case in many businesses, more and more managers are giving their employees the right to make decisions on their own. This allows employees to act quickly in response to the needs of their customers. Such independence can result in employees being more highly motivated and more productive. It can also result in more satistied customers, which is very important in the highly competitive business world of today.

As you learned in Chapter 3, employees who know that they are working in a safe and healthy environment are also more likely to produce a better quality of work and take less time off. The kind of teamwork and personal responsibility that is practiced at Boeing (page 110) also increases employees' self-esteem and enables them to do their best work.

In addition, employees have a better attitude towards their work when they feel they are working for a company that is committed to fairness, quality, lifelong learning, and trust. In the Canadian Tire profile (page 63), Brian Toda noted that the best companies create "a sense in an organization that when people come in to work at that company, it is worth a day of their life each day." It is the company's attitude towards its employees that makes the difference.

At Hewlett-Packard, this attitude has been developed into a company philosophy that affects the entire company. Dore Thompson, a Learning

Ranking of Aspects of Workplace Satisfaction

Rank	Aspect
1	Quality of decision makers
2	Work ethic
3	Personal growth opportunities
4	Communication between manager and employees
5	Level of innovation
6	Relations between managers and employees
7	Level and range of responsibility
8	Physical work environment
9	Flexible about personal needs
10	Training opportunities
11	Salary
12	Job security
13	Service/product quality
14	Work hours
15	Attitude towards environment
16	Benefits
17	Relations among employees
18	Amount of time off

Figure 4-19 An October 1999 study on Workplace Satisfaction in the Private and Public Sectors found that employees gave this ranking to aspects of the workplace. Why do you think the survey respondents ranked the aspects in this order? Does the ranking surprise you?

Technology Instructor with HP said that he learned from Dave Packard and Bill Hewlett's example "the belief that people will do well, if given the right tools and resources and treated with respect, trust and encouragement." People are motivated to be more productive when they feel that their work is appreciated and they themselves are valued. You will learn more about the effect of different management styles in Chapter 6.

Check Your Understanding

Knowledge/Understanding

1 Explain, in your own words, why good customer service is so important to a company's success.
2 List and explain some of the ways that businesses can make sure that their products meet quality standards.

Thinking/Inquiry

Skills
Appendix

researching

3 Work with a partner to investigate three recent product recalls. Using a chart, list the product and the manufacturer of that product, the reasons for the recall, and each company's response to the recall.

Communication

4 Create a poster of five of the quality products that you own or would like to own. Write captions for each product to explain why you judge it to be a quality product and which quality standards might have been used.

Application

Skills
Appendix

building an argument

5 Have a round table discussion, with a group of classmates, on the factors that affect your attitude and the quality of your work at home, at school, in the community, and in the workplace. After the discussion, independently rank the factors from most to least important to you personally and explain your ranking to your group.

Figure 4-20 How would Radical Entertainment's corporate culture affect employees' attitude and quality of work? What characteristics of this workplace might make it a place where you could enjoy spending each work day?

In the employee lounge at Radical Entertainment, an enormous log cabin is under construction. It will become an in-house theatre. In the nearby kitchen area, a handful of employees are helping themselves to a late breakfast—one employee eats Fruit Loops and another spreads cheese on a bagel. All the food in the kitchen is provided at company expense.

On the other side of the airy, bright space, another employee is taking a 10-minute time-out on a large couch, one of several provided for relaxation. Employees who prefer to exercise when they relax can head for a fully equipped gym, and take a shower afterward. And those who find nature relaxing can gaze at the spectacular view of the Coast Mountains from the building's top floor.

Radical Entertainment is one of North America's leading developers of digital entertainment. At the company's new eight-storey building on the eastern edge of downtown Vancouver, taking care of employees gets as much attention as taking care of business. That, says CEO Ian Wilkinson, is because the two are so closely linked. Wilkinson says the new workplace is integral to the company's identity and the success of its product, video games for clients like Sony Corp., Fox Interactive, and Microsoft Corp.

Working up a sweat on a stationary bike while he talks, Wilkinson says most of the people who work at Radical are just big kids, including himself. Nurturing that kind of energy and creativity is crucial to keeping the company competitive, he says. "We spend money when there is value to it, in human capital or revenue," Wilkinson says. "If creating a good place to work means that the people who work here will be inspired and that they will stay with us, then it's worth the cost."

So far, Wilkinson's corporate culture is working. In December 2000, Radical Entertainment was named one of Canada's Top 50 Best-Managed Private Companies. The award is presented by

Arthur Anderson, the Canadian Imperial Bank of Canada, and the National Post. In order to win the award, a company has to have revenues over $5 million, have shown strong growth over the past three years, and be more than 50 percent owned by Canadians.

One of the management practices that Radical was recognized for was its open and regular communication between management and employees. Employees are asked for their opinion on everything from which technologies the company should adopt to what food it should stock in the kitchen. The Chief Financial Officer holds a seminar four times a year to explain the company's financial performance to employees. This practice helps employees understand where the company earns money and where it spends its revenues.

Radical Entertainment was also praised for the healthy, creative, and respectful work environment it provides for employees. The new Idea Review Senate (IRS) is one of the company's revolutionary business practices. The IRS is a team of nine employees drawn from all divisions, so it represents various viewpoints. Employees are encouraged to present their creative ideas to the IRS. If the team recommends that an idea be developed at Radical, then the employee and the company begin to do so.

If Radical does not develop the idea, it gets passed back to the employee who created it. This is revolutionary. In many companies, creative ideas thought up by employees are left to gather dust. But at Radical, the employee who created the idea can either develop it independently or even sell it to another company. The idea belongs to the employee.

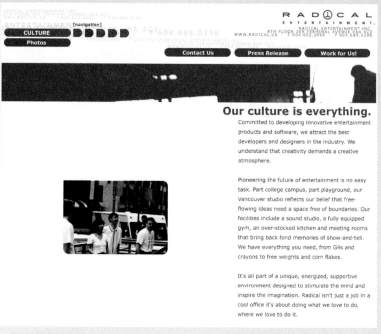

Our culture is everything.
Committed to developing innovative entertainment products and software, we attract the best developers and designers in the industry. We understand that creativity demands a creative atmosphere.

Pioneering the future of entertainment is no easy task. Part college campus, part playground, our Vancouver studio reflects our belief that free-flowing ideas need a space free of boundaries. Our facilities include a sound studio, a fully equipped gym, an over-stocked kitchen and meeting rooms that bring back fond memories of show-and-tell. We have everything you need, from G4s and crayons to free weights and corn flakes.

It's all part of a unique, energized, supportive environment designed to stimulate the mind and inspire the imagination. Radical isn't just a job in a cool office it's about doing what we love to do, where we love to do it.

Figure 4-21 Visit Radical Entertainment's web site to learn more about the company's corporate culture.

In their very competitive market, Radical knows that it has to attract and keep the best employees it can get. The company believes it can do so by offering employees the kind of workplace where they are encouraged to use their imaginations and explore new ideas.

ACTIVITIES

1 Why would a company like Radical Entertainment need to foster creativity in its employees?

2 Investigate the digital entertainment industry. What are some of the advantages of working in this industry? What might be some of the disadvantages?

3 If you worked for Radical, which of the company benefits would you enjoy? What would motivate you? Think of a place you have worked or volunteered. What, in addition to getting paid, made you want to do good work there?

Chapter Review

Points to Remember

- A successful business responds to change, fills a market niche, and understands demographics.

- A successful business person takes risks, has vision, passion, and perseverance, and can work in teams.

- Business compete for customers by providing good customer service, finding out what customers want, and providing quality products

- Employee attitudes and work quality affect the success of business.

Activities

Knowledge/Understanding

1 Identify and describe the following:
   a) the qualities of a successful business
   b) the qualities of a successful business person
   c) how businesses compete for customers

2 Develop a list of five niche markets in teen's clothing, fast food services, and describe one factor or characteristic of the product that relates to its niche.

3 What are two industries or business sectors, not given as examples in the chapter, that have had to respond to change in the last two years? What did they change? What caused the change?

Thinking/Inquiry

1 Read two articles from Canadian business magazines about a successful business or a businessperson. Identify the qualities of the successful business and business person and how the business competes for customers. Do these qualities and characteristics match any of the data you collected in Knowledge Activity 1.

2 Think of a store or company in your community that has gone out of business. Why do you think the company closed? Was the cause external or an internal, something that the company itself did?

3 Ask someone you know about teamwork in their workplace . Find out what the person does as a team member and get a specific example. Ask what the person likes about teamwork and what the person finds hard about it. Write a report on what you learned.

Skills
Appendix

analysing media.

Communication

1 With a partner, conduct a survey of students in your school who hold part-time jobs with the goal of identifying factors that influence employees' attitudes and the quality of their work.
   a) Brainstorm with your partner possible survey questions that you might ask your fellow students.
   b) Draft and revise your questions, making sure that they will serve your purpose and be clear to your audience.
   c) Conduct your survey of other students in your school.
   d) Tabulate your results and draw conclusions from your findings.
   e) Compare your findings with what you've learned in this chapter.
   f) Give a brief oral report of your findings and compare your findings with those of your classmates.

Skills
Appendix

building an argument

Application

1 Develop a poster listing the top ten initiatives that you would implement in a business that wants to achieve the following:
   a) success of the business
   b) success of the people in the business
   c) high quality customer service and products
   d) positive employee attitudes and high-quality work

Present your poster to the class and explain why you believe your initiatives will work.

2 Write a five paragraph essay on how Bombardier's business activities have contributed to the success of that company.
   a) Draw up a plan for your essay based on your findings from Knowledge Activity 1.

Skills
Appendix

writing reports

b) Outline your essay by deciding on your main idea (thesis). Be sure that you offer supporting evidence for this main idea.

c) Write a first draft of your essay based on your outline, and share your draft with an editing partner.

d) Review suggestions from your editing partner, then revise your essay and produce a final good copy.

Internet Extension

1 Visit a number of e-business Web sites and analyse the components of the businesses in terms of their customer service, quality standards, and attitude towards their employees.

Skills
Appendix

researching

5 Market Conditions and Business Environments

KEY TERMS

law of demand
complementary goods
substitute goods
supply
law of supply
equilibrium
business cycle
prosperity
inflation
recession
depression
recovery
consumer protection
false advertising
misleading advertising
illegal pricing
competition

Specific Expectations

After studying this chapter, you will be able to

- analyze the forces of supply and demand and explain how they affect market prices and the willingness of businesses to produce products

- explain how the number and quality of competitors in the market place can affect a business

- describe reasons for government policies and actions relating to the regulation of markets and business activity

In this chapter, we will investigate the conditions that affect the Canadian economy and market for business. The inter-connections between the forces of supply and demand are important factors in the economy. To be successful, businesses must be able to predict what consumers will demand and what price they will be willing to pay for goods and services.

The state of the economy and changes in the business cycle also affect demand and supply, as will the number and quality of competitors in the market. Competition in the marketplace should be fair, and both federal and provincial governments have laws to try to ensure that the rights of both sellers and buyers are protected.

Tim Hortons

The Tim Hortons franchise chain has become a Canadian success story largely because it has continued to stayed focused on supplying the demands of its market. Today, with 60 percent of the market, the company is the largest coffee and fresh-baked goods restaurant chain in Canada.

Tim Horton, the popular Maple Leafs' hockey star, opened the first Tim Hortons coffee and donut restaurant in Hamilton, Ontario, in 1964. Ron Joyce, a retired Canadian navy and police officer, became the first franchisee. After Tim's sudden death in 1974, Ron became president of the company.

Tim Hortons became popular because of growing consumer demand for the kind of products and services that it offers. Many Canadians–from Whitehorse in the Yukon to Cape Breton in Nova Scotia–stop at some point in their day for a Tim Hortons fresh-baked goods and a coffee. The company has also established itself as a meeting place in many communities–serving another consumer need, building up a loyal customer base, and gaining an advantage over its competitors.

Today, the more than 1900 Tim Hortons in Canada and 120 in the U.S. continue to focus on quality and consistency in their products and their service. They supply their market with fresh coffee, fresh baked goods, innovative products, and good service. As consumer tastes have changed over the years, so have Tim Hortons' products, from the introduction of low-fat muffins in the early 1980s, to Cappuccino coffee in the 1990s, to hot chicken soup in an edible bread bowl in 2000.

In the highly competitive franchise food services industry, Tim Hortons franchises are very much in demand. So much so that a license fee can cost up to $400 000. The company also differentiates itself from the competition through its successful marketing campaigns–the Roll Up the Rim to Win promotion and true-story TV commercials.

As you read about market conditions and business environments in this chapter, consider how Tim Hortons managed to supply consumer demand by offering the service that consumers wanted when they wanted it.

Figure 5-1 Tim Hortons is a successful franchise because it has been able to predict what consumers want. Can you think of a new product or service that Tim Horton's offers to its consumers?

Supply and Demand

The operation of any market depends on both demand and supply. For a healthy economy to exist, the people who buy, or create demand, and those who sell, or supply that demand, must exchange money (or something of value) for a good or service.

For example, the hotdog vendor outside a school during lunch sells hotdogs and pop because students want them. There is a demand for them. She is willing to supply the hotdogs and pop because she can charge a price that covers her costs and lets her make a profit.

Because demand and supply influence each other and are each affected by so many factors, the relationship between them is complex. To make discussion easier, we will look at them separately.

Demand

Demand is about you, the consumer, and your needs and wants, as you learned in Chapter 1. Demand refers to the quantity of particular goods or services that the market—which includes you and other consumers—is willing to buy. The **law of demand** states that when the market demands a high quantity of a good or service, the prices for that good or service will be high. When the market demands a low quantity, the prices will be low.

For example, when a new blockbuster movie first comes out, many people want to see it. The market demand is high. A multi-screen theatre complex may charge $2.00 over the regular ticket price and may show the movie on four screens at once. And people will line up to buy tickets in spite of the higher price. However, once many people have seen the movie or a new blockbuster comes out, the demand for the first movie will go down. The market demand is low, and so the price drops back to the regular movie ticket price or even below.

Consumers' demand for a good or a service depends on a number of factors:

- the price of the good or service
- the prices of *substitute* or *complementary* goods
- consumers' *income*
- their *future expectations* about either income or price
- their *taste* or desire for the good or service

In order to understand how demand works, we'll look at each of these factors as though they changed separately. In the real world, all these may change at the same time and may be influenced by other factors. A change in one factor will often affect another.

Price of Goods

Karen has finished her training to be a lifeguard and will soon start a summer job at the local pool. She is delighted but will need to buy herself at least two and preferably four good-quality, fast-drying bathing suits. If she has to jump into the pool to rescue a child, she'll get soaked. All of the guards keep at least one extra dry suit on hand in case they have to change.

First, Karen decides she has find out the price of bathing suits. She checks manufacturers' Web sites on the Internet and finds that they don't list prices, so she goes to a few of the retail Web sites. They list their prices, but she finds quite a range.

The problem is that the prices are high for the type of bathing suits that Karen needs. She has $80.00 saved for her purchase. The best price she can find, at the moment, is $40.00 per suit. So, she can buy two if she makes her purchase today. Or she can wait to see if the price will go down. If the price dropped to $20.00, she could buy four suits. Waiting for a sale can be risky, however, because other people may buy the available suits. Stores tend to order a limited number of seasonal goods.

Consumer Behaviour

In general, consumers have a sense of the value of each good or service they want. They may pay so much and no more. They are likely to

Figure 5-2 Although price is an important consideration for a consumer who is purchasing a good or a service, it isn't the only factor. What are some of the other things you have to consider as you make a purchase?

buy if they expect the price of a good or a service to rise soon, or if they think the item will sell quickly. They may wait to buy a good or service if they expect that the price will go down, or if they think the manufacturer will soon make a special offer, such as a bonus gift with a purchase.

Sometimes consumers decide they can't wait. If they have a deadline, such as a trip, they may be motivated to pay more than usual or to get something they wouldn't usually buy. At other times, consumers will pay much more for an item because of the prestige attached.

However, if enough people think that a price is too high and they stop buying, the demand for the good or service will go down.

Price of Substitute Goods

A good that can easily be replaced by another is called a **substitute good**. Examples of substitutes would be tea for coffee and margarine for butter. When the price of a good such as coffee increases, consumers will switch to tea, a substitute good. The result is an increase in the quantity of tea demanded, and a decrease in the quantity of coffee demanded.

Sometimes goods are substituted when the price goes down. When the price of portable compact disc players decreased, people began to substitute them for tape cassette players. Demand for the compact disc players increased, and demand for the cassette players decreased.

Price of Complementary Goods

Two goods that are usually used with one another are called **complementary goods**. Demand for one of these products will affect the demand for the other. For example, compact disc players and compact discs are complementary goods. If you have a compact disc player, you are going to need compact discs. When the price of the players decreased and more people bought them, the demand for compact discs increased.

Consumer Income

Generally, the more money consumers have to spend, the higher will be their demand for goods and services as they satisfy wants as well as needs. This also applies to communities and countries.

Our lifeguard, Karen, may have been able to afford only two bathing suits when she started her summer job. However, by the end of her first month she may be able to buy the two others she wants because she will have income from her job. If Karen works overtime and earns extra pay, she may buy a $60 bathing suit made from a very quick drying fabric.

In Chapter 2, you learned that consumers' level of income has a direct effect on their standard of living and quality of life. As the level of income in a region or a country increases, so does the demand for goods and services. The higher level of income usually results in the purchase of costly items. When incomes decrease, the demand for luxury items decreases.

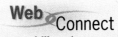
Web Connect
www.school.mcgrawhill.ca/resources/
Using Statistics Canada data, compare the current Canadian level of income with that of a year ago. How might the change affect consumer demand?

Tastes and Preferences

Individual tastes and preferences—what consumers like or choose—also affect demand. Consumer trends, such as an increased emphasis on health and fitness, have influenced the demand for certain goods and services. As Figure 5-4 shows, consumers still want the convenience of foods that can be prepared quickly. But as they become aware of the need for healthy foods, they also want the convenience food to be healthy, and may choose a frozen dinner labeled as "low-fat."

Image influences some people's choices. Loose roomy pants are the choice of many skateboarders, or of those who want to have that image. Some students like a "vintage" look and shop at second-hand stores styles popular in the past.

Advertising also influences consumers' tastes. The primary goal of advertising is to increase consumer demand for a particular that good or service. If a good or service is frequently advertised, the purchasing behaviour of consumers will likely be affected. For example, the demand for popular toys is created largely by television commercials aimed at children.

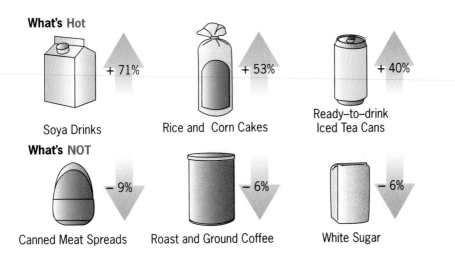

What's Hot

Soya Drinks + 71%

Rice and Corn Cakes + 53%

Ready–to–drink Iced Tea Cans + 40%

What's NOT

Canned Meat Spreads − 9%

Roast and Ground Coffee − 6%

White Sugar − 6%

Figure 5-3 Canadian shoppers increasingly want foods that are both convenient and good for them. People are buying fewer food products that they think are not nutritious. What effect is this trend likely to have on the manufacturers of food products?

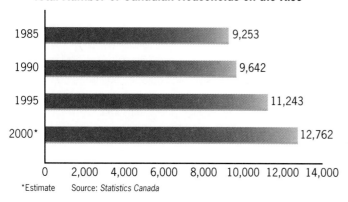

Total Number of Canadian Households on the Rise

Year	Households
1985	9,253
1990	9,642
1995	11,243
2000*	12,762

0   2,000   4,000   6,000   8,000   10,000   12,000   14,000

*Estimate   Source: *Statistics Canada*

Figure 5-4 More Canadians are living alone or as members of smaller families. Each of these family units is considered a household.

Demography and Demand

In Chapter 4 you were introduced to demography, the study of statistics relating to populations or communities. Businesses study demographic trends to try to predict which goods or services will be in high demand among consumers.

For example, the Food and Consumer Products Manufacturers of Canada (FCPMC) have noted that Canada has a growing number of households. The FCPMC predicts that this trend–along with the large number of women in the workforce–will continue to boost the demand for more prepared foods.

Another growing demographic group is people 65 years of age and older. Statistics Canada estimates that more than 16 percent of the population will be 65 or older by 2011. This increasingly important consumer group will eventually need more retirement and health care services. Some businesses recognize the opportunities in this demographic trend and realize that as an aging population will cause an increased demand for new products and services. Businesses that specialize in fitness, for example, would be wise to develop gentler exercise programs.

Demand Curve

Price (P)

$80

$60 ....

$40 ....**D**

$20 ....

0
    1   2   3   4   Quantity (Q) Demanded

Figure 5-5 Notice how demand decreases as the price goes up and increases as the price goes down. Remember that we are assuming that income and other factors remain constant.

Charting Demand

To illustrate the relationship between price and demand, economists use a graph called a **demand curve**.

Let's look again at Karen's situation as she shopped for those bathing suits for life guarding. She had $80.00 to spend. At a price of $40.00 per suit, she was able to buy two suits. If the price had been $60.00 or $80.00 for each suit, she could only have bought one suit. And, if she had been very lucky and found a good sale price of $20.00, she could have bought the four suits that she wanted.

The demand curve in Figure 5-5 illustrates the relationship between price and the quantity of suits Karen will demand as a customer. Price or P is charted on the y-axis, and quantity or Q is charted on the x-axis. The line drawn between the points is called the demand curve (though the line may not have a curved shape).

In calculating the demand of a whole market—rather than of an individual—the total number of buyers determines the total amount of a good or service that is purchased.

Supply

If demand is the consumer side of the market, supply is the producer's side. **Supply** refers to the quantity of goods and services that producers and sellers are willing or able to sell consumers. There is a direct relationship between the price of a good or service and the quantity offered for sale. The **law of supply** says that as prices rise, the quantity supplied by producers tends to increase. In turn, as prices fall, the quantity supplied tends to decrease.

Sometimes the cost of bringing a product to market may be too high compared with what consumers are willing to pay. In this case, suppliers drop out of the market. For example, in recent years, the cost of wheat farming has become so high relative to what farmers could earn that many farmers have stopped growing wheat.

Several factors in addition to price affect supply. A producer's decision to supply a good or service depends on

- the *costs* of producing the good or service
- changes in *technology* that affect the costs
- the producer's *desire* to own and operate a business
- *environmental* and *other conditions*

To see how the supply process works, let's catch up with Karen after she graduated from college. She decided to come an entrepreneur and produce high-quality, long-lasting swimsuits for lifeguards and professional swimmers. Karen called her company SwimSuit Pro.

For the business to succeed, Karen needs to sell enough of the kind of bathing suits that professionals want, at a price they will pay. She will have to earn enough revenue to cover her costs and allow her to make a profit. Price will be a big consideration for prospective buyers, so she has to find a balance between the price and earning a profit. If she can get a higher price, she will make more profit.

Biz.Bites

In 1999 and 2000, the forces of supply and demand were at work in the increase of natural gas prices in Ontario. Just a few years ago, many people converted to natural gas furnaces. Natural gas was cheaper than electricity. By 1999, demand for natural gas had increased, but supplies were low. The same low gas prices–in 1997 and 1998–that had encouraged consumers to switch to gas also discouraged gas producers from drilling for more supplies.

Web Connect

www.school.mcgrawhill.ca/resources/
If you were running your own business, how would you figure out the price to charge your customers for goods? for services? What are some of the ways you might cut your production costs and still produce quality products?

Production Costs

Karen needs to consider **production costs** on everything involved in making her swimming suits. She needs a place to manufacture the bathing suits. She will need materials and equipment: fabric, sewing machines, and office equipment. She will need to hire skilled employees, which means paying wages and benefits and buying insurance in case of accidents.

At some point, she will have to decide if she can afford to make changes. What would happen to Karen's costs if a new chlorine-resistant fabric is discovered? The material is likely to be expensive, at least initially. But if it results in superior products that her customers would want, Karen will need to use the material. The higher costs of this fabric will probably mean that the price of those suits will have to increase. She may decide to manufacture fewer suits at first, and the supply will be less.

Labour is one of the highest costs a supplier has. A wage increase to employees leads to an increase in the cost of supplying the product. In such circumstances, a supplier may be willing to continue supplying the market only if the selling price of the product is increased.

The change in any of these costs can affect the supply that Karen, or any supplier, makes available to the market.

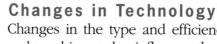

Figure 5-6 What would computerized production systems add to your production costs if you were running a manufacturing business?

Changes in Technology

Changes in the type and efficiency of technology and machinery also influence the supply of goods and services. For example, the introduction of computers and other communication and information technologies has had a major effect on industry. Some manufacturers use robotics to reduce labour costs. Others use databases to keep track of inventory, or goods they have on hand, and to cut down on the length of time they need to store raw materials to make products. This saves storage and other costs. The savings in production costs means producers can make more profit, so they may want to increase the quantity of the goods or services that they supply to their markets.

Owner's Desire

Some people assume that people and businesses supply goods and services only because they want to make money. In fact, people start businesses for a variety of reasons. Some want the control and flexibility of being their own boss. Others want to try out an innovative idea. Karen wants to draw on her knowledge of swimming to earn an income.

Although all businesses must make a profit to survive, these other reasons for going into business affect supply. For example, some people open small, specialized boutiques, even though they may not make as much money as a larger store would. These retailers want to sell the products they like in an environment that they create.

Environmental Conditions

Environmental circumstances can also have an effect on a producer's ability to supply a good or a service. As you learned in Chapter 3, cod fishers off the east coast of Canada weren't able to supply cod to their markets because there were so few fish left.

Seasonal weather conditions can also affect supply. For example, too much rain or not enough sun can have a very serious effect on Ontario farmers' ability to supply strawberries to markets in the early summer. On the other hand, just the right amount of sun and rain can result in an abundant supply of strawberries.

Charting Supply

To illustrate the relationship between price and supply, economists use a graph called a supply curve. Supply curves are used along with demand curves to demonstrate balance in markets.

Let's look again at Karen's situation at SwimSuit Pro. Karen has decided to sell her suits directly to customers over the Internet. By selling directly, she won't have to discount the price as she would if she sold to retailers. If she charges $40.00 per suit and sells 200 suits per season, she can cover her costs and make a decent profit.

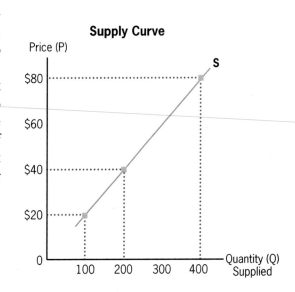

Supply Curve

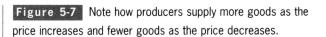

Figure 5-7 Note how producers supply more goods as the price increases and fewer goods as the price decreases.

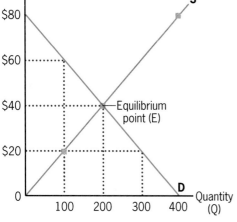

Equilibrium Curves

Price (P)

$80 ··· S

$60 ··············

$40 ············· Equilibrium
point (E)

$20 ·····

0
    100   200   300   400   Quantity (Q)
                              D

Figure 5-8 As you can see, consumer demand and SwimSuit Pro supply are balanced—or in equilibrium—at $40.00 per suit.

Market research tells her that if SwimSuit Pro charges more than $40.00 per suit, consumer demand will decrease. And, if she sells them for less than $40.00, her profits will disappear, and she won't be able to cover all of her costs.

Equilibrium

Economists use the concept of **equilibrium** to describe the point where the forces of supply and the forces of demand are balanced. Think of demand as a market force that tends to increase the price of a good or service. Supply is the force that tends to reduce the price.

When the two forces are in balance, or equilibrium, prices tend to remain stable. Consumers can afford and are willing to buy a product at the price charged. Producers can afford and are willing to supply a product at the price consumers will pay.

The equilibrium of supply and demand can be shown in a supply and demand chart, as in Figure 5-8.

Check Your Understanding

Knowledge/Understanding

1 Explain, in your own words, the concepts of demand and supply.
2 Give five examples of the costs involved in supplying the market with a product or service. You could choose from goods such as racing bikes or posters, or from services such as hair styling or tennis lessons.

Thinking/Inquiry

3 You are a summer camp counsellor and have to organize the food for a barbecue. You must provide hamburgers and hot dogs to 100 children. Work out a system to predict the things the camp needs to buy, and in what quantities, to satisfy everyone's needs but not have a lot of leftovers. What conclusions can you draw about predicting demand?
4 Brainstorm the ways that a drop in availability of a natural resource would affect supply and demand. What would happen if a country supplying a

Skills
Appendix

critical thinking

rare metal had a civil war? Or if a province declared that a forested area
was to become a conservation area?

Communication

5 Write a paragraph explaining how demand and supply interact to produce
the right amount of goods at the right price. Draw a supply and demand
chart to illustrate your explanation.

6 Using the newspaper, find articles relating to events that create demand.
Choose one and summarize it. How do you know the article discusses
demand? What is the relationship between price and demand in the article?

Application

7 Working with three other students, write and perform a role play to illustrate the impact on a consumer and a supplier who owns a retail store
when a factor that affects demand or supply changes. You could work with
the price of substitute goods or services, consumer tastes, production
costs, or changes in technology.

Skills
Appendix

brainstorming

The Business Cycle

The economic condition of a person, family,
town, or country never remains at the same
level. Economies move from prosperity to
inflation to recession, sometimes into
depression, and then to recovery. The term
business cycle is used to refer to this series
of changes.

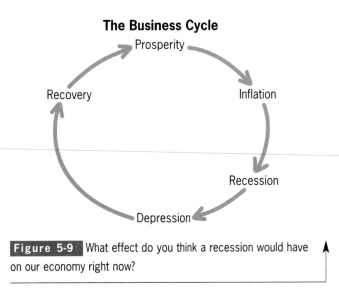

The Business Cycle

Prosperity

Inflation

Recession

Depression

Recovery

Figure 5-9 What effect do you think a recession would have
on our economy right now?

Prosperity

Good economic times are called periods
of **prosperity**. During them, the economy
is doing well, levels of employment are
high, and workers are well paid. As businesses grow and flourish, companies that
supply them also experience prosperity.

Connecting Business with  *Ecotourism* ....

North Nahanni Naturalist Lodge

As the part owner and operator of the North Nahanni Naturalist Lodge, Ria Letcher has brought to life her dream of sharing the beauty of the Nahanni Region. The Lodge is part of one of the fastest growing segments of the tourism industry: ecotourism. It also offers "world-class accommodations in the middle of nowhere."

Ecotourists demand sites that show respect for fragile environments and that allow them to interact with the local people and learn something about their traditions and culture. Because Ria, her husband, Loyal, and other aboriginal people own and operate the lodge, their Dene culture is part of daily life at the lodge. Guests are welcome to participate in Dene music, dance, and traditional crafts.

Visitors from around the world stay at the lodge to enjoy the region's glacier lakes, the Nahanni mountain range and deep 3000 to 4000 foot canyons. Guests that go out on guided hiking, fishing and skiing expeditions are likely to see grizzly bears, trumpeter swans, woodland caribou, and bald eagles.

However, getting the lodge operating was no easy task. Ria and her family knew that the demand existed for the services their lodge could offer, but they did not foresee all of the challenges that they would face as suppliers of that service.

Construction in remote areas is difficult. Although local people provided the labour and took building materials from nearby forests, the other supplies had to be brought in by plane or boat. That was costly and resulted in a number of frustrating delays. Ria and her husband kept reminding themselves that "a plane takes off against the wind." They persevered and completed their lodge in 1998.

Figure 5-10 "We felt that we shouldn't be the only ones to experience this scenery. The air is so fresh. The water freezes and is so clear, you can see the rocks at the bottom of the lake. The northern lights are breathtaking and visible all winter." (Ria Letcher)

ACTIVITIES

1 How have Ria Letcher and her family responded to the demands of today's ecotourists in running North Nahanni Naturalist Lodge?

2 How might production costs, changes in technology, the lodge owners' desire, and weather conditions have affected the process of opening the lodge and of keeping it functioning? Consider both the pluses and the minuses of these different supply-side factors.

Businesses spend money on research and development and often expand their facilities to supply the markets that want their goods and services. People start new businesses.

When people have jobs that pay well, they are willing to borrow money to make large purchases, such as houses. They are confident that their incomes will allow them to pay back the loans.

Society as a whole benefits from the strong demand for consumer goods. The increased amount of tax dollars from successful businesses mean that there is money for social programs, education, health care, and the arts.

Inflation

Prosperity, however, can lead to inflation. **Inflation** refers to a rise—over time—in the price of goods and services. Because they can earn more money, businesses are willing to increase the quantity of goods and services they supply.

Inflation also increases the cost of doing business. The prices that businesses pay for supplies go up. This is not a problem when people can pay the new prices and have money left for other needs and wants. However, if wages do not go up at the same rate as prices, employees don't have the income to buy the same quantity or types of goods and services. Then suppliers end up with unsold stock and lose money. Sometimes a competitor from another country offers similar goods at lower prices, and the domestic supplier's profit drops.

Recession

In a **recession**, the whole economy slows down and business no longer creates as much wealth as it did during the period of prosperity. A recession occurs for a number of reasons. The government may introduce changes, such as price controls, to fight inflation. Or a shift in the economy may affect a large number of businesses at the same time.

Businesses may feel under pressure because of the cost of the wages paid to workers. When businesses can no longer afford higher wages, they stop hiring and may lay employees off. Consumers are reluctant to spend money because they are not sure their jobs are secure. They already feel uneasy because their incomes no longer keep up with the

Biz.Bites

In 1918, a typical Canadian family–father, mother, and three children–needed about $20 a week for such basics as food, lighting, and rent. The family spent about $10.00 for food. Since then, some prices have gone up 1000 percent. In 1918, a pound of cheese cost about 30 cents. A quarter pound (113 g) of coffee cost 10 cents.

Biz.Bites

The last two recessions in Canada occurred in 1982 and 1990. In the 1982 recession, GDP dropped 6.7% over a period of 18 months. In the 1990 recession, GDP dropped 3.2% over 12 months.

cost of living. As demand drops, so do prices (although usually not immediately).

Both businesses and individuals pay less income tax because their earnings have dropped. At the same time, governments need more income because more people need government assistance. Thus, the overall standard of living drops during a recession.

Depression

If a recession is severe or lasts a long time, it may become a depression. A **depression** occurs when economic activity is very low and unemployment is very high. Few people are able to buy goods and services, and companies cannot stay in business.

The demand for government services is very high, but, because the main source of government revenue is from taxes, social services suffer. The need for welfare and unemployment insurance rises sharply, and drastic cuts must be made to other social services. The quality of people's lives is often greatly reduced.

During the Great Depression, from 1929 to 1939, prices dropped drastically. In spite of the low prices, people could not afford to spend their limited money on anything but the most basic necessities. With demand so low, fewer and fewer goods were supplied by a shrinking number of companies.

So many people lost their jobs and so many companies went out of business that there was too little commercial activity to start a recovery until the outbreak of the Second World War in 1939. The need for military equipment stimulated industry and created new demand that helped the economy grow stronger.

Recovery

A **recovery** occurs when the economy starts to improve. The fall in national income lessens. Manufacturers slowly begin production again. However, unemployment remains high until businesses feel confident enough to hire more employees.

After doing without for so long, people are interested in spending again. Cautiously, businesses begin to produce a few more goods and services and to hire employees. People begin to feel a bit more optimistic. The economy gets healthier, although the process is usually slow.

Competition in the Market Place

Competition has a strong influence on the market because of its effect on prices and choices of goods and services. **Competition** in business is a rivalry among suppliers of a good or service. Each supplier tries to make a profit by best satisfying consumer demands. New suppliers enter the market because they believe that the market is large enough for them to earn a profit. But if they want to succeed, businesses have to offer consumers an attractive alternative to the goods or services that are already in the marketplace. That is why businesses use all the means at their disposal to convince consumers to buy from them and not from their competitors.

Let's suppose you are in the market for a new stereo system. You can choose from six electronic stores and each one is trying to convince you to buy from them.

- One store offers lower prices than another.
- A second offers products of a higher quality.
- A third provides better service, perhaps an extended warranty or free installation.
- A fourth has a location that is the most convenient for you.
- A fifth stays open the longest.
- A sixth has a convincing advertising campaign on radio, television, and the Internet.

What would influence your choice of store?

Number of Competitors

The number of competitors in a market affects consumer demand and supply. For the consumers, fewer suppliers often means less choice. For example, when large suppliers try to win customers by cutting prices, small suppliers may not be able to keep up with the price cuts. The smaller businesses—even if their products are better than the competition's—may not have the financial resources to survive a period of lower profits.

Having few competitors in the market can cause problems for the consumer. In 2000, Air Canada and Canadian Airlines merged. Air Canada became the only major airline in Canada. Since the merger, customers have complained loudly about everything from prices for tickets to lost luggage and long lineups at airport check-in counters. Some consumers believe that because Air Canada has little competition it does not need to hurry to provide better service for its customers.

On the other hand, what happens when the number of competitors in a market increases to the point where the supply is much greater than the demand? The answer can be major problems for the supplier. In February 2001, Cineplex Odeon announced that it would be shutting down many of its theatres in Canada. Movie-goers had not come out to the theatres in the numbers that Odeon had expected. The decline in number of patrons and the building of multi-screen theatres meant that more movie theatres existed than the number needed to meet consumers' demand. There was just too much competition for the same pool of customers.

Figure 5-12 How does this editorial cartoon reflect some Canadians' frustrations with not having many competitors for air service in Canada?

Quality of Competitors

The market defines quality differently for different products. So, suppliers who compete for the same customers have to be aware of how those customers define quality for their products. Remember those MP3 players in Chapter 4. What were consumers most interested in? Quality of sound and length of playing time? Once MP3 suppliers provide consumers with these two features, the suppliers have to find other ways to differentiate themselves from their competitors.

As you saw in the Business Profile that opens this chapter, Tim Hortons has built a successful reputation and business by differentiating itself from its many competitors. For over 35 years, it has provided fresh coffee, a community environment, and products that matched consumers' demand. The company has continued to change its product line to adapt to changing consumer needs and wants. Because Tim Hortons has been consistent in providing quality goods and services, it has loyal customers who keep coming back for more.

Differentiating yourself from the competitors can be tough. Kellogg Company, General Mills, Inc., and The Quaker Oats Company all sell breakfast cereals. Many of the products sold by one of these large companies are similar to those sold by the other two. The products also cost about the same. So, to compete for consumers, the cereal suppliers advertise that their products are the highest quality, the best tasting, or are the most nutritious.

Sometimes competing in a new market can be very difficult, even for a company with a well-established reputation for quality in its own market. In March 2001, Roots, the Canadian fashion company, opened Roots Air. Roots had formed an alliance with Skyservice Aviation. By May 2001, Roots Air was out of business, after Air Canada bought a 30 percent interest in Skyservice.

Check Your Understanding

Knowledge/Understanding

1 Explain, in your own words, prosperity, inflation, recession, depression, and recovery.
2 What is the relationship between the number of competitors in the marketplace and consumer supply and demand?

Thinking/Inquiry

3 If a recession began today, what kind of businesses do you think would be affected first? Explain your opinion.
4 Work with a partner to predict how consumers' purchasing decisions would change during each stage of the business cycle. Discuss your conclusions with another pair of students and then revise your original conclusions if need be.

Skills Appendix
building an argument

Communication

5 Create a diagram with illustrations to represent each stage of the business cycle.
6 Find an article–in a Canadian newspaper or in an online newspaper from another country–on the state of the economy. The article could discuss

Skills Appendix
analysing media

inflation, depression, recession, or recovery. Summarize the article and present it to your classmates in a 1-minute radio report.

Application

7 If you wanted to buy a pizza, a coffee, or a new pen, what would influence your decision? List the factors. Create a chart comparing similar choices and service in three stores. Identify the one you would shop at.

Consumer Protection

As a consumer, you try to find reliable, dependable products that will do what they are supposed to do and satisfy your needs or wants. Yet, no matter how carefully you research your purchase, things sometimes go wrong. It is not always possible to discover the truth about every aspect of every good or service you buy.

When unscrupulous business practices and fraud are added to this situation, the need for **consumer protection** is obvious. In Canada, the federal and provincial governments try to protect consumers by making sure that the buying and selling of goods and services is fair. You have rights as a consumer, and you should know what they are.

Federal Legislation

At the federal level, the agency that primarily oversees consumer protection is the Office of Consumer Affairs, which is a department of Industry Canada. Regional offices across Canada handle consumer complaints and help consumers in the marketplace.

The Office of Consumer Affairs tries to make sure that the marketplace is fair and that it supports and advances the interests of Canadian consumers. The office researches and analyses consumer products and passes on information to consumers.

The Office also publishes its warnings and findings on its Web site. A recent investigation covered email hoaxes. The Web site even lists the names of offenders. For example, air carriers who do not maintain airplanes properly or who fail to follow the rules about noise levels, can be fined and have their names posted on the site.

Competition Act

The Competition Act is a federal law that governs advertising and business practices. Anyone who violates this law may be prosecuted in criminal court. A conviction will result in a fine or imprisonment.

A large part of the Competition Act is concerned with mergers and acquisitions, but it is also devoted to controlling unfair business practices that eventually hurt consumers. The Act outlaws false and misleading advertising and illegal pricing practices.

False and Misleading Advertising

Advertising is legal, but advertisements have to be truthful. Consumers can have difficulty detecting advertising that is deceitful. A good rule to remember is that if something sounds too good to be true, it probably is. **False advertising** is making an untrue statement about a product or service. Unfortunately, false advertising is not usually clear-cut. A store that advertises that its purses are all leather might be selling purses made of a synthetic which looks so much like leather that the ordinary consumer cannot tell the difference.

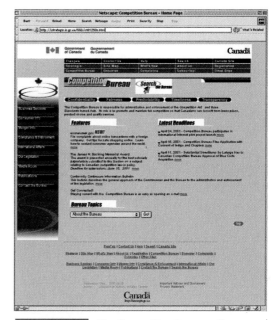

Figure 5-13 The Competition Bureau offers services for businesses and consumers in both domestic and international businesses.

Misleading advertising is also hard to detect. **Misleading advertising** distorts the truth about the goods being offered so that consumers are led to believe one thing through wording or promises, but something else turns out to be true. Imagine this scenario. A sale is advertised in which an item is being sold at 70 percent off the regular price. When you get to the store, the item is sold out. The rule is that a retailer has to keep the same number of products in stock as they would sell in a normal day. But, in fact, only a few of these items were available and were quickly sold. It is also misleading advertising to announce a 20-percent-off sale when all the prices in the store were raised by 20 percent just before the sale. Obviously, there is no sale. The goods are being offered at their regular price.

Illegal Pricing Practices

Illegal pricing practices lessen competition and give consumers less choice than they should have. The following are some examples of such practices.

Figure 5-14

A set of universal warning symbols has been created, and the appropriate symbol must appear with the written warning to inform consumers of the danger.

 Health Canada   Santé Canada

Do you know what these symbols mean?

They are symbols (or pictures) that mean DANGER!

You will find them on the labels of products in and around your home. You will see them on paint thinners, drain cleaners, windshield washer fluid and different kinds of polish.

Look for them on labels. Learn what they mean.

 CORROSIVE This can burn your skin or eyes. If you swallow it, it will damage your throat and stomach.

 FLAMMABLE This product or the gas (vapour) from it, can catch fire quickly. Keep this product away from heat, flames and sparks.

 EXPLOSIVE This container will explode if it is heated or if a hole is punched in it. Metal or plastic can fly out and hurt your eyes or other parts of your body.

 POISON If you swallow or lick this product, you could become very sick or die. Some products with this on the label can hurt you even if you breathe (or inhale) them.

Safety Tips

- Teach children that these symbols mean **Danger! Do not touch**.
- Keep all products with these symbols where children cannot SEE or REACH them.
- Read the label and follow the instructions. If you have trouble reading the label, ask for help. Do not cover up or remove the labels from these products.

Copy emergency phone numbers from the first page of your phone book. Keep the numbers close to the phone.

If someone is hurt by a product that has these symbols on the label:
- Call the Poison Control Centre or your doctor right away.
- Tell the person who answers the phone what the label says.
- Bring the product with you when you go for help.

For more information, contact the Product Safety Bureau, Health Canada, at:

Vancouver, British Columbia (604) 666-5003	**Hamilton, Ontario** (905) 572-2845	**Moncton, New Brunswick** (506) 851-6638
Edmonton, Alberta (780) 495-2626	**Toronto, Ontario** (416) 973-4705	**Dartmouth, Nova Scotia** (902) 426-8300
Calgary, Alberta (403) 292-4677	**Ottawa, Ontario** (613) 952-1014	**St. John's, Newfoundland** (709) 772-4050
Saskatoon, Saskatchewan (306) 975-4502	**Montreal, Quebec** (514) 283-5488	
Winnipeg, Manitoba (204) 983-5490	**Quebec City, Quebec** (418) 648-4327	http://www.hc-sc.gc.ca/psb

To order more copies: by telephone **(613) 954-0609**, by fax **(613) 941-8632**, by e-mail **eh_publishing@hc-sc.gc.ca**

Cat. H46-2/99-228E

ISBN 0-662-27824-0

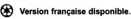 **Version française disponible.**

 Canadä

This material can be photocopied.
Revised September 2000

- *Price fixing* is an agreement between or among businesses to charge the same price for similar products rather than competing on price. When prices are fixed the consumer can't choose among alternative products based on price.
- *Price discrimination* is the practice of selling goods more cheaply to one person or business than to another. If you own a retail store and your competitors can buy goods more cheaply than you can, you may be forced out of business.
- *Predatory pricing* is the practice of charging very low prices in order to reduce competition. Predatory pricing can put companies out of business. Once there are fewer competitors in the market, the businesses that remain can increase their prices again.
- *Resale price maintenance* means that a manufacturer sets the price at which wholesalers and retailers must sell the product.
- *Bait and switch* occurs when a business offers a product at a very low price to draw customers. Once customers arrive they are told the product is sold out and are offered another product at a higher price.

Hazardous Products Act

The Hazardous Products Act was passed to ensure consumer safety. The Act is concerned with the labelling, advertising, and sale of hazardous products. It prohibits the manufacture and sale of very dangerous products and regulates the sale of products that might be harmful.

Products such as cleansers, bleaches, and polishes may be hazardous to both children and adults and must be labelled with warnings that show the danger. The product label must also contain first aid information. The labels are intended as a warning only. The user of the product is responsible for using the product as directed and for keeping it out of the reach of children.

Textile Labelling Act

With the development of synthetic fibres came the need for more information. Natural fibres–cotton, silk, wool, and linen–have certain qualities and require certain types of care. Synthetics such as nylon, acrylic, polyester, and rayon have different qualities and require different care. Consumers can check the labels to see if the product will fit their needs. For example, a marathon runner might check a label to be sure that the material is light and durable.

The Textile Labelling Act requires that the labels of all clothing, household textiles, and fabric sold by the piece include information on
• the types of fibres contained in the fabric
• the amount of each fibre present in a quantity of 5 percent or more
• the identity of the dealer by name and address or identification number

Consumer Packaging and Labelling Act

The Consumer Packaging and Labelling Act establishes guidelines for the packaging and labelling of all consumer products sold in Canada. Packaging can be misleading. The Packaging and Labelling Act prohibits the packaging of a small article in a large box in order to make the consumer believe that the package contains a greater amount than it does. Some package sizes have been standardized to avoid confusion.

According to this Act, labels must contain the following information:
• all ingredients listed in descending order by proportion or as a percentage on food products
• information in both French and English
• net amount in metric units
• the name and address of the company responsible for the product in case consumers have any questions, complaints, or comments about the product
• a best before date on most perishable foods, except fresh fruit and vegetables

Nothing added,
nothing taken away
Pasteurized
**Keep refrigerated
between
0°C and 4°C.**

Entièrement naturel,
rien de plus,
rien de moins
Pasteurisé
Garder au
réfrigérateur
entre 0°C et 4°C.

NUTRITION INFORMATION NUTRITIONNELLE
per 175 mL serving / par portion de 175 mL
Energy / Énergie .... 80 Cal
                                                    330 kJ
Protein / Protéines .... 0.5 g
Fat / Matières grasses .... 0 g
Carbohydrate / Glucides .... 20 g
    sugars / sucres .... 17 g
Sodium .... 0 mg
Potassium .... 320 mg
PERCENTAGE OF RECOMMENDED DAILY INTAKE
POURCENTAGE DE L'APPORT QUOTIDIEN RECOMMANDÉ
Vitamin C / Vitamine C .... 88 %
Folacin / Folacine .... 26 %

We thank you for buying Tropicana.
Merci d'avoir acheté du Tropicana.

Your comments are important to us.
1-800-237-7799
Vos commentaires
sont importants pour nous.

Tropicana Products, Inc. Bradenton, Florida 34206 U.S.A.

Figure 5-15 Look over this label carefully and identify the items required by the Consumer Packaging and Labelling Act. Are there any that you can't find? Why might that be?

Food and Drugs Act

The Food and Drugs Act regulates harmful products that could cause injury or illness if not used properly or if swallowed. The Act also regulates matters such as packaging and advertising of food and drug products.

The Canadian Food Inspection Agency

The Canadian Food Inspection Agency (CFIA) is Canada's federal food-safety, animal-health, and plant-protection enforcement agency. It enforces regulations on a wide variety of food related products such as dairy products, fresh fruit and vegetables, honey and maple syrup, livestock and poultry.

The Agency was created in April 1997 to bring together inspection services for four federal government departments. It now has inspection programs related to food, animals, and plants. Its activities range from inspecting meat-processing facilities and looking for foreign diseases in imported foods to enforcing practices related to fraudulent labelling. The CFIA also ensures the humane transportation of animals and performs laboratory testing and environmental assessment of seeds, plants, feeds, and fertilizers.

Provincial Legislation

Every province has passed laws to protect consumers. A Consumer Protection Act usually includes the following regulations on credit charges and door-to-door sales.

Consumers who sign a contract to make a purchase on credit must be told the total credit charges in dollars and cents, as well as the true rate of interest. If you're buying a car, you'll need to know if you can afford all the payments. You'll learn more in Chapter 12 about the benefits of comparing interest charges on credit cards and loans.

Door-to-door salespeople must be licensed to protect buyers from fraudulent selling and misleading sales. The consumer, however, must ask to see the licence. The Act provides for a cooling-off period. During this time, consumers may cancel the contract, but must do it in writing. The law does not apply to sales made in the seller's place of business, because the buyer always has the option of leaving. The length of cooling-off periods ranges from two days in Ontario to 10 days in Newfoundland.

All provinces have a Trade Practices or Business Practices Act, which outlines unfair or misleading business practices, such as

- claiming service or repairs are needed when they are not
- claiming that a product has a specific use when it does not
- using a celebrity to endorse a product if he or she does not, in fact, use it
- misrepresenting the price at which a product is sold

If a consumer can prove that a contract involves an unfair practice, he or she has the right to cancel the contract. These Acts also establish ways for consumers to claim compensation if they have been subjected to an unfair business practice.

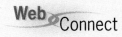

Web Connect

www.school.mcgrawhill.ca/resources/
Go to Ontario Ministry of Consumer and Business Services site and investigate some current consumer protection issues.

Check Your Understanding

Knowledge/Understanding

1 How does the Hazardous Products Act protect consumers?
2 How does the Textile and Labelling Act protect consumers?

Thinking/Inquiry

3 Identify the unfair business practice in each of the following situations:

- Alain receives an advertising flyer that offers leather boots at 70 percent off the regular price. When he gets to the store, there is only one pair, in a small size.

- Gina reads an advertisement for a ten-carat gold chain. The price is only $10, so she sends away for it. When she later receives the chain, she realizes it is definitely not gold.

- Paul travels across town to a sale featuring 30- to 50-percent price reductions on stereo equipment. When he gets to the store, he is told that there was only one model on sale and that was sold a day ago.

Communication

4 In groups of two or three, prepare a collage or bulletin board display on the theme of consumer protection. Collect materials from magazines, newspapers, and the office of Consumer Affairs. Present your collage to the class, explaining your choices.

Application

5 Work with a partner to retell an anecdote of your own experience with misleading or false advertising. You may want to focus on the advertisement in the media or false statements on packaging or in labelling. Practice your oral storytelling techniques to make the story vivid and interesting. Then tell your story to a larger group.

Issues Affecting Business

Environmental Factors

What's for Dinner? Globalization Gives Farmers New Challenge

Like his neighbours, grain farmer Marcel Bouchard had assured himself all summer that he could look forward to a good crop in 2000. He knew he wouldn't get as much for his rye as in other years. Grain prices were down because of good crops around the world. Also, the U.S. and European countries were supporting their farmers with government grants or subsidies. But Bouchard thought that a good crop with a high yield might help offset the low prices. That might be enough to get him through another year." These fields were looking really good," Bouchard said. "Really good."

Then the fog rolled in. A light mist, really. It blew around the Prairies for three or four days around Labour Day, just as the harvest was getting under way. Until then, the expected good crop was coming in as planned. But the rain that followed the mist forced farmers off their fields when they needed to be there most. They could only watch as the cool, wet days ruined their hopes. By the time the sun finally allowed farmers back on their fields, their worst fears were coming true.

As their combines cut through fields of grain, farmers could see that the once bountiful kernels had begun to sprout. They had taken the wet fall weather as a signal to start germinating. Those kernals that hadn't sprouted were bleached by the damp weather. In a little over a week, bad weather reduced a very promising crop to animal feed.

The price of Bouchard's rye, which he had expected to bring about $2 a bushel, dropped to less than a dollar in a matter of days. Other farmers growing other grains saw their crop values drop the same way. At one time, a bad crop could be at least partly offset by higher prices as reduced supplies failed to meet demand. But no more.

Figure 5-16 Marcel and Konner Bouchard's livelihood, like many Canadian farmers, depends on economic as well environmental factors.

Today's farmers compete on the world market, with countries that have government subsidies that Canada doesn't match.

"We don't take care of our farmers," Bouchard said. In other parts of the world, the harvest was good this year, with the U.S. reporting ideal growing conditions and large crops in the American midwest. That was enough to keep prices down for all farmers. It was the second year in a row that wet weather and bad prices have caused farmers to lose money.

In 1999, the wet weather came at the start of the year. Severe flooding in the spring kept farmers in southern Saskatchewan and Manitoba off their land during the crucial planting season. More than 2 million acres went unplanted, including three-quarters of Bouchard's 4500-acre farm. These conditions forced the federal and provincial governments to come up with a $1 billion subsidy package.

Bouchard didn't get a cent. He was told that because he had a livestock operation, he didn't need any money. "I guess they figure that the cattle offset the grain," he said, shaking his head, unable to grasp how he could be denied aid. "I'm still trying to figure it out."

In 1999, farmers took to the highways in their combines to protest the low level of aid they were offered. They held rallies in Regina and Ottawa, with one farmer driving his combine to Parliament Hill in a plea for more help. But their protests didn't do any good.

The central issue to Bouchard and other farmers is heavy subsidies in other countries. Canadian farmers have no problem competing on the open market. They just want a level playing field. And that, say Canadian farmers, means that if Canada cannot convince the U.S. and Europe to cut their subsidies, it must match them.

Figure 5-17 George Godenir, another Canadian farmer, was involved in farm protests in 1998. He says that protests don't do any good though. He believes Canadian farmers need more government support.

ACTIVITIES

1 Briefly describe the problems faced by Canadian wheat farmers.
2 How has global competition influenced the supply and demand for Canadian wheat?
3 Should our government provide more financial subsidies to farmers? Will this make them globally competitive? Write an opinion on this issue and include factual evidence to support your opinion.
4 With a partner develop an economic solution that will help farmers achieve their goals of turning profits. Report your solution to the class.

Chapter Review

Points to Remember

- Supply and demand and their inter–relationship influence market activities and the economy.

- The level of demand affects the health of a market. In general, the lower the price the greater the demand.

- The supply of goods and services produced relates to price. Generally, the higher the price, the greater the supply.

- An economy changes over time. The typical business cycle starts with prosperity, and then moves through inflation, recession, depression, and finally recovery.

- The number and quality of competitors in a market has a direct effect on the market.

- The federal and the provincial governments have passed acts to protect consumers.

Activities

Knowledge/Understanding

1 Name the federal government agency that regulates consumer protection, and describe its function.

2 Why is there a need for packaging and labelling regulations for food?

Thinking/Inquiry

1 In your local newspaper or a magazine, find an article on the regulation or restriction of business by government. Summarize the article and discuss how it benefits consumers.

2 Identify the factor of supply that each of the following situations demonstrates.
  a) A neighbourhood store is going out of business because a new one charges less than it can afford to charge.

Skills
Appendix

critical thinking

b) Electronic calculators, which used to cost hundreds of dollars, are now being given away by businesses as gifts.

c) A manufacturer warns that increased taxes could result in layoffs.

d) Insects have destroyed the coffee crop in Colombia.

e) Kwok says he doesn't care how hard he has to work at his doughnut franchise. It's better than the job he left.

3 Marie works as a computer programmer in a medium-sized company. Her husband, Doug, is also employed, and they have two small children. Day care has always been a hassle. Marie and Doug agree that their quality of life would be much better if one of them could take the children to day care in their workplaces. They decide to find out how many other people at their work are in this position.

a) How can they learn whether there is any demand for day care at the places they work?

b) What factors of demand are likely to affect day care?

c) What benefit is there to the company in providing day-care for its employees?

4 Obtain and read a copy of a consumer-oriented magazine or visit a consumer Web site that rates products and services by testing them. Choose a product that interests you and summarize the testing that was conducted. Include information about

a) the types of product and brand names tested

b) the kind of testing that was done

c) the results by brand names, listing them from best to worst buys

d) the relationship, if any, between price and quality

e) the relationship, if any, between the most popular brand and testing results

f) whether your perception of this product has changed as a result of the tests

What conclusions can you draw about the relationship between price and quality?

Skills

Appendix

researching

Communication

1 In small groups, identify three businesses that could be considered as competition for a movie theatre. Suggest how the theatre could attract customers. Create a newspaper advertisement that the theatre might run. With the rest of the class, prepare a bulletin board display of the advertisements.

2 In groups of two or three, compare the brand names, prices, and quality of three different products in different stores. Compare the stores' service and reputation. Visit at least one local store, a large department or grocery store, and two smaller specialty chain stores. Choose three products. Organize your findings in chart form and create a bar graph to compare the different stores on the scales of price, quality, service, and reputation.

Application

1 Your friend's parents operate a small retail clothing store in the local mall. They sell the same quality of goods as stores belonging to large chains, and they have difficulty competing because the big stores are so well known. Outline ways they can compete with the big stores and suggest how they should advertise.

2 Pilar operates a restaurant. Costs have been rising on all her supplies and business has not been good lately, but she has a plan. She will start to cut down on the size of portions she serves and raise her prices. Because she has regular customers, she believes she will make a higher profit this way. Advise Pilar.

Skills
Appendix

problem solving

3 At a factory, the workers are worried that there will soon be many layoffs. They have heard that management is considering buying a computerized production system to replace 50 people currently doing the production job. Form groups of three or four to discuss this problem and answer the following questions.
  a) What factors of supply are affected in this case?
  b) What has probably caused the company to consider this change?
  c) What options may be open to these workers if the company goes ahead with the plan?
  Write down the answers you come up with, and report these answers to the class. Individually, write up the discussion as a newspaper article.

Skills
Appendix

writing reports

Internet Extension

1 Using Internet resources, analyse how the forces of supply and demand are affecting some current market prices.

6 Human Resources and Management

Specific Expectations

After studying this chapter, you will be able to

- **describe the function of human resources and effective people management**

- **describe the role of management in business**

- **identify key employability skills**

- **describe a variety of business career paths**

- **compare the rights and responsibilities of employees and employers**

- **describe how different management approaches and styles can influence employee productivity**

Businesses must hire employees who will succeed, and help the business succeed. This is one of the functions of the human resources department. Other important functions are training and development, assessing employee performance, and compensating employees for their performance.

The management of a business must plan, organize, lead, motivate, control and evaluate the activities of the business. Management acts on behalf of the business itself, not primarily on behalf of employees. However, management is obligated to consider the rights and responsibilities of employees as well as its own rights and responsibilities when it makes decisions.

For a successful relationship, both employers and employees need to be aware of the nature of today's workplace and the skills employees need in order to get and keep jobs.

Carter Powis and Targetnet

Carter Powis's friends couldn't understand why he suddenly quit his corporate job to help run Targetnet Inc., a Canadian Internet company started by a 19-year-old. "They all said, 'You're doing what? You're going where?'" he recalled. At 37, Powis had an enviable résumé than included an MBA from a school in Switzerland, and management experience at Colgate-Palmolive Inc. and McKinsey & Co., a consulting firm.

When Powis joined Targetnet in 1999, it had just eight other employees and a little money to get started. The company had been launched in 1998 to create and sell banner ads for Web sites. It also delivered targeted e-mail and wireless messages, mainly advertising, to consumers on behalf of corporate clients.

Like many other new Internet companies, Targetnet had lots of employees with technical skills. It needed someone like Powis–who had marketing and administrative experience—to introduce sound business practices, assemble an executive team, organize the company for growth, and generally give the firm the polish required to attract bigger investors.

Powis says that the time that he has spent at Targetnet has been a huge learning experience. One challenge was creating a budget. Old-economy companies can project future performance by looking at past sales. New economy companies—like Targetnet—have no idea what their sales will look like next year, or even next month. Old economy companies know what they do and whom they do it for; new economy companies often change focus and markets very quickly.

In addition, Powis now works with a much more diverse group of employees. "At Colgate-Palmolive or McKinsey, you work with people who all look alike, who have similar backgrounds and interests." At Targetnet there's a much greater variety in employees' ages, experience, and skill sets. Powis enjoys that challenge. What might have been the challenges that Carter Powis faced managing the employees of Targetnet? What business practices would he have had to put into effect? What do you think his management style would be?

Figure 6-1 "It's an incredible experience to participate in something that probably hasn't been seen since the Industrial Revolution. I'm not looking at it from the sidelines. I'm living it." (Carter Powis)

The Role of Human Resources

Most companies say that their greatest strength is their people—the men and women they employ. Because employees are as important to a business as its financial resources and productive resources, they are often called human resources. In business, **human resources**, as an activity, is that aspect of business operations that deals with hiring, developing, and keeping good staff.

Figure 6-2 JobsCanada is billed as "the Internet's most advanced employment website." Its Human Resources Database contains thousands of codes describing types of businesses, job skills, experience, and other qualities. Job seekers and employers can both enter data. The technology codes and matches information from both groups.

Recruiting Employees

To get the employees that they want, businesses must recruit them. **Recruitment** is a process that involves attracting people to apply for a job, checking applicants' qualifications, and hiring the person who has been chosen.

But before a company advertises a position, it often reviews the human resources needs of the department or company as a whole. Those in charge of recruiting first check if the job has changed, if a new employee is really needed, and if the company can afford to hire someone. This type of review keeps the company's competitive edge sharp.

Before it advertises, a business will also develop a **job description** for each position. A job description describes the requirements and responsibilities of a particular job. It includes the necessary education, skills, expertise, and experience.

These requirements are specific to the job. For example, a mechanic needs one set of skills and a teacher needs another. So the skills listed for their jobs will differ in many ways. Likely, though, they would also need some of the same skills. Both the mechanic and the teacher will need communication skills to be able to work effectively with clients and students, and with their employers.

Once a business knows the type of people it needs, it goes about recruiting, or attracting, them. When companies recruit internally, they try to hire someone who already works for them by posting a job notice or by word-of-mouth advertising. They may transfer a person from one department to another, or promote someone who has demonstrated a particular skill and is ready to take on more responsibility.

When businesses recruit externally, they reach out to the larger world by advertising in newspapers and trade publications, on the company Web site, or on employment Web sites. Some large companies go to job fairs, often held at colleges and universities. Businesses may hire a third party to recruit talented employees. These professional recruiters are often referred to as "head hunters."

Figure 6-3 Job fairs are great places to seek work because you meet and interact with potential employers. Meeting people, and allowing them to meet you, can sometimes open the door to a job placement.

Selecting Employees

When a company is ready to select an employee out of a group of candidates, it usually follows a step-by-step process. The first step is asking the candidate to submit a résumé and in some cases fill out an application form. The company identifies the applicants who most closely fit its requirements. Next, the applicants have one or more interviews with the person who will directly manage them. Some businesses administer tests to determine a candidate's skill in a particular area. In many instances, the company will check to make sure the candidate actually has the education and job experience described in his or her résumé. It is costly to hire the wrong person, so businesses usually take this part of the selection process seriously.

Training and Developing Employees

The training and development of employees usually begins on the first day of the job and can continue as long as the employee is with the company. The goal is to improve company productivity by improving an

employee's ability to perform. **Training** is teaching skills that are learned by practice. On-the-job training can begin the day the employee joins the company and end at a specific date, usually once the person can do the job comfortably. If an employee is promoted to a new job, training may begin again.

Development, on the other hand, is a long process of upgrading an employee's performance over time by giving him or her opportunities to grow. Methods include job-related technology training, management seminars, and workshops in time management or communications. Companies select training programs to meet their own need for excellence in specific areas.

Assessing Employee Performance

Most companies **assess** how well employees do on the job. This process is called **assessment**. One of the first steps in assessing employee performance is to tell employees what is expected of them—similar to the process you experience at school. These expectations are known as **performance standards**, and they must be specific, measurable, and easily communicated. For example, "The employee behaved properly at all times" is not a standard against which performance can be judged. However, "The employee consistently met deadlines over a 6-month period" is a measurable standard.

In addition to having supervisors or managers assess employees, many businesses ask employees to assess themselves. Then the employee and supervisor or manager discuss the results and agree on an action plan for improvements, changes, or promotion.

Biz.Bites

One of the golden rules of management is: Criticize people in private.

Web Connect

www.school.mcgrawhill.ca/resources/
Visit the JobsCanada Web site to investigate some types of jobs you might be interested in either for your present or your future careers. Look carefully at the job descriptions and identify the key employability skills that would be necessary to do the job.

Compensating Employees

Managing compensation programs is a major function of human resources. In order to employ people, a company must pay them to work. But it also wants to manage its costs carefully. It is estimated that employee **compensation**, which includes wages and benefits, makes up the single largest operating cost of running a business. (You will learn more about wages and benefits in Chapters 9 and 10.)

Management determines the amount that a person will be paid, as well as the form the payment will take.

- Some people are paid a salary, a fixed amount that they receive on a regular basis (weekly, biweekly, or monthly).
- Retail workers are usually paid by the hour. Mechanics are often paid on a flat rate basis—an hourly rate multiplied by the number of hours a job should take.
- Other people are paid commissions—a percentage of the sales they negotiated for the company. Real estate agents, for example, earn a percentage of the purchase price of a property they helped someone buy or sell.

Biz.Bites

In the past decade, pay for women has remained "stuck" at about 65 percent of men's earnings.

Check Your Understanding

Knowledge/Understanding

1 Using your understanding of the role of human resources management, indicate which of the following activities match with the steps listed.

Human Resources Activities	Steps
job descriptions	selecting
commissions	training and development
workshops for employees	recruiting
performance standards	compensating employees
skill tests and résumé checks	assessing performance

2 Write a brief paragraph explaining the role that human resource management has in business.

Thinking/Inquiry

3 Work with two other students to prepare a chart listing the advantages and disadvantages of three types of compensation. Then examine the chart and decide which form of compensation would most likely motivate you as an employee to perform better at work.

Communication

4 Assessing an employee's performance on the job can be a challenging task. Imagine that you are part of a management team put in charge of developing performance standards for retail employees at a clothing

Skills
Appendix

working in groups

CHAPTER 6 *Human Resources and Management* • MHR **161**

store. In small groups, create a list of performance standards and indicate how you would measure them.

Application

Skills
Appendix

decision making

5 You are a human resources manager in a large company trying to find someone to fill a clerk's position. You have narrowed the choice to two people. One person has lots of clerical skills and has completed high school. The other has some clerical skills and a law degree. The person with less education seems ideally suited to the job. The one with the law degree might be overqualified for the job. On the other hand, the legal knowledge could be of use at your company.

How will you decide which candidate to hire? What questions will you need to ask yourself to help you make this decision?

The Role of Management

You've probably heard someone's job referred to as a "management position." You or your friends may have older brothers or sisters who intend to study management at university. But what is management? **Management** is the function of directing and administering all, or part of, a business. Managers set goals and handle the company's human, financial, and productive resources to achieve its goals.

While management once meant a rigid distinction between managers and employees, managements styles have changed. **Management style** is a combination of the techniques a person uses to take charge of something and of the manner in which he or she takes charge.

Management styles have undergone a revolution ever since global competition and evolving technology forced companies to respond to market needs more rapidly and with more creativity. Today, employees at every level—not just the managers— are expected to contribute ideas.

Figure 6-5 Encouraging employees at every level to contribute ideas makes good business sense.

Connecting Business with *Lifelong Learning*

Will You Be a Lifelong Learner?

According to Human Resources Development Canada's Offices of Learning Technologies, learning is undergoing a revolution. You may not go to school for the rest of your life, but you may be learning from now until you retire.

Consider the revolution in information technology that has occurred in the last 30 years. Before that time, there were no photocopiers, computers, or fax machines. Imagine how difficult it was for the people who had worked for years on these systems to tackle word processing, e-mail, and the Internet.

So you feel you know it all now? Hold on a minute. The revolution has only begun. Over your lifetime, you may witness four or five more major changes in technology as well as in other areas of life. Because technology, economy, politics, and social values are interrelated, the challenge to adapt will come from all sides, says the Offices of Learning Technologies.

What are the issues in lifelong learning? The first issue is the need. Today goods and services are being produced in a new way—often by teams of people working in different parts of the globe. Employees at all levels are expected to contribute ideas, use their judgement, and make decisions.

The second issue is how to deliver lifelong education. Some countries are forging ahead with plans. Japan has announced its intention to wire every school, home, and office with fibre optic cable by the year 2015. The European Union is investing millions of dollars in research funds to support distance education in the health care field. In Canada, the Canadian On-Line Exploration and Collaborative Environment for Education (COCEE) Alliance has announced that it wants to develop and operate an open network of education, training, and lifelong learning resources.

The last issue is how to overcome barriers to lifelong learning. One of the main barriers is poverty, which denies children basic education or sets them up for failure in learning. As people mature, barriers to lifelong learning persist. One barrier is the cost of adult training. When Canadians were recently surveyed on why they did not get more training, 30 percent of them cited expense as a reason. Another issue is accessibility. Ideally, lifelong learning should be accessible at home, at work, or in the community. Some of the new approaches being proposed include the virtual classroom and on-line tutorials, customized training for specific needs in specific situations, and "just in time learning," which aims to meet the immediate needs of an employee.

ACTIVITIES

1. Give three examples of new technologies (other than the ones in this feature) that have affected our offices or homes.

2. What new skills did people have to learn to use these new technologies?

3. Think of a job that you would like to have. What changes might happen in that industry or profession? Write a paragraph describing the change and the training you would have to take to continue doing that job.

Managers must be able to communicate and interact effectively with everyone in the business. They need leadership qualities, including the ability to inspire, motivate, and delegate. Effective managers, like the people they manage, help to ensure that a business is productive and profitable. Without them, a business will surely fail.

Planning

Planning is the first critical step for managers to take. The planning process involves forecasting the future and usually begins with research. Will the goods or services produced by the business be necessary in the future? Will tomorrow's need be greater than today's? What tactics should the business use to meet those needs? Managers involved in this kind of planning have to watch for trends and changes in the business environment. Once management understands the big picture, its sets the **objectives**, or goals, for the business and creates a business plan.

The business plan will list the goals for the company as a whole and for each area. It will describe strategies to achieve these objectives, the resources the company will use, and the schedule for reaching those goals. The plan will also identify who is responsible for various parts of the plan.

Organizing

Having a plan is important, but so is **organizing** the company, in other words, having the structure and the right systems to implement the plan. The **structure** of an organization is the arrangement of employees according to their positions and responsibilities. If the organizational structure is solid, employees will be working at jobs that suit them and they will understand how their work is contributing to the company goals.

To get work done, many companies establish **systems**, or procedures. If systems have been thought out, people will find them effective and easy to follow, and they will help the company to achieve its goals. Many fast food restaurants have strict systems for cooking food so that everyone prepares the quality of food customers expect. You may recognize ineffective systems in your own school life. If your system for getting your homework done consists of opening a book in front of the television and taking regular breaks to chat with your friends on your cell phone, you would have to describe it as an ineffective system.

For Better or for Worse

© UPS Reprinted by Permission

Management must also ensure that a company's resources are used wisely. You have already learned about a company's human resources. In addition to human resources, a company has financial resources and productive resources.

A company's financial resources are its money and assets, such as cars, furniture, and computers. Investors in a company provide the necessary cash for the purchase of these materials and equipment. (When a company is small it may have only one investor—the owner.) Naturally, companies must protect their financial resources so that there is enough money both to meet daily needs and to invest in the future. Managing and tracking a company's financial resources is the work of accountants and bookkeepers. Their roles will be examined in Chapter 8.

Many companies also have machinery and equipment for producing goods and services. These are known as productive resources. When machinery is bought or acquired, it must be used efficiently and maintained properly. Outdated or poorly maintained equipment could result in costly downtime while repairs are made, or in quality control problems. A manufacturing company cannot afford to have a large number of products rejected because they do not meet specifications. So it might develop a plan for regularly inspecting and repairing equipment.

Human, financial, and productive resources are interrelated. All resources must be managed effectively in order to accomplish the goals of the company. Suppose a business is experiencing a sales slump. One of the first things the company will want to know is—Why? What is the problem? Could it be external? Perhaps there is a recession, and sales are slow for all businesses. Or the problems might be internal. Perhaps

Figure 6-6

While encouraging employees to take initiative may be a good idea, it can also be a challenge. How could the problem that this manager now faces have been avoided?

Biz.Bites

Today, the knowledge used to achieve the company's goals is called a productive resource.

some employees are unmotivated or unresponsive to the management style of the people in charge. If that's the case, they may not be very productive. Maybe the equipment is old or out-of-date; and the products rolling off the assembly line are poorly made or unattractive. Perhaps the business needs to invest in some new equipment. It might be able to save some money by closing on the one night of the week when sales are slow. The bottom line is that good organization lets a company use its resources effectively in order to maximize its profits.

Leading

The third function of management is leading, or leadership, one of the most talked about areas of management. **Leading** is setting a direction for others. It involves giving assignments, clarifying roles, explaining routines, and providing motivation and feedback. Is a good leader someone who gives people orders or one who inspires them to do their best work? You will read more about this topic in "Do Men and Women Thrive under Different Management Styles" (page 179). One thing is certain, however. A manager's leadership style can affect the performance of employees and the atmosphere in a place of business.

There are three main leadership styles.

- The autocratic leader is "in charge." He or she clearly directs people, states how things are to be done, and does not allow employees to criticize or alter systems or provide feedback about their job.
- The democratic leader is clear about his or her expectations, but allows employees to give feedback about their work.
- The laissez-faire manager does little to direct employees and leaves them to make their own decisions.

It may surprise you to learn that all three types of managers can be effective in specific situations, and ineffective in others. Although it may seem less stressful to have a manager who leaves you alone, such a person might not give you the necessary direction and could blame you when something goes wrong.

Motivating

Another aspect of managing involves **motivating**, or encouraging employees to act. A manager may use methods that are positive, negative, or a mix of both. This is external motivation. A manager must also encourage others to develop internal motivation that comes from within the person. Internal motivation is usually a stronger force than external motivation. You are already familiar with what motivates you—for example, fear of failing a course (motivation to study for a test) or a desire for a certain stereo system (motivation to stick to your part-time job).

Motivation is tied to the theory of human needs described in Chapter 1. Abraham Maslow, who created the theory, believed that people were motivated to satisfy their unmet needs. The most basic are physical and safety needs. Millions of people around the world work to satisfy their basic needs and those of their children. They do not have the luxury of thinking about how work could satisfy their higher needs.

In the developed world, however, employees often expect work to satisfy their growth needs—the social, esteem, and self-actualization needs in Maslow's hierarchy. For example, employees might experience the need

- to be part of a team
- to grow in knowledge and skill
- to be mentally challenged
- to feel they are making a real contribution
- to have prestige

Knowing what's important to an employee is the key to motivating him or her. But it's not the whole picture. Managers often have their own bias about what motivates people. One theory holds that managers think one of two things about employees. The first type of manager assumes that the average employee dislikes work, is naturally lazy, has no ambition, wants to be told what to do, and is motivated by fear and money. The second type of manager assumes that the average employee likes work, is naturally inclined to setting goals, seeks responsibility, likes to solve problems, and is motivated by many different rewards, not just money or fear. (See Figure 6-9)

Studies have also shown that while their level of pay is important to people, it is not the only factor that motivates them to work. In fact, many people are willing to take less pay for better working conditions. Figure 6-9, shows how managers' biases influence the ways in which they motivate employees. (Note that some of these assumptions and motivators are meant to be negative because they reflect negative biases on the part of management.)

Management Assumptions and Motivators

Assumptions	Motivators
All Lucy cares about is her pay cheque.	Offer Lucy overtime if she performs well. (This manager considers other factors, such as job satisfaction, irrelevant.)
All Bruno cares about is leaving work at 5.	Threaten Bruno with having to stay late if he slacks off during the day. It's the only thing that will keep him on track.
All Sally cares about is being told what to do.	If you have to give Sally a big job, break it down into small pieces and assure her that she won't have to think.
What Angela cares most about is creative problem-solving	Give Angela opportunities to problem-solve as well as feedback on her success. Invite her to share her problem-solving stategies.
What Isaac cares most about is maintaining excellent relationships with team members.	Nominate Isaac for the quarterly company award for best team player and tell him why you did so.
What Ayesha cares most about is setting her own goals.	Encourage Ayesha to set goals for the next six months, along with an action plan. Throughout the process, inquire if she needs anything from you (her manager) to attain her goals.

Figure 6-8 How would you react to these managers' tactics for motivating employees? Which of these management styles is likely to be most successful?

Controlling and Evaluating

Another management function is controlling and evaluating the performance of the company. **Controlling** means ensuring that company performance is going according to plan—that the objectives are being met.

Ultimately, profit is the measure of how a business has performed, but many things can affect company performance. Suppose a business falls short of its profit objectives? Many factors could contribute to this failure, but management is responsible to determine what they are. To do this, management evaluates what happened. Perhaps the expectations for the product or service were too high. Maybe production was not on schedule. Maybe the advertising was not as effective as it could be. Perhaps the sales force was overwhelmed and unable to perform well. Once management has determined the problem, it must figure out how to improve the company's performance.

Levels of Management

Depending on its size, an organization could have up to three levels of management.

Top management usually includes the president of the company and other key executives such as the chief executive officer (CEO), the chief financial officer (CFO) and chief operating officer (COO). It could also include a company's board of directors. These people are responsible for the overall management of the organization.

Middle management—division and plant managers—takes the overall plan and creates plans of action for their own divisions and departments. They pass these plans on to supervisors.

Supervisors are sometimes called first-line managers because they are the first level of management above the employees. They communicate directly with employees to ensure that tasks are completed efficiently, and they deal with problems that arise on a daily basis.

TOP MANAGEMENT
President, CFO, COO
Vice-presidents
Governor, Chancellor, Mayor

MIDDLE MANAGEMENT
Plant managers
Division heads
Branch managers
Deans

SUPERVISORY (FIRST-LINE) MANAGEMENT
Supervisors, Foremen,
Department heads
Section leaders

NONSUPERVISORY
Employees

Figure 6-9 Levels of management in a traditional organization.

Check Your Understanding

Knowledge/Understanding

1 Explain, in your own words, why planning and organizing are important in a business or organization.

2 What is involved in the management functions of leading and motivating? How are the two functions connected to each other?

Thinking/Inquiry

3 Work in a small group for this activity. Use the functions of management— planning, organizing, leading, motivating, controlling, and evaluating. Prepare a list of characteristics and skills that make a manager effective, and explain to the rest of the class how these would help employees do better in their jobs.

Skills
Appendix
decision-making

Communication

4 According to his manager, Greg is not performing well. He has been late a number of times, and customers have complained that he is rude. The manager has observed Greg and thinks he is not willing to change. With a

partner, role-play a conversation in which the manager attempts to talk to Greg about his behaviour. Suggest ways in which company training might be used to prevent problems like this one.

Application

5 Sales have dropped at Mindful Manufacturing. Recent financial results indicate that company performance fell considerably short of targets. Further investigation reveals several things

   - little communication among the department managers of sales, finance, marketing, and production
   - a lot of employee absenteeism in the factory
   - poor morale with workers saying management does not know what is going on. They say that they hear "through the grapevine" that massive layoff are about to occur.
   - senior management feels their memos to employees are clear, and that the workers are lazy

      You and your group are management consultants who have been hired to improve the situation. Discuss the problems at Mindful Manufacturing using what you have learned in this chapter. Create a plan to improve management style, communications, and motivation. Explain how the problems have resulted in poor sales and company performance. Present your solutions to the class.

Careers in Business

Whatever career path you choose, it will probably be connected to business. Even if you decide to be an artist, you will need to market and sell your work (unless you are independently wealthy). If you decide to be self-employed, you will have to make many business decisions. What hourly rate will you charge? What expenses will you need to record? How will you set up your home so you can work satisfactorily?

If you work for a company, you will need to accept or adapt to that organization's management style, approach to assessing employee performance, marketing plans, production efficiency, and creativity. No matter what you end up doing during your career, business skills will be indispensable in helping you succeed in a company environment.

You can study business now, in high school, and later in college or university. You can graduate with a diploma or degree in business and start your own business, join a small company, or work for a large company.

Starting Your Own Small Business

As you learned in Chapter 3, a big change in employment took place in the 1980s and 1990s when more people opened their own businesses. For some people, being self-employed worked out well; others failed in their businesses. Like other forms of self-employment, working for yourself has its advantages and disadvantages.

For the person who likes independence, self-employment is satisfying because he or she can be their own boss. Someone who wants the freedom and time to try creative ideas may find many aspects of self-employment satisfying. For others being able to have flexible work hours is very appealing.

There are also challenges in being self-employed. Money may be a big concern. Self-employed people don't get regular wages. Freelancers need to complete projects in order to be paid. Occasionally, a client may be very late in paying or not pay at all. If an entrepreneur doesn't have enough money to live on until the company gets established, he or she might have to close before really testing his or her business idea.

People who became self-employed because jobs were scarce, may not have the qualities needed for self-employment. They may discover they don't like to work alone. Or they may find that they work better when someone else provides a structure and encouragement.

Figure 6-10 The growing popularity of home-based businesses means that there are more stores selling office equipment to consumers.

Working for a Small Company

Working for a small company has its advantages and disadvantages.

Since there are fewer levels of management, you will likely have more responsibility than at a large company. Some small companies are highly flexible about roles. If everyone gets along well, you could be invited to step outside your job description and perform a variety of business functions. In a small company, the general rule is that employees pitch in and do whatever needs to be done. This can give you valuable experience. There may be fewer rules and restrictions, less reporting to do to management, and less structure. Many small companies have an informal atmosphere, which many young people appreciate.

On the other hand, small companies may have few opportunities for promotion because they have no "middle management." You may feel close to your boss because you work directly with her, but her job is not likely to become available. Many small companies cannot pay employees as much or give them as many benefits as a larger company can. Some companies do not have well-organized systems, which can frustrate people who prefer to know what they are required to do. Finally, small businesses are more vulnerable than large ones to economic downturns and business cycles. A small company may not know where its next contract is coming from, and that could mean less job security for you.

Working for a Large Company

Figure 6-11 Some people view large organizations as impersonal. Others like the hustle and bustle of large firms.

There are also advantages and disadvantages to working for a large company. Salaries paid by large businesses are generally higher than those small firms offer. Compensation packages frequently offer benefits, such as dental and vision care plans, long-term disability insurance, or a pension plan—things a small business may not be able to afford. There may be more job security because a large firm is not as vulnerable to business cycles as a small one. Large firms also have many departments, divisions, and branches, offering you opportunities to travel and acquire a variety of experiences. Promotional opportunities are more likely to exist, as there are many levels of employment and management in different areas. Many large companies also offer training programs, enabling you to acquire new skills that will always be useful.

However, working in a large company also has disadvantages. Many people feel uncomfortable in a huge organization that treats them impersonally and has numerous policies and rules. Big companies have the reputation for periodically laying off large numbers of employees in an effort to earn greater profits. Promotion may mean relocating to another part of the country or world. The layers of bureaucracy can make you feel as though no one at the top is even aware of you, let alone willing to respond to your suggestions.

Rights and Responsibilities of Employees and Employers

Both employers and employees have rights and responsibilities. Many of these are defined and enforced by federal and provincial governments' laws. Knowing the rights and responsibilities of your employer will make you a better-informed employee, one who can actively participate in your company and its culture. The knowledge will also protect you, especially when you first start looking for work.

Discrimination

In theory, everyone has equal access to employment opportunities and fair treatment in the workplace. **Discrimination** involves unfair treatment of individuals on the basis of these characteristics. The Ontario Human Rights Code makes it illegal for employers to discriminate against an individual on the basis of race, national or ethnic origin, colour, religion, age, sex, sexual orientation, marital status, conviction for an offence that has been pardoned, or physical handicap.

In theory, everyone should have equal access to employment opportunities and fair treatment in the workplace.

Access involves a wide variety of issues such as whether the building has elevators or ramps, making it a accessible for a person with a disability, or whether someone who is blind or deaf can bring a dog to work. Making changes to ensure access is known as altering the conditions of work to meet the needs of otherwise qualified people.

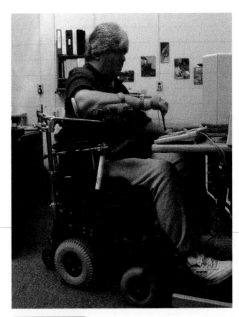

Figure 6-12 The Ontario Human Rights Code makes discrimination illegal. What are the consequences of the Code for employers and for employees?

In the Career Connect in Chapter 3 (pages 76-77), you were introduced to the Conference Board of Canada's Key Employability Skills. But how do you identify these skills? What do they look like?

Most people get a little nervous when they take stock of their skills. The good news is that you've probably got more skills than you realize. Everybody has skills. You use your skills at home, at school, at work, and in your activities in the community. And it turns out that the skills you need to make yourself employable are the same skills you use in your everyday life.

Let's look at how this identification process works using one of the Conference Board's "Think and Solve Problems" skills.

Skill Seek different points of view and evaluate them based on facts.

More detail about what this skill looks like
- Be creative and inclusive when trying to solve a problem
- Involve others when problem-solving to draw on their experiences
- Ask the right people the right questions to get the information you need

You can demonstrate examples of this skill in daily life by
- Asking salespeople at different stores why their computer is the best buy
- Having a family talk to find out why people don't seem to understand each other
- Asking a mechanic what is making the funny noise in your car
- Asking family members whether your music is too loud

You can demonstrate examples of these skills at school by
- Reviewing your lifestyle and work habits to see if some changes can be made to improve your marks
- Asking other students what arrangements they want for the school dance and checking the details for different options

You can demonstrate examples of these skills at work by
- Going to co-workers and asking for their suggestions on a project they are interested in
- Checking with peers and co-workers in developing a project plan or budget
- Asking for input when helping to schedule part-time work shifts

You can demonstrate examples of these skills in the community by
- Asking your sports team members for suggestions on how to improve your team's performance
- Surveying the neighbours to gather their input on plans for a new park

ACTIVITIES

1 Imagine that a prospective employer has asked you to demonstrate that you have this particular problem-solving skill. Choose an incident in your life that shows you have this skill and tell the story of what happened.

2 Go back to the list of Key Employability Skills in Chapter 3. Select one skill that you are particularly good at or that you are interested in getting better at. Then use the structure in this Career Connect (skill, more detail about the skill, etc.) to write an identification report on your selected skill.

In Canada many businesses require employees to retire at the age of 65. Some people view this as ageism or discrimination based on age because it suggests that people of a certain age are no longer capable of performing adequately on the job. Although human rights legislation does not mention mandatory retirement, the federal government and the provincial governments in Manitoba and Quebec have abolished mandatory retirement.

Employees can be fired for cause, that is, if they have failed to perform adequately, or have done something illegal, such as stealing from the company. In order to fire someone for incompetence, an employer must have documented the person's performance over a period of time. The employer must tell the employee of displeasure, and give the employee enough time and resources to improve.

Employees may be laid off or "let go" if the company simply has no further need for their services. But if employees feel that some type of discrimination has occurred, they can go to court and ask the judge to order the company to rehire them, or pay compensation for lost wages. Employees are entitled to be paid for the work they have done, in accordance with the terms of their employment contracts. However, if a company goes bankrupt, the employees may not be able to collect what is owed to them.

Harrassment

Employees may not discriminate against or harass other employees. An employer is obliged to act on reports of **harassment**, which means being repeatedly annoyed by someone. Harassment include accounts of verbal abuse, threats, unwelcome invitations, requests, or statements about a person's body, clothing, race, age, as well as leering or similar gestures, unnecessary physical contact and physical assault.

Affirmative Action

Affirmative action is the process of improving employment practices so that they are fair to people who may have been discriminated against in the past. The practice is sometimes called *employment equity*. Affirmative action includes giving women, minorities, and other groups preference in hiring. In addition to righting past wrongs, it is thought that affirmative action programs support the idea that everyone has the potential to be a good employee. It was too easy in the past for a company to say it had no female executives because there were no qualified women to promote. In fact, the situation may have existed because it had never hired women for management positions in the first place.

Those in favour of affirmative action say that it will improve the workplace quickly. Opponents say that the best person for the job is the one who should be hired or promoted, regardless of who they are. They feel that affirmative action programs might cause resentment in the workplace among qualified individuals who did not get a promotion because it was awarded to a woman or member of a minority group.

Workers' Compensation

As you learned in Chapter 3 in the section Safety in the Workplace, both employers and employees are required to maintain health and safety standards. And employers and employees must report accidents, injuries, and work-related illnesses to the Workplace Safety and Insurance Board (WSIB).

The workers compensation legislation also protects both the employee and employer when accidents or illness occur. If a heavy box falls on your foot, or you get sick from chemicals in a factory, you might need expensive medical treatment. WISB has an insurance plan to cover many of the costs. If you can't work, the plan also pays you a part of your regular wage. Your employer likely won't pay you while you are away. A worker who accepts compensation gives up the right to sue his or her employer for damages. This protects employers from long, expensive court cases. Employers pay premiums to the program based on the number of employees they have. Employees do not pay at all.

Web Connect

www.school.mcgrawhill.ca/resources/
To learn more about the rights and responsibilities of both employers and employees when it comes to safety in the workplace, visit the Web site of the Workplace Safety and Insurance Board in Ontario.

Employee Responsibilities

You have read about the responsibilities of managers and of businesses. But what about the responsibilities of employees?

All employees must follow company rules and guidelines, such as dress codes and security requirements. To make sure that a business stays well-organized, everyone must follow policies and procedures, such as methods for keeping track of deliveries and shipments. If you are part of a professional group, you will be expected to follow the rules set by your governing body.

Then there are the laws and codes of ethics to be followed. Laws against theft and fraud help protect businesses as well as individuals. Sometimes companies develop a code of conduct to make it clear to employees what is acceptable and what is not. For example, if you work in a store or in food services, you will learn that you are expected to provide good customer service. When it comes to secrecy, some businesses protect themselves by requiring employees to sign confidentiality agreements.

Then there are the basics. You are expected to arrive early enough to start work on time and to phone ahead if you are sick. Once you are told what your tasks are, you are responsible for following through and doing them well. Because you will be working with other employees, you have responsibilities to them. These include doing your fair share of the more difficult or tiresome tasks and helping a fellow-worker who is busy.

Check Your Understanding

Knowledge/Understanding

1 What are the advantages and disadvantages in working for (a) yourself, (b) a small company, and (c) a larger company.

2 Explain, in your own words, what constitutes discrimination in the workplace, according to the Ontario Human Rights Code.

Thinking/Inquiry

3 A music store that caters to young people is hiring. One of the applicants is clearly a middle-aged person. This person has a lot of experience and is very knowledgeable, but the owner is concerned that hiring this individual may hurt her business. Advise the owner on what she should do.

Skills
Appendix

decision making

Communication

4 Using the classified advertising section of the newspaper or an online jobs Web site, collect three advertisements for possible summer jobs or part-time jobs after school. Identify at least four of the following for each job: source of the advertisement, description of the job, education needed,

experience required, specific skills required, salary and benefits, and contact information on how to apply for the job.

Application

5 Imagine yourself in your dream career. If you could have any job, what would it be? Write a brief newspaper article about your accomplishments in your dream career. Describe your type of job, the type of company, your skills and the way you achieved success. Be sure to include a headline and a photograph or drawing of yourself.

Although more and more women are joining industry's ranks as sales managers, they sometimes have to tailor their management styles to the gender of their employees if they hope to be successful managers.

According to a study conducted by four university professors, both female and male sales personnel are starting to welcome the newcomers. However, Lucette B. Comer, assistant professor of consumer sciences and retailing at Purdue University, says there is a big difference between the management style male employees prefer and the management style that draws the best performance from them.

"I can remember not so long ago hearing men say they'd never work for a woman," she says. "Now, we're hearing men say they prefer a female management style. What's interesting is that those same men still perform better under the traditional, male-oriented, rewards-based management style."

Comer and her colleagues sent questionnaires to a random sample of 45 individuals (15 female sales managers, 15 salesmen, 15 saleswomen) to find out if salesmen and saleswomen respond differently to the leadership styles of female sales managers.

In particular, the researchers wanted to assess differences in salespersons' satisfaction with female supervision and differences in sales performance under female supervision. Comer and her colleagues identified two overall management styles used by sales managers.

"A transactional style is the more traditional of the two and is more typical of a male-oriented style of management," she says. "The transactional style of management relies on rewards and punishments to influence employees. Many of these managers are hands-off until something goes wrong. The philosophy is, 'When you're doing OK, you won't even know I'm around. But, when you mess up, I'll be right next door.'"

Women, Comer says, take a more hands-on approach. "The transformational style is a more individual-oriented style," she says. "Women managers tend to motivate by encouragement and individual attention. They relate to their employees with emotion and faith, and tend to encourage new ways of thinking."

Study results show that both men and women prefer a transformational, individual-oriented management style, Comer says.

> **"I can remember not so long ago hearing men say they'd never work for a woman . . . Now, we're hearing men say they prefer a female management style."**

"Men reported an appreciation for the considerate attention they received," Comer says. "It's possible that salesmen treat their work with female sales managers as an extended family or social relationship. In other words, in order to deal with having a female boss, the men view their manager in a familiar, non-threatening role, such as a helpful mother or wife."

Saleswomen, however, focused on the charismatic traits of their managers, rather than the considerate attention they received. "Actually, women were relatively unmoved by considerate treatment," she says. "Charismatic leadership was valued above any other trait. Perhaps that's because charisma is a definable trait that employees can identify when looking for role models."

Comer says she was surprised when performance levels were measured. "It's interesting that although men reported a preference for a relational management style (the transformational style), they performed relatively poorly under those conditions," Comer says. "When left to their own devices, however, men thrived."

Comer theorizes that men are so used to the traditional management style, they can't function under what appears to them to be constant surveillance. Women, on the other hand, preferred not to be left alone. That could be a reason women have had difficulty rising through the sales ranks to a sales manager position, Comer says.

"Women have had a difficult time adapting to the traditional male-oriented management style," she says. "As women enter into sales manager positions, I think we'll see saleswomen becoming more productive, and more women will move up."

But women sales managers won't be successful using an across-the-board transformational approach, Comer says.

"If women want to be successful as industrial sales managers, they'll have to employ two very different management styles—one for men and one for women," she says. "What it comes down to is managing the individual instead of the position."

ACTIVITIES

1 In the above study, what type of leadership style was reported to be the most motivating for salesmen?

2 According to the article, to what type of leadership style do women appear to respond best?

3 How do the transactional and transformational styles compare to the traditional leadership styles discussed in this chapter?

4 Work with a small group of students to debate the issues raised by Lucette Comer's theory. Do you agree or disagree with her conclusions? Summarize your group's arguments both for and against and present the arguments to the rest of your class.

Chapter Review

Points to Remember

- Human resources involves recruiting, selecting, training, assessing and compensating employees.

- Managing is the planning, organizing, leading, motivating, and controlling of business activities through people.

- Advantages and disadvantages exist to being self-employed or working for small or large businesses.

- Both employers and employees have rights and responsibilities.

- Affirmative action programs attempt to address unfairness in hiring and promotion.

- Workers' compensation protects both employers and employees.

Activities

Knowledge/Understanding

1 In your own words, explain each of the roles of human resources.

2 Create a comparison chart to show the rights and the responsibilities of managers and of employees. How are these rights and responsibilities similar and how are they different?

Thinking/Inquiry

1 Interview a relative or a friend of your family who works in a full-time job. Ask them about the experiences that they have had with the functions of human resources in their job. Record their responses under each of the five roles of human resources.

Skills
Appendix

working in groups

Communication

1 In small groups examine each of the functions of human resources. Identify the top ten human resources measures the ideal employer would use to recruit, select, train, develop, assess, and compensate his

or her employees. Give your company a name and develop a poster to show how your ten-step program will prove that your group's company has the best human resources program. Present your groups' ideas to the class.

2 Now that you have completed this chapter on the role of human resources in business, read over the opening Business Profile on Carter Powis and Targetnet. What do you think would have been his greatest challenge as he took on a management role at Targetnet? In role as Powis, explain to your classmates why you say that managing at Targetnet is such an "incredible experience."

Skills
Appendix

oral presentations

Skills
Appendix

problem solving

3 Work in small groups to create a role play demonstrating a specific leadership style. Your group can select from the scenarios below to develop your role play and demonstrate your group's assigned leadership style. Keep in mind that the leadership style may or may not match the situation. As a class, debrief after each presentation to determine the advantages and disadvantages of each leadership style in each situation. Also assess which leadership style had a positive impact on employee productivity.

a) You are at the scene of a dangerous chemical spill in a plant and people have been injured.

b) You must announce a mass layoff of employees.

c) You are coaching a Stanley Cup hockey team and your team is losing by one goal going into the last period.

d) An employee is having family difficulties and you must address his or her declining performance on the job.

e) The health inspector is coming to visit your restaurant tomorrow for a routine inspection. The result of the inspection will determine if your restaurant will be allowed to stay open.

f) Your two top salespeople have just been offered a great promotion and more money at a competitor's company.

g) Employees are failing to meet the deadlines that management demands. These deadlines are critical to serving your customers properly.

Application

1 Complete this activity in groups of four.

a) Each group chooses a different job from the following:

• day camp counsellor

- retails sales position
- server in a fast food outlet
- self-serve gas bar attendant
- cartoon character at an amusement park

b) One pair of students prepares the job description for one of these jobs, and the other pair writes a plan for training and developing the new employees.

c) Meet together to discuss the results of your descriptions and plans. Would the job descriptions and the training plans match? If not work together to create a match so that the training and development will help the new employee fulfil the responsibilities of his or her job description.

d) Finally, work together as a group to write some possible questions that you could use to interview your prospective employees. Keep your focus on your purpose and your audience as you write up these questions. Remember that you are looking for employees who would match your job description.

Internet Extension

1 How has job recruitment changed in the age of the Internet. With a partner, investigate some of the job Web sites and their contents, their purpose, and their audience.

7 Marketing

KEY TERMS

marketing
direct competition
indirect competition
target market
market research
marketing mix
brand name
trademark
packaging
labelling
channel of distribution
wholesaler
retailer
promotion
personal selling
telemarketing
AIDA
sales promotion
public relations
publicity
advertising
direct mail

Specific Expectations

After studying this chapter, you will be able to

- Describe the role and effectiveness of the following in marketing a product:
  - advertising display
  - distribution
  - research
  - packaging
  - selling methods

In this chapter, we will examine the importance of marketing and the reasons why a business must be knowledgeable about the marketing environment. Marketing involves understanding what your customer needs and wants, and demonstrating how you can satisfy your customer's expectations.

Marketing is not straightforward because there are many factors involved. Market research will reveal the demographics of your target audience, the social and cultural changes that are occurring, and whether there will be competition for your product. Understanding how your product should be packaged and advertised is also critical. These and other issues are explored in this chapter.

Cyndi Chooses a Web Developer

"You should go on the Web," Cyndi's brother told her. "Your party business would really grow if you were on the Web and if you had the right site. You could do all sorts of things to get people in and keep them coming–Cool Party Tip of the Week, Parties that Go Belly Up . . .you know. Grab them with humour. The point is to create a buzz around your business."

"I have been thinking about going on the Web," Cyndi said. "In fact, last week, I researched companies that will create a Web site for you. I stuck to the Canadian firms, but you should see how many there are and all the things they're doing! It's so confusing!"

"What's confusing? You want a Web page."

"Well, that's just it. According to the folks who market this service, it's complicated. There's everything from having a simple Web page to having e-commerce or even offering 3-D virtual tours."

"3-D Virtual Tours? You're kidding me."

"Well, that's just it. I don't need the 3-D stuff, thank you very much, but I would be interested in e-commerce one day. I really have to give this serious thought."

A few days later, Cyndi thought about the Web sites she had seen, and all the things the Web developers promised to do for her. She knew she wasn't a very big business. She decided to make a list of all the things she wanted her Web site to be, and do. Then she carefully reviewed the Web developers' sites one more time, this time paying attention to their "feel" as well as the content.

After making her list, Cyndi looked one last time at the sites of two Web developers. She had narrowed it down to these two. Read the captions beside the sample Web pages to find out which company Cyndi chose to develop her Web site.

My biography

A complete description of my services and prices

An on-line portfolio that shows some of the great work I've done

Party management tip of the week (will make my site look friendly I'm going to take my brother's suggestion!)

Testimonials from satisfied clients

Complete contact information, including telephone, address, and e-mail

Figure 7-1 Cyndi's Web site wish list

Figure 7-2 Cyndi continued to be in awe of this site. It just seemed to have everything, and the company did have a great online portfolio, just like the one she wanted. One other developer she had checked out offered a button for "work samples" and then told you to mail in your request for samples. Forget that! And the virtual tour offerings at Weblife 2000 were amazing. Cyndi started to wonder how one of her table arrangements would look in the "360° immersive imaging" offered by Weblife 2000. But she was fairly certain that the cost for such Web design services would be too high.

Figure 7-3 Cyndi eventually chose Blue Cat Design to create her Web site. She kept returning to the site because its image matched her image—colourful, whimsical, and a little funky. In addition, she was very impressed by all the helpful hints Blue Cat put on their site. She wanted her site to look as friendly. She also loved the individual biographies and photos of the team members, and the fact that Blue Cat's services were clearly laid out. In addition, Blue Cat also knew how to set up e-commerce if she ever wanted to do that. She had definitely found her developer. And now *she* would be marketing her business more effectively, with a brand new Web site!

The Importance of Marketing

Marketing is a process that includes many activities. The goal of this process is to create an exchange that will satisfy human needs and wants. Marketing involves planning, pricing, promoting, and distributing a good, service, or idea. Every time you buy something at the store or watch a television commercial, you are involved in a marketing activity. Marketing affects you all the time.

As you read magazines, view Web sites, or listen to the radio, you are being exposed to some very persuasive marketing techniques. Learning about marketing will help you become a more informed consumer. You will have a much better understanding of how a company promotes its goods and services. Understanding marketing strategies will also help you in any career you choose because every type of job involves persuasion. A teacher, for example, has to keep his class engaged—he has to figure out the most convincing way to present a concept. A nurse, on the other hand, might have to persuade a patient to do something that he or she really does not want to do.

Marketing activities are crucial to all businesses, no matter what their size. Even if a company has no marketing department, it has to promote the goods or services that will eventually earn revenues for the business. Producing a quality product or coming up with a good idea will not necessarily result in a company's success. Consumers must be convinced that the product fills their needs or wants—just like Cyndi was assured that a certain Web developer would fulfill her business needs and wants. Goods and services are brought to the attention of consumers through marketing activities.

The Marketing Environment

We are living in a world of rapid change. We are constantly being exposed to new technology and new products. These exciting times make marketing activities much more difficult and provide businesses with new challenges. Some changes are beyond the control of the business community. Yet in order to compete successfully, businesses must react to everything that's going on around them—marketing segmentation, changing demographics and economic conditions, new competition, social and cultural change, and new technology.

Find a need

▼

Conduct research

▼

Design a product to meet the need based on research

▼

Set a price and do product testing

▼

Determine a brand name, design a package and logo

▼

Select a distribution system

▼

Design a promotional program

▼

Build a relationship with customers

Figure 7-4 The marketing process

Market Segmentation

It's important for marketers to understand **market segmentation**, which is the division of a total market into specific groups relating to customer needs and characteristics. Not every consumer has the same needs and wants. Different people fall into different consumer groups.

Take the automobile market, for example. In Chapter 1, you read a feature on how women drive the automobile market. Women have specific needs and wants when it comes to purchasing an automobile. Manufacturers and retailers need to develop products and marketing plans to suit the individual characteristics of each customer group. The larger market can be divided into segments according to age, gender, income, family status, lifestyle, interest, language, and culture.

Demographics

In Chapter 4, you were introduced to the concept of demographics. Demographics are the characteristics of a population, categorized by criteria such as age group, sex, income level, and level of education. Demographic statistics help businesses target a particular group or market, for example, women between 18 and 54 or people over 65.

Canadian demographics change constantly. In the year 2000, for example, the number of people over the age of 65 was greater than the number of teenagers in the population. This kind of information helps businesses decide on the goods and services they will offer, the media they will use to advertise products, and even the price of certain products. As the population ages, it is likely that the price of retirement properties will increase, along with the supply of products aimed at people over 65. For this reason, you might expect advertisers to start using well-known older people to represent their products as a marketing strategy.

Business owners and marketers use demographics to help them understand their markets and try to predict the opportunities that might exist. If interpreted correctly, demographics can reduce the risk of business failure.

The Economic Environment

As you learned in Chapter 5, the business cycle refers to the changes in the economy as it moves from prosperity to inflation, sometimes into depression, and then to economic recovery. The economy never stays the same; it is always contracting and expanding.

When a business is engaged in marketing, it has to pay careful attention to the current stage of the business cycle. During a period of high unemployment in a recession, a business might reduce its advertising and emphasize essential goods and services for the consumer. Price is a very important factor during periods of high unemployment. People who don't have a job or who are worried about losing a job tend to become very price-conscious. During a time of prosperity, a company might emphasize the more luxurious aspects of its goods or services, especially if interest rates are low and people can borrow money easily to buy luxury items.

Competition

Competition can take many forms. **Direct competition** is the rivalry that exists when two or more businesses produce similar goods or services. For example, McDonald's and Burger King compete for customers who like hamburgers. Each chain has to persuade customers to buy its hamburgers, and not another chain's burgers. In addition, both chains compete with other chains selling different kinds of fast food, such as pizza and tacos. This is known as substitute or **indirect competition**. When developing a marketing strategy to compete for consumers, a company needs to consider the type of competition it will be facing.

Competition is good for you, the consumer. When two or more companies compete for the same market and try to anticipate your needs and desires, the end result is usually more excellence, more offerings for you to choose from, and a better price.

Social and Cultural Change

As consumers' lifestyles, values, and beliefs change, so do their needs and wants. As a result, they spend their money on different goods and services. A business needs to be aware of these changes and to be flexible in order to survive.

For example, when banks and other financial institutions introduced the first "bank machine" in the late 1970s, they were worried that customers would find these machines too impersonal. Up to this point, people had always gone to a bank teller—a real person—to make bank transactions, including

Figure 7-5 Many consumers embraced the convenience of automatic tellers.

simple deposits and withdrawals. But the banks soon discovered that people appreciated the flexibility of bank machines, and that they wanted more and more electronic services, such as telephone banking, Internet banking, and electronic debiting. There were more women in the Canadian workforce than ever before, and people were also working much longer hours. Most people welcomed the electronic banking revolution enthusiastically, even though they had to pay charges for many of the services. Banks stopped worrying about providing less personal service.

Another example of a social change occurred when gasoline prices increased dramatically in the 1970s. As a result of the price increase, consumers became more aware of the need to conserve energy. Many car drivers switched to smaller, more fuel-efficient cars. An added bonus was that these cars were more affordable than larger cars. Soon, automobile manufacturers stopped stressing the luxury of large cars and began to emphasize the affordability and fuel efficiency of smaller cars. As a result, these cars soared in popularity.

Technology

Technology has had a major impact on our lives and on the businesses that supply goods and services for our needs and wants. Many Canadian homes have a microwave oven, a videocassette recorder, and a computer. Twenty-five years ago, these appliances were not widely used or even available. Very few business people today are without cell phones, and the Internet is playing an extremely important role in marketing and advertising.

Technological breakthroughs have a significant effect on marketing:

- Technological innovations create new industries, which means new marketing opportunities. Of course, inventing a new product is not enough—the customer has to like it.
- Technological changes may alter or even destroy existing businesses. Compact discs have driven most vinyl records from the marketplace. Soon, digital may replace CD technology.
- New technologies can sometimes stimulate businesses in unrelated fields. For example, there is a direct relationship between the sales of VCRs and DVD players and the growth of the snack-food industry. Have you ever noticed how many video rental outlets sell popcorn, chips, candy, and pop?
- Technology opens the door to brand new ways of marketing, as you learned by reading about Cyndi in the Business Profile.

Check Your Understanding

Knowledge/Understanding

1 Explain, in your own words, why demographic statistics are important to marketers.

2 List two of your own examples of direct and indirect competition, and explain the marketing strategy that the competing companies use.

Thinking/Inquiry

3 As a consumer, why is it important for you to understand marketing?

4 Work with a partner to create a survey that would help a business understand the lifestyles, values, and buying habits of yourself and your classmates. Then, independently, write a one-page report describing how marketers could use the results of such a survey to promote their products or services to teenagers.

Communication

5 Look through magazines and newspapers and select two automobile advertisements. Review the visual components and the words in each. Then write a paragraph comparing the market segments that are being targeted by the two advertisements.

Application

6 Select a product and research the strategies that are used to market that product. You could consider packaging and labelling, advertising and promotional literature, Internet Web sites, or newspaper and magazine articles about the product. Then use what you have learned to prepare an illustrated report to predict the following:
- the demographic profile that fits the product
- ways that the economic environment might effect marketing for the product
- the potential or real direct competition for the product
- social and cultural changes that should be considered in marketing the product
- the effect of technological changes that might influence the marketing of this product

Skills
Appendix

writing reports

Skills
Appendix

analysing media

Career Connect — *Media Copywriting*

When students arrive for the first day of Humber College's media copywriting program, "every one of them dreams of writing that great television commercial," observes Wilf McOstrich, one of the program instructors.

During the year at the Toronto school, students learn that writing ads is hard work—much harder than most students think. At Humber, they learn how to develop creative strategies; write ads for print, television, radio, and the Internet; present ideas to clients; and perhaps most important, put together a portfolio or "book" to show prospective employers.

The one-year course, which accepts only students with a post-secondary degree, includes a two-month summer placement at an agency that may or may not pay the student a small salary.

Writing ads involves both skill and ingenuity. For example, during a recent class on direct mail, McOstrich reminded the students that, "The envelope has three seconds to live." That's how quickly someone decides whether to open a letter or toss it, so it had better grab the person's attention in a hurry," he says.

He holds up an "exceptionally clever" direct mail piece created by a student. In large bold type on the envelope are the words "Your latest issue of incredibly boring Vistas and Views has arrived! Featuring tremendously boring stuff from around the world!"

How could anyone resist? Inside, as promised, is a booklet with mundane photographs of a highway, a toll booth, and auto parts store. The pitch? "There are 1.1 million Canadians with visual disabilities who will never witness such incredibly boring sites. Help us promote a greater understanding of blindness."

Stephen Fogel, 25, created the fundraising letter and typifies the sort of irreverent personality drawn to the Humber copywriting program. Humber expects big things from Fogel. "Steve could get up and do an agency presentation tomorrow and he'd probably win the account," says McOstrich. "He's going to be president of an ad agency one day."

True or not, Humber students have gone on to senior positions in the industry since the program started in 1993. One of them is James Lee, associate director at Palmer Jarvis DDB in Vancouver. He won a Golden Lion at the prestigious Cannes International Advertising Festival in 1999 for a humorous shampoo commercial.

Other graduates credit Humber with getting them in the door at ad agencies. In the words of Rich Cooper, who now works as a writer for Roche Macaulay & Partners in Toronto: "More than any other writing program in the country, saying that you're a Humber copywriter does pull a lot of weight."

ACTIVITIES

1 How does the Humber College program prepare students for a career in marketing? What skills does the program focus on developing?

2 Create a poster that could be used for the visual disabilities fundraising campaign described in this feature. Keep in mind the purpose you want to achieve and the audience you want to persuade. Present your poster to a small group and explain how it would achieve the fundraising goal.

The Functions Of Marketing

Marketing has two main functions. First, it helps a business determine its target markets. A **target market** is a group of consumers the business wants to reach. The members of the targeted group will be similar in some way, such as in age. Every business needs to answer the questions in Figure 7-6 in order to sell a good, service, or idea.

To answer these types of questions, businesses frequently undertake market research. **Market research** is the gathering and analyzing of data to provide a business with information on consumers' needs and wants.

For example, if a business is making a new laundry detergent, it might interview supermarket shoppers and ask what brand they buy now and why. A beverage company might conduct a taste test to determine consumers' opinions of a new product. Or an advertising agency might phone people randomly to measure the effectiveness of a new television commercial. Market research has to be carefully planned and administered to give valid results. Validity means that the company can rely on the results and make generalizations about the rest of the population.

The second function of marketing is to give consumers what they want:
- A product they want (product)
- A product they want, when they want it (promotion)
- A product they want, when they want it, where they want it (place)
- A product they want, when they want it, where they want it, at a price they are willing to pay (price)

This what is known as the **marketing mix**—product, promotion, place, and price.

Marketing Functions

Questions	Strategies
• Who will buy this product or service?	Consider consumers by sex, age, income level, rural or urban distribution, or any other defining characteristic.
• When do they want to buy?	Consider season, time of day, time of month, or if the purchase is tied to another purchase.
• Where do they buy?	Consider whether they will buy in retail stores, discount stores, or over the Internet. Consider where they live in Canada.
• Why do they buy?	Consider whether the purchase is a necessity, a luxury, a planned purchase, or an impulse buy.

Figure 7-6 What does a business need to know about your buying habits?

The Marketing Mix

The components of the marketing mix vary for each product. One of the functions of marketing is to help a company design a program to reach the product's target market. The market will determine the make-up of the mix and the way each component is weighted in the final marketing plan.

Product

In marketing, the "product" is not just the good or service. The term, *product*, also includes an item's name, its packaging and labelling, and any guarantees that come with the product. Through research and development, many businesses invest a great deal of money developing products that they believe consumers want and will pay for.

Brand Names

A **brand name** is the name that identifies the goods or services of one business. It can be a word or words, number or numbers, letter or letters, or some combination of these elements. The visual elements of a brand—a logo, symbol, or other such design—are called brand marks. When these brand marks are registered so that no one else can use them, they are called **trademarks**.

Microsoft Windows' trademark is the stylized four-colour window that customers see when they open up the software. The brand name is "Microsoft Windows." It takes many years for a company to establish a brand loyalty. However, once a brand name has consumer loyalty, it can be used for a variety of products. For example, the Ivory name is used for hand soap, laundry soap, and dishwasher soap. Kleenex is so recognizable that it is used by many people to mean any disposable tissue.

Packaging

Packaging refers to the container or wrapper for a product, the design of the container, and the information printed on the container. The packaging must protect the product while it is on the way to the consumer and often during use by the consumer. A milk carton must not leak, even after you take it home.

CD cover | Information about production and recording credits | The artist thanks everyone involved | Titles of CD tracks | Lyrics to all the songs, continued on the next panel

The container also must attract the attention of consumers. The design of the container and the advertising printed on it can help sell the product. Packaging will often carry slogans, list special features, or provide useful information about the product, such as "fortified with vitamins A and D" or "contains no artificial preservatives." In fact, such phrases are examples of package advertising. Displaying the manufacturer's name prominently on the packaging is also a form of advertising.

Packaging is changing as a response to consumers' demands for less packaging material. More manufacturers are trying to package their products in smaller or reusable containers in response to criticism that packaging contributes to the waste problem. The ideals of "reduce, reuse, recycle" will probably continue to affect packaging in the future. In some instances, however, customers may come to expect more and more visual appeal, and more packaging features. For example, the evolution in CD packaging shows how a relatively simple format can become a design extravaganza because that's what consumers decide they want. Perfume and cosmetics are good examples of other products that attract customers because of their packaging.

Figure 7-8 This mock-up for an imaginary CD illustrates how elaborate the packaging can be. What other elements are sometimes included?

Labelling

Labelling is the part of packaging that provides the consumer with information, such as product ingredients. Many foods you eat carry labels indicating how much fat they contain, and the percentage daily requirement of nutrients a serving provides. Labels may vary from country to country, and will appear in different languages, depending on government regulations and the needs of consumers. In Canada, for example, labels on all products must appear in English and French.

A label can be as simple as the brand name "Chiquita" stamped on a banana or as detailed as a description of the recyclable products that were used to create a new product. Labels can also include information to help the consumer use the product more effectively (cooking instructions, assembly instructions, a picture of the product). Like packaging, labelling helps to sell the product.

Pricing

The price of a product will, in many cases, be determined by the demand for it. Price will play an important role in how successful the product is. Some businesses price their products low to sell more of them, and others price their products high, knowing that fewer will be sold but that a greater percentage of the selling price will be profit.

A business must always take into account the price that competitors are asking for similar products and how much consumers are willing to pay. Few consumers will pay five dollars for a doughnut, for instance.

Place

Even if consumers are pleased with a new product and its price, its success is uncertain unless it is where consumers can get it when they want it. The manufacturer's choice of channels of distribution is extremely important. A **channel of distribution** is the path a product takes from the manufacturer to the final consumer. The four most common channels of distribution are shown in Figure 7-9.

Manufacturers make products. They sometimes sell their products to wholesalers and sometimes directly to retailers, depending on the type of product and on the size of the retailer. For example, a cereal maker sells directly to large supermarkets (the retailers), as well as to wholesalers who, in turn, sell the cereal to smaller retailers such as convenience stores.

Wholesalers buy goods or services and sell them to other businesses for resale. Wholesalers usually buy products in large quantities from the manufacturers and sell them in smaller quantities to the retailers. By buying in larger quantities, wholesalers pay less per unit for a product than an individual retailer, who buys a smaller quantity of the product directly from the manufacturer. In turn, some of the wholesaler's savings are passed on to the retailer.

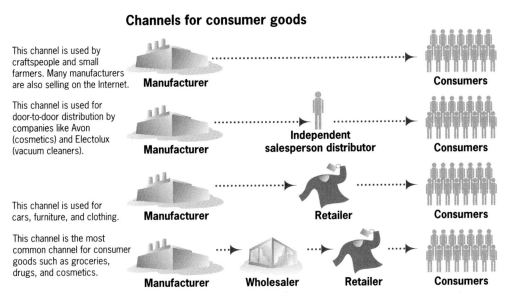

Channels for consumer goods

This channel is used by craftspeople and small farmers. Many manufacturers are also selling on the Internet.

Manufacturer → **Consumers**

This channel is used for door-to-door distribution by companies like Avon (cosmetics) and Electolux (vacuum cleaners).

Manufacturer → **Independent salesperson distributor** → **Consumers**

This channel is used for cars, furniture, and clothing.

Manufacturer → **Retailer** → **Consumers**

This channel is the most common channel for consumer goods such as groceries, drugs, and cosmetics.

Manufacturer → **Wholesaler** → **Retailer** → **Consumers**

Figure 7-9

Channels of distribution for different kinds of businesses.

Retailers sell goods or services directly to consumers. Retailers come in all shapes and sizes. They can be as large as Home Depot or as small as a mobile hotdog business. The consumer is the end user of the product or service. When you walk into your favourite store to make a purchase, you are the consumer, the end of a long chain. Manufacturers fight for "good" shelf space in the retail chains. Everyone wants to get your attention first.

The increasing popularity of the Internet means that there is one other way for manufacturers to reach consumers directly. Web sites connect manufacturers with their customers 24 hours a day, and customers can browse any time they please. Through the Internet, customers can select from a range of products, order products with a credit card, and have them delivered to their home.

Web Connect

www.school.mcgrawhill.ca/resources

Visit the Retail Council of Canada's Web site to read what retailers are saying about current consumer trends, developing technologies, and changes in the shopping environment.

Promotion

Promotions inform consumers about a product or service and encourage them to buy it. Promotion involves personal selling, sales promotion, publicity, public relations, and advertising.

Figure 7-10 Face-to-face selling involves paying close attention to the customer. Some experts have described it as "getting inside the customer's head."

Personal Selling

Personal selling is any one-to-one communication of information that tries to persuade a customer to buy a good, service, or idea. The owner of a corner store is using personal selling when he or she asks you if you need any help and then proceeds to sell you something. The sales representative, who tries to sell books to your teacher, is using personal selling. The representative of a charity, who asks you to make a donation, is using personal selling.

Personal selling often starts with "selling an idea." It may later lead to the purchase of a product. For example, a salesperson in a bicycle store may try to sell you on the idea of road safety first. Once he has sold you on the importance of safety, you are more likely to buy a helmet.

Personal selling has several advantages. First, it is a flexible method of promotion. Sales presentations can be tailored to suit the needs of individual clients. Second, sales efforts are focused on prospective buyers, eliminating unproductive efforts. Third, sales can be finalized immediately while the customer is interested in the product. Finally, the personal contact found in this type of selling can help a salesperson develop a long-term relationship with a customer.

However, personal selling also has several disadvantages. First, it's expensive to maintain a qualified sales staff. Studies have shown that the cost of one sales call can be as high as $200. This cost includes such items as salary and traveling expenses. Second, many companies have trouble finding and keeping qualified, competent sales staff. Selling is a high-stress job because there is the constant pressure to perform. Many people get burned out by personal selling and have to quit after a couple of years. These disadvantages have forced some businesses into considering alternatives to personal selling. Some stores and services have moved to self-serve operations such as those found at many gas stations. In return for not receiving personal attention, consumers often pay less for the good or service.

Alternatives to Personal Selling

Telemarketing is a popular alternative to personal selling. It uses telephone technology, including fax machines, to maintain regular contact with customers. Household services, such as carpet cleaning, duct cleaning, or window installation, are often promoted by telemarketing.

Another alternative to personal selling is the use of mail order. Some businesses, either by the nature of the business or the type of product being sold, use this form of selling. These businesses do not have retail stores. Potential customers are sent the catalogue, order their goods by mail or phone, and receive the goods by mail.

The AIDA Selling Formula

Many sales training programs teach those who do personal selling participants to use the **AIDA** formula. The word is made up of each of the first letters in the four steps of the basic selling approach:

- attract *attention*
- hold *interest*
- arouse *desire*
- take *action* to close the sale

The salesperson's first objective is to attract your attention. The salesperson must be sensitive to your needs and find some way of arousing your interest, perhaps by generating curiosity about the product. Once you're paying attention, the salesperson must hold your interest to explain the benefits of the product and create a desire in you to have the product or service. When the salesperson feels you have an interest in the product, he or she should start to close the sale. Before a sale can be closed, however, the salesperson has to overcome any objections you might have about the product or service.

Sales Promotion

Sales promotion covers all the activities designed to stimulate you to buy. Free samples, discount coupons, rebates, in-store displays, in-store demonstrations, and contests are examples of sales promotions. Some promotions, such as free samples left in your mailbox, are designed to get you to try the product. Free samples are usually products that are necessary household items, such as laundry detergent or shampoo. Other promotions are designed to get you to switch from a competitor's product to another company's product. One popular tactic is to challenge you to find a better price for the product and

Figure 7-11 Since its earliest days, the McDonald's Corporation has been highly skilled at using sales promotions like the one shown in this photograph, to stimulate the public to buy the company's products.

for the promoter to match the lowest price. Still other promotions, such as in-store displays, remind you of all your unfulfilled desires and may introduce a new product, sometimes at a special price.

Public Relations and Publicity

Public relations includes all the activities by which a business tries to maintain its good reputation and promote good will with the public. Public relations does not involve actually selling products. Instead, for example, a business becomes involved in charitable activities or sponsors local (or even national) sports teams. Large companies usually have a public relations department. Smaller companies contract out their public relations activities to a firm specializing in this area.

Publicity is the act of bringing company activities to the attention of the public. Publicity is not controlled or bought by the business and can be either good or bad. A business that is in the news for contributing money to a residence for senior citizens receives positive publicity. A business that is in the news for polluting a town's only source of drinking water receives negative publicity.

Check Your Understanding

Knowledge/Understanding

1 Briefly describe, in your own words, the four components of the marketing mix.
2 How does packaging and labelling influence consumer purchasing decisions?
3 In chart format select three products that you use everyday and identify the following: the product name, the manufacturing company's name, and the brand name.

Thinking/Inquiry

4 Research the marketing mix for a product that you are interested in purchasing. Explain how the four components of the marketing mix would contribute to influencing your purchasing decisions.

Communication

5 Using current media reports, identify a real-life situation where an individual, organization, or company has experienced some bad publicity. In

small groups, develop a public relations plan to deal with the situation and to get some positive publicity for the person or group. Present your group's ideas to the class.

Application

6 Develop a poster, radio, or television advertisement for a new product idea. Be sure that the advertisement clearly illustrates the following: the appropriate elements of the marketing mix, the target market, the AIDA formula, the brand name, and the trademark.

Advertising

Advertising is any paid use by an identified sponsor to inform a target market about a product, service, idea, or organization. The presentation of the message—the advertisement—can be oral, visual, or a combination of the two.

Advertising has three objectives:

- **Inform** The main purpose of informative advertising is to tell you about the product, its features, its unique attributes, how it works, and how to use it effectively. Informative advertising is often used to promote a new product or to suggest new uses for an existing product.
- **Persuade** Persuasive advertisements try to convince you to buy one particular company's product or service instead of the competitor's product. Persuasive advertising can appeal to your emotions, such as love, pride, or fear. An example of an emotional appeal would be a chewing gum ad that appeals to your concern about having bad breath. Some persuasive advertisments use testimonials in which a well-known celebrity or a member of an association endorses a product. For example, Silken Laumann, the Canadian Olympic bronze medallist in rowing, endorses Brooks Sports athletic wear. People who buy endorsed products hope that some of the celebrity's success will "rub off" on them.

Figure 7-14 Milk marketing boards in Canada and the U.S. have raised their profile among consumers by producing eye-catching, humourous advertisements designed to gently persuade people to buy their products.

Connecting Business with *Art*

Graphic Design

Graphic design is a growing field that includes illustration, type design and typesetting, formatting, and photography. Since 1975, when IBM produced the first laser printer, computer technology has revolutionized the way graphic designers work. However, technology is no substitute for talent.

Figure 7-12 The lips that didn't work

Figure 7-13 The final product

Marketers and advertisers rely on the skill of graphic designers every day. Through the use of memorable graphics and eye-catching typography, these designers make sure that you remember what you see. With so many products for sale, the challenge is to create advertising that is memorable. How do graphic artists rise to the challenge?

Here's how one Canadian design firm approached an assignment. The task was to create an animated character that would act as a guide during a three-minute video for a shopping mall that was getting a facelift. The character had to walk, talk, and look happy.

Simon Tuckett, the designer, began by thinking of a concept. He had an "idea of a 3D smiley face," which he sketched out on paper with a pencil because "I can't design directly on the computer. I always feel so constrained there."

Then he used a computer program to model the character in 3-D, creating a head, eyes and eyelids, and skin texture. Tuckett also used the computer program to ensure that the eyes had just the right sparkle and the mouth moved. He created the lips in a separate file, but when he moved them to the face, he realized they would need adjustment: "I was looking at one of those horrible images of an astronaut in training, straining against G forces," he said.

After completing the face, Simon created arms and legs. Because the legs would have to move, he created a skeleton using another computer program. The skeleton showed how the limbs would move, bone by bone. Next, he tested how the character moved to ensure it was realistic. He added flesh to the bones, and refined the appearance and colour so that the final character would be appealing. During this phase, Tuckett shared his progress with his client and asked for feedback.

ACTIVITIES

1   Why would the animated smiley face be effective as a video host? What sort of marketing appeal would this character have?

2   What did Simon Tuckett do to ensure that the character he created would be an unforgettable marketing tool?

- **Remind** Many advertisements are designed to keep the product or organization visible to the public. This method of advertising is often called institutional advertising; its main purpose is to promote goodwill for the company. Advertisements for charitable organizations, such as World Vision, are one example of reminder advertising.

Once marketers know what they want from their advertising campaign, they choose a type of medium to carry their message. Should the company use radio, television, the Internet, newspapers, magazines, billboards, direct mail, or other media? Each medium has its advantages and disadvantages.

Types of Media

Newspapers

Newspapers provide advertisers with a timely and flexible medium. Advertisers can select which among many regional and local newspapers appeal to their target market. A business that operates only in London, Ontario, might advertise in the *London Free Press*, whereas a national business would run advertisements in the daily newspapers of all large cities.

Newspapers offer advertisers the advantage of responding quickly to local economic and social conditions and being able to change their advertisements on very short notice. For example, as interest rates change, banks and mortgage loan companies can advertise the new rates to potential customers. The cost of producing a newspaper advertisement is relatively low, but its life is quite short since papers are normally discarded a day or two after they have been read.

Magazines

Magazines offer advertisers a high-quality medium for their advertising. Compare an advertisment in the newspaper with one in a magazine printed on glossy paper. What do you notice about the visual effect of the two advertisements? How clear are they? How vivid are the colours?

Because many special-interest magazines exist, advertisers can be selective and can focus advertisements on target markets. For example, a garden equipment manufacturer would likely advertise in *Canadian Gardening* rather than in a news magazine such as *Maclean's*.

Magazines are usually read in a leisurely fashion, so an advertiser can send a lengthy or complicated message to the reader. People usu-

Figure 7-15 Yogen Früz's brilliantly coloured magazine advertisements are very carefully designed to take the best advantage of high-quality paper and colour production values.

ally keep their magazines longer than they keep newspapers. Magazines are also often read by a number of people. Because magazines are published less frequently than newspapers, more time is available for the preparation of the advertisement, but the flexibility associated with newspapers is lost.

Radio

Radio is a popular advertising medium. It is relatively inexpensive and allows advertisers to reach a target market because individual stations cater to specific groups of people. An advertiser can place a message on a station aimed at teenagers, a country-and-western station, or a station that plays classical music. A rock concert might be advertised on a radio station that plays rock music, but a 10 kilometre run to benefit a youth orchestra might be advertised on a classical music station.

Radio is a medium that reaches people anywhere, which is an attractive feature for advertisers. People can listen to the radio while sitting on the beach, while jogging, or while driving in their cars. Advertisers pay a lot of money for airtime in the morning and evening rush hours.

Although most radio advertising is not expensive, advertisers must repeat their message frequently. Many listeners tend to use the radio as background and do not really concentrate on what is being said. People also tend to remember what they see better than what they hear.

Television

Television is the only medium that offers the advertiser a combination of sight, sound, motion, and colour. The people who create advertisements for television can use a wide range of effects to attract the viewer's attention.

Because people tend to remember what they see, advertisers ensure that their product appears in the commercial. Its method of use or application can be demonstrated, sustaining the viewer's interest. Television also allows the advertiser to select demographic markets. A negative aspect of television for the advertiser is the high cost of producing commercials and advertising, so this medium tends to be used primarily by large corporations.

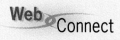

Web Connect

www.school.mcgrawhill.ca/resources
Take a look at the Canadian Code of Advertising to see some of the challenging issues faced by consumers and businesses in today's multimedia advertising environment.

Your Learning Partner

Figure 7-16

McGraw-Hill Ryerson's banner ad at its Web site contains the company's logo and name. The ad appears at the top of each page at the company's site.

Internet

Advertising takes a twist on the Internet, where new gimmicks can attract the attention of even the most seasoned media watcher. What would you do if you were on the World Wide Web and a box suddenly appeared that looked like your personal e-mail? What if it said you had one new message? You would probably open it—only to find that it's a marketing pitch. Messages that claim you've just won something are also marketing pitches from companies that want you to order more of their products. In both instances, the advertisers anticipate your behaviour on line.

Banner ads are advertisements that appear at the top or bottom of a Web site. They may "scroll" or flash with a series of different boards. The latest high-tech banner advertisements function as mini-Web sites and let customers order products without having to go to another Web site. As a result, marketers on the Internet are increasingly able to target people when they have the impulse to buy. This is the one huge advantage of advertising on the Internet.

An inviting home page is also an effective form of Internet advertising. Companies can sell their products on line, and buyers can access reviews and testimonials about products, for example, the editorial and customer book reviews offered by Indigo.com, which distributes toys, books, videos, and music.

Advertising is generated on the Internet every time someone reaches a Web site, so it's always in a company's interest to be listed in the search engines. Since the top 3 percent of the search engines generate 90 percent of traffic on the Web, companies are advised to focus their attention on the big search engines, such as Yahoo, Google, Lycos, and other top performers.

Web Connect

www.school.mcgrawhill.ca/resources
Review some of the current forms of advertising being used on the Internet. Watch for changes in techniques and features of these advertisements. Why is it that some of the most interesting and advanced media techniques are developed for advertising?

Direct Mail

Advertising pamphlets, brochures, leaflets, and flyers that are delivered in the mail make up a medium called **direct mail**. Because direct mail can be selective, the advertiser can tailor the advertisement to its target market. A business that buys the subscription list of a fashion magazine to market mail-order clothing knows that the magazine subscribers are more likely to be interested in fashion than people who do not subscribe to fashion magazines. As well, direct mail gives the advertiser a way to distribute samples of their products to potential customers. However, direct mail can be expensive and is sometimes considered as "junk mail." It is often thrown out without being read. Also, mailing lists can quickly go out of date.

Outdoor Advertising

Billboards, bus-shelter ads, and advertisements on public transit and on the sides of trucks are forms of outdoor advertising. These advertisements tend to be seen by people on the move who are not focusing on the advertisements around them. It is a medium most appropriate for short messages. An advantage is that outdoor advertisements are seen by a large number of consumers, but a drawback is that it is impossible for advertisers to target their market.

Figure 7-17 Mobile Vision is a Canadian company that specializes in creating advertising for trucks and tractor trailers. The company developed its own vinyl product that allows billboards and vehicles to be "wrapped" in a fraction of the usual time, and at a low cost.

Check Your Understanding

Knowledge/Understanding

1 Identify and describe the three objectives of advertising.
2 Using an organizer, identify the advantages and disadvantages of using each media type for advertising and marketing.

Thinking/Inquiry

3 Compare one form of Internet advertising with advertising in a different medium. Chart the advantages and disadvantages of each medium and explain the type of products and services best suited to each medium.

Communication

4 Create an advertisement that would convince an employer to hire you. As you plan your advertisement, keep your purpose—to market yourself— and your audience in mind.
5 Work with a small group of students to plan and design an advertising campaign for a local retailer, charity, or club. Be sure that your campaign covers the objectives of advertising. Decide which media type would help you reach your objectives.

Application

6 Develop an advertisement for a product that you enjoy using for a hobby or a sport. Identify the medium you would use for your advertisement. Create your advertisement as a storyboard, a layout for a print or Web page, or a script for a radio commercial.

Skills
Appendix

analysing media

Skills
Appendix

building an argument

Marketing to children poses some unique opportunities and some serious ethical challenges. As marketing has grown, so have concerns about society's responsibility for its children's health and safety.

In the United States, parents and educators are becoming more and more critical of Channel One, a marketing company that "delivers two minutes of advertising and ten minutes of news" to about 8 million students in 12 000 schools every day, according to Commercial Alert, a watchdog group.

Canadian schools have so far managed to keep out Youth News Network, a 12–minute educational program that comes with two minutes of commercials. The Canadian firm that created Youth News Network offered schools free computers, televisions, and VCRs if they picked up YNN, but teachers, parents, and students "just said no."

Exclusive contracts between soft drink companies and school cafeterias are also becoming popular. The school gets a percentage of the money from the soft drink sales, if it promises to sell only that brand name in the school. In the United States, the number of exclusive soft drink contracts in schools has increased 300 percent in the last two years. In Canada, many schools have opted for soft drink vending machines and are benefiting from exclusive contracts with soft drink companies.

Promotion of the brand name is also an important marketing strategy. In both the United States and Canada, it is illegal to aim cigarette advertising directly at young people. The result has been that cigarette companies often promote messages *other than smoking*, but rely on the association of their brand name *with smoking*.

Figure 7-19 A student drinks coke sold at a vending machine in a Vancouver school

In the Unites States, Phillip Morris recently distributed 13 million schoolbook covers as part of an anti-smoking educational campaign. *Advertising Age* noted that the design of the cover looked "alarmingly like a colorful pack of cigarettes." The textbook covers also promote the Philip Morris brand name—synonymous with tobacco and smoking—to children.

According to Commercial Alert, branded book jackets are an effective way to increase brand recognition among schoolchildren. "When Philip Morris promotes its name among children, it increases its brand recognition, and builds a relationship with them that can help sell tobacco products," says Commercial Alert. "This is especially troubling given that Marlboro, a Philip Morris brand, is the Number One brand of cigarettes among children."

While some parents are concerned about specific products being marketed to youngsters, others are more concerned about children's privacy in an age of electronic marketing techniques. Most of this concern focuses on the Internet.

Recently, the Canadian Marketing Association amended its Code of Ethics to "better guide its members and protect the interests of children." The CMA noted that some marketers collect far too much personal information from children on the Internet by asking them questions directly. The CMA now requires its members to

- obtain consent (given explicitly, either orally or in writing) from a child's parent or guardian before collecting, retaining or transferring a child's personal information, e.g., a name, address or telephone number.
- use clear and simple language that takes into account a child's inexperience and credulity.

In additional guidelines for parents, "Protecting Children's Privacy in the Information Age," the CMA pointed out that "most children are more cyber-savvy than their parents. They tend to have a trusting and curious nature that can lead them to give up their personal information without realizing it."

Another danger involved in on-line marketing is the ability of marketers to track children's behaviour on-line. "Cookies" are files that are automatically placed on a computer when someone is browsing. These files allow companies to create profiles of people who visit their sites. As a result of this profiling, marketers

Figure 7-20 Children may be more cyber-savvy than their parents, but they may also give up more personal information willingly.

learn what children are interested in and can aggressively pitch products to them. You can eliminate "cookies" by changing the options in their browser so that a Web site must get permission to place a "cookie" on their computer.

ACTIVITIES

1 What are some of the ways that companies market their products to children?
2 What policies has the Canadian Marketing Association put in place to protect children while they are on the Internet?
3 Working with a partner, research the issue of privacy on the Internet. Create a concept web or other diagram to demonstrate the complexity of this issue. Post your visual on a bulletin board or school Web site along with a caption that offers a possible solution for this problem.

Chapter Review

Points to Remember

- Marketing is the process of discovering what customers want and need and then providing them with products that meet or exceed their expectations.

- A marketing environment results from the influence of several factors.

- The four components of the marketing mix are product, price, place, and promotion.

- A channel of distribution is the path a product takes from the maker or developer to the final consumer.

- The promotional mix is made up of a variety of approaches.

- Advertising informs the target market of goods and services and tries to persuade it to buy them.

- Advertising media includes print and electronic media as well as outdoor advertising.

Activities

Knowledge/Understanding

1 Create a comparison chart to demonstrate the advantages and disadvantages of the following types of advertising media: newspapers, magazines, radio, television, direct mail, and outdoor advertising.
2 List and give examples of the four Ps of the marketing mix.
3 List the three main objectives of advertising and explain their purpose in your own words.

Thinking/Inquiry

1 Select two packages from similar types of products. One package should illustrate your idea of packaging that is not harmful to the environment. The other package should illustrate what you consider to be packaging that is harmful to the environment. Discuss the reasons for your selections and suggest ways to improve the harmful packaging.

Skills
Appendix

analysing media

2 Collect examples of sales promotion material that you receive at home over a one-week period. Bring the examples to class. With a partner, evaluate their effectiveness. Would you or your family buy any of the advertised products? Why?

Communication

1 Collect examples of sales promotion material that you receive at home over a one-week period. Bring the examples to class. With a partner, evaluate their effectiveness. Would you or your family buy any of the advertised products? Why?

Application

1 Work with a small group of students to brainstorm a list of questions that could be included in a survey to determine which brand of shoes young consumers use most. Include questions that might help you find out why they prefer one brand over another.
Prepare a one-page summary of the outcome of the survey, showing the brands available, consumers' choices, and the reasons for their choices. Which is the most popular brand for each product? And why?

Skills
Appendix

critical thinking

Internet Extension

1 Work with a partner to write a slogan and draft of a marketing plan for a new brand of product with which you are familiar. Research different kinds of slogans on the Internet and decide which one you think would be most effective for the kind of marketing your product will need.

8 Accounting

Specific Expectations

After studying this chapter, you will be able to

- **describe how effective accounting and financial statements contribute to the success of a business**

In this chapter you will learn how accounting enables a business to measure its financial performance. All businesses in Canada are expected to keep their financial records according to generally accepted accounting principles so that the records can be read and understood by people who are not involved with the business. These financial records or statements are created using the fundamental accounting equation, which ensures that all financial transactions of the business are accounted for. The two key financial statements are the balance sheet, which shows the present financial worth of a business, and the income statement, which shows how much money the business has earned during a given period. Owners, managers, investors, lenders, and governments rely heavily on financial statements to assess the value and performance of a business. In recent years, accounting software has reduced the amount of time required to produce financial statements.

Marie-Celeste and Accounting

Marie-Celeste, owner of The Hair Port, was hearing a lot of different opinions about what she should do with her business. The more she heard, the more confused she felt.

It all started on a quiet Tuesday morning in January. Marie-Celeste was sorting the mail. A semi-annual newspaper from the Board of Education featured an announcement that might have a major impact on her business. She showed the notice to her employee Selvana and to Ravi, the sales representative from Professional Beauty Supplies Ltd.

"It says here that the Board is proposing to expand Eastern Collegiate this summer," she explained. "They can finally afford to close the Portable High School. Three hundred more students will come here."

Selvana immediately understood what this news meant for the Hair Port. Eastern Collegiate, across the street, had over 700 students. The collegiate accounted for about 60 percent of the Hair Port's business.

"You'll need more help, " Selvana replied, "My cousin finishes his apprenticeship this summer. He's talented and you'd like him."

"You will end up buying over $1000 worth of supplies each month, which means that you will qualify for our lowest wholesale prices," Ravi pointed out. "Your business will be more profitable, based on that fact alone!"

A customer spoke up. "You don't have enough chairs or sinks as it is, Marie-Celeste! Even now, when my daughter comes here to get her hair done before a big social event, she has to wait an hour. Either she gets her hair done during her spare at 2:00 p.m. or she arrives really late at the dance. Then she gets home late and— "

The phone rang. Marie-Celeste's sister Jeanne, who had also read the notice, phoned to suggest that Marie-Celeste should get a bigger sign. She had read in a business publication that a bigger sign had helped a hairdressing business in Fort Frances.

Figure 8-1 Business owners face dilemmas. Most business opportunities come with a price. Is it worth paying? The businesses past performance, as shown by its records, is a good place to start looking for the basic information.

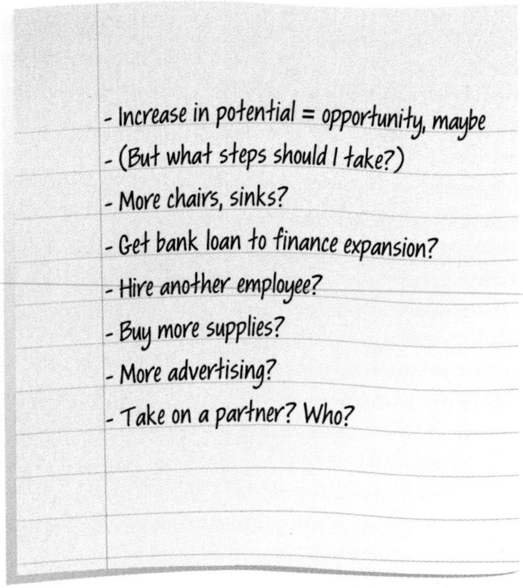

- Increase in potential = opportunity, maybe
- (But what steps should I take?)
- More chairs, sinks?
- Get bank loan to finance expansion?
- Hire another employee?
- Buy more supplies?
- More advertising?
- Take on a partner? Who?

Uncle Emile phoned too. He had heard the news and was convinced that The Hair Port should expand. He suggested that Marie-Celeste should take on a business partner. If a partner bought into the business, she could use the partner's money for the cost of expansion. She would not need a bank loan.

Marie-Celeste was glad that people were taking the time to tell her what they thought. The information she was receiving was interesting and useful. But it did not add up to answers to her key questions.

The Eastern expansion project created a dilemma for her business. She would need to expand her salon to cope with increased business, especially during social events. But where would she get the money? Should she take on a business partner? Or should she get a bank loan? What if she expanded the salon and the Board's expansion project got delayed? Would that be a disaster or only a minor setback?

Would there really be enough extra business to justify hiring Selvana's cousin? She did not want to hire him and then let him go.

Professional Beauty Supplies' lower prices for high-volume customers were attractive. But if Marie-Celeste took a bank loan, she needed to set her own prices correctly, so that she could pay off the loan but keep her customers.

She wasn't sure that she needed a bigger sign. However, Jeanne was right about her main idea. The salon's advertising budget should be increased, to convince new students to try the Hair Port. She could offer a temporary discount too. But how would that affect paying off the bank loan?

She respected Uncle Emile's opinion. He had succeeded in business and retired on a comfortable income. But his business had been a gas station/lunch counter. Would the same ideas work for a hair salon?

That evening, as Marie-Celeste was sweeping up, she began to see where the answer lay. "I've heard lots of opinions. But there is only one solution. I must study the financial records of my business. Those accounting records will provide me with a lot of the information I need to make the right decisions."

Why do you think Marie-Celeste expects to find some answers by studying the accounting records of her business? In what ways might those answers differ from the opinions she has been hearing?

How Effective Accounting Contributes to Business Success

Accounting is the system used by an organization to keep a record of all the money that comes in and goes out. Payments received from customers, wages paid to employees, and the purchase of a computer are all recorded. Even the cost of the pizza and pop that the company orders for employees who work late must be recorded.

Figure 8-2 Most civilizations have used accounting records in business. The ancient Egyptian scribe prepared accounts on papyrus (paper made from rushes) with a calamus (a reed pen). In an account from a picture in the tomb of Chnemhotep we are told, "Minute care is not only taken in the case of large amounts, but even the smallest quantities of corn or dates are conscientiously entered." Is keeping careful track of even the smallest quantities the most effective way to do accounting?

However, accounting is more than a written record of how money is received or spent each day. Accounting records are kept according to strict principles and rules. The same principles and rules are used by all businesses. This fact has two important results:

- A person who is not involved with a business can understand key aspects of its financial activities or performance by studying the company's accounting records (*books*).
- A person can use accounting records to compare the financial activities or performance of different types of businesses, such as a pizza franchise and a music store.

There are two types of accounting: financial accounting and managerial accounting. Financial accounting is the subject of this chapter. It is the process of recording and analyzing information about the financial position of an organization. A company's financial *position* is its standing with its owners, including shareholders, and its creditors. Company management, shareholders, creditors, customers, suppliers, governments, financial analysts, and many others use the information created by financial accounting to make decisions about the company. You will learn more about this later in the chapter.

Managerial accounting is used within a company to help decide questions like what to charge for a new product or whether to enlarge a factory. The usefulness of both kinds of accounting depends on accurate financial records.

Accounting records are published in the form of *financial statements*. **Financial statements** are formal documents that use a standard

Web Connect

www.school.mcgrawhill.ca/resources/

You can learn more about possible careers in accounting through the Canadian Institute of Chartered Accountants, Certified General Accountants Association of Canada, and the Society of Management Accountants of Canada.

format to provide the key information about a company's financial position. This chapter introduces two types of financial statement: the balance sheet and the income statement.

Effective financial reporting, based on accurate financial statements, is the best way to ensure that a good business remains profitable. It is also the first step towards helping a struggling business recover. The struggling business can identify and deal with problems before it's too late.

Previewing Financial Statements

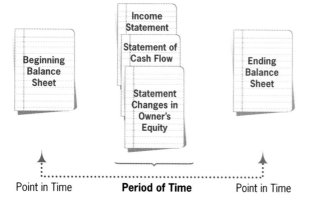

Point in Time   **Period of Time**   Point in Time

Figure 8-3 The balance sheet shows an organization's total worth on a certain date (a point in time). The income statement shown here updates the balance sheet by adding net income (or subtracting in case of net loss). The two other documents shown, the statement of cash flow, and the statement of changes in owner's equity assist in preparing the income statement or the balance sheet.

Generally Accepted Accounting Principles

The **Generally Accepted Accounting Principles** or **GAAPs** are the guidelines developed by professional accountants for the way accounting records and financial statements are prepared. These guidelines ensure that financial information is presented in a standard form so that organizations' performance may be understood and compared. Here are some key GAAPs.

Business entity concept

The finances of the business are kept separate from those of its owner. For example, Wanda Kowalchuk, owner of Kowalchuk's Interior Design, buys many items of furniture to resell through her business. These purchases are business transactions. But when she bought a sofa bed for her own apartment, she did not treat the purchase as a transaction of her business. Her sofa bed is a personal possession, not a business asset. It does not appear in her business's books.

Time period concept

An accountant uses time periods of equal and appropriate length to measure the financial health of a business. For example, Gracie-Ann's Ski and Swim Wear showed a big profit in the winter and the summer. But the business barely covered its expenses in the spring and fall. An accountant will prepare financial statements that show the whole business year, not just the profitable seasons.

Cost principle

The actual cost of a business purchase is recorded as the cost in the books. For example, Bobby Fuller, owner of Bobby's All-Star Renos, got a great deal on a truck. He paid only $16 000 for a truck that would usually cost $18 000. Which price is recorded in the books? An accountant would insist on recording $16 000. For accounting purposes, the truck is assumed to have the financial value that Bobby actually paid.

Consistency principle

Accountants apply the same rules, methods, and procedures from one financial period to the next. For example, during a very warm year, Gracie-Ann's Ski and Swim Wear showed big losses from ski wear but big profits from swim wear. Can Gracie-Ann report only the swim wear results and pretend that she never even tried to sell ski wear? No, the consistency principle requires that she use the same reporting methods from year to year. Only if she decides to stop selling ski wear can she stop reporting its results.

Financial Statements

The purpose of financial statements is to provide accurate information on a regular basis, according to generally accepted accounting principles. Statements may be produced each week, month, or quarter, depending on the need. Sole proprietorships, which you learned about in Chapter 2, often produce statements only at the end of a year of business (a *fiscal year*).

The **fiscal year** or accounting year for an organization is a period of 12 consecutive months, at the end of which the business produces its annual financial statements.

Incorporated companies do not always use the calendar year for their financial year. For example, Kathy-Ann Leon, owner (sole shareholder) of Kathy-Ann's Guided Caribbean Tours, Inc., found December 31 an inconvenient date to end the financial year. She was nearly always out of the country at that time. She chose July 31, which is the off season for her business.

"Ceremony of the Pipe"

Figure 8-4 The accounting records of the Hudson's Bay Company, established in 1670, provide valuable information about Canadian business. For many years prior to Confederation, in what is now western Canada, people did not use currency. They used beaver pelts instead of dollars when they wanted to buy or sell items. A blanket was worth four beavers. For one beaver, you could get a brass kettle.

All business organizations—sole proprietorships, partnerships, and corporations—are required by law to produce financial statements, to verify income for income tax purposes. Canada Customs and Revenue Agency provides blank income statement forms that enable a self-employed person to construct an income statement. Private individuals or organizations that do not offer stocks or bonds to the public do not need to share financial information with anyone other than Canada Customs and Revenue Agency, the income tax gathering agency. There is one exception to this: a financial institution may ask for financial statements if a business is trying to borrow money. Public corporations must by law publish their financial statements because they issue stocks and/or bonds to the public.

Personal Balance Sheet

A balance sheet is a statement of net worth. **Net worth** is the difference between what you *own* (assets) and what you *owe* (liabilities). It is sometimes called owner's equity or owner's capital. Preparing a personal balance sheet can help you understand the concept of net worth. On the following page is Michael Abramov's personal balance sheet (Figure 8-5). Because Michael's net worth is the difference between what he owns and what he owes, his balance sheet can be summed up in an equation:

Assets – liabilities = net worth.

Therefore, using the mathematical rule for transposing equations

Assets = liabilities + net worth.

This is called the **fundamental accounting equation** because accounting is based on it. Because it is an equation, the two sides must balance. In Michael's case, the balancing figure is seen to be $2 675.00. When accounts do not balance, an error has been made. The accounts are said to be "out of balance." The error must be found and corrected.

Michael Abramov
Balance Sheet
June 15, 2001

What Michael Owns (Assets)		What Michael Owes (Liabilities)	
Savings account	$275.00	Owed to Dad for computer	$500.00
Clothes	$600.00	Owed to Ibrahim at school	$20.00
CDs	$300.00	Pledge to Read-a-thon	$50.00
Bicycle	$500.00	**Total Liabilities**	**$570.00**
Computer	$1 000.00		
Total Assets	**$2 675.00**	**Net Worth**	**$2 105.00**
		Total Liabilities and Net Worth	**$2 675.00**

Figure 8-5 Michael Abramov is a student in Kingston, Ontario. This statement expresses the financial value of his possessions, after his debts are subtracted. It is his net worth as of June 15, 2001.

Check Your Understanding

Knowledge/Understanding

1 What is a GAAP? Why is it important?
2 What is the fundamental accounting equation?

Thinking/Inquiry

3 A friend offers to let you invest in her company. She shows you a sales order book listing all the orders for her products. What financial information does her sales order book not tell you? Why do you need this information in order to make a decision?

Communication

4 Assume that you are a business advice columnist. You have received e-mails asking for advice on how the generally accepted accounting principles apply to the following situations. In each reply, identify the generally accepted accounting principle that governs the business situation.
  • Help! I own Unique China and Gifts in Barrie. I recently attended an estate auction. I found two boxes of great antique china. No one else at the auction knew their value, so I got them for $20! Why won't my accountant enter them in my books at $1200 when I know that I will probably find a client who will pay that much? – *Baffled in Barrie*

Skills
Appendix

problem solving

- Hi, I'm Toula Karalambos. I own Toula's Blossoms Flower Shoppe in Pembroke. I got a great deal on a flowering tree for my apartment's sun parlour when I attended the Tropics North exhibition hosted by a supplier. That was a business event. So is this a business transaction? I'm not sure. – *Puzzled in Pembroke*
- Hey, I started my part-time snow ploughing business on October 1, but that turned out to be a big mistake. The year was unusually warm so no snow fell until December 15. Why won't my accountant agree to ignore the ten weeks when there was no snow? If I could get her to agree to move the date, my business would look a lot more profitable to the bank. – *Mystified in Meaford*

Application

5 Develop a personal balance sheet for yourself. Include only assets (things you own) that belong to you personally. Include only liabilities (debts) that you are expected to pay personally. Identify your net worth. Remember to include your name and the date.

The Balance Sheet for a Business

Your personal balance sheet shows your financial net worth on a given day. In business, a **balance sheet** is a financial statement that shows the company's assets, liabilities, and net worth (owner's equity) on a given date. Sometimes the balance sheet is referred to as the *statement of financial position*. It is a snapshot of a company's financial affairs at a single point in time. It is usually prepared on the last day of the month. A business owner, or other interested person, could compare the balance sheet with those of the previous months to determine whether the organization's assets or liabilities are growing.

A balance sheet is also prepared at the end of the financial year. That balance sheet can be compared with the balance sheets of previous years. Figure 8-6 shows a year-end balance sheet for a business, Fast Forward Computer Repair Services, a company owned by sole proprietor Chris Alexanderssen, who repairs home computers in her basement in Cornwall, Ontario.

Fast Forward Computer Repair Services
Balance Sheet
December 31, 2000

Assets		Liabilities	
Cash	$ 7 400	Accounts payable	$ 1 100
Canada Savings Bond	1 000	Loan payable	5 100
Supplies	3 600	Total liabilities	6 200
Office funiture	2 000		
Equipment	7 000	**Owner's Equity**	
Motor vehicle	20 000	C. Alexanderssen, Capital	34 800
Total assets	$ 41 000	Total Liabilities and Owner's Equity	$ 41 000

Figure 8-6 Like all balance sheets, Fast Forward's sheet lists the types and dollar amounts of assets and liabilities, and the owner's equity as of a specific date. Recall that in the fundamental accounting equation, assets = liability + owner's equity.

Assets

Assets are anything the company owns that has a dollar value. The purpose of assets is to earn income for the company. Studying Figure 8-6, note the assets Fast Forward owns: Cash, Canada Savings Bond, Supplies, Office furniture, Equipment, and Motor vehicle. Each has a dollar value and therefore all are considered assets of Fast Forward.

For convenience, assets are subdivided into several categories, as follows:

Current Assets are cash or any asset that can quickly be turned into cash, usually within a year. Cash includes cheques. It also includes the Canada Savings Bond because the bond can be cashed within the year.

Accounts receivable is the most important current asset of many companies. **Accounts receivable** is money for which a company has billed its customers, but has not yet received. Accounting rules require the company to assume that this sum will be paid. Therefore, accounts receivable is treated as an asset, even though the company has not yet received the cheques.

Then why do you not see Accounts receivable in Figure 8-6? When Chris Alexanderssen started Fast Forward, she marketed mainly to private individuals. She insisted on customers paying her by cash or cheque when their computers were repaired. Therefore, the balance sheet for 2000 shows no Accounts Receivable.

In the summer of 2001, however, Fast Forward started servicing small businesses. It began billing customers, using *invoices*. These invoices listed the services Fast Forward had provided, requesting that the customer pay the agreed amount within 30 days. Therefore, the balance sheet for 2001 shows an asset called Accounts Receivable, right under cash. See Figure 8-7 on the following page.

Fast Forward Computer Repair Services
Balance Sheet
December 31, 2001

Figure 8-7 Fast Forward keeps detailed records of accounts receivable—the money that customers owe to the business. But only the total amount appears on the balance sheet.

Assets		Liabilities	
000Cash	$ 7 400	Accounts payable	$ 3 100
Accounts receivable	16 000	Loan payable	5 100
Canada Savings Bond	1 000	Total liabilities	8 200
Supplies	6 600		
Office furniture	3 000		
Equipment	6 000	**Owner's Equity**	
Motor vehicle	14 000	C. Alexanderssen, Capital	45 800
Total assets	$ 54 000	Total Liabilities and Owner's Equity	$ 54 000

Liabilities

Liabilities are debts owed by an organization or person to another organization or person. The most common liability is *accounts payable*. **Accounts payable** is the money that the business owes to other businesses that supply it with services.

Fast Forward keeps detailed accounting records of the money owed to suppliers. But, just as you observed for accounts receivable, these individual accounts payable records do not appear on the balance sheet. Only the total amount owed to all creditors of a certain type is listed on the balance sheet.

Liabilities, like assets, are divided into different types.

Current liabilities. Accounts payable is called a *current liability*, which means that it must be paid within a year.

Long-term liabilities. A debt or portion of a debt that does not have to be paid within a year is a long-term liability. When Chris Alexanderssen started Fast Forward in January 2000, her brother gave her a loan of $5100, telling her that she did not have to pay him back that sum for five years. Therefore, she can treat the loan as a long-term liability.

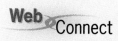

Web Connect

www.school.mcgrawhill.ca/resources/
The financial statements of publicly traded Canadian companies are available through the System for Electronic Document Analysis and Retrieval (SEDAR). Identify a company that has been making news headlines recently and find its financial statements.
www.sedar.com

Owner's Equity

Owner's equity is the amount of money the owner invested when starting the business, plus any accumulated profits (or minus any accumulated losses and money the owner takes out to live on (drawings)). If you recall the accounting equation, owner's equity is what is left over after the liabilities have been deducted from assets. For example, in 2001, Fast Forward had $54 000 in assets and $8 200 in liabilities. Therefore, it had equity, or net assets, of $45 800. How does that compare with its owner's equity in 2000 (Figure 8-6)?

You can learn a number of things about Chris Alexanderssen's business by studying the balance sheets. You know what type of assets the business owns and how much it owes, short and long-term. But there are some things you cannot discover. For example, can you conclude that because the owner's equity has increased, the business is a good one to own? Remember, the business exists to earn income for its owner. How much income did Chris Alexanderssen take out of the business to live on? The balance sheet in Figure 8-7 does not tell you that. It tells you that the business grew in owner's equity by $11 000 (from $34 800 to $45 800). But assume Chris took no money out of the business to live on, but rather worked at a job during the day in order to support herself? In that case, although the business has increased in value, it is not yet very successful. To tell us how profitable the business is to its owner we need another kind of statement: the income statement. The next section deals with the income statement.

Biz.Bites

If the organization is a corporation, instead of "owner's equity," you will see "shareholders' equity" on the balance sheet. The shareholders own the company. Their equity includes common stock and retained earnings.

Check Your Understanding

Knowledge/Understanding

1 Under what circumstances would Accounts Receivable not appear on a balance sheet?

2 What does Cash mean on a balance sheet? Is Cash a Liability or an Asset?

Thinking/Inquiry

3 The balance sheet can tell us a good deal about a business. What can it tell us? What does it not tell us?

Communication

4 Sarkus Markarian owns a small building supply firm. He has asked you to explain to him whether the following items should be on his balance sheet. Provide an oral explanation, stating whether the item is an asset, a liability, or not part of the business.

Skills
Appendix

oral presentation

- Stock of sand, cement, bricks, valued at $30 000
- Sarkus's pet dog Snap (his presence often prevents theft of materials)
- $2 250 owing from a customer for work completed
- Cash in hand, $1 400
- $2 500 owing to Aunt Anna, who says that Sarkus need not repay her for four years
- Ticket for charity draw given to Sarkus by a grateful customer

Application

5 If assets are $15 000 and liabilities are $3 475, what is the owner's equity?

6 If owner's equity is $52 900 and assets are $100 000, what are the liabilities?

7 If liabilities are $33 782 and owner's equity is $17 619, what are the assets?

The Purpose of the Income Statement

Biz.Bites

A quarter is three consecutive months, January–March, April–June, July–September, and October–December. Businesses commonly report their "quarterly" earnings using these time periods.

The **income statement** is the financial statement that reports a business's income and expenses for a fiscal period. A fiscal period is a period of time over which the earnings of a business can be measured. It tells you the company's profit or loss during that period. It is sometimes called the *profit and loss statement*, the *statement of income and expenses*, or the *statement of earnings*. Commonly chosen fiscal periods for the income statement are a month, a quarter, or a year. An annual income statement is required for income tax purposes.

Income (sometimes called revenue) can be earned by the business from a variety of sources, including sale of goods, services, rent, fees, interest payments on savings or bonds, royalty payments, or dividends from stock held. For a not-for-profit organization, government grants and private donations may be the main sources of income.

Expenses are the money the business has spent in order to produce income. The most common expenses include employees' salaries and benefits, rent, daily operating costs, and the cost of supplies used to generate sales or service fees.

What is the difference between expenses and liabilities? The main difference is this: Expenses have already been paid. Liabilities have not. Expenses appear on the income statement because they must be subtracted from the income earned during a given period, in order to get a true picture of a business's profits. Liabilities appear on the balance sheet because they are a claim by creditors against the value of the business itself until they are paid.

The income statement helps to answer the question that was not answered directly by the balance sheet in Figure 8-7. How profitable is the business to its owner? Figure 8-8 shows a simplified income statement for Fast Forward.

Fast Forward
Income Statement
For Year Ended December 31, 2001

Income		
Computer repair income	$ 58 940.53	
Interest income (Canada Savings Bond)	$ 35.00	
Total Income		**$ 58 975.53**
Expenses		
Advertising expense	$ 3 024.75	
Bank charges	$ 234.25	
Conference and trade show expense	$ 2 135.00	
Delivery expense	$ 3 018.63	
Equipment maintenance	$ 487.23	
Maintenance expense	$ 301.87	
Motor vehicle operating expense	$ 6 087.23	
Office expense	$ 40 301.87	
Professional association membership	$ 200.00	
Supplies expense	$ 2 927.31	
Telephone	$ 1 523.23	
Total Expenses		**$ 59 939.50**
Net Income		**$ 963.97**

Figure 8-8 The income statement, like the balance sheet, gives a total for each category. Detailed documents and accounting records support these figures.

What the Income Statement Tells You

As you can see, the net income of the business is the total income minus the total expenses. It looks as though Fast Forward provided a reasonable income for Chris during this period, considering that the business is only two years old. She can take out enough income to live on ($28 036.03) and still leave $11 000 in the business to help it grow. The income she takes out is called *drawings*.

Notice the type and amount of Fast Forward's expenses. You can learn important things about a business by studying its income statement's expenses. For example, notice how much Fast Forward spends on delivery expense. Fast Forward's delivery expense is high because Chris frequently uses expensive "rush order" services. Perhaps if she forecast her need for replacement parts for clients' computers more accurately, she could economize on delivery expense.

Income statements can help forecast the future of a business. Notice the item called "Maintenance expense." Chris assigns a portion of her household expenses to her business. That is because she works from her own basement. She can operate the business much more cheaply that way. Her income statement tells you that her business is profitable mainly because she has kept her expenses down. But if she decided to move her business downtown, she would face a great increase in her expenses, including office rent and business taxes.

Figure 8-9 shows what might have happened if she had decided to move to a fashionable business centre in 2001, her second year in business. Assume that she did the same amount of business.

Fast Forward
Income Statement
For Year Ended December 31, 2001

Income		
Computer repair income	$ 58 940.53	
Interest income (Canada Savings Bond)	$ 35.00	
Total Income		**$ 58 975.53**
Expenses		
Advertising expense	$ 3 024.75	
Bank charges	$ 234.25	
Conference and trade show expense	$ 2 135.00	
Delivery expense	$ 3 018.63	
Equipment maintenance	$ 487.23	
Motor Vehicle expense	$ 6 087.23	
Office expense	$ 40 301.87	
Professional association membership	$ 200.00	
Supplies expense	$ 2 927.31	
Telephone	$ 1 523.23	
Total Expenses		**$ 59 939.50**
Net Income		**($ 963.97)**

Figure 8-9 Here what would happen if Fast Forward rented a luxury office in the year 2001. The company is showing a net loss for the year, displayed as the amount in brackets. Fast Forward cannot afford a fashionable office at its current level of business.

The income statement updates the balance sheet. The net income Chris leaves in the business (Figure 8-8) will increase the assets and the owner's equity on the balance sheet at the same time. In the case of net loss (Figure 8-9), the net loss will decrease both the assets and the owner's equity. In either case, the balance sheet will still be in balance.

Analyzing a Trend

Marie-Celeste's hair salon, The Hair Port, had a busy April. The students' council of a nearby high school held a big graduation dance and other social events as well. Many students who attended sported very flashy hairstyles that cost an average of $50. When she tallied up the receipts on Saturday night, she found that the net income for the month of April 2001 was $7 750 (income of $12 850 minus expenses of $5100). That's not a bad profit for one month. Would you advise Marie-Celeste to expand her business based on that profit?

Chances are, you will want to know first what her profits are like in the summer, when the school is closed and no dances are held. Marie-Celeste must pay her rent, her business taxes, and her two employees whether she gets business or not. In July 2001, she took in only $5 000 but she still had to spend $4610 for a profit of only $390. Does this mean her business is failing? Should she close her salon?

Like most business people, Marie-Celeste knows that income goes up and down from month to month, but many expenses are fixed. Before making decisions, she assesses her financial results over longer periods of time than one year. Figure 8-10, for example, shows the five-year trend of Marie-Celeste's business. A trend is a business pattern over time. Based on what you see here, do you think she should add another two salon chairs and hire a part-time person?

Biz.Bites

The Industrial Revolution in the 19th century created a need for accounting methods that could handle the information needs of mass production in factories. Owners of the companies realized that no one person knew everything that was going on from day to day. Therefore accounting and financial statements became very important.

Hair Port Net Income for the Year	
1997	$37 001
1998	$38 237
1999	$27 093*
2000	$39 344
2001	$40 272

* The school was closed from January through March due to a gas leak.

Figure 8-10 Users of financial statements pay attention to the notes at the bottom of the statement. They usually contain important information. What does the note at the bottom of Figure 8-10, in relation to the figures, add to your understanding of Marie-Celeste's business?

Check Your Understanding

Knowledge/Understanding

1 Identify four common sources of income for a business.
2 Explain the difference between expenses and liabilities.

Thinking/Inquiry

3 Based on what you have learned so far, would Fast Forward gain any benefits from operating from an office rather than the owner's basement? What benefits?

Communication

4 Marie-Celeste Camero, owner of the Hair Port has expressed the view that "The business has been growing steadily every year except for the year of the gas leak. Really, I should get about $20 000 in financing and expand the business!" Draw a line graph of The Hair Port's income trend over five years, plotting the net income against the year (Figure 8-10). Assume an average inflation rate of 3% per year. How much has the business grown when inflation is factored in? Write a memo to Marie-Celeste Camero to accompany the graph, explaining what it shows. Should Marie-Celeste go into debt to expand the size of her salon, on the grounds that her income is increasing? Explain your opinion.

Application

6 Calculate your personal income statement for last month. Use the heading format shown in Figure 8-8. Under Income, list the money you received by sources of income (for example, allowance, babysitting, chores, part-time job, etc.) Under Expenses, list what you paid out of that sum by type of expense (for example, donations, gifts to others, snacks, transit tickets). Estimate amounts where necessary. What is your "net income" or "net loss"?

How Financial Statements Are Used

As you can see from what you have learned in this chapter, financial statements provide a great deal of information about a business. One thing that they provide is an accurate picture of how well—or poorly—a business earns income for its owners. As a result, the statements of businesses, whether large or small, are studied carefully by four main types of users: business owners and managers, investors, lenders, and government. Each group is looking for different things.

Career Connect *Actuary*

Should young people pay higher car insurance rates? Should smokers pay higher life insurance rates? Is there a real difference in injury or sickness, or are these just unfair stereotypes?

Finding out the answers to questions like these is actually a job. The professional who looks for answers is called an actuary.

An actuary uses the mathematical theories of statistics and probability, current trends, and the principles of finance to predict the likelihood of illness, accidents, and catastrophes. Actuaries also formulate strategies for companies and governments to deal with these events.

For example, drivers under 25 suffer more collisions than older drivers because they have less experience. Smokers get more illnesses at an earlier age than non-smokers. These are facts, not stereotypes, so actuaries must set a higher price for insurance. But the price must still be fair. The actuary considers mortality rates, illness, injury, disability, and property loss to arrive at a fair price.

Actuaries calculate large, public risks as well as personal risks. Over 500 Canadian companies,

not-for-profit corporations, and governments employ actuaries. These organizations include railway companies, mining companies, workers' compensation boards, pension boards, investment firms, the Canadian Wheat Board, and Canada Customs and Revenue Agency.

All these different organizations have one thing in common: They need to know how to deal with changes or crises that are foreseeable but not preventable. For example, when 329 people died in the 1985 Air India bombing, an actuary was hired to calculate the lost future earnings of the victims, to compensate their relatives in court.

Becoming an actuary requires not only good math skills but the ability to understand a wide range of medical, legal, environment, and other issues. Actuaries continue to upgrade their knowledge and take exams long after they leave university. However, the good news is that actuarial science is one of the best-rated careers in North America. Actuaries often hold senior management positions in the firms that rely on their advice.

ACTIVITIES

1 What do all the organizations that hire actuaries have in common?

2 What questions might a railway company ask an actuary to research?

3 During the 20th century, Canadian life expectancy increased from 61 for women and 59 for men in 1920-22 to 81 for women and 75 for men in 1990-92 (see Figure 9-16). With a partner, brainstorm questions that the following types of organizations might ask actuaries about how this trend affects them: (a) Life insurance (b) Government health insurance (c) Government pension plan (d) Private pension plan (e) Workers' compensation board (f) Travel insurance

Business Owners and Managers

Biz.Bites

Auditing is the examination of the financial data, accounting records, business documents, and other documents to determine the accuracy of an organization's financial statements. An independent accountant usually conducts an audit.

Business owners and managers need accurate information to make decisions for the business. They might ask

- Is our income high enough? Are we charging enough for our goods or services?
- Should we add a line of business—sales, perhaps, as well as service?
- Are our expenses reasonable? Can any be reduced?

Chris Alexanderssen, for example, decided to market to small business as well as to private individuals. What difference did that decision make to the growth of her company? Compare Figures 8-6 and 8-7. Was it a wise decision? The figures on the balance sheets show whether the company grew as a result. She also spent $6087.23 on the operating costs of her company van in 2001 (see Figure 8-8). Would a different model cost significantly less to operate? The figures on the income statement provide a basis for research when she must buy a new van.

By examining the balance sheet and the income statement from one fiscal period to the next, owners and managers can compare company performance, and note the changes that have occurred. They can respond to trends. For example, if expenses have risen but prices have not, income will be lower. If the company cannot reduce its expenses, it may have to raise prices.

Comparing statements from year to year can also identify situations that are not really a trend. The Hair Port experienced a business problem in 1999 (see Figure 8-10, note), but it was clearly not a trend.

Investors

Investors need financial statements as much as owners do, perhaps more. For example, Marie-Celeste works in her business and knows when the busy times can be expected. Because she has set her prices carefully, she knows that when the salon is busy, the business is earning a good income. Her uncle Emile, however, is in a different position. He is considering investing some retirement money by becoming a partner in her business, but he knows nothing about hairdressing. He would therefore be a "silent partner," providing only capital. He believes that The Hair Port is a good business opportunity because the school board has decided to increase the high school's enrollment by 300. His investment would enable The Hair Port to add more chairs and staff. But is the business profitable now? If not, he might lose his money by investing in it. Financial statements can answer his questions.

Lenders

If Uncle Emile was not able to invest in Marie-Celeste's business, she might try to get a loan from a bank in order to expand. The bank manager will then ask to see her financial statements. Banks and other lenders need to know that they will be repaid by a business that owes them money. The income statement will show a lender if a business is producing enough income to pay the debt. The balance sheet shows lenders how much the business owes others and whether any assets could be sold, if necessary, to pay the debt.

Government

Much of the financial information prepared by a business is for income tax purposes. All individuals and businesses, with the exception of non-profit organizations, pay income taxes on their earnings. The government checks an organization's financial statements to make sure that all income has been reported and that all expenses claimed were allowable. In addition, the financial statements show the government what the business owns and owes, because these items affect the amount of income tax the business pays.

The four groups listed above seek accurate, specific information to help them make decisions. Large organizations have accounting departments to ensure that information is accurate. By contrast, small business owners sometimes have a hard time learning to prepare financial statements themselves. However, computer accounting programs, which you will learn about in the next section, can assist small businesses as well as large ones to ensure that information is accurate.

Computers and Accounting

Preparing financial statements became much quicker and easier with the widespread introduction of computer technology.

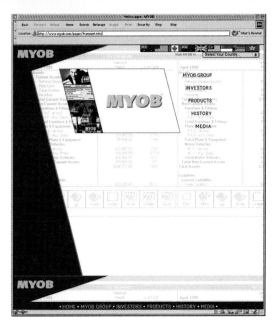

One advantage of computer accounting is that it reduces errors, mainly in two ways:

- Computers do not make arithmetic errors, which is a common cause of the accounts being out of balance in a manual system.
- A computer accounting program will not permit the user to enter a transaction that puts the fundamental accounting equation out of balance. For example, if Marie-Celeste adds $673.71 to her Supplies account, her program will prompt her to either deduct the same amount from the Cash (Asset) account if she paid by cash or cheque, or add to the Liabilities account if she bought on credit. The software program will insist on balancing the accounting equation before accepting the transaction.

Figure 8-11 Many accounting programs are aimed at small business. How is this Web page designed to make accounting look easy if you use the advertised system?

Computer accounting systems do not prevent every possible mistake. Marie Celeste might accidentally place hairdressing supplies in the Equipment account instead of the Supplies account. The software might accept this because the accounting equation will still balance as long as payment is recorded in the correct way. However, that does not mean that nothing is wrong. The picture of the business's assets is now inaccurate. A mistake like this will most likely be discovered when the financial statements are being prepared at the end of the year. Marie-Celeste will realize when she studies her assets on the balance sheet that she did not buy a new piece of equipment for $673.71. A search through the paid invoices will reveal what the $673.71 really paid for. Then the accounts will be adjusted correctly.

Another advantage of computer accounting systems is that they can provide immediate accounting information. For example, when all the transactions for a fiscal period are entered, the program can automatically print out the income statement and balance sheet. Some programs also enable the user to automatically reconcile a bank account if access to the account is available via the Internet. Others automate tax preparation. Many programs allow the user to construct pie charts or other graphics that illustrate business performance or trends.

Web Connect

www.school.mcgrawhill.ca/resources/
Go to the sites of accounting software companies whose products are commonly used in small business. Identify features of business record-keeping and accounting that the system automates. Identify ways in which each site's material makes accounting look easier if you use the advertised software system.

Specialized financial management software designed for specific types of businesses, for example, travel agencies, trucking companies, or restaurants, enable a company to keep its accounting records efficiently and effectively. However, general programs for all types of small business (see Figure 8-11) also have modules that can be customized, depending on the type of business.

This is an advantage for keeping records. For example, The Hair Port does not charge its customers for hairstyling supplies. The customer is charged a flat fee that includes the use of supplies. By contrast, Fast Forward orders parts for customers' computers and lists each installed part on the invoice at its cost price. Chris's labour is charged separately from parts. Because these two businesses use different pricing practices, they might choose to customize accounting software in different ways. However, the fundamental accounting equation remains the same for both businesses.

Some computer accounting functions may be critical to a particular business and others may just be extras. With accounting software, as with every other business purchase, the user must decide what functions are needed for the purpose of providing accurate accounting records.

OPTICIANS

"The business-recovery plan from our accountants - it just says make the sign bigger."

Figure 8-12 Accounting firms become very knowledgeable about the financial affairs of businesses that are their clients. As a result, they are often asked for advice on improving business performance. What do you think of the accounting firm's advice in this case?

Knowledge/Understanding

1 Name the four groups that seek information from financial statements.

2 Give an example of a mistake that computer accounting would not prevent. How might such a mistake be discovered?

Thinking/Inquiry

3 Would Uncle Emile be wise to become a partner in Marie Celeste's business, based on what you have learned?

4 If Uncle Emile became a partner in Marie Celeste's business, would his investment be recorded as part of the business's Liabilities or its Equity? Which account would increase if Marie Celeste borrowed expansion money from the bank instead? Which Asset account would increase in either case?

Communication

5 "Accounting principles are a waste of time. Now that computers do all the work, who needs to know the principles?" Roz declared. Based on what you have learned in this chapter, write a paragraph explaining how knowledge of accounting principles helps us to interpret business success and failure.

Application

6 Place your personel balance sheet and income statement in a spreadsheet and use the formulas to calculate them correctly.

Skills
Appendix

critical thinking

Skills
Appendix

writing reports

Chapter Review

Points to Remember

- Accounting is the system used by an organization to record all the money that comes in and goes out.

- Financial statements are formal documents that use a standard accounting format to provide the key information about a company's financial position.

- The generally accepted accounting principles or GAAPs ensure that financial information is presented in a standard form.

- Assets are what a business owns; liabilities are what it owes.

- A balance sheet reports a business's assets, liabilities, and owner's equity.

- An income statement reports how much a business has earned during a fiscal period.

- Fiscal periods are reporting periods of an equal length that are reasonable for the type of business.

- An annual income statement is required for income tax purposes.

- Owners, managers, investors, lenders, and government need financial statements to understand a business's financial picture.

- Computers assist in preparing financial statements by automating the work and making accurate arithmetic easy.

Activities

Knowledge/Understanding

1 Describe the contribution that accounting information can make to business success.

2 Explain why the generally accepted accounting principles enable people who do not work in a business to understand its basic financial position.

3 Give the three categories of financial information on a balance sheet.

4 What is the relationship between the balance sheet and the income statement?

5 Why is it important to analyze a trend in the financial statements?

6 Name four groups who use financial statements and explain why each one seeks information.

7 Does customizing an accounting software program change the fundamental accounting equation?

Thinking/Inquiry

1 Why do business organizations depend on the fundamental accounting equation to understand their financial transactions? Why isn't it enough just to keep a record of all transactions?

2 The list below includes some names of accounts of a company, Rush Rush Delivery Service. Some are fixed assets, some are depreciable assets, and some are current assets. Some items are not assets at all. Some do not even belong on a balance sheet. List the items that are assets, and state which kind. If items are appropriate entries for a balance sheet, state what kind of entries they are.
- Business building
- Cash at bank
- Cash in hand
- Membership fee, Downtown Business Association
- Telephone expense
- Creditors
- Debtors
- Fixtures and fittings
- Office machines
- Hydro bill
- Rent from business tenant
- Loan from Mary
- Mortgage
- Motor vehicles
- Office supplies
- Donation from the business to the United Way
- Canada Savings Bond

Communication

1 Prepare to debate one side of the following proposition: "Business is really about imagination. Paying too much attention to accounting data can stifle a good idea." Use any examples you can find in the textbook or from other sources to strengthen your arguments.

Application

1 Assume you have $200 to lend. Three students have approached you separately. Each wants to borrow the money to help start a summer lawn mowing business. The money would enable one of the students to add a lawnmower to the business and hire another student to help. Here is the basic information for each student:

a) Jonas's Lawn Care: Assets: Cash $100, Supplies $57.80, Lawnmower $200, Bubblejet (for printing/designing flyers) $200. Liabilities— short term: $57.80. Owner's Equity: ?

b) Shiraz's Lawn Service: Assets: Cash $1000, Bricks $270.00, Supplies $12.80, Lawnmower $317.45. Liabilities—long term: $317.45. Owner's Equity: ?

c) Liam's Lawns: Assets: Cash $50, Flyers $75.02, Rake $10. Liabilities $75.02 (to Speedy Flyers). Owner's Equity: ? *Note:* Can borrow neighbour's lawnmower, but only sometimes.

Construct a simple balance sheet for each of the students, showing the owner's equity. Studying the balance sheets, explain which of the students you would lend the money to and why. Assume that all three live in neighbourhoods where lawns are plentiful.

3 Personal Finance

Overall Expectations

By the end of this unit, you will

- distinguish the various ways in which individuals and households can acquire income and other benefits

- develop skills in managing personal income effectively, such as skills in budgeting, planning, saving, and investing

- analyse the role and importance of consumer credit

As a consumer you will deal with many businesses, but you must earn income in order to meet your needs and wants. Over time, you will also want to build wealth in order to afford the lifestyle of your choice. Building wealth requires wise decisions about how to earn, save, invest, donate, spend, and borrow money. To make wise decisions, you need personal financial goals, a financial plan, and a budget.

The most likely way that you will earn income is by working. This unit discusses the factors that determine how much you can earn from a job or business. You will also learn about the benefits that jobs and businesses offer, apart from wages or salary. Knowing these things can help you find the job or business that is right for you.

In order to build wealth, people need to invest some of their income. A variety of types of investment are available to Canadians. You will learn about the most common ones in this unit. You will also learn how Canadians use a tax shelter (an RRSP) to reduce their taxes while they save for retirement.

Most consumers need to borrow money at some point in order to build wealth. For example, students who finance postsecondary training, diplomas, or degrees often require student loans. Homeowners usually require mortgages. In this unit, you will learn the principles of wise borrowing (consumer credit), so as to stay on track with your personal financial goals.

9 Income and Benefits

Specific Expectations

After studying this chapter, you will be able to

- summarize the various ways in which individuals and households can acquire income
- describe the major factors that can influence a job's income level
- describe other benefits of a job in addition to income

To meet most of your personal needs and wants, you must have money to pay for goods and services. Most of us get money by earning income, and there are a number of ways to get it: employment, saving, investing, and social programs. The most common method is through employment, or having a job. Most people would like to earn a high income from their work. But what we actually earn is not determined by what we would like to have. The income we earn is determined by our experience, education, personal performance, and unique abilities, and by the success of a business, the type of business, and the economy. Employment also provides many benefits in addition to income, for example, skill development and self-fulfillment, pensions, health insurance, and employment insurance. In this chapter, you will consider the many ways you can acquire income and its benefits.

Successful Financial Goals and You

Bobby Fuller, a popular Grade 12 student at Newmarket's Portland Heights Secondary School, knows he is the kind of guy who doesn't get excited about programming computers, like some of his classmates. "Sure, I wish I was another Bill Gates and could start a company like Microsoft, but I'm just not," he likes to say. Bobby is pretty good at building things, though, and he often works from his own designs. He is also well organized and punctual and gets along well with people. But his mother keeps telling him, "You can't make a good career out of building things and getting along with people."

For a long time, Bobby thought that if he couldn't become a professional—like a programmer or an engineer—he would end up operating the cappuccino mill at a coffee shop that catered to people who could. One day his uncle Roy, an electrician, heard him say this and told him to think again. "There's going to be a shortage of workers in the skilled construction trades in Canada in the next 15 years," Roy explained, "Do you know how old the average person in some skilled trades is? About 50 years old! Lots of them will retire soon."

Okay, but is that because they won't be needed, Bobby wondered. He was smart enough to know a skill must be needed before he can use it to earn income. So he did some reading, and found out something that surprised him: ➤

Figure 9-1 Bobby found that a part-time job in the construction industry gave him a chance to learn a few things before he starts his apprenticeship. However, he did have to give up spending a lot of time with his friends. ▼

Toronto's population is expected to nearly double between 2001 and 2016. Bobby soon realized that he could take advantage of a business opportunity and earn a good income. New homes, office renovations, conversions of old factories into lofts — they all need skilled tradespeople.

Bobby realized that he could either work for someone else as a skilled tradesman or become an independent general contractor. People who need homes would hire him to oversee the project: He would find, supervise, and pay carpenters, electricians, plumbers, bricklayers, and landscapers.

Uncle Roy encouraged him. "For starters," he said, "Get your carpentry certification. That way, you can always get work. You can learn enough about the other trades to be a contractor by taking courses and getting to know skilled tradespeople." Certification means that Bobby must complete a three to four-year apprenticeship program or a combination of over four years of carpentry work experience, plus high school, college, or industry courses. Bobby plans to start after Grade 12.

In order to apply for apprenticeship, Bobby has to be working in the building trades. Roy has already found Bobby a part-time position for $10.00 an hour helping drywall construction projects. Bobby hopes to learn a lot even before he starts formal training. Besides, he needs the money. He must budget and save for his courses. His mom, a low-income single mother, supports his two younger sisters and cannot help him much financially. And once he starts apprenticing, he will earn a lot more while he studies.

Sometimes, though, Bobby isn't sure if the effort is worthwhile. Instead of hanging out with his friends Mike and Mario, he spends a lot of time drywalling. Mike and Mario have told him to forget it and live for today. "You don't know whether your idea will really work out," they say, "And being the boss is a big headache." But Bobby knows for sure the kind of future he does—and doesn't—want. He asks himself, "I wonder if Bill Gates had this problem?"

As you read this chapter, identify the factors that determine how much money a job or business pays. Can an individual influence or change these factors in any way?

Suppose you made the same amount of money no matter what you did for a living. What job would you prefer to have?

Acquiring Income

Where do you see yourself in five years? Ten years? Twenty years? After graduation will you go into the work force? To community college? University? What sort of job or business will you have?

Do you think you will rent an apartment or own a house? Take the bus or drive a car? Will you take courses? Travel? Each of these goals requires income. Some require a higher income than others. To achieve higher income goals, you must plan carefully.

Earning a high income is rarely a matter of luck. Some people get big inheritances or win lotteries. But most people who earn a high income had goals and strategies for getting what they want.

When asked, self-made millionaires said that the three factors most important to their success were being honest, being well-disciplined, and getting along with people (Figure 9-2). They rated these skills for living ahead of luck, inheritance, intelligence, or knowing the right people.

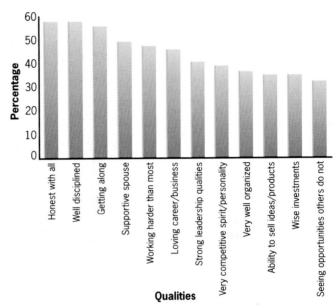

Qualities that Helped Self-made Millionaires Become Wealthy

Figure 9-2 733 self-made millionaires were asked what qualities helped them become wealthy. Which qualities did you expect to see? Which ones surprised you?

Sources of Income

The most common sources of **income** are
- employment (including self-employment)
- saving money you have earned but do not owe to anyone
- investing, including borrowing money to invest
- lending money and receiving it back with interest
- social programs that help you if you run into difficulties

What do you think are the advantages and disadvantages of each of these sources of income?

Employment Income

Some jobs pay a lot more than others. But money isn't the only reason people take jobs. The job described in the margin note pays US$12 per hour. What factors besides money might motivate people to apply?

How Employment Income Relates to Quality of Life

In general, you will want to choose a career that you enjoy, that also pays a good income, and that lets you enjoy a good standard of living and quality of life. But your income is only one of the factors that determine your standard of living and quality of life. Recall from Chapter 3 that your standard of living is the level of goods and services that your income can buy. However, having quality of life does not just mean spending money on material things. As the United Nations rating system which you learned about in Chapter 3 suggests, it also means being able to spend money on education, fitness, travel, and causes you support.

In other words, if all your time were spent earning money for food, clothing, and shelter, you would have a low quality of life even if you had a high standard of living. You might earn enough income to eat expensive food, but if you had no time for physical fitness, your health would deteriorate anyway. Career choices must take into account quality of life as well as income. That might be one reason to think carefully about the alligator wrestling offer. Study Figure 9-3 to see what pay rate some other jobs offer.

Do any of the jobs in Figure 9-3 pay more than you thought? Less than you thought? Think about the factors that might determine what a job pays. You will learn more about this later in the chapter.

Average 1999 hourly earnings of various occupations in Canada.

Job Title	Average Starting Wage	Average Hourly Wage
Financial/Investment Analyst	$19.81	$33.51
Electrical Engineer	20.55	29.78
Computer Systems Analyst	19.52	27.68
Computer Programmer	17.19	22.72
Registered Nurse	17.85	21.73
Bricklayer	15.17	21.67
Medical Radiation Technologist	17.23	21.08
Auditor/Accountant	16.97	21.03
Accounting Clerk	12.10	15.37
Truck Driver	13.19	14.96
Secretary	11.89	14.23
General Office Clerk	10.79	13.18
Restaurant/Food Service Manager	9.34	11.46
Cook	8.44	9.48

Source: "Ontario Job Futures 2000" Wage figures as at March 1999.

Figure 9-3 A skilled bricklayer earns nearly as much as a registered nurse. What market force is probably at work here?

Developing Skills That Earn Income

If you are unsure whether you have the right skills for a given occupation, see your school guidance counsellor. Guidance counsellors usually have skills and aptitude tests that students can take to learn what areas of employment work best for them. Remember that if you did a test a few years ago, you may have developed new skills and aptitudes since then. Or, if your school offers a co-op program, you could discover if you and a job suit each other by working in the field.

Also, as you learned in Chapter 3, skills can be developed. Go back and take another look at Employability Skills on page 76.

Remember that, according to the Conference Board of Canada, you need to develop your employability skills in everything you do: at school, in volunteer work, in sports, in clubs, and at home. Don't wait till you have a paid job. Many of the skills that you learn in everyday activities can be transferred to work.

Volunteer jobs for student council, a science fair, or a school show, for example, are an opportunity, not a burden. They help you to develop and display skills. If you successfully organized a Hot Dog Day, you can put that on your first résumé. It shows your ability to take charge. Or, if you put up the tent and got the barbecue going, you displayed valuable technical skills.

Web Connect

www.school.mcgrawhill.ca/resources/
Do you need to earn while you learn? Check out the Skills Canada and Co-operative Education in Canada Web sites for ways to finance your education.

Saving

People save money for many things: vacations, education, retirement, and emergencies. **Saving** means putting away a portion of your income today, in order to have money in the future. You choose not to use money for something you want now, so later you have it for something you want much more. For example, you take your lunch to school during the year so that you will have money for tennis lessons in the summer.

By putting money in a savings account, you can make a kind of income called interest. **Interest** means that the bank pays you a small fee so it can use your money while it is in the account. However, it is important to observe how this fee is calculated. Very few savings accounts pay simple interest; most pay compound interest. Simple interest is added to the principal (the sum deposited) but compound interest is added to the principal plus the previous interest. Figure 9-4

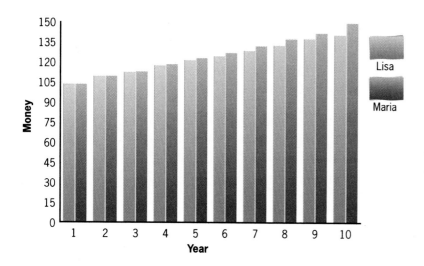

Figure 9-4 Simple versus compound interest. Lisa deposited $100 in a bank account at simple interest. Maria deposited $100 at yearly compound interest for the same period. Both got 4%. Who came out ahead after ten years? Why?

shows the difference. You will learn more about compound interest in Chapter 11.

Why does a bank or other financial institution want to use your money? Because the institution lends it to other people. It charges them a higher rate of interest than it pays you. It keeps the difference, and so makes a profit.

Sometimes, saving to earn interest income doesn't really pay. To make sure it does, ask how the interest is calculated when you open a savings account. Banks compete for your business and may offer different plans to attract customers. Also watch that your bank's **service charges** (the fees charged for transactions) are not so high that they reduce or eliminate the value of your interest income.

Investments

You cannot earn much income from savings account interest unless you have a really large amount of money. You would make more income if you invested the money. **Investment** means that you give up the use of the money for a period of time in exchange for a chance to make more. Here is the difference between investment and savings: When you are saving money, you can take the money out of your savings account at any time, and use it. But when you invest, you buy an investment. If you don't want it any more, you must sell it if you can.

The two most common types of investments are bonds and stocks. Other names for these investments are *debt* and *equity*.

Bonds

When governments and companies want to raise money for projects, they often issue **bonds**. They borrow a sum of money from you and agree to pay it back, with interest, on a certain date. The government or company is in debt to you for the whole sum, including the interest. Because they are debts, bonds are known as *debt instruments*. Bonds usually pay you higher interest than savings accounts. However, you must do research to ensure you are getting the best rate available.

Because you know exactly how much interest you stand to make on a bond, it is called a fixed income investment. What you originally paid is called the **principal**. But, as with savings, you come out with more money than you originally paid for the bond when you cash it in. The difference is your income from bonds, which is called interest.

The best known bonds, purchased by many Canadians, are Canada Savings Bonds. These are very popular because you can buy one for as little as $100 and can cash it in at any time. Most government bonds, as well as corporate bonds, cost much more, and can't be cashed in until a specific date, called the maturity date.

Figure 9-5 To vacationers, Disney is entertainment, but Disney is also a company earning money for its shareholders on the stock market.

Stocks

Stocks are the money organizations raise by selling ownership in the company in the form of shares. When you purchase stock, or shares, you become one of the owners or shareholders of that company. As you learned in Chapter 2, shareholders are not responsible for the debts or decisions of the company. If the shares go up in value, you can receive income. You can sell your shares for more than you paid and keep the difference. The company may also send you a small share of the profits (a dividend). Shares are sold on stock exchanges such as the Toronto Stock Exchange and the Vancouver Stock Exchange.

Stocks are a riskier investment than bonds because if the company does poorly, you can lose money. Take a look at this share price trading chart for Walt Disney Company in Figure 9-6. Look also at Amazon.com (Figure 9-7) and Nike (Figure 9-8) on the next page.

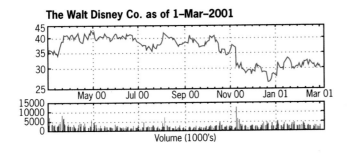

Figure 9-6 How would you feel in March 2001 if you had bought Disney shares in May 2000? You would probably feel better than the people who bought shares in May 2000 of Amazon.com, an Internet entertainment retailer.

Amazon.Com Inc. as of 1–Mar–2001

Volume (1000's)

Figure 9-7 Stocks prices can change rapidly; this happened to many dot.com companies (companies that depend on the Internet) in 2000 and 2001.

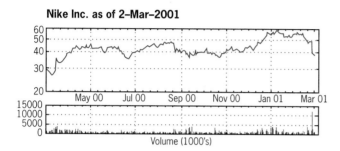

Nike Inc. as of 2–Mar–2001

Volume (1000's)

Figure 9-8 March 2001 was a particularly bad month for North American markets. Is Nike up or down from a year ago? When would it have been best to sell your Nike shares? Or should you keep them? Investors make these decisions every day.

So, why take the risk? Why not just keep your money in the bank? Because if a company does well, you can make a lot more than you could from savings or bonds. Look at some results from sports footwear and fashion company Nike (Figure 9-8).

Social Programs

In Canada, government **social assistance** programs provide income for people who are unable to work due to illness, layoffs, or age. Provinces and the federal government provide various programs. Each province provides social assistance to people who, due to misfortune, are unable to provide satisfactory levels of income for themselves. However, they usually provide a lower standard of living than most Canadians would like. People who have other sources of income are not eligible for most social programs.

Federal income support programs also provide income for people who are unable to work due to disability, layoffs, age, or other circumstances. Some examples of federal income support programs are employment insurance benefits, pensions (Canada Pension Plan and Old Age

Web Connect

www.school.mcgrawhill.ca/resources/
Do you think you might be eligible for a
Canada Millennium Scholarship someday?
Check out criteria.

Security), War Veterans Allowance, Guaranteed Income Supplement, allowance for the survivor, and Canada Student Loans (including the Canada Millennium Scholarship).

The most significant federal programs for wage or salary earners are the Canada Pension Plan (CPP) and Employment Insurance (EI).

Canada Pension Plan

The Canada Pension Plan (CPP) protects you and your family against the loss of income due to retirement, disability, or death. With very few exceptions, every person in Canada over the age of 18 who earns a salary must pay into the plan. You and your employer each pay half of the contribution. At age 70, you stop contributing, even if you have not stopped working.

These mandatory contributions, as well as CPP investments, provide retirees with pensions. Some young people are concerned that a heavy tax burden will be put on them to support the huge generation of baby boomers who will be drawing on CPP when they retire over the next 20 years.

The Canada Pension Plan offers three kinds of benefits:
- disability benefits (which include benefits for disabled contributors and benefits for their dependent children)
- retirement pension
- survivor benefits (including the death benefit, the survivor's pension, and the children's benefit).

The Canada Pension Plan operates throughout Canada, although the province of Quebec has its own program, the Quebec Pension Plan. The Canada Pension Plan and the Quebec Pension Plan work together to ensure that all contributors are covered.

Employment Insurance

You can receive regular income through employment insurance if you meet the requirements of the plan. You must
- have lost your job through no fault of your own
- apply for employment insurance
- be actively seeking but have not yet found suitable work
- have paid into the government's employment insurance account through payroll deductions
- have been without work and without pay for at least seven consecutive days

- have worked the required number of hours based on the region where you live and the regional unemployment rate

Employment insurance applicants must have worked a minimum of 420 to 700 hours to qualify, sometimes up to 910 hours. They may receive payments for between 14 and 45 weeks, depending on their circumstances. However, the basic benefit rate is usually 55 percent of average weekly insured earnings up to a maximum. Self-employed people don't pay employment insurance and therefore are not eligible for employment insurance benefits.

Check Your Understanding

Knowledge/Understanding

1 Describe the sources of income available to Canadians.
2 Explain briefly the differences between stocks and bonds.

Thinking/Inquiry

3 Are there reasons that Bobby (see page 245) might be happy as a general contractor even if he makes only an average income from it? Explain.
4 Ella reads that the average Canadian will have three to five different careers during the course of working life. If she is likely to change jobs, Ella sees no reason to learn any specific skills. Ella also thinks there is no point in identifying careers that interest her now. Is she right? How would you advise Ella?

Communication

5 Compare the qualities you bring to group projects with the top 12 qualities valued by self-made millionaires (Figure 9-2). (a) Write a point-form list of the qualities you think you have. (b) Explain briefly how they help you. (c) Also list at least one quality you are still working on and explain why you need it. (d) Present your list to a small group.
6 While people invest in firms to make a profit, ethical issues may motivate them to sell their shares. Some international garment firms are accused of using materials made in sweatshops (factories with harsh and unfair working conditions, and low wages). Debate the following proposition: Canadians should not invest in firms accused of using sweatshops.

Skills
Appendix

building an argument

7 Make use of what you have learned about demographics and about what your classmates like in sportswear and entertainment. (a) Chart the probable future of the stocks of Nike and Amazon.com. (b) Assume that overall consumer spending is high and companies are well managed. Which stock will probably do better? (c) Explain your opinion.

Skills
Appendix

building an argument

Income Level Factors

If you look back at Figure 9-3, you will see that some occupations do not pay as much as others, even if the employee or self-employed person works hard and does a good job. Why is this so? Seven factors usually determine how much a job or business pays.

The following four factors, which you first encountered in Chapter 3, relate to the person seeking a job. They affect your chances of getting an interview:

- education, including continuing education
- experience
- personal performance
- uniqueness of abilities

The following three factors relate to the job marketplace:

- type of business
- success of the business
- economic conditions

Even if you cannot control the last three factors, you can respond effectively to them. For example, you can learn about the sector you work in by reading newspapers, watching business news segments, and searching the Internet. Is more demand predicted for your industry's type of business? Or less? If you know that reduced demand is certain, you can slowly move into a different industry. You can also monitor the success of the business you work in. If your company is not profitable, but other companies in the industry are, you may want to seek a new job with a competitor. If you know that overall economic conditions are good or poor, you can compare how your business and industry are doing with how others are doing. You will now have a better basis for making a wise decision.

Factors That Relate to the Job Seeker

Education

A good education and high marks won't guarantee you a job, promotions, or a rising income. However, they will almost always get you an interview ahead of those who have less education or lower marks. Getting the interview gives you a chance to get hired. As a result, university graduates are only half as likely to be unemployed as others. As Figure 9-10 shows, graduates usually make more than dropouts as well. Figure 9-11 shows that 54 percent of new jobs will require at least some post-secondary education.

Average Earnings by Highest Level of Completed Schooling, 1995

Less than grade 9	$19 377
Grades 9-13 without graduation	$18 639
Grades 9-13 with graduation	$22 846
Less than university degree	$25 838
University degree	$42 054

Source: Statistics Canada, 1996 Census Nation tables.

Figure 9-9 People who never attended grade 9 actually earned more per year than those who did. Does that mean that you would be better off to forget grade 9? What characteristic might be true of most people who never attended grade 9?

Where New Jobs Will Come From, 2000–2005

• Management (includes education, experience, and training)	11%
• University degree required	25%
• Post-secondary education (not university)	29%
• Skilled trades	10%
• No secondary school diploma (short on-the-job training)	10%

Source: Statistics Canada

Figure 9-10 What percentage of new jobs require education or skills training?

Experience

Have a look at classified job advertisements in the newspaper. Do any say "salary commensurate with experience"? It is common for job advertisements to say this. It means that if you have specific experience, you can expect a higher salary.

The more experience you have, the more valuable you are to a business. People who are already experienced at doing a specific job can begin to produce income for the company quickly, after a short orientation. They may also have valuable contacts from their previous job. By contrast, less experienced people have to be trained. Training ties up other employees, takes time, costs money, and involves risk. If you come with experience, the company can afford to offer you more.

Personal Performance

When you rank very high in **personal performance**, it usually means that you are doing more than is needed just to keep the job. When you are adding value to a company or project, you can feel secure about asking for a raise at some point. You are also much more likely to be considered for a promotion. Similarly, if you are self-employed you can charge more if you provide a high quality of goods or services. Put yourself in your boss's or client's shoes. What would impress you if you were on that side of the desk?

An important factor in personal performance is having a high "EQ." That stands for **emotional quotient**." EQ includes self-awareness, altruism, personal motivation, empathy, and the ability to love and be loved. High EQ people achieve rewarding careers and lasting relationships, according to Daniel Goleman, author of *Emotional Intelligence.*

EQ includes learning how to manage anger so that it does not interfere with achieving your goal. For example, Sabitri and Jared applied for the same after-school job shelving books at the local library. Sabitri was offended when the stern and unfriendly interviewer pointed out that "a workplace is not a social club" and warned her against letting her friends "hang out" there. She reminded herself that the job would help her get into Information Science at the local university, so she remained polite and friendly. Jared, by contrast, scowled angrily when told the same thing, and the interview was cut short. For weeks afterward, he told friends he did not even want the job. Sabitri, who got the job, discovered that most of the other librarians were friendly and helpful. Which of the two, Sabitri or Jared, had the higher EQ? (See also Figure 9-12.)

Emotional intelligence is not fixed; you can develop it with practice. It may be even more important to career and financial success than IQ (intelligence quotient), as Sabitri's and Jared's example shows.

Test your EQ

You are on an airplane that suddenly hits extremely bad turbulence and begins rocking from side to side. What do you do?

a) Continue to read your book or magazine, or watch the movie, trying to pay little attention to the turbulence.

b) Become vigilant for an emergency, carefully monitoring the flight attendants and reading the emergency instructions card.

c) A little of both a and b.

d) Not sure–never noticed.

Answer: Anything but d)—that answer reflects that you lack awareness of your habitual responses under stress. Actively acknowledging your stress and finding ways to calm yourself (i.e., engage in a book or read the emergency card) are healthier responses.

Figure 9-11 How would you handle a possible emergency?

Uniqueness of Abilities

Tiger Woods's Professional Golf Association (PGA) earnings up to 2000 were $20 411 835. He has made much more than that over the years from endorsements and other opportunities that his fame has attracted. Does this mean that you should aim to be a professional golfer? Can you, like Canadian Mike Weir, hope to compete with him? Mike won his first tournament at 16 (Ontario Juvenile).

Kiso Tanaka isn't famous, like Tiger Woods or Mike Weir, but his skill as a DJ means that he earns five times more than his classmates earn. Is it unfair that one young person makes so

Web Connect

www.school.mcgrawhill.ca/resources/
If you are interested in learning more about emotional intelligence, you can take an on-line ten-question quiz. Emotional intelligence is a lifetime project—most successful people are always learning how to listen better and relate better to others.

Figure 9-12 At 13, Mike sought advice from golf champion Jack Niklaus. Should he switch to playing right-handed? Niklaus told him to stick to his natural swing. He has since earned $5 519 148.

much and others make minimum wage? Remember that sports and entertainment are businesses. The star athlete, or even a local celebrity like Kiso, enables many other business owners to make money.

Sports owners, food concession owners, and sellers of public space, fashion, and equipment gladly buy into a good investment. In other words, you are a good investment if people will buy tickets to see you or if they will buy a product because you endorse it. Also, remember that unique gifts may not last. Bobby Fuller can still be a general contractor at 50 and Tiger and Mike may still be golf champions in their 40s. However, a teen pop star's career may be long over. The star's agent includes that fact in negotiations and financial calculations.

Factors That Relate to the Job Marketplace

Type of Business

Sometimes jobs that are very similar pay very different amounts of money. The difference may depend on what the business can afford. Consider the following example.

Sofia and Peter, who are both administrative assistants, meet on vacation. Peter is surprised to learn that Sofia makes $20,000 a year more than he does, plus a large year-end bonus. Not only that, Sofia admits that her job is not even as demanding as Peter's. What is the difference?

Sofia works for a well-known financial advisory firm in downtown Toronto. Headlines in the business section of the newspapers scream the huge sums the firm earns.

Peter, by contrast, is the administrative right arm of a family doctor who runs two nine-staff clinics in Kenora. Peter knows he is doing a good job and he enjoys his work. But he wouldn't dare ask for a raise because health care cutbacks have sliced the clinic's budget. Moving to a different doctor's clinic would not help. They all get the same government funding.

Success of Business

No matter how good you are at your job, if the company doesn't make much money, neither will you. Many businesses with good products fail, often because they are not properly managed. A lower level employee does not have any control over management. Of course, the employee could move to a better managed firm. Note that Peter, above, cannot do that; to improve his income, he would have to seek work in a different type of business altogether.

Economic Conditions

In Chapter 5 you learned about the business cycle. Our economy moves in cycles. It moves from recessions when jobs are hard to find to boom times when they are plentiful—and back again. A recession is a slow-down or *downturn* in the economy. Businesses shrink, so they let staff go. Because there is more demand for each available job, employers don't have to offer as good a salary. Even skilled workers have trouble getting hired. The good news is that recessions always seem to give way to boom times eventually.

Check Your Understanding

Knowledge/Understanding

1 What factors that determine income relate to the job seeker? What factors that determine income relate to the job market?
2 Give some examples of how unique abilities can enable a teen to earn a high income in a business environment.

Thinking/Inquiry

3 How does having a high emotional quotient (EQ) help in the following areas: (a) sharing the work, (b) sharing the credit, (c) sharing the blame, (d) explaining what is wrong with someone else's work and how to fix it, (e) accepting criticism of one's own work, (f) giving bad news.

Communication

4 Write a short report for your teacher comparing the relative benefits of a part-time summer job at a local fast food franchise and a summer-long job as a junior camp counsellor. (a) Assume the income is the same (minimum wage). (b) Consider issues such as educational value for the future, promotion opportunities, level of responsibility, and free time. (c) Explain which you would prefer.

Skills Appendix

writing reports

Application

5 Suppose that, in order to make society fairer, a province wanted to pass a law requiring Canadian teen sports stars and celebrities to work for the minimum wage. Working in groups, prepare an oral presentation from the point of view of the teen stars. Use what you have learned so far about business to frame your arguments.

Other Benefits of a Job

You will spend the bulk of your adult life working. Thus, it is important to consider the **benefits** of work, apart from income. What makes people happy in their choice of a job or career? Psychologists who study motivation say that money isn't always at the top of the list. Recall Maslow's Hierarchy of Needs from Chapter 1. Once we have acquired necessities like food and money, we seek **self-actualization** or *self-fulfillment.* That is why psychological benefits, such as a sense of control, become very important on the job. But many benefits are not only psychological; they have a financial value, for example,

- skills development
- pension
- health insurance
- stock options and bonuses

Why do employers provide these benefits? Employers sometimes use the term "human capital" to refer to employees, because employees are not just an expense. They make money for the company. For example, in the computer engineering industry, without the information that is inside the engineer's brain, the company wouldn't exist.

Therefore, employers provide benefits to keep employees from leaving. Keeping employees—and keeping them happy—is particularly important in fields where there is high demand for specific skills.

Self-Fulfillment

What leads an employee to feel fulfilled? Peter, who administers the two medical clinics in Kenora, feels fulfilled even though his income is less than Sofia's, because he knows he makes an important contribution to the health of his employer's patients.

No matter how much money you are paid, you won't feel fulfilled without some sense of control over your environment, responsibility for your work, and the respect of your colleagues. These are sometimes called "intangible" benefits, because no dollar value is attached to them. For example, at some companies employees who wanted to **telecommute** (work from home and send their work through the Internet) found that management feared that they "wouldn't really work" if they were not being watched. They were quite disappointed to discover that their bosses did not really trust them. Do you think that those employees enjoyed their jobs more when they discovered that?

The higher the level of job you have, the more of these intangible benefits you will likely receive. That's one reason that employees seek promotions. But a higher position also means greater accountability. Accountability can mean that you will be expected to work long hours and shoulder the blame for things that go wrong in your department, even if you didn't make the mistake.

Figure 9-13 What benefit is the music teacher enjoying?

Skills Development

People need to continually retrain and upgrade their skills over their working life. Because new technology makes workplaces more efficient, it is in the employer's interest to pay for staff to upgrade their skills. Many employers will pay for employees to take training on their own time, as well as provide training courses in the workplace. Self-employed workers must also upgrade their knowledge and skills continuously to serve their clients better.

Biz.Bites

A recent study found that 87 percent of new media workers (Internet and CD-ROM builders) spend an average of 13.5 hours per week learning new skills. It pays off. They make over $60 per hour.

Biz.Bites

In 1889, German Chancellor Otto von Bismarck (1815–1898) offered the Old Age Pension to Germans over 70. The average life expectancy was less than 50.

Although retraining might seem tedious, it is important to take advantage of programs offered by the employer. Promotion may depend on it. If you must seek a new job, it is also important to be up-to-date. Otherwise, you may have a hard time finding work and may have to accept a lower income.

Pension

Company **pension** plans enable employees to continue receiving income after they have retired. But employees who have a job with a pension plan are lucky. Fewer employers offer pensions today than 30 years ago. One reason is that to operate some kinds of pensions, a company needs a very large workforce. That is because retired employees receive their pension payments partly from the premiums that will be paid by younger people just starting out. But most companies nowadays are cutting their workforce.

If a smaller company has a pension plan, it usually depends on returns from investments. The popularity of Canada's Registered Retirement Savings Plan (RRSP) has caused many employers to leave pension responsibility to the employee. Some companies offer to pay a portion of an employee's yearly RRSP investment, as a form of bonus.

Life Expectancy in Canada, 1920–22 through 1990-92

Canada	Males	Females
1920–22	59	61
1930–32	60	62
1940–42	63	66
1950–52	66	71
1960–62	68	74
1970–72	69	76
1980–82	72	79
1990–92	75	81

Source: Statistics Canada, Catalogue no. 82F0075XCB

Figure 9-14 Can you see why retirement savings have become an important consideration for all working Canadians? This chart is updated every 10 years. What do you expect the figures for 2000–2002 to show?

Health Insurance

Many employers offer group health insurance plans that pay a portion of the costs of dentistry, eyeglasses, and some other medical services. Many offer life insurance for employees and their dependants. Some also offer extra holidays or membership in a health club. When assessing the value of these benefits, employees must consider what the overall package of income plus benefits is worth to them. For example, dental benefits are valuable, but if you are already covered under another plan, they will not be an incentive to choose a particular job.

Stock Options and Bonuses

Stock options are the right to buy shares in a company. In addition to salary, a company may give an employee stock options. A **bonus** is an extra amount of money paid to employees, usually once a year. The bonus is often higher if the company did well. It recognizes that the employees were an important part of the reason that the company did well.

At one time, stock options and bonuses were offered almost exclusively to executives. In the Information Age, employers began offering these benefits to other employees. The employers wanted to motivate knowledge workers by offering valuable benefits. Employees, in turn, were demanding higher compensation for their valuable skills.

The trend caught on. Now employees in many industries negotiate both stock options and bonuses when the company makes more money. Employers have come to see these benefits as incentives to motivate all employees to help make the company successful.

Benefits as Income

Benefits that have a financial (dollar) value may be considered part of the employee's income and thus be taxable. For example, if the employer gives the employee $2000 at Christmas as a bonus, the money is part of the employee's income. If the employer gives the employee a car, the value of the car is income too. However, if the employer installs an exercise room on the site, using it is not considered part of income. Fitness is important, but in this case a dollar value is not assigned to it.

With careful planning, you can find a career that you enjoy, that pays you well and provides both material and emotional benefits. The more you learn about your company, your industry, and the economy, the better your chances of finding the right job for you, in terms of job satisfaction, income, and benefits. Whatever the choice, the way you use your money after you earn it is the next important decision.

Check Your Understanding

Knowledge/Understanding

1 List at least four types of benefit that employees may receive. Explain briefly what the benefit is.

2 What major social change has made retirement savings more important to employees? What marketplace change caused employers to offer non-management employees stock options?

Thinking/Inquiry

3 Natasha is annoyed because her boss wants to send her on a course during working hours, to learn to update the flower shop's Web site. Natasha feels it's not fair because she gets only minimum wage. Why should she go to the trouble of learning new skills? What would you tell her?

4 Anil's boss does everything "the old-fashioned way" in his grocery store. Anil likes him, and wants to stay there "for 10 years." His friend Gina is worried about that. Why do you think she might be worried? What do you think?

5 Carlos joined a firm that offers stock options. His friend Jerry thinks that a dental plan would be a more valuable benefit. He reasons that the value of Carlos's company's stocks might go down. But dental care will always be costly. What do you think?

Communication

6 Based on what you have learned about factors that determine income in this chapter, develop a presentation on "Success in Today's Workplace." Use audiovisual aids or current media materials available to you. Assume that Natasha, Anil, and Ella (page 254) are in the audience. Ensure that your material addresses their situations.

Application

7 Interview someone who has a "home office." (a) Ask how they keep in touch with clients, employees, or employers. (b) Identify the business communications equipment they use. (c) Write a short report on "Business Equipment Used in a Home Office." (d) Working in a group, compare your findings with others. (e) As a group, answer this question: How necessary is modern business communications equipment to working at home?

Skills
Appendix

oral presentations

Young part-time employees of a toy store got interested in retirement benefits when the store's benefit plan gave them a chance to play the stock market.

Toys-R-Us (Canada) Ltd. had an average employee age of 26. Sixty-four percent of employees were under 25 and 33% were under 20. Would they be interested in a pension plan?

"We wanted to build a plan that would be open to everyone," said Shirley Murray, vice-president, human resources. "What the average 16-year-old wants isn't necessarily what the 67-year-old or the executive wants." Most young people were willing to take more risks, she explained.

To enroll more employees in the group RRSP pension plan, the company management offered six investment choices, instead of choosing funds for the employees. Employees could find out how their investments were doing by looking in the financial section of a daily newspaper. As an employment benefit, Toys-R-Us also matched the employees' RRSP contributions by 50%, up to a maximum of 2% of total earnings. After two years, the plan was portable (could be taken elsewhere).

The younger employees signed up in record numbers for the plan because, according to Toys-R-Us management, they liked the idea that they could actually see what was happening to the money they had invested. Randy Helander, the national training and recruiting manager, said, "As the world gets more interactive, young people have come to expect choice."

Source: *Benefits Canada* Magazine, May 1996 copyright Maclean Hunter Publishing Ltd.

ACTIVITIES

1 What change did Toys-R-Us make to the pension fund, in order to interest younger employees?

2 If an employee was dissatisfied with the performance of a pension fund investment, what could he or she do about it?

3 "As the world gets more interactive, young people have come to expect choice." Do you agree or disagree with this opinion? Write a response, giving examples from your own life. Compare your response with other students' responses in a small group.

4 Working with a partner, research the National Secondary School Stock Market Competition, available through the Toronto Stock Exchange. Report to the class on registration, rules, awards, and recent school champions. Recommend whether your class should take part, and explain why or why not.

CHAPTER REVIEW

Points to Remember

- The main source of income for most Canadians is employment, including self-employment.

- Saving, investing, borrowing and lending money to earn interest, and social programs are also sources of income.

- Employment income depends on the employee's education, experience, personal performance, and unique abilities.

- Employment income also depends on market factors such as the type of business, the success of the business, and economic conditions.

- Apart from income, employment may offer financial benefits such as skills development, pension, health insurance, stock options and bonuses.

- Employment may offer psychological benefits as well, such as control over environment, responsibility for work, and the respect of colleagues.

Activities

Knowledge/Understanding

1 Explain briefly the difference between savings, bonds, and stocks as sources of income. Use a three-column table that shows one advantage and one disadvantage of each.

2 Why is it important for employees to understand the market factors that determine their employment income? How can employees use this information?

3 Why is it important to consider benefits as well as income when deciding whether to accept a job?

Thinking/Inquiry

1 Using the business section of a daily or online newspaper or Web sites of banks, list five financial institutions that offer savings accounts. Record the interest rates they offer, along with any other conditions listed (minimum deposit, for example). State which account you think is best and why.

2 Check the financial section of a newspaper or government bond Web sites for information on bonds available from a government (Canadian, provincial, or foreign). List four, and report the interest rate and how long the money is tied up in each bond. If you had $10 000 to invest, which bond would you choose? Why? Assume that your money is equally safe.

Skills
Appendix
critical thinking

Communication

1 Referring back to the profile of Bobby Fuller, and based on what you have learned in the chapter, prepare a two-minute talk to present to a discussion group on one of the following topics:

- Are Mike and Mario right? Should Bobby forget his plans and live for today? Is being the boss just a big headache? Why or why not?
- List the factors that you think will determine how much money Bobby can make. Rank them in order of importance.
- Suppose Bobby gets a construction industry job for a while before starting a contracting business. Are there benefits to a skilled job besides money?

Skills
Appendix
oral presentations

Application

1 Interview three to four employed or self-employed adults about their retirement plans.
  a) what proportion of their retirement income will come from
   - a company plan
   - Canada Pension Plan (mandatory government plan for employed persons)
   - Old Age Pension (social assistance plan)
   - personal savings and investments
  b) Ask them whether their situation is the same as that of their parents. If it is different, ask them how. If they think your situation will be different from theirs, ask them to explain how. Work in a group to compare your findings. Prepare a report that summarizes the group's results, omitting the names of the respondents (the people who answered your questions).

Internet Extension

1 How do investors know whether they should invest in a company that offers shares for sale? They can research how well the company's shares have done in the past.

Skills
Appendix
researching

10 How You Use Your Money

deductions
gross pay
disposable income
net pay
discretionary income
income tax
total income
taxable income
tax credit
property tax
sales tax
mortgage
down payment
warranty
guarantee
financial institutions
capital
pre-authorized payments
guaranteed investment
certificate
mutual fund

Specific Expectations

After studying this chapter, you will be able to

- **distinguish the various ways of using income**

- **identify the types of expenses, including taxes, that individuals and households typically incur**

- **identify the criteria required for making effective purchasing decisions**

- **evaluate the products and services offered by major Canadian financial institutions**

In Chapter 9 we considered how individuals and households acquire income. In this chapter we discuss how income is usually spent. Wouldn't it be nice if the sections of this chapter had headings such as Fashion, Movies, Vacations, and Sports! The reality is that most people use income on the less exciting necessities—taxes, utilities, phone bills, savings, investing, donations, insurance, food, and basic clothing. In order to have money left to satisfy your wants, you need to make wise decisions when buying to satisfy your needs. Your needs include saving and investing, so you also have to know about the products and services of Canadian financial institutions.

Wildflower Farm

In 1988, Miriam Goldberger decided that she would leave the corporate world and the steady income that it provided. Instead, she would earn her living doing what she loved best: gardening. Today she is the president of Wildflower Farm in Schomberg, Ontario. She and her husband, a former advertising executive, do it all: landscape gardens, design meadows to attract butterflies and songbirds, and sell low-maintenance wildflowers that they grow in their greenhouses.

Before she started her farm, Miriam did a number of jobs, but they weren't satisfying to her. As she says, "I have a low tolerance for jobs that don't feed big parts of me." Every day she used to come home, change out of her business clothes and run out to work in her garden. Finally, she decided that doing what she loved was what was most important.

When her husband left his job in advertising to join her in her business venture, Miriam and her family were without a stable income. They had to scale back their lifestyle while their seasonal business got on its feet. They had to learn to shop carefully and make effective purchasing decisions. No one starved or went without new clothes, but annual vacations were replaced with the occasional day trip. On the other hand, because their income was lower, they had fewer expenses and paid less income tax.

It wasn't easy to transform her passion for gardening into a successful business that provided steady income for her family. She started with a part-time, wholesale dried-flower business. This grew into a pick-your-own operation in 1992. Today, Wildflower Farm is Canada's largest wildflower nursery, specializing in low maintenance lawns and gardens. The company's online catalogue and growing guide is one of the top wildflower sites in North America.

As you read this chapter, identify reasons why using income wisely is just as important to achieving your goals as earning it.

Figure 10-1 For one Ontario couple, a decision to change careers meant learning to use their money wisely.

Source: Adapted from "Take this job and love it," *Chatelaine*, October 1999, page 97 ff.

How Income Is Used

Maybe you just want a simple life. Perhaps you would go without CDs, fashionable clothes, books, concert tickets, and other luxuries, so you don't have to work in order to buy them. But, unfortunately, even the first level of Maslow's hierarchy of needs—meeting your basic needs for food, clothing, and shelter—doesn't come cheap in our society. You need a good income just to get by!

In this section, we will consider the four main ways in which you will use that income: spending, saving, investing, and donating.

In Chapter 9 you learned how you can acquire and increase your income through employment, saving, and investing. In Chapter 10, we consider how to spend, save, invest, and donate from your income to help provide yourself and others with a good future.

Figure 10-2 Most of the income that Canadians earn by working is spent on basic needs, saving, investing, and donating.

Spending

Do you remember the first time someone paid you for doing a job? When you got your first pay statement or stub, what did you do with the money? Did you see a difference between what you earned (*gross income*) and what you got to keep (*net income*)?

Look at the pay statement in Figure 10-3. It belongs to Lawrence Li, 28, who started working in construction at 18 and is now a construction superintendent at DelMarco Contractors. The company did not pay him all the money he actually earned in the month. There are *deductions* from his wages.

Deductions are the money that an employer takes from your salary before giving you the remainder. *Mandatory* deductions are amounts that the federal government requires your employer to deduct. When you examine Lawrence's paycheque statement (stub), you see that these are Canada Pension Plan, Employment Insurance, and income tax. An employee may also allow the employer to deduct non-mandatory or *voluntary* deductions from pay, for example for a charity. In Figure 10-3, identify Lawrence's voluntary donation.

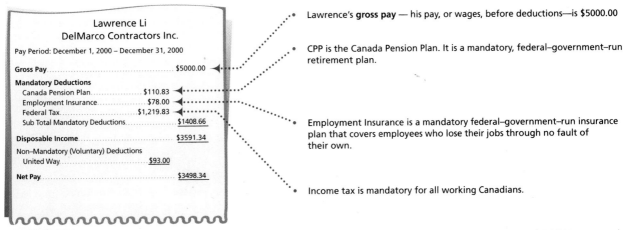

Lawrence Li
DelMarco Contractors Inc.

Pay Period: December 1, 2000 – December 31, 2000

Gross Pay..$5000.00

Mandatory Deductions
   Canada Pension Plan....................$110.83
   Employment Insurance.................$78.00
   Federal Tax.................................$1,219.83
   Sub Total Mandatory Deductions................$1408.66

Disposable Income...........................$3591.34

Non–Mandatory (Voluntary) Deductions
   United Way.................................$93.00

Net Pay..$3498.34

- Lawrence's **gross pay** — his pay, or wages, before deductions—is $5000.00

- CPP is the Canada Pension Plan. It is a mandatory, federal–government–run retirement plan.

- Employment Insurance is a mandatory federal–government–run insurance plan that covers employees who lose their jobs through no fault of their own.

- Income tax is mandatory for all working Canadians.

Figure 10-3 Here is Lawrence's paycheque statement for December 2000. As you can see he makes (12 x $5 000) $60 000 a year, and gets paid every month. What is the biggest deduction on Lawrence's paycheque?

Lawrence's **disposable income** is the money he has available to spend ($3591.34) after mandatory deductions. His voluntary charitable deduction is deducted from his disposable income. So, in the end, after deducting all of his compulsory and voluntary deductions, Lawrence's **net pay** or net income is $3498.34.

By far, Canadians spend the greatest part of their disposable income on necessities.

Lawrence's biggest spending priority for his disposable income is his rent. He pays $750 per month for rent on his one-bedroom apartment in Orangeville. He also pays $400 a month for food. Lawrence has all the furniture and most of the clothes he needs so he spends only about $122 a month on these things. However, he must pay telephone and Internet of $140 per month, and $260 a month for truck pool or rental. Lawrence does not own a truck just now. He drives a company truck at work.

He also takes adult education courses in construction trades. These activities cost $200 per month. So let us look at his monthly expenses on necessities in Figure 10-4.

Lawrence has $1626.34 left over. This amount is called discretionary income. **Discretionary income** is the money Lawrence can spend in whatever way he wishes.

Lawrence's monthly spending
of his net pay

Net Pay..$3498.34

Expenses
   Rent.........................$750.00
   Food.........................$400.00
   Truck pool/rent............$260.00
   Telephone & Internet......$140.00
   Adult Education............$200.00
   Clothing/Toiletries/
   Furniture...................$122.00 $1872.00

Left for discretionary spending, savings,
investment, further donations......................$1626.34

Figure 10-4 Lawrence's monthly spending of his net pay, or disposable income. Can you see any expenses that Lawrence could cut down on in a financial pinch?

Connecting Business with *Crafts*

The One Of A Kind Show

"People don't want plastic any more," says one woman strolling through the maze of booths. She is shopping for unique Christmas presents – Santa Claus figurines made of driftwood; hand-blown glassware, stationary, hand-painted silk scarves, or handmade toys not advertised on television. These may not be conventional goods, but they are good business.

Since it began in 1974, the One of a Kind Craft Show has drawn over 2 million visitors and over 6000 artisans from every province in Canada. With one show in late November, and another each spring, it's the largest craft venue in the country.

"We're not talking about hippies selling beads," says one seller. The total sales for all Canadian craft shows is now about $100-million each year. Overall, the craft business in Canada is a growing industry estimated at $600 million yearly. One of a Kind takes in more than $1 million per day.

Buyers—whether they are collectors, shop owners, or bargain hunters—are attracted to the unrivaled range of quality, selection, value, and convenience offered by the nearly 600 sellers at One of a Kind. The buyers pay $10 to get in. Sellers are charged from $2000 to $4000 for the 11 days of each Toronto show. At those rates, some craftspeople rent space for only half of the time. Sellers are sometimes advised that if they are not making ten times the booth fee, they're not profitable.

Booths that sell small, less expensive items such as soap, pottery, ornaments or foodstuffs do the liveliest business. These items are the most affordable and make good gifts year-round. Some sellers barely break even, but come back every year. These sellers usually have other jobs, and the One of a Kind show offers a special outlet for their creativity. Others travel the craft show circuit year-round, but make their largest revenue here. Each booth doubles as an advertisement for its artisans, who often receive orders later in the year from customers who saw their goods at the show.

Contemporary Craft Shows Ltd. organizes seven One of a Kind Craft shows like the one in Toronto in five other North American cities. The company's owner, John Ladouceur, says, "The exhibitors are not corporations. Here, you're dealing with individuals." Clearly, the businesses featured at the One of a Kind Craft Show are owned by people who love what they sell, and sell what they love.

ACTIVITIES

1 Would crafters want machines that produce thousands of identical copies of a craft item? Explain.

2 Is earning money important or unimportant to a crafter? Or somewhere in between? Explain the role of earning income in a business pursued partly for enjoyment.

3 Think of a business that you would enjoy. Give your business a name. Design a business card that promotes your business.

Saving

Lawrence could plan a luxurious weekend getaway on what is left over. But he has goals for which he will need the spare money. He used to take a lot of vacations. But, now that he's reached the age of 28, he wants to buy a house. Years ago, he also started putting aside some money for his retirement.

Lawrence is a careful money manager. He arranged with his bank to move $300 per month out of his chequing account into his savings account. The savings account paid an average of 4.5 percent daily compound interest over the years.

He saves more than the average Canadian. Figure 10-5 shows that many Canadians do not save much and save much less than they did two decades ago.

Because Lawrence has income left over after necessities, he must think about savings, investing, and donations.

Personal Income and Savings

Year	Personal Saving Rate (Total Personal Saving/ Total Personal Disposable Income)
1982	18.5
1983	15.1
1984	15.0
1985	14.0
1986	11.7
1987	10.1
1988	10.5
1989	11.2
1990	11.1
1991	11.4
1992	11.2
1993	10.0
1994	8.0
1995	7.4
1996	5.4
1997	2.1

Source: Statistics Canada

Figure 10-5 Canadians' savings rate declined from 18.5 percent in 1982 to 2.1 percent in 1997. Why do you think the decline might have occurred?

Investing

Like many Canadians, Lawrence has a Registered Retirement Savings Plan (RRSP). You will learn more about RRSPs later in this chapter. For now, note that an RRSP is not the same as the Canada Pension Plan. Here are the differences:

- The Canada Pension Plan (CPP) is a mandatory plan operated by the federal government. An RRSP is a private retirement plan that an investor, in this case Lawrence, owns.
- The money that Lawrence is required to contribute to CPP is taken directly from his paycheque, as you saw in Figure 10-3. But Lawrence can decide whether or not he wants to contribute money to an RRSP for his retirement. The amount does not appear on his paycheque because it comes from his discretionary income (see Figure 10-4).

He contributes $200 per month to his RRSP. Some of the people who work with Lawrence think that it is funny that he is contributing to an RRSP—a retirement plan—when he is only 28. But Lawrence knows that he isn't going to stop living when he is older. In fact, he thinks he may want to retire early and travel. Or go to university. He didn't have the money for a degree in archaeology when he was 18. He was also unsure whether it would lead to a job. But if he invests wisely, he will have the money as an older adult.

Lawrence's Discretionary Monthly Spending

Item	Amount	
Discretionary income		**$1626.34**
Savings for a house	$300.00	
RRSP investments	$200.00	
Donations		
UNICEF	$20.00	
CWF	$20.00	
		$540.00
Left for luxuries		**$1086.34**

Figure 10-6 Could Lawrence save, invest, or donate more money than he does? Should he?

Web Connect

www.school.mcgrawhill.ca/resources/

Canada's supersite for the non-profit sector contains over 3000 pages of news, jobs, information and resources for executives, job-seekers, staff, donors, and volunteers. If you are looking for information on worthy causes, check this out.

Donations

Lawrence gives to charities because he believes in investing in society. He donates $93 a month to United Way. He allows that amount to be deducted from his paycheque. In addition, before he buys any luxury goods or services, he donates $20 a month to UNICEF. He also sends $20 a month to the Canadian Wildlife Federation. The government gives Lawrence a *tax credit* when he contributes to a registered charity. You will learn more about tax credits later in the chapter. (See Figure 10-6)

So it turns out that Lawrence has $1086.34 per month left. If he wants to buy holiday gifts, birthday gifts, a truck, or a vacation, he will have to budget and save most of that money. In the next section, we will look more closely at Lawrence's taxes and expenses. Can you think of ways he might use his income more wisely?

Check Your Understanding

Knowledge/Understanding

1 Explain the meaning of the following terms: gross income, net income, disposable income, and discretionary income.

2 Identify two mandatory deductions from paycheques and explain their purpose.

Thinking/Inquiry

3 Why do you think Canadians do not save very much? (See Figure 10-5). If you can think of several reasons, rank them in order of importance.

Communication

4 Working in a group, compare your lists of reasons why Canadians do not save very much. Choose up to three reasons that appear on everyone's

list. Think of illustrations of these reasons. Give a short oral presentation, ensuring that every group member speaks.

Application

5 Lawrence invested his RRSP money in safe investments provided by his bank. Check with a financial institution to find out what safe investments it offers. List three of them and attach a sample brochure for at least one.

Types of Expenses

In the previous section, you learned how much of an employee's disposable income was really available for spending, saving, investing, and donating. You also observed in Figure 10-3 that a portion of Lawrence's income went to income tax.

All levels of Canadian government—federal, provincial, and municipal—have taxes and fees that fund their activities and programs. These include property taxes, sales taxes, and licence fees.

You also know from Figure 10-4, which shows how Lawrence spends his pay, that he has many other expenses he can perhaps reduce, but not avoid—for example, rent, food, truck pool, and telephone. Some consumers are tempted to use credit cards in an inappropriate way as a form of discretionary income. You will learn more about consumer credit in Chapter 12.

Figure 10-7 The first time Lawrence had to fill out and send in an income tax return, he picked up an income tax form (a T1) from the local post office. Now the government sends him one every year. His tax information is not very complicated, so he can do his taxes himself. He will need a document from his employer called a T4 (discussed below) and the receipts from his charitable donations, his adult education, and his RRSP.

Taxes

The four main types of Canadian taxes are income tax, the goods and services tax (GST), sales tax, and property tax. Income tax and the GST are federal taxes; sales tax is provincial; and property tax is municipal (city or township).

Income Tax

Income tax is the share of the cost of government programs and services that is paid by those who earn income. Federal government expenses include Parliament, federal programs such as the military, and payments on the national debt, as well as many social programs.

For all provinces except Quebec, the federal government also collects the provincial income taxes, and distributes them to the provinces. (Quebec collects its personal income tax). Provincial governments spend tax money mainly on health, social welfare, education, and payments on the provincial debt.

When Lawrence gets his pay, he has already paid his income tax. His employer deducts it and sends it directly to the federal government.

Businesses also pay income tax but in a different way than Lawrence, an employee, pays his. Because a business (a sole proprietorship, partnership, or corporation) cannot determine in advance how much it will earn, it usually pays every three months (quarterly installments), based on how much it earned in the previous tax year.

Individual taxpayers like Lawrence must send the Canada Customs and Revenue Agency (CCRA) an income tax return each year. This return, called a T1, tells the government the taxpayer's income (sometimes called revenue) for the previous year. The return must be filed by April 30.

Lawrence is careful, so he gets his return in on time. He uses the figures that his employer gives him on a document called a T4. (See Figure 10-8.) Figure 10-9 shows key figures on his return.

Income from all sources includes not only salary but also commissions, dividends from stocks, or interest received from deposits. Lawrence's sources of income are salary ($60 000) and the interest portion of his $29 000 savings for a house ($1396.79). The figure for all sources of income that Lawrence must report is the line called **total income**.

Income tax deductions are expenses that Lawrence is entitled to subtract from his income. Lawrence does not have child care expenses, moving expenses, or the extra expenses of living in the far North, which are three examples of allowable expenses. He did, however, invest $2400 in RRSPs, as we saw earlier. So he enters the RRSP information in that line. His total income ($61 396.79) minus his deductions

Figure 10-8

Lawrence's T4 for his 2000 tax return. This form shows that Lawrence has already paid federal tax of $14 637.95, as well as mandatory deductions for Canada Pension Plan and Employment Insurance.

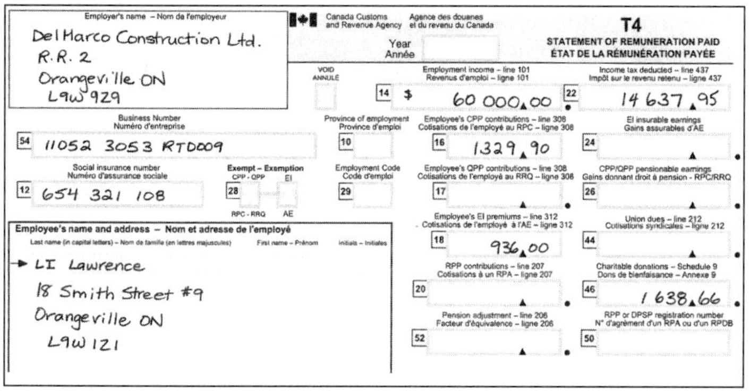

($2400) gives his *net income* ($58 996.79). Because Lawrence has no additional deductions to declare, his net income is his **taxable income**.

Canada has a graduated tax system, which means that the more money Lawrence earns, the higher the percentage of his income he will be expected to pay in taxes.

However, Lawrence does not pay taxes on this amount of $58 996.79. He now applies *tax credits* to his total tax payable. A **tax credit** is an amount of money that can be deducted from tax payable.

Note the difference between tax deductions and tax credits. Tax deductions are deducted from total income in order to determine taxable income, while tax credits are deducted from tax payable.

Lawrence is allowed a basic tax credit of $7 231 for himself on his 2000 return. If he had a dependant spouse or child, or if he were over 65 years old or severely disabled, he would receive additional tax credits.

Lawrence also receives federal credits for his CPP and EI payments, charitable donations, and adult education expense. The amount of these credits is subtracted from his total tax payable, according to formulas supplied on the tax form.

Property Tax

The federal government and provincial governments raise money primarily through income taxes, as discussed in the previous section. But the local level of government, municipal government, does not raise money in this way. Instead, municipal government raises money from *property tax*. **Property tax** is the tax that property owners pay to cover the cost of municipal services, such as maintenance of roads, snow removal, electricity and water, garbage collection, and sewers. Owners of residences (places where people live) pay realty tax. Businesses pay realty tax plus business tax, so they actually pay more. Renters pay property tax too—it is one of the expenses that are built into their rent. One of the most important purposes of property taxes is to finance the elementary and secondary school systems.

Biz.Bites

Here are the tax brackets for an Ontario resident for 2000:

If you make		Federal	Ontario
$30 004 or less	you pay	17%	+6.37%
$30 004 to $60,009	you pay	25%	+9.62%
over $60 009	you pay	29%	+11.16%

Lawrence's Final Tax Figure

Total Income		
Employment income	$ 60 000.00	
Interest Income	1 396.79	
TOTAL INCOME		**$ 61 396.79**
Net Income		
RRSP Deduction		$ 2 400.00
TAXABLE INCOME		**$ 58 996.79**
Tax paid		$ 14 637.95
Tax owed		
(after credits are subtracted)		$ 13 704.19
Tax refund		**$ 933.76**

Figure 10-9 Lawrence's taxable income is $58 996.79. He paid $14 637.95 in taxes. He only owed $13 704.19, so he is entitled to a refund of $933.76.

Property Taxes pay for

- Ambulance Services
- Animal control – dog and cat licences
- Building permits and inspections
- Construction and maintenance of roads, sidewalks, and sewers
- Fire protection and prevention
- Garbage and recycling collection
- Libraries
- Parks – day camps
- Planning services
- Police protection
- Public health services
- Recreation programs – children's and seniors' programs
- Snow and sidewalk clearing
- Street lighting
- Transit, including bus and streetcar shelters

Figure 10-10
Here are some of the services that property taxes pay for. If your municipality did not provide the services, what would your quality of life be like?

Different municipalities levy different amounts of property tax, depending on the number of services they provide and the cost of the services (See Figure 10-10). In general, bigger, more expensive properties pay more tax. If a property owner improves the property in a way that increases its market value, property taxes will increase proportionately. The municipality also collects taxes on behalf of the Board of Education.

Sales Tax

Whenever you make retail purchases in most parts of Canada, you must pay **sales taxes**. There are two types of sales taxes, provincial sales taxes (PST) and the federal Goods and Services Tax (GST). (The GST was introduced in 1991, to help pay down Canada's national debt.) These taxes are a percentage of the purchase price collected by the seller on behalf of the provincial or federal government. The PST is charged only on goods, whereas the GST is charges on goods and most services. In some provinces, the GST is calculated on the cost of the goods without the PST and in others it is calculated on the cost of the goods together with the PST. The seller who has collected the tax money for the government must then remit the sales tax, or send it in at regular intervals. There are some exceptions to these taxes. For example, dental care is exempt from the GST.

Licencing

Another way that governments raise money is through the sale of licences. A resident of a province is required to purchase a driver's licence if he or she drives a motor vehicle on public roadways. The owner of a vehicle driven on public roadways must also purchase a licence plate for the motor vehicle. Liquor licences, and hunting, fishing, and firearms licences may also be required, depending on the province and the circumstances. Municipalities sell dog and cat licences as well. Licencing is a form of taxation.

Biz.Bites

According to Statistics Canada, the proportion of households with a cellular phone increased to 32% in 1999 from 26% in 1998. Average spending on computer equipment and supplies in 1999 for households reporting, was about $920.

Other Expenses

After taxes, households pay for the expenses of food, shelter, clothing, personal care items, transportation, utilities, entertainment, and savings from their income. We looked at Lawrence's expenses earlier in this chapter in a very general way. Here are things Lawrence has learned.

Be careful about hidden costs. Sometimes it does not appear that a household is paying for something when it really is. For example, some households' utilities are included in their rent. That does not mean that the household is not paying for utilities. It means that the property owner is including an estimated utilities figure in the rent. The property owner's figure could be higher or lower than the true expense. There may be no simple way of knowing. A business proverb says, "There is no such thing as a free lunch." In situations where people think they are not paying, they may really be paying more in hidden costs.

Needs are not flexible but wants are. Household expenses are based on both needs and wants. For example, if a household of eight orders pizza, the expense can be eight times the cost of a single person ordering pizza. However, the household of eight might decide to make stew and biscuits instead, and spend only twice as much as one person ordering pizza.

When households try to save money or economize, they usually reduce the amount of money spent to satisfy wants. Often, the reason for saving money is to acquire something that is of greater value to them. For example, Lawrence may economize by not eating out if he wants to buy a house.

If you own more you must spend more. Sometimes, when people acquire a higher income or more property, their needs increase as well as their wants. For example, Lawrence does not buy insurance on his belongings because they are not valuable. But if he buys a house, he will have to buy insurance because he will own a valuable building. He may suddenly need to finance expensive repairs like a new roof. He won't be able to manage without budgeting and planning. You will learn more about personal budgeting and financial planning in Chapter 11.

How do your personal expenses compare?

- Households spent an estimated $6100 on food, up 3 percent from 1998. This includes spending on restaurant meals.

- Spending on clothing increased 6 percent to an average of $2330, mostly owing to an increase in spending on women's and girls' wear.

- Amounts spent by all household members on personal care services (but not supplies and equipment) such as hair grooming, facials, manicures, and tanning salons increased 4 percent from 1998 to an average of $370.

Source: Statistics Canada, *The Daily*, December 12, 2000

Figure 10-11 How do these findings compare with your personal expenses? Do you think Canadians could have spent their money more wisely in 1999? What advice would you give?

Check Your Understanding

Knowledge/Understanding

1 Distinguish between tax deductions and tax credits.
2 Name five services that municipal governments are responsible for.

Thinking/Inquiry

3 Identify possible sources of hidden costs in the following offers: (a) Complete all-in-one package vacation. (b) Parking free with your rent. (c) Third pair half price if you buy two pairs at the regular price.

Communication

4 Pierre and Pam are talking. Pierre complains that his take-home pay was only $1000 for the two-week pay period, even though he actually earned close to $1800 during this time. "What happens to all my money?" he wants to know. "I get nothing out of it; I feel like I am throwing it away." In the role of Pam, explain to Pierre what he gets for his tax dollars.

Application

5 Obtain an income tax return (a T1). Examine it and note the following: Which section would Lawrence fill out if he owned his own unincorporated business? What kinds of expenses does that section require information about?

Making Effective Purchasing Decisions

Early in 2001, Lawrence decided to buy a house. Two events spurred him to make this decision. His parents offered to lend him $15 000 that he did not have to repay for 10 years. If he added that to his own savings of $29 000, Lawrence had $44 000. Second, mortgage interest rates had dropped.

"Once you have paid for the house, you don't have to pay anybody for the right to live there," his mother said, "If you rent, you are going to pay $750 a month for the rest of your life."

In the areas near Lawrence's work sites, $44 000 was not nearly enough to buy a house. A house cost more like $200 000, mostly because land is very valuable in a growing urban area. Should Lawrence just keep saving until he has that much money? That would take a long time. And house prices might rise while he saved. In Lawrence's area, house prices had tripled since 1970. The trend in house prices varies across Canada, as Figure 10-12 shows, but Lawrence's community wasn't unusual.

Instead Lawrence chose to take out a **mortgage** (loan for a house or business) to buy the house. That means that he would use the $44 000

House Price in Canadian Cities, 1961 and 1999

City	Median House Value 1961	Median House Value 1999	Percent increase
Toronto	$17 301	$249 972	336
Vancouver	$13 932	$200 559	334
London	$13 128	$146 542	237
Windsor	$10 349	$109 864	220
Halifax	$14 716	$ 95 143	95
Quebec	$13 673	$ 85 374	88
Canada	$11 021	$115 027	215

as a **down payment**, and a bank would lend him the rest. He would then pay back the mortgage loan, making a payment each month for a number of years. When he paid off the loan, he would own the house outright.

It was a good time to look: house prices were not rising, and mortgage interest rates of about 6.5 percent per year were available.

Lawrence knew that buying a house is a big decision, and he wanted to choose the right one. He made a list of his seven criteria for effective purchasing decisions to help him make a good decision. DelMarco used this method when buying new equipment and commercial buildings. Industry experts said that good decisions were one of the reasons for DelMarco's business success, so Lawrence reasoned that it would work for him.

Figure 10-12 The percent increase in this chart takes into account the difference in the cost of living between 1961 and 1999.

1. Money Available

First Lawrence needed to be sure he could get a mortgage. This is called getting pre-approved. It would be risky to try to buy a house if he was not sure that he had the money available. He had to know in advance how much money he could borrow.

He researched financial institutions for a competitive interest rate on mortgages. He discovered several things. Because he was considered a good financial risk, banks were competing for his business; they felt sure he would pay back his loan. He was considered a good risk because he had $44 000 down payment, an RRSP, a salary of $60 000 a year, and a ten-year job history with a well-established company.

Lawrence was glad to hear he qualified for a mortgage of about $180 000. He now knew how much he could pay: about $224 000 (his down payment plus the mortgage loan, added together). Each month he would pay approximately $1170 for 25 years until the mortgage was paid off. He could afford this amount if he was more careful with his income. For example, he could start taking his lunch to work instead of eating out every day.

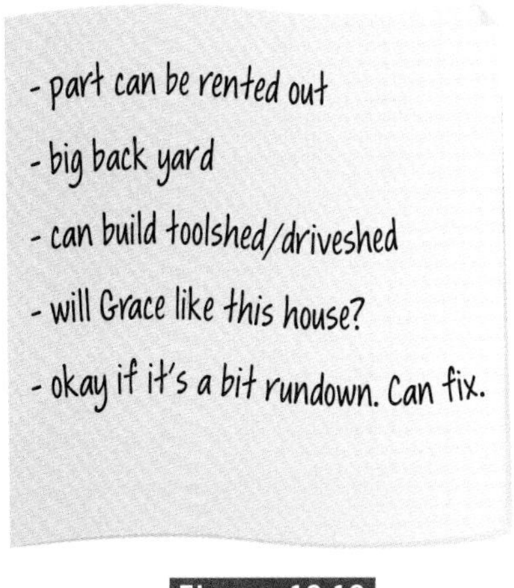

- part can be rented out
- big back yard
- can build toolshed/driveshed
- will Grace like this house?
- okay if it's a bit rundown. Can fix.

Figure 10-13 Lawrence started by writing down his goals and concerns.

2. Cost

Lawrence's friend Burt, an administrative assistant, said Lawrence also needed to think about the costs involved. The costs, Burt explained, were the monthly expenses that Lawrence would have to pay to keep up the house. Wouldn't he regret paying $1170 on the mortgage, plus utilities of $380, maintenance costs of about $200, and property taxes of $280 every month, for a total of $2030 per month? That did not even include the cost of improvements and renovations. When you figured all the costs in, said Burt, Lawrence was getting in over his head.

But Lawrence had thought carefully about the costs. He planned to buy an older house and fix it up, using his construction knowledge. He knew where to get recycled materials cheap. He planned to put in a legal basement apartment. Because friends would help him on weekends and after work, he could keep costs down. He knew that the rental income of about $500 per month would pay part of his costs.

Lawrence also pointed out that he would no longer have some of his current costs, such as rental expense of $750 per month.

He had already decided not to buy his own truck for a while; he used a company truck for work and was able to rent or pool expenses at other times. He showed Burt an item he had clipped from the newspaper on the high cost of driving.

Burt agreed that vehicles were expensive, but said he could never get along without his status car. He preferred to continue renting an apartment, and said that if he bought anything, it would be a condo downtown. But for now he wants to have fun with his money.

3. Buyer Behaviour

The friends' different outlooks are an example of how people's wants and needs affect their buying decisions or buyer behaviour. Lawrence viewed a house as a benefit while Burt viewed it as a burden. Lawrence needs to know about buyer behaviour so he can predict who might want to compete with him for a house and maybe bid the price up.

Advertising influences buying behaviour. Burt had seen a glossy brochure showing beautiful loft condominiums full of attractive people lounging by a pool, or eating desserts at a party. Because he hates the thought of mowing lawns or shovelling snow, he is attracted to the condo lifestyle. Thousands of people agree with him. They won't compete with

Lawrence for a house. Therefore, Lawrence doesn't need to worry about competition from them. Lawrence needs to be aware of those other buyers who would look for an older house to fix up.

Although Burt's buyer behaviour differs from Lawrence's, he will have the same challenges if he decides to buy a condo. He too must make an effective purchasing decision. Both of them will need to remember an old business rule—*caveat emptor*, a Latin saying that means, "Let the buyer beware."

Why does the buyer need to beware? Advertisers are only required to make truthful statements. They do not have to explain the disadvantages of an option, product, or service. Nor does a salesperson need to know whether a decision is right for the customer. It is the customer's job to find out whether a buying choice is right, and to learn about any disadvantages that may affect him or her.

Figure 10-14 An older home that needs work may offer good value to a buyer with know-how.

4. Quality

Lawrence had concerns about some of the decisions he would have to make. While he trusted his own judgment on the overall quality of construction in houses, there were many areas in which he was not an expert. He would certainly have to buy his tenant a fridge, but knew little about refrigeration technology. How would he distinguish a reliable refrigerator from one that would require many costly repairs?

Lawrence knew that, as a rule, if he paid more he would get higher quality. But he only needed a certain level of quality. Beyond that, paying for higher quality would be a waste. For example, he did not want to pay for an ice-cube maker.

He might rely on buying a trusted brand name. But he knew that some large department stores put their own brand name on a product manufactured by a large brand-name firm. Often, the store's brand name sells for less.

Web Connect

www.school.mcgrawhill.ca/resources/
A number of consumer organizations will give you unbiased information on products. For example, you can search on topics (for example, milk or sports utility vehicles) at the site of Consumers Union, a non-profit American consumer organization, or at Consumers' Association of Canada/Association des consommateurs du Canada.

5. Comparison Shopping and Product Information

Comparing the products and services available to you in terms of features, quality, and price is called *comparison shopping*. Comparison shopping is particularly important when making large purchases like houses. If Lawrence's choice turns out to be wrong for him, selling it again and buying a new one would be expensive and time-consuming.

But how can Lawrence compare houses? It's not like comparing snacks. Each home has a thousand different details to consider. One way is to use a comparison matrix. Figure 10-15 shows the matrix Lawrence drew up.

Lawrence expected to eventually narrow his search down to about three houses, and then rank them from 0 to 5, according to his needs. Zero would mean that the house didn't meet his expectations in a category. Five would mean it exceeded his expectations.

Lawrence then got down to finding a good house. He was interested in an area where he could get a good-sized house for his money. He got on the Internet, clicked on the Multiple Listing Service (MLS) through the local real estate board, and searched out houses in a city north of Toronto. The MLS showed most of the houses for sale, usually with a photo and a description of their features, as well as their price.

For two weeks he walked around a pleasant suburban area, visiting houses that were for sale. He looked for houses that were somewhat run down—but not too badly.

Comparison Shopping Matrix

Criteria	House A	House B	House C
Structurally sound (according to structural engineer)			
High basement ceiling (for apartment)			
Bathroom in basement, so no need to install pipes			
Easy to ensure two separate basement apartment entrances (safety requirement)			
Convenient to shopping and main roads			
Safe neighbourhood			

Figure 10-15

Here is Lawrence's comparison shopping matrix for his top six categories. He will fill it in when he visits houses. What is Lawrence's major concern? Why does his list of needs not mention an elementary school? Why does it mention "convenient to shopping and main roads"?

6. Service

Like most home buyers, Lawrence needed the services of a real estate agent. He met Fatima Akbarali at an open house. An open house is an event at which prospective buyers can see the interior of a house.

Like all real estate agents, Fatima was licenced to help people buy and sell houses. She impressed Lawrence because she seemed more interested in helping him find the right house than making a quick sale. For example, she told him that, given his needs and wants, he was looking in the wrong neighbourhood. There were lots of things Lawrence could do with a house, she said, but moving it to another neighbourhood was not one of them.

She recommended a nearby urban area. Young people just starting in the work force in a new commercial development might want to rent his apartment. Although he would have to buy a smaller and older place for his money, it would probably retain or increase its value better than houses in the new suburban area in which he was looking.

Comparison Shopping Matrix – Filled in

Criteria	House A	House B	House C
Structurally sound (according to structural engineer)	4	5	3
High basement ceiling (for apartment)	4	5	5
Bathroom in basement, so no need to install pipes	5	1	5
Easy to ensure two separate basement apartment entrances (safety requirement)	5	2	1
Convenient to shopping and main roads	4	3	1
Safe neighbourhood	3	4	3
	25	20	18

Figure 10-16 The houses were rated from 1 to 5 on each quality. Which of these houses do you think Lawrence should buy?

Several more weeks of searching with Fatima followed, and soon Lawrence had filled in his matrix (see Figure 10-16).

7. Warranties and Guarantees

Lawrence hired a DelMarco structural engineer, who had a small business on the side, to do an inspection and tell him if there were any structural flaws that he hadn't noticed. After receiving the generally favourable report, Fatima told Lawrence to offer the seller (vendor) less than what he was asking, because he had installed plumbing pipes himself. Therefore no *warranties* were available.

A **warranty** provides after-sales service on a product for a specified period of time. Some new product warranties will state that the owner can bring back defective merchandise and have it replaced. Others will supply labour and parts during a specified number of years of ownership of the product.

There were also no *guarantees* that the vendor had done the plumbing according to government or industry specifications. A **guarantee** is a formal promise or assurance, especially that an obligation will be fulfilled or that goods are of a specified quality and durability. Lawrence asked the vendor to sign a guarantee that he had installed copper plumbing pipes.

If Lawrence discovered, when renovating, that some pipes were not copper, he could sue the vendor. If Lawrence hadn't required this guarantee, and the pipes turned out not to be copper, he could not sue.

Lawrence's offer of $220 000 for the house was accepted.

Check Your Understanding

Knowledge/Understanding

1 What is an advertiser required to do? What is an advertiser not required to do?

2 What is the difference between a warranty and a guarantee?

Thinking/Inquiry

3 Compare your buyer behaviour for snacks with that of other members of a small group. Ranked out of five, how big a role do the following qualities play? Price? Nutrition? Brand name? Another issue (explain)?

Communication

4 Using the results from question 3, prepare two advertisements—one that appeals to your buyer behaviour for a snack and one that appeals to a buyer whose score is the opposite of yours. (If you gave economical price a 5, the other buyer gave it a 1.)

Application

5 Develop a comparison matrix for three brands of an article of clothing you wear. Work with a partner to develop five points of comparison that are relevant to the product category, and then rate the brands. Declare a winner.

Skills
Appendix

brainstorming

Products and Services of Financial Institutions

Financial institutions are companies that are permitted to hold savings deposits, offer loans and mortgages, issue credit ratings, exchange currency, and offer stocks and bonds for sale. These institutions include Canadian and foreign banks, trust and mortgage loan companies, credit unions (in Quebec *caisses populaires*), life insurance companies, pension plans, investment funds, and securities dealers.

Banking

Banks are financial institutions that use money deposited by customers for lending and investment. Banks are divided into two groups: The Schedule I banks offer a wide variety of banking services, especially to consumers. This is called *personal banking*. The Schedule I banks are nicknamed the "Big Six." They are The Royal Bank, TD Canada Trust, The Bank of Nova Scotia, CIBC, The Bank of Montreal, and the National Bank. These account for about 90 percent of all bank assets in the country. In 2000, that added up to over $1.3 *trillion dollars*.

Schedule II banks, such as the State Bank of India and Hongkong Bank of Canada, seek mostly business customers. A business's banking is called *commercial banking*.

Recently, *virtual banks* have also come to Canada. A virtual bank has no physical branches; instead, it operates electronically and by telephone. ING Direct, a Dutch bank, is an example. Most banks today are fully equipped for electronic transactions, via automated banking machines (ABMs), also known as automated teller machines (ATMs), and debit cards. It is possible to use many of your institution's services daily without ever setting foot in a branch.

Trust companies offer services similar to those of banks. In addition, they operate pension funds and act as transfer agents for company stocks, as trustees for company bond issues, and as administrators for estates and trusts.

Credit unions offer services similar to those offered by banks and trust companies. Unlike

> **Biz.Bites**
>
> Early in Canada's history, banks, trust companies, the insurance industry, and the securities industry could only sell certain products and services. For example, banks were not allowed to sell insurance or own securities companies. In 1992, new legislation let them offer services that other types of institutions sold. Then banks started to buy securities companies.

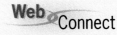

Web Connect

www.school.mcgrawhill.ca/resources/

Have a look at the products and interest rates offered by the Big Six Canadian banks. Do they differ in type or emphasis? Type of offer?

banks and trust companies, however, they are non-profit organizations. They have owner-members who invest a small amount of money to join. (See Chapter 2.)

Savings Accounts

Most bank customers need a personal savings account and a personal chequing account. A savings account is a bank account that pays interest. The customer is expected to use the account to save money, and to write few or no cheques on it. Millions of Canadians' savings accounts together provide a large pool of **capital**, or money available for investment or lending. Financial institutions lend this money to businesses and consumers if they seem able to pay the money back.

Financial institutions make money primarily in two ways: through service charges and by charging interest on loans. The institution charges more interest on its loans than it pays to its customers. The difference, after expenses and taxes, is the bank's profit. The bank is said to be making money on the *spread* (a term for the difference between interest charged and interest paid). Compare the Savings Rate (interest paid on savings accounts) with either the Prime Lending Rate or the Conventional Five-Year Mortgage Rate in Figure 10-17.

Chequing Account

A chequing account is a bank account against which cheques may be written. It is used mainly for paying bills. Bills can be paid by writing paper cheques or by using **pre-authorized payments**. When you agree to preauthorized payments, you allow a company, government, or charity to take money on a regular basis from your chequing account. This is a convenient arrangement if you are making the same payment each month. Increasingly, bank customers pay bills via the Internet using PC banking, but the principle of the chequing account remains the same.

Chequing accounts generally pay little or no interest. Most charge transaction fees (service charges). As a result, bank customers try to keep just enough in the account to pay their usual monthly expenses, plus a little more for safety. Accidentally writing cheques that "bounce" (are not honoured by your bank because there is not enough money in your account) is not only embarrassing but can cause people to lose confidence in you.

Persons who write cheques for which they know they do not have the funds are considered guilty of *fraud*. Fraud occurs when a person

Average Annual Canadian Interest Rates

Rate	Prime Lending Rate	Savings Rate	5-Year Mortgage Rate
1988	10.83	5.69	11.65
1989	13.33	8.08	12.06
1990	14.06	8.77	13.35
1991	9.94	4.48	11.13
1992	7.48	2.27	9.51
1993	6.10	0.77	8.78
1994	7.25	0.50	9.53
1995	8.65	0.50	9.16
1996	6.06	0.50	7.93
1997	4.96	0.50	7.07
1998	6.60	0.24	5.47

Source: Bank of Canada

deceives another for financial gain. This serious criminal offence can result in a jail sentence, even if the sum of money involved is small.

Current accounts are a form of chequing account used by businesses and other organizations, such as student councils. They are strictly chequing accounts that pay no interest. Fees are charged for all cheques, and a monthly statement is issued, with cashed cheques included. The current account appeals to organizations because they need a record of all money deposited and spent that can be easily examined when needed.

Figure 10-17 Notice how average savings account interest rates fell drastically around 1993, and continued to be low. Do you think the banks were making a good spread? Many bank customers look for better interest rates by using interest-bearing investments such as Guaranteed Investment Certificates (GICs). You will learn more about GICs in this chapter and Chapter 11.

Mortgage Loans

One of the most important functions of a bank or trust company in Canada is to lend money for mortgages, so bank customers can buy property. Mortgages are loans for property with very long terms—usually 25 years. However, because mortgage loan rates change over the years, mortgages can usually be renegotiated after three to five years, depending on the agreement. Earlier, we learned that Lawrence Li needed a mortgage loan to buy a house. Two basic types of mortgage are available in Canada: Closed mortgages cannot be repaid or renegotiated before the term without a penalty. Often, the homeowner may make some extra payments, but only certain amounts or on agreed dates. Open mortgages can be repaid or renegotiated at any time, without penalty.

Closed mortgages are usually offered at a lower interest rate than open mortgages for the same term. Lawrence Li chose a closed mortgage to save on interest. But some bank customers prefer open mortgages. For example, Sophia DelMarco, Lawrence's boss, has an income that changes from year to year, depending on the profits of her business. After a good year, she will make extra payments on her mortgage. She hopes to make up for her higher interest rate by paying the mortgage off faster. If she can, she will not have to pay as much total interest on the loan.

When Lawrence takes out a mortgage, the house itself is used as *collateral* against the loan. Collateral is something of value that the lender can seize if payments are not made. The house is the only valuable thing Lawrence owns, so it must serve as collateral for the mortgage.

The rate of default (non-payment) of mortgages in Canada is very low. As a result, financial institutions consider mortgages very safe investments. Therefore they have the lowest interest rate of any loan made by a lending institution, lower, for example than car or vacation loans. You will learn more about loans in Chapter 12.

Investment Services

Banks and other financial institutions provide a variety of investments. One important type is the guaranteed investment certificate (GIC), usually sold by a bank or trust company. A **guaranteed investment certificate** guarantees a fixed interest rate on a sum of money deposited at the financial institution for a fixed term. The interest is generally higher than what the same institution would pay on a savings account.

Figure 10-18 Homeowners can save thousands of dollars if they are willing to take the time to research mortgage offers.

The reason that the interest rate is higher is that the money cannot be withdrawn from a true GIC before the term is up. This investment is suitable for customers who know that they will not need the money until then. GICs are a staple of Registered Retirement Savings Plans because RRSPs cannot be used until the customer is a senior citizen. The money that banks lock into GICs is then made available for mortgage loans. You will learn more about GICs in Chapter 11.

Another type of investment is the mutual fund. A **mutual fund** is a fund in which the contributions of many individuals are combined and invested by a professional fund manager in a variety of stocks and bonds. The profits are split according to the number of units each investor owns. Mutual funds are often chosen by customers who do not have much knowledge of the stock or bond market. The risk of making a bad choice is reduced because the money manager invests in a wide range of funds. You will learn more about mutual funds in Chapter 11. Many mutual funds can also be registered as an RRSP.

Safety Deposit Boxes

Another service that financial institutions provide is the rental of safety deposit boxes for the safekeeping of important documents or other

Biz.Bites

Why do experts say you should store your household insurance policy in a safety deposit box, *not* in the house?

valuables. Jewellery, stock certificates, bonds, insurance policies, mortgage documents, deeds, passports, or rare collectibles can be stored in safety deposit boxes in the vault of a bank or trust company, usually for a small annual fee.

Travellers' Cheques and Currency Exchange

Although many people use credit and debit cards when travelling, *traveller's cheques* are still popular. They are a form of international currency that can be purchased from a financial institution. The traveller does not need to carry a lot of cash because traveller's cheques can be used like cash, but with this difference: They will be replaced if lost or stolen. A financial institution will also provide currency exchange services. Travellers can buy foreign currency or sell it in exchange for Canadian currency. Sometimes the institution can do the exchange immediately. But for currency that is rarely exchanged or that changes value often, the transaction may take a few days.

Credit Cards

Banks and other financial institutions also sponsor *credit cards*. A credit card is a card issued by a financial institution that allows you to obtain goods or services on credit. The reason you do not have to pay at the time of purchase is that your promise to pay later is accepted by the institution that gave you the card.

If you pay the bill before a certain date, the credit card costs you nothing except, perhaps, a small annual fee. But if you do not pay the bill before that date, the card turns into a temporary, expensive loan. Interest charges on credit card balances are very high, in some cases 2 percent per month. That is over 24 percent per year of compound interest on the unpaid balance. You will learn more about credit and credit cards in Chapter 12.

Check Your Understanding

Knowledge/Understanding

1 Explain what a guaranteed investment certificate is.
2 Explain what a credit union is.

Thinking/Inquiry

3 Ayesha is a sales representative who works on commission. Her income varies between $40 000 and $70 000 per year. She could get a mortgage loan from her bank to buy a condo at 6 percent per year closed or 8 percent open. Based on what you have learned so far, which is better for Ayesha? Explain.

4 Ayesha accepts the position of national sales trainer and makes a salary of $55 000 per year with no commission. Faced with this change, which mortgage option is better for her? Explain.

Communication

5 Debate the following point: RRSPs are only good for older people. Young people should not tie up their money when they might need it for businesses, homes, and travel. Be sure to use what you have learned in Chapters 9 and 10 to frame your arguments.

The Day Business Left Town

When a community in a remote area loses population, businesses may not survive. Then the need to find goods and services forces the remaining residents to leave. The town becomes a *ghost town*.

Many Ontario towns have become ghost towns due to changes in economics that forced businesses to close. An example is Andrewsville, close to the Nicholson Locks in the Rideau River. It did well in the 19th century, but died when the railway passed it by. Another is Byng Inlet on Georgian Bay. Once a thriving town, it was doomed when its single industry, the lumber mill, closed. Byng Inlet is now used as a recreation area by Georgian Bay residents.

This fate threatens the town of Clearwater (population 65), in an agricultural community near the southern border of Manitoba. The population has been dwindling for years, and the town has already lost its hardware store. In 2001 came word that the owners of the grocery store were retiring. The nearest supermarket is 100 kilometres away. Residents would have to make a 200-kilometre round trip every week for perishables such as milk and vegetables, even during the winter.

Because residents did not want to abandon the town, they decided to get together and buy the grocery store. Forty-five residents got together and raised $30 000 in 24 hours.

One shareholder is Heather Gardiner, who invested $650. "It's important to me to try and keep the life of our community going," she explained. Shareholders volunteered their labour to renovate the store by adding a bakery and deli.

Teri Richard, who manages the store, is learning from scratch because she has no experience in the grocery business. If the venture succeeds, she will offer jobs to others. The owners of the business will also get dividends on their shares.

(Source: Written by CBC News Online staff Web posted, May 13, 2001).

ACTIVITIES

1 Why do you think the business is called Solo Grocery, even though there are 45 shareholders?

2 As a shareholder, would you encourage high, low, or medium prices for the groceries? Explain.

3 Think of a suitable slogan for Solo Grocery. Prepare a logo to go with it.

Chapter Review

Points to Remember

- Most Canadians have mandatory deductions taken out of their gross income.

- Disposable income is left over after taxes and deductions; discretionary income is left over after meeting basic needs.

- Many Canadians save large amounts of money for a down payment on a home.

- Many Canadians put money in registered retirement savings plans (RRSPs).

- Donating to charities and cultural organizations is an investment in society. The donations can also help lower income taxes.

- Four main types of taxes collected in Canada are income tax, the Goods and Services Tax (GST), sales tax, and property tax.

- Effective purchasing decisions consider factors such as money available, cost, buyer behaviour, quality, comparison shopping and product information, service, and guarantees and warranties.

- Financial institutions offer savings and chequing accounts, mortgages and loans, investment services, credit cards, safety deposit boxes, traveller's cheques, and currency exchange.

Activities

Knowledge/Understanding

1 What tax benefit does the federal government offer to encourage Canadians to save for their retirement? What type of tax benefit is it?

2 What tax benefit does the government offer to encourage Canadians to continue to educate themselves? What type of tax benefit is it?

3 Explain how you would apply the seven criteria of effective purchasing decisions to shopping for a new winter coat.

4 What is the consequence of not paying off the balance on your credit card by the due date indicated on the credit card statement?

Thinking/Inquiry

1   Go to the Web site of a local real estate board or company. Find a couple of houses in your community that are offered at an average price for your area. Compare their prices with similar houses in two communities in other parts of Canada. Working with a partner, look up information about the two communities. Brainstorm reasons for the difference in prices.

Skills
A p p e n d i x

researching

2   Next to a house, a motor vehicle (car, truck, or van) is the biggest single purchase item for most buyers. List five reputable sources of information that compare competitive models. Your sources can be books, magazines, or Web sites, as long as they are independent (not sponsored by a manufacturer or dealer).

Communication

1   Write a script for a short play (no more than 10 minutes) on an incident that occurs as a result of one of the following situations:
    *   There are no longer charities or cultural organizations in Canada. There are still government services but private citizens do not help others or develop our culture.
    *   Municipal government vanishes. Because citizens refuse to pay taxes, they do not get services.
    Perform your play with a group, if asked to do so.

2   With a partner, role play a dialogue between Lawrence Li and a financial counsellor. Lawrence has consulted the counsellor because he wonders how to make a wiser use of his discretionary income, now that he has bought a house. Perform your dialogue. Use your own experience of living within a budget.

Skills
A p p e n d i x

oral presentations

Application

1   Obtain an income tax form (T1) and accompanying information booklet and study it. Answer the following questions:
    *   Lawrence was given a document from his bank that stated the exact amount of interest he earned on his savings in 2000. What is that document called? What is he supposed to do with it?
    *   If Lawrence has a tenant, will the rent that the tenant pays him be considered income? Where does Lawrence enter the information about rent?

How You Manage Your Money

Specific Expectations

After studying this chapter, you will be able to

- **explain how fluctuations in interest rates affect saving, investing, and spending decisions**

- **identify various types of investment alternatives**

- **compare the benefits of saving and investing**

- **demonstrate an understanding of the factors that will affect the value of money over time**

- **demonstrate personal-budgeting and financial-planning skills, and produce a personal budget and a financial plan, using appropriate software**

In Chapter 9 you learned about acquiring money through income. In Chapter 10 you learned about options for saving, investing, spending, and donating that income. In this chapter you will learn to decide how much to save, invest, and spend of that income, and which methods to use. This process of deciding is called managing your money or financial management. It includes understanding how to use your money to make more money. You will learn how economic factors such as interest rates and the future value of money affect your financial position. You will also learn the basics of personal budgeting and financial planning, which are essential to effective financial management. When you have a clear grasp of these concepts, you will see why those who make use of financial management techniques can earn more with the same amount of money than those who rely on luck.

The Birth of a Great Small Business

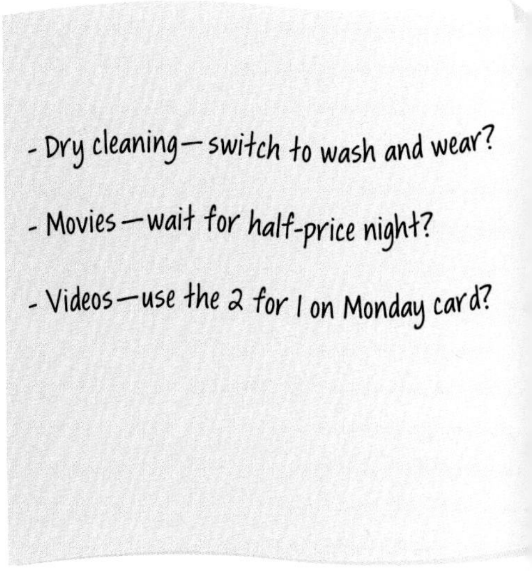

Natasha dived for the empty stool beside her friends, Gina, Anil, and Ella.

"So...what have you been doing lately?" Gina wanted to know. "Your telephone line is always busy."

"I know," Natasha replied. "I got your messages. Sorry I didn't call back. When a person starts a business, it can really take over their life."

"You? A business?" Anil looked really surprised. "Do you have enough experience or capital to start your own florist shop?"

"Well, in the first place, I am not starting a florist shop. I am starting a home-based Web design business. And," turning to Gina, "I was on the Internet, doing my course and looking for ideas."

"I thought you were mad at your boss for making you take that course," Ella said. "You have to attend on your own time."

"Well, I realized later that my boss is actually paying for me to learn something useful, when I would otherwise have to pay myself," Natasha replied. "I'm good at Web design. Here is my strategy: I will do a really good job on the flower shop's Web site—the best in Ottawa! My boss agreed to pay for advanced courses too. It's win-win, you see. Winning a local Web design award would give her free publicity and help my business get started."

"Aren't we getting ahead of ourselves?" asked Anil, "Do small businesses really want all this high-tech stuff?"

"My boss does. She even wants shopping-cart technology so people can order through the site," Natasha replied. "But let me explain my business idea—and my problem."

"My business idea is to put up user-friendly sites for small businesses like my boss's, at a package price they can afford. My problem is, I need about $6000 worth of equipment."

"You don't have much chance on minimum wage," said Ella sadly.

"Let's be creative here!" cried Gina. "She can budget. Reducing expenses is as good as making money. Let's do some figuring. Who's got a clean napkin?"

As you read this chapter, think about the ways in which people can manage their money to help.

- Dry cleaning—switch to wash and wear?

- Movies—wait for half-price night?

- Videos—use the 2 for 1 on Monday card?

Figure 11-1 Managing money includes examining expenses to get the best use from the money.

The Effect of Changes in Interest Rates

As you learned in Chapter 9, interest is the amount of money a financial institution will pay you to keep your money on deposit. To borrowers, the **interest rate** is the rate a financial institution charges for the money it lends. The rate rises and falls (fluctuates), and the changes affect savings, investing, spending, and donating.

What Causes Changes in Interest Rates?

Biz.Bites

The Bank of Canada, Canada's central bank, is the institution that manages our money supply by raising or lowering the bank rate, or interest rate at which it lends money to its members.

A number of circumstances cause interest rates to rise and fall. The most common reason is the health of the economy. When Canada's economy is doing well, a large number of consumers and businesses want to borrow money to improve their lifestyle or expand their operations, so they compete for the money. The Bank of Canada responds by causing interest rates to rise. Thus, if you save your money as the economy moves toward the peak of a business cycle, you will benefit from higher interest rates because you will earn more interest.

By contrast, when Canada's economy is doing poorly—this is called the trough of a business cycle—few people want to borrow money. There is not much competition, and the Bank of Canada makes changes that let interest rates drop. The Bank of Canada does this to encourage borrowing, to stimulate the economy. Thus, if you negotiate a loan during a slow economy, you will benefit from lower interest rates.

The Bank of Canada adjusts interest rates to keep the changes in the business cycle from affecting average Canadians too severely. But it can do only so much. For example, it cannot prevent world-wide economic trends from affecting Canada.

Managing Your Personal Finances When Interest Rates Change

To manage your personal finances effectively, you must understand what changes in interest rates mean to you. High interest rates increase your income from savings and investments. If you save for college, university, or travel, you will want the highest rates available.

But they also increase what you must pay in interest if you borrow money. When interest rates go up, for example, a car will cost you more if you need to borrow in order to buy it. If you have a credit card and don't pay it off each month, you will have to pay more interest.

By contrast, low interest rates decrease your income from savings and investments. But they also decrease what you must pay in interest if you borrow money.

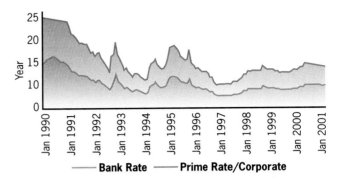

Historical changes in Canada's bank rate

— Bank Rate   — Prime Rate/Corporate

Figure 11-2

The bank rate is the rate the Bank of Canada charges other banks. The prime rate is the rate the banks charge their best customers. What is the relationship?

Effect of Interest Rates on Savings

The interest rate on your savings account isn't fixed. The rate depends on how many people would like to borrow from the financial institution and how the Bank of Canada influences the interest rate.

Savings and Inflation

Inflation refers to an increase in the price of goods and services that occurs as an economy approaches a peak in the business cycle, as discussed above. (See Chapter 3 for details on inflation.) As we will see, one effect of inflation is that it forces financial institutions to pay more to get people to save money.

Consider the following examples: Suppose a dollar you saved in 2000 (a 2000 dollar) will still buy $1.00 worth of goods in 2005. The saver has lost nothing to inflation in the five years that passed. So the interest rate only needs to remain high enough to encourage him or her to save money.

But if, due to inflation, a 2000 dollar will buy only $.90 worth of goods in 2005, then the person who agrees to keep that dollar in the bank must be paid an interest rate high enough to make up for the loss of purchasing power. Otherwise, savers would be smarter to spend the money when they have it.

Suppose that a period of **deflation** (costs and prices fall) occurs. Thus, in 2005, a 2000 dollar buys $1.10 worth of goods. Financial institutions would offer lower interest rates during the period of deflation because money that was saved would increase in value without interest.

Biz.Bites

How do you know you will be able to get money from your financial institution if it is always lending the money? Your financial institution is required to keep enough money on hand so it is available when you need it. Also, the institution is unlikely to be short of money because it is constantly receiving payments, plus interest, on the loans it has made.

Web Connect

www.school.mcgrawhill.ca/resources/

To calculate the effects of inflation on savings and investment, visit the Bank of Canada Web site and use the Investment Calculator.

Historically, Canada has had a lot more inflation than deflation, so financial institutions have had to pay interest rates that are high enough to offset expected inflation.

To summarize, the **future value** of savings is generally assumed to be more than the present value. However, the precise future value depends on inflation and deflation as mirrored in interest rates.

Savings and Future Value

Suppose the interest rate on your savings account drops or increases by 2%? Will that make much difference? First, let's go back and look at Figure 9-4, Maria's yearly compounded 4% interest savings account after 10 years. She ends up with $148.02. A faster way to figure this out is to use the

Future Value Formula

Figure 11-3 If you have access to a spreadsheet or calculator that can provide you with a "to the power of" formula, use it to quickly figure out how much Maria will make in 10 years. Use the following formula, called the future value formula:

$$FV = PV \left((1 + r/n)^{(nt)}\right)$$

Where

FV = future value of the investment after t (t = the number of years you invest the money for)

PV = present value of the investment (how much money you put in, in the first place)

r = annual compound interest rate (expressed as a decimal number)

n = number of times per year the interest is compounded (daily? weekly? monthly?), and

t = term your money is tied up (expressed in years)

Since Maria's account is credited only once a year, the number of **compounding periods** per year, or n, equals 1.

This is how we would plug in Maria's information.

1 FV = future value of the investment after 10 years

2 PV = $100.00 (initial principal put in savings account)

3 r = .04

4 n = 1

5 t = 10 years

Or

$$\$148.02 = 100 \left((1 + .04/1)^{(1 * 10)}\right)$$

Thus, the future value of Maria's $100.00 is $148.02.

Future Value Formula in Figure 11-3. Figure 11-4 shows what happens to Maria's interest income on her savings of $100 for 10 years if the interest rate on her account goes down to 2 percent, or up to 6 percent compounded annually.

Future Value When Interest Rate Changes

Future Value of Maria's $100.00

Present Value	Rate	Future Value	No. of Compounding Periods Per Year	Term
$100.00	0.02	$121.90	1	10
$100.00	0.04	$148.02	1	10
$100.00	0.06	$179.08	1	10

Maria obviously makes a lot more money at a higher interest rate. So she would want to research institutions that offered the best rate.

Figure 11-4
What happens to Maria's savings of $100 for 10 years if the interest rate goes down to 2%, stays at 4%, or goes up to 6%.

Future Value and the Yield from Compound Interest

Suppose Maria's interest rate remains at 4 percent, but the number of compounding periods per year is changed to twice a year or even to every month. The interest she gets as a result of the interest payments being added back into the principal is called the yield.

Future Value When Compounding Periods Increase

Future Value (FV)	Present Value (PV)	Rate ®	Number of Compounding Periods Per Year (n)	Term (t)	Yield
$148.02	$100.00	0.04 (4%)	1	10	4.80%
$148.59	$100.00	0.04 (4%)	2	10	4.86%
$149.08	$100.00	0.04 (4%)	12	10	4.91%

Figure 11-5 Does the number of compounding periods per year make a difference?

Here is the formula for Yield:

$$\text{Yield} = \frac{(FV - PV)/t}{PV} \times 100$$

Where

FV = Future Value

PV = Present Value

t = term

This gives the true yield that the account pays due to compounding. Notice that the greater the number of compounding periods, the higher the yield (Figure 11-5).

Yield isn't significant for savings of $100. But what if the savings account had been $10 000? The difference in the number of compounding periods would have resulted in the difference between $14 908 and $14 802 or $106.

As you can see, both interest rates and compounding periods determine how much money Maria will end up with after 10 years. We will now look at the role that interest rate fluctuations play in determining the performance of investments such as bonds and stocks.

On Investing

Recall that construction superintendent Lawrence Li saved $29 000 in a savings account over a period of 10 years, in order to buy a house. He was getting a good interest rate, but he might have got a better rate by putting his money in a form of investment such as Canada Savings Bonds. Interest rates affect investing just as they do saving.

Interest Rate Fluctuation and Bonds

You will recall from Chapter 9 that governments and corporations issue bonds in order to raise money. The organization pays you a higher interest rate than a savings account would, to use your money for a fixed period. Federal or provincial government bonds are considered a relatively safe investment because Canada is a stable country where governments can raise money to honour their financial commitments through the tax system.

However, fluctuations in interest rates can change the market value of bonds. Suppose Maria has saved $1000 and decides to invest in a 6% government bond, compounding bi-yearly, with a term to maturity of 10 years. We can figure out its future value, using the future value formula given above (Figure 11-5).

Maria has increased her money by 1.8 times and probably stayed well ahead of inflation.

What happens if she needs to sell the bond? In that case, Maria will be competing with other really safe investments that have higher (or lower) interest rates. For example, what if government bond interest rates go up to 7 percent the week after Maria buys her bond? Maria would end up

Biz.Bites

Cash is called a liquid asset because you can spend it at any time. Canada Savings Bonds, provincial savings bonds, and any guaranteed investment certificate (GIC) or bond that ties up your money (has a term) for one year or less, is also referred to as "cash" or "cash equivalent."

Biz.Bites

The financial industry uses many unusual, sometimes humorous terms. Here are some examples:
Air Pocket Stock – A stock that plunges unexpectedly, similar to an airplane which has hit an air pocket
Bear Market – A market that is doing poorly, where investors hold back like a bear staying in its cave
Bottom Fisher – An investor who looks for bargains among stocks whose prices have recently dropped dramatically
Bull Market – A market that is roaring ahead, like a charging bull

FV = future value of the investment after 10 years

PV = $1 000.00 (initial principal invested)

r = .06

n = 2

t = 10 years

Or

$1 000 ((1+.06/2))(2*10) = $1 806.00

Figure 11-6 The future value of Maria's $1000.00 is $1806.00. See Figure 11-3 for the future value formula.

wishing she had waited to buy. Why? Because the value, or true yield, of her bond has gone down.

It is important to understand that if she keeps the bond to maturity Maria will still get the interest and principal promised on the 6 percent bond she bought ($1806). That is a guarantee. The guarantee explains why bonds are considered a safe investment.

But if Maria wants to sell her 10-year bond she has a problem. No one will buy the 6 percent bond from her for $1000 when they could get a $1000 bond paying 7 percent instead. She will have to sell the bond for less than she paid.

The interest rate rule for bonds is this: When interest rates go up, the value of the bonds you own goes down. When interest rates go down, the value of the bonds you own goes up.

Interest Rate Fluctuation and Stocks

Stocks are riskier than bonds because they are tied to the fortunes of companies. As you saw in Chapter 9, people may—or may not—buy clothes from companies like Le Chateau. There is no guarantee. So, if you could get 8 percent interest in a safe investment like a medium-term Government of Canada bond, why risk your money on whether people will buy Le Chateau products?

During periods when the economy features high interest rates, stock prices tend to fall. That is because, for example, people who are not sure whether Le Chateau clothing lines will sell well and keep the company share price high just buy bonds instead.

However, suppose the economy changes and interest rates fall. New bond interest rates drop significantly. Then money flows back to the

Biz.Bites

If Maria is willing to invest her $1000 in a 20-year bond, she might get a higher interest rate than if she agrees to tie up her money for only 10 years. However, she might not. Lenders may think that interest rates are going to fall, or rise, over the next 20 years. But no one really knows what will happen over the long term. For that reason, the interest rates on long-term bonds are figured out differently from short- and medium-term bonds.

stock market. People take a chance on the manufacturer that sells the latest sportswear line if they can see no chance of making a significant amount of money from bonds.

The general interest rate rule for stocks is this: When interest rates go up, the price of stocks goes down. That is because buyers of investments sell stocks to buy new bond issues. When interest rates go down, the price of stocks goes up. Notice that this is the opposite of the general rule for bonds you own. Generally, the small investor is better to buy relatively safe stocks in periods of rising interest rates. But he or she must also be prepared to hang on to stocks over the long term in order to earn income.

In general, the investment market is driven by people's beliefs about products, the interest rate, the future of industries, what demographic trends mean, and many other things. It really comes down to you putting your money on your opinions.

On Spending

Interest rates affect saving and investing. But do they also affect spending? Yes, directly and indirectly.

Most people must go into debt for the biggest purchases they make. Lawrence will need a mortgage to buy his house. Burt got a loan to buy his status car. When interest rates are high, more household income is needed to pay debt. As a result, higher interest rates reduce the income people have available to spend on other items. For example, during the early 1980s when interest rates went as high as 17 percent some homeowners could not afford groceries because the cost of paying their mortgage interest had risen by thousands of dollars per year, but their incomes had not. Many people lost their homes. Review Figure 11-2.

When interest rates are low, consumers spend more on wants (nonessentials) or expensive items. One reason Lawrence decided to buy a house was that mortgage rates had just come down. In fact, he was able to get a mortgage for five years at 6.25 percent. If mortgage rates had been as high as 14 percent (see Figure 10-19 for five-year average Canadian mortgage rates since 1988), Lawrence's monthly mortgage payment would have been closer to $2 118, as opposed to the $1 170 he now pays. This would have meant a lot more "belt-tightening" for Lawrence. How might this have affected his savings and RRSP contributions? He would have been better off to wait to buy a house.

Biz.Bites

Borrowers renewing mortgages in 1996 and 1997 saved over $1.4 billion as a result of declining mortgage rates.

Lawrence's five-year mortgage doesn't mean that he has to have the $176 000 all paid off in five years, but rather that he has to come back to the bank in five years to renegotiate the terms (i.e., interest rate) of the remaining mortgage.

Remember, the interest rate is not in itself good or bad. The wise manager of personal finances knows what the interest rate is and makes decisions accordingly.

Mortgage Rates

Financial Institution	Interest Rate % 3 yr term closed	Interest Rate % 5 yr term closed
Bank of Montreal	7.1	7.5
Bank of Nova Scotia	7.1	7.5
Canadian Imperial Bank of Commerce (CIBC)	7.35	7.75
Duca (credit union)	6.35	6.45
ING Direct	5.95	6.3
President's Choice Financial*	6.74	6.64
Royal Bank	7.1	7.5
TD Canada Trust	7.35	7.75

Figure 11-7 On a single day in May 2001, the following mortgage interest rates were offered by financial institutions. Do tiny differences add up to much on a $100 000 mortgage? Is researching mortgage rates worthwhile? (Note: President's Choice Financial operates from a supermarket, but its services are provided by Canadian Imperial Bank of Commerce.)

Check Your Understanding

Knowledge/Understanding

1 How do interest rate changes affect bonds that an investor already owns? How do they affect new bond issues?

2 How do interest rate changes affect stocks that an investor already owns? How do they affect whether an investor will buy stocks or bonds?

3 How do interest rate changes affect household spending? How does household spending affect the stock market?

Thinking/Inquiry

4 Look back at Figure 11-4 on the future value of Maria's 6 percent bond, with a term of 10 years. Figure out what the future value would be of a 7 percent bond with the same term. What about 5 percent? Explain, using your figures, what would happen to the value of Maria's 6 percent bond if the interest rate fell to 5 percent the week after she bought it, and she had to sell her 6 percent bond. State what you think would be a fair price for Maria's bond. Explain your reasoning.

5 The Future Value Formula is mainly used to determine the future value of bonds, not savings accounts. Why might that be the case?

Communication

6 In this section, you encountered the following statement: "The interest rate is not in itself good or bad. The wise manager of personal finances knows what the interest rate is and makes decisions accordingly." Develop a point-form presentation, perhaps using PowerPoint, Corel Presentations, overheads, or a flip chart, that explains how interest rates affect bonds, stocks, and household spending.

Application

7 Go back and look at Figure 10-14 that deals with the increase in housing prices in Canada. Suppose an investor had faced the following choice in 1961: A provincial government will sell the investor a 38-year bond at 5% interest compounded daily for the sum of $17 301. a) In 1999, when the bond matures, would the investor have been better or worse off to have purchased an average house in Toronto? Show the figures. b) Now assume the same offer but use the average house price in Vancouver.

Investment Alternatives

In Chapter 10, you learned about the products and services of financial institutions. In addition to savings and chequing accounts, financial institutions offer a number of investment alternatives. Two that you have already learned about are bonds and stocks.

These investments are sometimes called **financial instruments**. To make the best use of your investment money, you must understand each

Convenience for Customers

Many people enjoy the convenience of managing their accounts and paying their bills via the Internet, using a home computer. Internet banking has been growing by 10% per year since 1994. One reason for the growth is that advances in encryption have made Internet banking reasonably safe. Banks use encryption—the scrambling of messages—and digital signatures that verify the user, along with a personal password. By 1999 there were 2.5 million computer banking customers in Canada. Banks without branches, such as ING Direct, are becoming common.

Electronic banking of all kinds, including telephone banking, ABMs, debit cards, and mobile banking (banking by cell phone), now accounts for 85% of transactions.

But Internet banking offers an important benefit other than convenience and safety for your financial transactions—it offers the opportunity to find information to make a wise decision, using the Web sites sponsored by financial institutions.

For example, suppose you get a chance to go to Florida on your spring break. You must buy travel medical insurance because your Ontario health coverage may not cover all your expenses if you become ill or suffer an injury in Florida. Many Canadian financial institutions sell travel medical insurance, but which one offers the best deal? You can get quotations on line.

On a particular day in May, 2001, the following three offers were available from major financial institutions: Bank A offered every applicant under 41 years of age one week of coverage for $24.00. Bank B gave the applicant the option of entering his or her actual age. If the age was 16, the quote was $20.00. Bank C also permitted the applicant to

enter the age of 16 and offered travel insurance for $16.68. The plans offered by the three banks may not be of equal value, so the applicant must review the benefits offered. The specific advantage that the Internet provides is the opportunity to get competitors' information quickly and easily. By contrast, phoning a number of institutions for information might take so long that you would end up accepting the first offer that sounds reasonable.

You can use the same strategy to research student loan offers, savings account rates, and credit card interest rates. You can also get currency exchange rates, financial or economic news, and even current news about an industry you are interested in through the Web sites of financial institutions. Because of its information-gathering capacity, the Internet is your most powerful tool for ensuring that your money is used wisely.

ACTIVITIES

1 Explain the specific advantage the Internet, as compared with the telephone, provides to the consumer.

2 Assume that a student used an Internet search engine to locate all offers of "travel medical insurance." Would this be a quicker, easier, or safer strategy than comparing offers on the Web sites of large Canadian financial institutions? Explain.

3 Go to the Web site of a major financial institution and find out today's rate of foreign exchange between the Canadian and the U.S. dollar, and the Canadian dollar and the Mexican peso. How can monitoring the rate of exchange help you if you receive foreign currency?

Stocks versus Bonds

Bonds			
Type	**Safety**	**Income**	**Growth**
Short-term	Best	Very steady	Very limited
Long-term	Next best	Very steady	Variable

Stock			
Type	**Safety**	**Income**	**Growth**
Preferred	Good	Steady	Variable
Common	Often the least	Variable	Often the most

Source: Canadian Securities Institute

Figure 11-8 Notice that no one type of investment offers all the advantages. Can you see why smart investors make sure they have some of every kind of investment?

financial instrument and how to use it correctly. No matter what financial instrument you use, the following are the most important objectives:

- safety of the principal (the amount of money you invested)
- a good return on your investment
- an increase in the capital. This happens if a stock or bond becomes worth more than you originally paid
- avoiding unnecessary taxes (usually by using a registered retirement savings plan for investments)

Guaranteed Investment Certificates (GICs)

GICs (Guaranteed Investment Certificates), which you first learned about in Chapter 10, are savings certificates sold by banks and trust companies. They guarantee a fixed rate of interest but they also usually cost a minimum of $1000, which is tied up for an agreed term. GICs are usually a short- to medium-term deposit instrument, which means that the investor buys them for perhaps three to five years.

Interest on GICs can be paid in a number of ways: monthly, quarterly, semi-annually, or annually, or compounded semi-annually or annually and paid at maturity. You could use the future value formula, which you learned earlier, to figure out the future value of your GICs. But the financial institution will usually give you that information.

Many Canadians use GICs when they are saving for tuition or a down payment on a house. For example, if you know that it will be three years before you can enroll in a college or university, your savings might earn more money in a GIC than a savings account. Remember, if you change your mind, you cannot always cash a GIC early. You may have to pay a penalty, or may not be able to cash it until it has reached maturity.

Also, remember that the value of the GIC depends on what happens to interest rates. If you buy a GIC for three years when the interest rate is 4% and the savings account interest rate climbs to 6% in Year 2, you will wish you had not tied up your money. Smart investors buy GICs when interest rates are high.

Safety

Bank accounts and GICs are considered to safe investments. That is partly because Canada Deposit Insurance Corporation (CDIC) insures them, subject to certain conditions: You don't have to apply. You are automatically covered for up is $60 000 in principal and interest per member institution. Deposits at different branches of the same member institution are not insured separately. If you had $100 000 spread over five different branches of a bank, $40 000 ($100 000 minus $60 000) would not be covered by CDIC if the bank had to shut down.

Biz.Bites

To be eligible for CDIC (Canada Deposit Insurance Corporation) deposit insurance protection, your money must be held in Canadian currency, payable in Canada, and repayable no later than five years from the date of deposit.

Bonds

You have already learned that governments and companies issue bonds as a way of borrowing money from the investing public. The government or company agrees to pay you back your principal plus an agreed rate of interest on agreed dates. Bonds are the most common type of lending investment traded in the financial markets.

Two main factors affect the return investors can earn on bonds: the current interest rate and the risk associated with the government or company. The risk is that the government or company would not be able to pay back the money when the bond has reached maturity.

The highest bond rating is AAA (triple A). This rating goes to the most stable governments and well established companies. It is as close to an absolute guarantee of payment as you can get. Next is AA, then A, then BBB, and so on. The higher the rating, the lower the interest rate the bond needs to offer to attract investors.

A poor credit rating means investors are taking more of a risk. They might not get paid when the bond matures. Therefore they demand a higher interest rate. The riskiest bonds are those with a rating lower than BB. These "junk bonds," are often issued by companies that have not made steady profits. Figure 11-9 gives examples of bond ratings.

Debentures

The word "bonds" is sometimes used to refer to both bonds and debentures. But a debenture is a different kind of financial instrument. The fixed assets of the issuer secure a bond; only the general credit worthiness of the issuer secures a debenture. For example, a railway company might issue bonds, with its cars backing them. The cars could be sold to pay the bond-

CHAPTER 11 *How You Manage Your Money* • MHR **305**

Company/Government	Rating
Algoma Steel	B
Bell Canada	A (high*)
Bell Mobility	BBB (high*)
Cadbury Schweppes	A
Canada Mortgage & Housing Corp.	AAA
Canadian Tire Corp.	A
DaimlerChrysler AG	A
General Electric	AAA
Halton, Regional Municipality	AAA
Hudson's Bay Company	BBB
Newfoundland & Labrador, Province	BBB
Ontario, Province	AA
Peel, Regional Municipality	AAA
Rogers Wireless Communications	BB
Star Choice	B (high*)
Toronto, City	AA (high*)

* "high" means something like a + on a report card.

Figure 11-9 Bond rating agencies rate bonds. If the organizations listed above issued bonds today, for which would you expect the highest interest rate? The lowest?

holders. But when technology companies want to borrow money, they often issue debentures to raise money, because they have no material assets. The company's main asset is its credibility. Many junk bonds are actually debentures.

Savings Bonds

Savings bonds are another popular way to earn higher interest than most savings accounts. The most popular is the **Canada Savings Bond**, which you may have seen advertised on television. When you buy a Canada Savings Bond, you are lending money to the federal government.

Canada Savings Bonds (CSBs) are very safe for two reasons: The government of Canada guarantees that they will be paid on maturity. For more than 55 years, all maturing Canada Savings Bonds have been paid.

Secondly, CSBs are fully cashable—you can cash them in for their accumulated value shortly after purchase. That is unusual for a bond. The smallest unit of CSBs you can buy is $100. They are a good place for a Canadian investor to begin, but you must buy them between October and April.

The Province of Ontario also issues savings bonds. Ontario Savings Bonds are released each June and are available only to residents of Ontario. The smallest bond you can buy is also $100.

Some people believe that bonds are safe and stocks are risky. But that is not strictly true. As you have seen, some bonds are risky too. There are ways of reducing the risks associated with the stock and bond markets. One of these is called the mutual fund.

Mutual Funds

A **mutual fund** is a financial instrument in which the contributions of many individuals are combined and invested by a professional fund manager in a variety of stocks and bonds. The fund is broken up into units, and the profits are split among investors according to the number of units owned.

Many mutual funds are sponsored by financial institutions. Customers who do not know the stock or bond market well pay the financial institution's fund manager to make the decisions. The customer monitors only the overall performance of the fund, not every investment it makes.

Mutual funds are often very specialized. For example, a number of funds invest only in bonds. But one may be a global bond fund, another may buy only Canadian bonds. Some funds buy and hold mortgages. Others invest in the Pacific Rim.

The financial institution charges the customer a management fee for managing the mutual fund. These fees usually range between 0.75% and 4%. The fee can make quite a difference on the fund's return. For example, a fund that returns 8%, but has a fee of 3%, has a real return—what the customer actually earns—of 5%.

Stocks

Because of a rise in disposable income over the past 40 years, many Canadians now place some money in stocks. The Internet has made investing in stocks easier by enabling investors to quickly get information on how stocks are performing.

Compared to GICs, bonds, and mutual funds, stocks are risky. But a wisely chosen stock can also be much more profitable than other investments. For example, Figure 11-11 shows a stock that did quite well.

The Bank of Montreal's performance was not unusual during this period. Between December 17, 1995, and March 20, 2001, average Bank of Montreal share prices rose from $22.63 to $49.89 in US funds. Average dividends rose from $.44 to $.56, which kept up with inflation.

Investors have many theories about how to manage stocks. Some people buy and keep them for years, believing that, even if the value falls at times, ups and downs will average out and they will do well. Others look for a quick profit. "Day traders," for example, sell stocks within a couple of days, or even hours, of buying them. How can you determine the right strategy for you?

Web Connect

www.school.mcgrawhill.ca/resources/
The Investment Funds Institute of Canada is a good source of information on mutual funds. An area for young people, called Mutual Funds 101, explains everything you need to know about mutual funds.

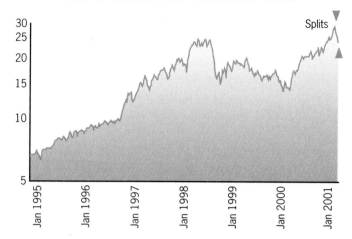

Bank of Montreal as of March 17 2001

Splits

Figure 11-10 Those who kept their Bank of Montreal shares from 1995 onward found that share prices tended upward. Dividends tended upward too.

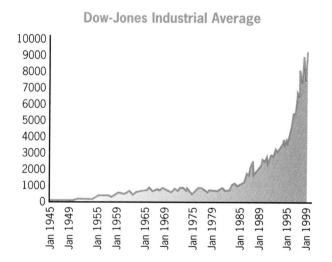

Dow-Jones Industrial Average

Figure 11-11 The Dow-Jones Industrial Average is watched carefully by investors. What does it tell you about the North American economy since 1945?

Stock Exchanges

Fortunately, stock exchanges provide information that helps you make purchase decisions. Each exchange posts an indicator called an average or index to reflect its overall performance. Most exchanges have Web sites that make it easy to find the indicator and other information as well.

One of the most important measures of how well stocks are doing in North America is the American **Dow Jones Industrial Average**. The Dow Jones is one of the oldest and most famous measures of stock performance. It was established in 1896 and reflects the share price of just 30 of North America's "blue chip," or very successful and profitable, companies. Figure 11-11 shows the Dow Jones Historical Trend since January 1945.

The Dow Jones Industrial Average suddenly started rising through the 1950s and shot up during the 1980s. This period coincided with great economic expansion. The population of North America greatly increased after World War II. During the 1960s and 1970s, parents of the baby boomers started to invest for retirement. Then baby boomers themselves, a very large, well-paid, well-employed group began investing through the 1980s and 1990s.

The most watched Canadian indicator is the **TSE 300** composite index, which reflects the share price of 300 Canadian companies listed on the Toronto Stock Exchange. Its fluctuations are similar to the Dow Jones Industrial Average. (See Figure 11-16)

You learned in Chapter 9 that stocks are shares in a company. Each share represents a small portion of ownership in the value (equity) of the company. Depending on the type of shares you own, you can expect to be paid a dividend—a portion of the profits for a given year. You may also have the right to vote at the company's annual general meeting. A single share will not give you much influence or big dividends, because many companies have more than 100 000 000 shares.

Costs of Using the Stock Market

Investors must pay to use the stock market. If you wanted to buy shares, you would have to go through a broker—a company licensed to trade on stock markets—and must pay a brokerage fee on each trade. Discount brokers charge the lowest fees for a trade. But they require investors to do their own research. Most small investors who use discount brokers do their trades and buy bonds through the Internet. If you want advice from a broker, you have to pay for it. The broker may charge per trade or may charge a monthly fee to manage your portfolio, or both.

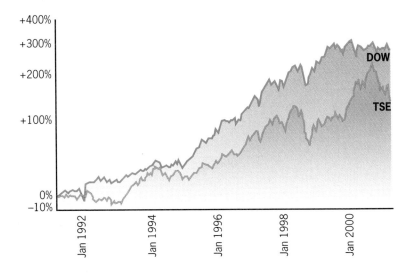

Toronto 300 Composite Index as of 16 March 2001

Figure 11-12 If you heard on the news that the Dow Jones Industrial Average was predicted to head down, what might you think was going to happen to the TSE?

Registered Retirement Savings Plans (RRSPs)

As you have learned in Chapters 9 and 10, the Canadian government created the Registered Retirement Savings Plan program to encourage Canadians to put money aside for their retirement.

An RRSP is not a specific type of investment. It is a **tax shelter**. That means that the government does not count the money you put in the RRSP as income for the purpose of computing your income tax for the tax year for which you made the contribution. Many types of investment—even a simple savings account—can be placed in an RRSP.

You saw this with Lawrence's income tax in Chapter 10. His taxable income (see Figure 10-9) would have been $61 396.79. But he contributed $2400 to an RRSP, so his taxable income fell to $58 996.79. That

Biz.Bites

When the Dow Jones Industrial Average was first published in May 1896, it comprised only 12 companies, of which General Electric is the only remaining one. Companies have been added or removed based on how well they represent an industry and how frequently the company's stock is traded.

RRSP Contribution	Lawrence's 2000 Taxes Payable
$2 400.00	$13 601.71
$6 000.00	$12 286.10
$9 000.00	$11 189.78

Figure 11-13 What if Lawrence contributed more to his RRSP?

meant that he was paying a lower amount of tax. If he had put more in his RRSP, he would pay even less tax. (See Figure 11-13.)

Lawrence will never have to pay tax on the $2400 or any of his accumulated RRSP savings as long as it is in the tax shelter. However, during a year in which he withdraws money from an RRSP, the withdrawal is treated as income. If he manages his investments wisely, he will not withdraw the money until he is retired.

Should you tie up as much money as possible in an RRSP every year? Not necessarily. You may need to have cash savings as well. In the next section, we will compare the benefits of saving and investing.

Check Your Understanding

Knowledge/Understanding

1 What is a mutual fund? Why do many investors like mutual funds?

2 What is the Dow-Jones Industrial Average? What is the TSE 300?

Thinking/Inquiry

3 Make a chart showing the advantages and disadvantages to the investor of GICs, Canada Savings Bonds, regular low-risk bonds, mutual funds, and stock in established companies.

4 Suppose the investor puts the investments in 4 in an RRSP for 30 years? Are any of the investments above a bad idea? What proportion of $50 000 would you allot to each of these types of investment? Explain your reasoning.

Communication

5 Miroslav said, "It's not worth saving for retirement. Old folks just sit around anyway. I'd rather spend all my money when I'm young and can have fun!" Do you think Miroslav is right? Before you respond, look at some magazines aimed at people over 50. Note the lifestyles that are promoted. Are they active or inactive? Is travel involved? Socializing? Education? What sort of income do these lifestyles require? Now compose an e-mail to Miroslav explaining whether you agree or disagree, based on what you have learned, and why.

Skills
Appendix

critical thinking

Skills
Appendix

building an argument

Comparing the Benefits of Saving and Investing

As you've learned, the key difference between saving and investing is liquidity. You can readily withdraw money from a savings account. But you will encounter penalties if you suddenly change your plans for money you have invested.

For example, you get no interest if you cash a Canada Savings Bond within three months of buying it. You may not be able to cash a Guaranteed Investment Certificate until its maturity date. If you sell a regular bond before it matures, its value may be reduced if interest rates have gone up in the meantime. If you sell units in a mutual fund or shares in the stock market when their value happens to be low, you simply lose money.

In general, investors must stay in the market over the long term to make money. So you must be reasonably certain that you will not need your investment money for something else. But how will you know? One way is to write up a budget and a financial plan for yourself. Later in this chapter, you will learn how to prepare a budget and a financial plan.

When Is It Important to Have Cash on Hand?

Should investors put all their money in investments to get the highest interest rate? Not necessarily. Sometimes liquidity (having cash on hand) is very important. Consider Lawrence Li's situation from Chapter 10. When he wanted to buy a house, the bank manager asked Lawrence if he had savings or any asset that could easily be converted into cash (Canada Savings Bonds, for example).

She was not interested in hearing about Lawrence's retirement savings in RRSPs because he is not supposed to use these tax-sheltered savings except for retirement income. So it is a good thing that Lawrence did not tie up all his money in a non-liquid investment for a long period. The bank manager could see that he had a substantial amount of money on hand. That made it safe for the bank to give him a mortgage.

A few weeks after he bought his house, Lawrence saw a sign in front of a commercial building that said *MOVING TO VANCOUVER. Building Materials, Kitchen/Bathroom Cabinets, and Fixtures for Sale. CASH ONLY.* Lawrence realized that he needed these materials for his basement apartment, so he bought $600 worth. Lawrence estimated that by buying secondhand, he saved about $1500. He was very glad that he had the money on hand. As you can see, the wise investor does not choose between savings and investment, but tries to manage both carefully.

Personal-Budgeting and Financial-Planning Skills

You have learned about saving, investing, and wise spending as critical areas of personal financial management. But the budget and the financial plan are the tools that give you the power to control your financial future. A **budget** is a plan of how you will spend your money and includes both a list of expenditures and estimates. Usually a budget covers a set period such as a month or a year. A financial plan is a forecast of how much money you will need to achieve a given future financial goal. Although keeping records may seem time-consuming at first, it makes achieving goals much easier. Decisions are easier to make when you have information you can trust. Also, if you need money for a training course or college or university tuition, you definitely need a financial plan.

Biz.Bites

A budget helps you:
- live within your income
- meet expenses
- identify spending priorities
- meet financial emergencies
- reduce credit use
- reduce uncertainty and conflict about money
- gain a sense of control over money
- reach your goals

Producing a Personal Budget

Suppose you want to produce a personal budget. The first step is to identify how you now earn and spend your money. (See Figure 11-14).

Identifying Financial Problems

If you didn't do well enough on the Reality Check to have any savings, you should examine a number of issues, including the following:

- Are you earning enough money? If not, don't assume that the solution is simply to increase your working hours. Check out what friends charge for a service like the one you provide (babysitting or lawn mowing, for example). If you charge much less than they do, you may need to increase your rates.
- If you are charging market rates and cannot work more hours without harming your schoolwork, then you must examine your expenses. Decide where you can cut down.

Developing a Budget

A budget can be constructed using the categories you developed for Reality Check. The difference is that in a budget you must spend no more than an allotted sum in each category. For example, if you have decided to save $75 per month towards a mountain bike or tuition, you must subtract that amount from your spending on other items.

Lawrence Li found that he really needed a budget after he bought the house. He had to make sure that he had enough money for his mortgage payments and for hydro, gas, water, and heat.

Let's have a closer look at Lawrence's budget. Some entries remain the same as in his earlier budget, before he bought the house. However, some items have changed. Lawrence no longer has to pay rent; he has rental income instead. Because he is renovating his house, he decided not to take an adult education course at the same time. But he must pay mortgage, mortgage insurance, property tax, utilities, and household insurance. He pays the same amount for truck rental/pool, as well as telephone and Internet. But in the other categories, Lawrence has had to make a number of adjustments.

Reality Check

Income per month
Take Home Pay (part-time job, babysitting, etc.)
Other Income (allowance, gift)
Total Income

Expenses
Clothes
Magazines
Video Rentals
Eating Out (school lunches, dinner, soft drinks)
Entertainment (movies, sports, games, etc.)
Hobbies
Transportation (taxis, public transportation, cars)
Other Expenses (computer games, Internet access)
Other
Total Expenses

Remainder
(Income minus expenses)

Source: Canadian Bankers Association

Keeping this record for a month should give you an idea of where your money is going. If your remainder is a negative number, that means you spend more than you earn.

Figure 11-14 Fill this in with your personal information and keep it. Take out any categories that do not apply to you and add any that do.

Lawrence Li's Monthly Budget	After Buying the House
Net Pay	$3 498.34
Rental Income from basement apartment	538.00
Total Income	$4 036.34
Expenses:	
Mortgage	$1 170.00
Mortgage Insurance	40.00
Household Insurance	23.50
Hydro (monthly average)	110.00
Gas (monthly average)	120.00
Water (monthly average)	15.00
Property Tax	125.00
Truck Rental/Pool	260.00
Savings	350.00
Loan Payment*	230.70
Telephone / Internet	140.00
Food	200.00
Clothing / Toiletries / Furniture	105.00
Household	150.00
RRSP Investments	500.00
Charitable donations	100.00
Total Expenses	**$3 639.20**
Remainder for Entertainment, Vacation, Unforeseen Expenses	$397.14

* Lawrence took out a home renovation loan for $5000 to be paid back over three years at an interest rate of 10%. You will learn more about this in the next section.

Figure 11-15 Lawrence Li's monthly budget after buying the house. Lawrence has increased his savings, his RRSP contributions, and his charitable donations. The reason he has made these changes will be explained in the next section, "Producing a Financial Plan."

Note that Lawrence discovered that he needed a $5000 personal loan to ensure he had cash on hand to complete the apartment renovation. He took a personal loan for 10% per year for this purpose. He also found that owning a house required him to own a lawnmower, rock salt, and fertilizer. He built picnic tables and a barbecue to entertain friends and co-workers. Various expenses of this kind cost him $105 per month in the budget category Household. There were additional surprise household costs. For example, when his tenant Burt got a cat, Lawrence bought and installed a cat door.

Producing a Financial Plan

Lawrence did not realize until too late that he should have reduced his down payment by $5 000 and not taken a personal loan. His mortgage was only 6.25% interest but the loan interest is 10%. The loan will end up costing him $536.80 in interest charges. But at the mortgage rate of 6.25%, the same amount would have cost only $331.60 in interest. Making this mistake helped Lawrence realize why he needed a financial plan. A **financial plan** differs from a budget because it includes savings for a goal.

After he had prepared a financial plan, Lawrence increased both his RRSP contribution and his charity donations. (See Figure 10-20.) Lawrence realized that he had not contributed nearly the amount to his RRSP that the government would have allowed on his 2000 earnings. So he had not reduced his taxable income by nearly as much as he could have. Also, he felt that he should really give more to charity, to help out more in his new community. As it happens, his donations will increase his charity income tax credits.

How did Lawrence decide how much to put in each category of his budget? Some entries are fixed expenses. These include mortgage payment, property tax, loan payment, insurance, truck rental/pool, telephone, Internet, and utilities. The Clothing/Toiletries/Furniture category was a reasonable estimate, as was food. However, for savings, RRSP, and charity donations he made a financial plan, to avoid putting things off or forgetting.

Simple Financial Plan

A financial plan can be fairly simple. The plan shown in Figure 11-18 is a plan for a young person who wants to buy a mountain bike and go to college.

Figure 11-16
Home ownership usually involves many new types of expenses.

Financial plans may have more goals than the one above, but in general they follow the same format. Lawrence Li's plan has several goals:

1. He wants to pay down as much of his mortgage as possible. (The agreement he made with the bank allows him to pay down 20% of the principal every year. Remember that once he pays off the mortgage, he will no longer spend $1170 per month, but he will still get $538 per month from his basement apartment.)

2. He wants to save on taxes by contributing more to his RRSP.

3. He wants to give more to charity.

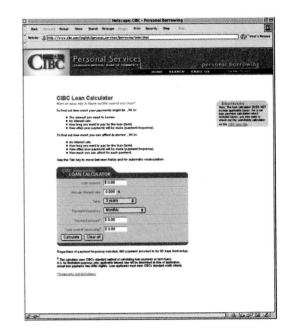

Figure 11-17 A loan calculator like the one on the CIBC Web site will let you figure out how much Lawrence's loan would cost if he changes the repayment term from 2 years, as it is now, to 3 or 4 years.

Financial Plan

Short-term goal	Present Cost	Forecast Cost*	Expected Purchase	Save per Month
Bicycle	$400.00	$430.00	12 months from now	$430.00/12 = $35.83
Medium-term goal				
College	$2 000.00 per year	$2 800.00 per year	48 months from now	2 800/48 = $58.33
Need to save each month				$94.16**

* Forecast cost at average estimated inflation rate. Use Bank of Canada's investment calculator.

**Put this in as the savings category to be deducted from your gross income, in your budget.

Figure 11-18 Do these figures seem realistic to you? Why or why not?

Using Software

After using a spreadsheet to make all his budget and planning calculations shown in Figure 11-19 Lawrence decided that, when he had time, he would investigate software that helps a person budget and plan.

While you can budget and plan without a computer, a spreadsheet program can save you time by performing calculations quickly and accurately. Also, most spreadsheet programs have a budget template with common budget items prepared in advance.

You can link numbers from your financial plan to your budget or any other financial list you've created.

People who need to keep track of their cash and assets sometimes use financial software programs. This type of software can be linked to banking and investment Web sites. When a cheque is cashed, the reduction in your balance will show on your home computer when you go into your personal finance information. Similarly, some software lets you download information from an online investment portfolio. Many people also use income tax software to do their returns, and submit their taxes online.

Software systems require some concentration to learn but they can save you a great deal of time in keeping track of your finances and help your achieve your financial and other goals.

Figure 11-19

Lawrence's short-term financial plan for RRSP, Charity Donations and Savings. He transferred each of these new calculations to his budget.

Short term financial plan for RRSPs

Lawrence's short-term financial plan for RRSP, Charity Donations and Savings. He transferred each of these new calculations to his budget.		
Goal	Optimum Yearly Investment	Need to Save per Month
RRSP Contribution	$6 000.00	$6 000/12 = $500
Charity Donations	$1 200.00	$1 200/12 = $100*
Saving to pay down mortgage	$4 200.00	$4 200/12 = $350

*in addition to his payroll deduction for United Way.

Knowledge/Understanding

1 What is the key difference between a budget and a financial plan?

Thinking/Inquiry

2 Explain why Lawrence should have reduced his down payment by $5000 instead of taking out a loan to pay for the costs of renovating his basement.

3 Lawrence could have reduced his taxable income by turning his savings account into an RRSP. Explain why that would not be a wise decision if he wanted to buy a house.

Communication

4 You are planning to go on a French class trip to Quebec City for four days. Make a checklist of expenses you would need to budget for. How much money do you need to have?

Application

5 Make a list of expenses that Lawrence might need to budget for when he buys a house, in addition to the actual cost. Estimate the amount of each expense. Talk to some people who have bought a house about these expenses, to help you provide an estimate. Provide a figure for the savings Lawrence should have in addition to the amount that goes into the down payment on the house.

Skills
Appendix

problem solving

In 1992, a rare event occurred in the mining industry. Geologist Michael de Guzman, who was prospecting at Busang Creek on the Island of Borneo, Indonesia, said he had found underground deposits estimated at "60 million tonnes with a gold content exceeding 3.5 grams." When geologists say that a region contains gold, the find is considered major if there is a concentration of more than 2 grams of gold per tonne of rock.

One person who noticed was Canadian David Walsh. A Calgary-based businessman, Walsh was someone who believed in using "other people's brains … other people's money." Walsh owned a mining exploration company, Bre-X Minerals Limited. He decided to buy the Busang claim from an Australian mining company who had owned it for years. Because potential investors would need more proof that there was this much gold, Bre-X put geologist John Felderhof in charge of the Busang site and had new core samples taken. By 1995, Bre-X was reporting much higher quantities of gold than originally estimated by de Guzman – 6.38 to 6.5 grams per tonne. If these estimates were accurate, Bre-X owned the largest gold find of the twentieth century.

By now gold fever had begun to grip the nation. Investors wanted a piece of the Bre-X miracle. According to an article in Time Magazine: "Bre-X stock soared from a few pennies a share, before the company said it had struck gold … to more than $200 at its peak … De Guzman cashed in options and sold shares for several million dollars. David Walsh and his wife later raked in $20 million. John Felderhof made $29 million."

Trouble loomed, however. When Felderhof's core samples were re-tested by independent experts, they seemed to have been "salted." This

Figure 11-20 Bre-X owners when the gold mine looked like a sure thing.

means that amounts of gold had been added to the rock taken out of the ground to make the samples seem richer than they actually were. One expert reported that the gold in the samples was "a man-made alloy of copper and gold not found in nature."

And there were more signs that something was awry. One Toronto geologist-engineer who visited the mine in 1996 wrote, "the office was a dump and the guy running it was a weirdo." When a team of Australian investors went to visit the Borneo site, they were prevented from entering the gold mine's outer gates. One of these investors later told Forbes, "We won't buy anything we can't visit, so we didn't invest."

By July 1996, the mine's work permit had expired. On October 4, 1996, a Globe and Mail

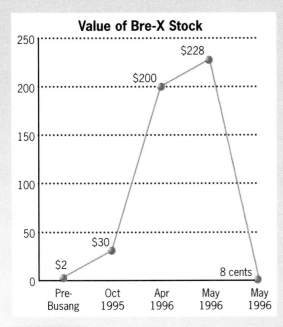

Value of Bre-X Stock

$228

$200

$30

$2

8 cents

| Pre-Busang | Oct 1995 | Apr 1996 | May 1996 | May 1996 |

Figure 11-21 When Bre-X's mine proved worthless, investors lost millions.

article reported the growing doubts about Bre-X. The next day, a massive rush to sell Bre-X shares caused the Toronto Stock Exchange to crash for 90 minutes.

In January 1997 a mysterious fire at the mine destroyed the building that contained all of the suspect core samples. Now there was no way to check the original samples to prove if they had been salted or not. For the thousands of small investors who had put their life savings into Bre-X, this was a major tragedy. There was no gold, and no way to get their money back.

Ironically, in March 1997, just when Walsh and Felderhof were about to be honoured as "the

Prospectors of the Year," their colleague Michael de Guzman jumped from a plane over the Borneo jungle. Circumstances around his death are still unexplained. Stocks dropped to 60 cents a share, and Bre-X was taken off the market in May 1997. Many people had lost millions. The Ontario Teachers Fund lost $73 million. It was one of three Canadian pension funds that invested in Bre-X and lost. Only a few, like Walsh and Felderhof, had become millionaires. No gold had ever been taken out of the ground.

This was the largest mining fraud in Canadian history. Many small investors joined forces to file a class action suit against Bre-X. David Walsh died of a heart attack in 1998, and John Felderhof moved to the safety of the Cayman Islands. He passed a polygraph test in September 1997. The trial of Felderhof, the last remaining suspect, continued into the twenty-first century.

ACTIVITIES

1   What evidence supported the view that Bre-X's Busang mine was the biggest gold find in the twentieth century?

2   Construct a timeline of the Bre-X gold scandal, using the events outlined. What information apart from the expert findings pointed to a serious problem? Explain.

3   Stories like this are often made into movies. Choose one event from your timeline and write dialogue for the characters.

Chapter Review

Points to Remember

- Fluctuations in interest rates occur as a result of inflation and deflation caused by boom and bust phases in the business cycle.

- The Bank of Canada changes the rate at which it lends money to Canada's financial institutions (the bank rate) to even out the effect of economic changes.

- Interest rates affect what you earn from your savings and how much you must pay to borrow money. That affects how you spend money.

- The four main investment alternatives are guaranteed investment certificates, bonds, mutual funds, and stocks.

- Investors who want to invest but do not know too much about bonds or stocks often choose mutual funds.

- An RRSP is a tax shelter. The government does not tax income if it is contributed to an RRSP.

- In deciding between savings and investment, the investor needs to keep financial goals in mind. Savings are more liquid than investment but earn less interest.

- A personal budget helps the investor manage day-to-day expenses or save for a purchase. A financial plan helps the investor achieve long term goals.

Activities

Knowledge/Understanding

1 What is a bull market? A bear market?

2 Why might the face value of a bond differ from its market value?

3 What is the difference between a bond and a debenture?

Thinking/Inquiry

Skills
Appendix

problem solving

1 Using the Future Value formula, determine which bond will return more money on $500.00 in 10 years. A 5.36% bond compounding monthly for 10 years or a 5.50% bond compounding once a year for 10 years. Show the results of your calculations and round out your answer to a whole number. Why did the two bonds show this result?

2 Find the Future Value of a 6.00% bond a) compounding daily for 10 years, b) compounding monthly for 10 years, c) compounding twice a year for 10 years, and d) compounding once a year. The pv is $20000.00 for 10 years. What is the difference in the return of the bond that compounded once a year and the bond that compounded daily?

Communication

1 You inherited $10 000. How would you invest it, why, and in what amounts? Pick at least three financial instruments.

2 Your friend Jean-Guy, who has not taken business courses, has been watching the business segment on TV evening news. A recent downturn in the stock market has convinced him that a huge financial depression is certain. "For example," he says, "Not only have stocks dropped but interest rates have been going up, and that's hard on families who want to buy houses!" Prepare a short report on the business cycle for Jean-Guy. Explain the usual relationship between stock prices and interest rates. Use charts to illustrate the relationships. Suggest wise investments to hold during a period of high interest rates.

Application

1 Using the Internet, the library, local news stands, and bookstores, prepare a resource list of books, magazines, and Web sites that will help you to
- develop a financial plan and budget
- save money on necessary purchases using tested consumer advice
- compare investments
- develop an investment portfolio
- research publicly traded companies

Prepare a table that provides a brief description of each resource, who provides it, its availability, its cost, and how you think it might help you. Especially note the bias of the source: Is it a consumer group evaluating student loans, or is it a financial institution promoting its own product? In your final version, rank the resources in each subject category by degree of general usefulness.

Internet Extension

1 So you think you know about money? Test your money smarts at the Canadian Bankers Association Web site and find out more about budgeting and protecting your money.

KEY TERMS

consumer credit
appreciate
depreciate
capital improvement
credit rating
limit
annual fee
co-sign
credit bureau
credit history
default
consolidate
pre-authorization
personal line of credit
installment plan
collection agency
garnisheed
bankruptcy

Specific Expectations

After studying this chapter, you will be able to

- **explain the advantages and disadvantages of consumer credit**

- **describe the process of establishing a personal credit rating and applying for and obtaining credit**

- **calculate the total cost of credit on a variety of loans**

In chapter 12, we investigate consumer credit, when to use and avoid it, how much it costs, and how it can either help or ruin a financial plan. Credit can help you achieve your financial goals if you use it to acquire assets that you can afford, based on your income. Credit can also help you build wealth if you use it to acquire training that improves your income or assets that increase in value. However, credit can create misfortune for those who try to "charge" a lifestyle that their income cannot pay for. In this chapter, you will learn how to establish a credit rating and how to maintain a good credit rating. You will also learn about the real costs of different types of loans.

The Wheels of Fortune

Bobby and Lawrence had stopped for lunch after drywalling Lawrence's basement apartment on a rainy Saturday morning. Burt, Lawrence's friend, had dropped over to see how they were doing because he was going to rent the apartment. Bobby began talking about buying a truck.

"My business teacher says that if you are self-employed and use a truck in your business, part of the expense is borne by the business. You subtract the business truck expenses from the business's gross income. Only my personal use of the truck would be a personal expense. If I get this weekend basement renovation business going, I can afford a truck."

"In fact, if you work for homeowners, you have to have a truck," said Lawrence. "It's not like working at DelMarco. You have to provide everything for the customer. But you charge the customer for that too. Just make sure you research all the costs and set your prices right."

"For sure. I'm working on a business plan in one of my classes. What I'd like is an F250 pickup with ..."

"Hey, Bobby, choosing a truck is the easy part! Me, I'd like a Chevy S10 with a crew cab. That's what I'm aiming for when I buy, maybe three years from now. Once I have paid my mortgage down a bit and paid off my reno loan, I can afford a little consumer debt."

"A crew cab? Wow! Are you planning to get married and start a family?"

Figure 12-1 A big purchase like a truck requires a carefully thought out financial strategy.

"For your information, Bobby, a four-seater is really handy when four guys go fishing."

Burt listened, but did not have much to say. He was thinking about finances too, but he had big problems. His status car, which cost $43 000 when he bought it, had cost him a lot recently. It was beautiful, the envy of all his friends. But it was expensive to maintain and insure, and he hadn't even finished paying for it. When he got short on cash a while back, he had begun using his three credit cards for as many expenses as he could, thinking he could deal with them later.

As an administrative assistant, he had an adequate salary, but not enough for the lifestyle he was living. It was years since he had paid off a balance on his charge cards. The compound daily interest was making the balance rise much more rapidly.

He was trying to get control. He stopped putting so many frivolous expenses on the cards. No more restaurant bills. Just necessities and regular car expenses. But then a big car repair expense put him over the limit on one of his cards.

Right now, he was negotiating a bank loan to clear the charge card debt. The bank would only charge him 10 percent interest, compared to the average of 16 percent interest on his cards. But that same bank gave Lawrence a mortgage loan at only 6.25 percent! Why the big difference?

Burt did not feel like sharing his problem with Lawrence and Bobby, because he was so embarrassed. To try reducing his debt, he had decided to work a lot of overtime. He knew he had to do something because the bank manager wasn't sure about giving him the loan. She expressed surprise that he was nearly 30 and had no assets.

"Don't you count the car?" he asked.

"Well, because it's four years old, it has a bit less than $16 000 value left," she explained. "Cars aren't like houses. They lose value every year you drive them. We bankers say that the asset *depreciates*. What you need are assets that *appreciate* — for example, investments that earn interest every year. Burt, you are on the wrong side of compound interest. Let's get on the right side!"

Burt promised to think about it.

What does the bank manager mean when she says that Burt is on the "wrong side" of compound interest? As you read the chapter, note how the same compound interest that increases the value of investments can work in reverse and empty bank accounts. Will getting a bank loan be enough for Burt? What other steps may he need to take?

Consumer Credit

Over the past 30 years, Canadian consumers have been using credit a great deal (see Figure 12-2 below). Is this a bad thing?

The answer is not a simple yes or no. If being in debt were always a bad thing, Lawrence would be much worse off than Burt. Lawrence owes over $176 000 on his house. Burt is only about $30 000 in debt because of his car and credit card expenses. But the bank manager thought that Burt, not Lawrence, was in big trouble. Why do you think that is?

Here is how the bank manager sees it: Lawrence's house will probably keep its value. In fact, its value will rise if more people move to his community. By putting in a legal basement apartment, Lawrence is further increasing the house's value, and will earn money from it. When he has paid off the house he can live there inexpensively and still collect rent. So, the house is a smart investment. The mortgage loan is a necessary expense for the investment. The bank manager was happy to lend Lawrence the money at 6.25 percent.

But what about Burt's car? It is a big expense to him. It does not earn him any money. Its value goes down every year. True, he needs a car to get to work, but a much less expensive car would provide the same service. Although the bank manager might lend money to Burt because he has a steady job, she wants a much higher interest rate. Burt's car was not a smart investment. Spending more money on the problem is not a good idea.

An important question to ask about debt is this: Will borrowing eventually create income or savings, or will it simply create more debt?

What Is Consumer Credit?

When consumers borrow money for mortgages and personal loans, and when they pay for purchases with credit cards, they are using **consumer credit**. Lawrence has used two types of consumer credit for his house: a mortgage and a personal renovation loan. Burt also has two kinds of credit: a car loan and

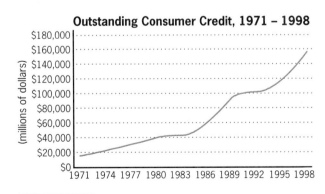

Outstanding Consumer Credit, 1971 – 1998

Figure 12-2 What factors in our society encourage people to buy on credit? Which of these factors is most important?

Biz.Bites

Who uses credit? According to Statistics Canada, 50% of households in which the main income earner is between 25 and 34 owe money on credit cards or installment plans.

credit card debt. Credit card debt, almost without exception, carries the highest interest rate.

Generally, apart from emergencies, you should borrow money only to acquire something that will do one of two things:

- **appreciate** (go up in value)
- earn income.

You should not borrow for things that

- **depreciate** (go down in value) or
- run up a lot of extra expenses.

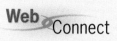

www.school.mcgrawhill.ca/resources/
On their Web sites, the Canadian Automobile Association and Rogers Media have excellent information on owning a car in Canada.

Lawrence's house, for example, was likely to appreciate and earn money. Burt's car was certain to depreciate and run up a lot of extra expenses.

This does not mean that a house is always a good investment or that a car is always a bad one. A poorly chosen house can depreciate. Borrowing money for a car can be smart. Burt, for example, would have been smart to borrow money for a modest car when he got his job. A car that he could afford would be a good investment because it would help him get to work to earn income and would not put him into serious debt.

Advantages of Consumer Credit

Credit can help you achieve your financial goals if you use it wisely. For example, assume Lawrence tried to save up all the money to buy a house. He might be an old man before he reached his goal. He would have the expense of paying rent and would not have the income from an apartment. House prices in his area might even rise faster than he could save. For him, consumer credit was a wise choice, based on a financial plan and a budget.

You will recall from Chapter 11 that Lawrence also took a personal loan of $5000 for the renovation. He would have been better off to take a larger mortgage, because the mortgage interest rate was lower (10 percent for the renovation loan vs. 6.25 percent for the mortgage). But in general, he hasn't made a big mistake. After all, the "borrowed" money meant he was able to buy inexpensive building materials. Also, he used the loan for a **capital improvement**. That is, he used it to build something—an apartment—which adds value to the house (causes it to appreciate).

A student who needs to go into debt for tuition faces similar decisions. The student needs to ask whether the training, certificate, diploma, or degree will lead to a job or another type of benefit that will justify the loan's expense.

The fact that credit card debt carries the highest interest rate doesn't mean that credit cards provide no advantages. *Misuse* of credit cards is the problem. A credit card comes in handy for a wise purchase when you don't have cash. It is very valuable if you find yourself stranded somewhere. However, as you learned in Chapter 10, you should pay off your credit card balance as soon as you receive your statement in the mail. *Carrying a balance* costs a lot because credit card interest is very high.

Disadvantages of Consumer Credit

The greatest disadvantage of consumer credit is that you may be tempted to borrow money to finance purchases that depreciate, and to live a lifestyle whose expenses your income cannot pay for. You won't be building wealth because you have to pay off purchases with high interest rates.

For example, Burt's financial future is threatened by unwise use of consumer credit. He really could not afford the car of his dreams. But Lawrence and Bobby, who manage their financial affairs wisely, will buy vehicles they want without sacrificing their income and credit rating. Each of them has a plan for managing consumer credit to his advantage. Lawrence will wait till his assets are high and indebtedness is low. Bobby will use the vehicle largely in his business, which means that most of the expense for his truck is a business expense and is subtracted from what he earns before his income tax is calculated. He will also have the personal use of the vehicle. You will recall from Chapter 8 that the business entity principle of accounting requires that the business bear its own share of the vehicle's expenses.

Figure 12-3 The debtors' prison. For many centuries, failure to pay debts was a crime, punishable by imprisonment. The establishment of the modern credit system in the 19th century ended imprisonment for debt.

Note that you are responsible for using credit to your advantage. The financial institutions that let you have credit cards or lend you money do not have to do your financial planning for you. Because Burt had a steady job, financial institutions lent him the money for the status car and let him pile debt on his credit cards. The fact that he was not getting ahead financially was his problem, not theirs. They will only refuse him money if they think he cannot ever pay them back.

Figure 12-4

Many factors can increase our desire to shop; attractive surroundings are one. The design of Toronto Eaton Centre, which opened in 1979, has been widely imitated because it lures credit cards out of wallets. How do shopping plazas in your area do this?

Check Your Understanding

Knowledge/Understanding

1 What is appreciation of an asset?

2 What is depreciation of an asset?

Thinking/Inquiry

3 Give an example of an asset that will probably appreciate. Find one that is not in the text.

4 Give an example of an asset that will probably depreciate. Find one that is not in the text.

Communication

5 Anna would like to take the four-year registered nursing course at a local university. Her math and science marks are good. She could live at home, but she must go into debt for tuition. Her mother thinks she should take a two-year health care aide course instead. A friend took such a course and is now making $18 per hour. "You say you could make $30 per hour as a nurse," her mother says, "But you might not get a job. And you will have a much bigger debt. You can't afford to take risks like that!"

Write a note to Anna giving your perspective. Use what you have learned in Chapter 9 on the factors that determine income and what you have learned in this section on consumer credit. (a) How big a risk is Anna taking? (b) Are there risks that her mother is not considering? (c) What do you think these risks might be?

Skills
Appendix

critical thinking
building an argument

Application

6 Bobby plans to write off the business portion of the cost and operating expenses of his truck. List the types of expenses that Bobby should expect. If you are unsure, ask people you know who own a motor vehicle.

Establishing a Personal Credit Rating

Your **credit rating** is your reputation for paying back money you owe. A good credit rating is important for managing personal finances. After high school, you will likely need a good credit rating if you want to rent an apartment or borrow money to buy a car. Protecting your good reputation with money is important.

Applying for Credit

Credit ratings pose the same problem for students as job experience: You must earn a credit rating—but how can you earn it if people won't give you credit? Many young people start to earn a credit rating by getting a phone in their own name while living away from home, perhaps at college.

Credit Cards

Another way that students develop a good credit rating is by getting a student credit card that they use sparingly and pay off every month. They may be invited to apply for a card at a display set up by a financial institution during registration. Or they fill out the application and hand it in at the financial institution. A young person who has a steady job is also eligible for credit in most cases.

Most first-time credit cards have a low limit. A **limit** is the amount of money the financial institution that sponsors the card is willing to allow you to charge to it. If you pay your balance promptly, they may give you a higher limit. If you develop a very good credit rating and have a high income, your limit might reach $10 000. Most cardholders would not want a higher limit than this, in case their card was stolen. As a rule, they would not need a higher limit because, as you learned, a different form of credit is used for very large purchases such as homes or cars.

Biz.Bites

How did credit cards get started? In the late 1940s, several U.S. banks started giving their customers specially issued paper that could be used like cash in local stores. The successor, credit cards, are now widely used and available throughout the world. Each year, they account for well over a trillion dollars worth of purchases.

```
CHARGE WORLD
INCORPORATED
STATEMENT DATE                                          ACCOUNT NUMBER
01 02 01    Orangeville ON    1 800 123-4567 1314 1516 1718 1920
 M  D  Y


 01 02 01 Gifts for the Whole Family Christmas Shoppe        805.72
 01 04 01 Gov't of Ontario Motor Vehicle Plate Fee - 2 yrs   148.00
 01 07 01 PetroCanada 2 Orangeville                           28.29
 01 11 01 Groceries on the Go Delivery Stoufville             57.01
 01 16 01 Pamper's Car Care Service                          197.00
 01 19 01 Fab! Fabrics Dry Cleaning                           29.00
 01 21 01 PetroCanada 2 Orangeville                           27.42
 01 24 01 Groceries on the Go Delivery Stouffville            72.01
 01 29 01 Hank's Import Auto Service Markham                3511.02


          BALANCE ON LAST    TOTAL CREDITS   TOTAL DEBITS   TOTAL INTEREST
            STATEMENT
   6000     2089.45 -           0        +   4875.47    +    29.12    =   6964.92

ANNUAL INTEREST  DAILY INTEREST  PAYMENT DUE DATE  PAST DUE/OVER LIMIT  CURRENT DUE
    RATE            RATE
  18.5%           .05068         01 28 01          120.00       +   352.98   =   472.98
```

Figure 12-5 This is the statement for Burt's highest interest charge card, and he forgot to make a payment last month. He charged the auto service on this one because the others were already near their limit. Which of the types of expenses on this card could Burt reduce? Eliminate?

Interest rates vary a lot on cards. The interest charged by a bank can be as low as 10 percent. But many retail stores and outlets, such as The Bay, Canadian Tire, or Petro Canada, issue their own cards, known as *retail* cards. They can charge as much as 30 percent per year on their cards. Some cards also charge an **annual fee**, usually between $10 and $100 per year. Others charge a monthly fee for services such as insurance in case the card is stolen. When you are offered a credit card, ask about all charges before you accept the offer.

When you apply for a credit card, the financial institution may ask you to find a person who already has a good credit rating to **co-sign** your application. The co-signer agrees to pay your debt if you don't live up to your responsibilities.

You must keep within your credit limit and make the minimum payment each month, usually 5 percent of the total outstanding balance, by the due date. If you don't, further purchases or cash advances may be declined (turned down). This can be very embarrassing in a restaurant or a busy store.

Keep in mind that when you use a credit card, the financial institution is advancing money *to the owner* of the business for *your* debt. Once the business deposits the charge slip to get the money, you owe the money to the financial institution. If you don't pay, the financial institution will stop paying your debts, and may take other actions, as discussed below.

Are credit cards a bad thing? In 2000, over half of Canadian credit card holders paid the entire outstanding balance each month on their credit cards. For them, the credit card was a short-term, zero-interest loan. The other half did not pay off the balance. For them, the credit card became a very high-interest loan. That's what happened to Burt (see Figure 12-5).

The Credit Rating

Some people who can't pay their credit card bill try to get new cards from other financial institutions. Do they succeed? To try to prevent this, institutions use the services of *credit bureaus*. **Credit bureaus** are companies that gather and provide information on the credit history of potential customers. **Credit history** is the history of paying back debts. Financial institutions provide this information to the credit bureau, which in turn shares it with other financial institutions for a fee.

Credit bureaus keep a record of your credit rating for the last seven years. A lender or property owner who wants to do business with you may pay to find out your credit rating. They want to know if you are a "late payer" or, worse, *in default*. **Default** means that a debt has gone unpaid for so long that the creditor wonders if the money will ever be paid.

A reputation as a bad credit risk can be very serious—you could be denied a loan for a car, for example, even if you need it to get to a new job. Property owners may refuse to rent to you. Stores may insist on cash.

Burt was in serious danger of developing a bad credit rating. After several years, he could barely pay the interest on his charge cards, let alone pay down the principal. Luckily, he realized that his situation signalled a serious financial problem (see Figure 12-6).

Why Burt's Debts Were Becoming Unmanageable

	1997	1998	1999	2000
Bert's net pay	$40 000.00	$42 000.00	$45 000.00	$45 000.00
Car payments/year	10 860.96	10 860.96	10 860.96	10 860.96
Total charge card balances (3 cards)/year	1 000.00	5 000.00	11 000.00	17 000.00
Rent/year	14 400.00	15 120.00	15 877.80	16 672.80
Other expenses/year	10 000.00	10 000.00	11 500.00	8 000.00
Surplus savings/(shortfall)	$3 739.04	$1 019.04	-$4 238.46	-$7 533.76

Figure 12-6 These expenses show why Burt's debts were becoming unmanageable by 2001. He has three credit cards, each with a high limit, and no budget. A luxury apartment, a luxury car, and a matching lifestyle meant hardly any savings or investments. Burt put many expenses, including car-related ones, on his credit cards and often carried balances from month to month. He forgot to make a payment last month, and a big, unexpected expense put him over the limit. Can you see why the bank manager told him he was on the "wrong side" of compound interest?

Credit Counselling

After receiving the statement shown in Figure 12-5 for one of his credit cards, Burt sought confidential advice from a local credit counselling service. The not-for-profit agency, which is supported by financial institutions, is one of a network of organizations across Canada that helps people deal with debt problems. The counsellor did not lecture Burt about his lifestyle, but did help him understand the significance of the figures shown in Figure 12-6. Then he helped him develop a realistic budget to reduce his debt.

One option was for the agency to contact the financial institutions and arrange a payment plan that let Burt take longer than usual to pay off his debt. Burt would pay the money to the agency, and they in turn would pay it to the creditors. Meanwhile, the creditors would promise not to send threatening letters or try embarrassing tactics like phoning Burt at his work.

Web Connect

www.school.mcgrawhill.ca/resources/
Take a look at the different rates charged by credit card companies in Canada, and decide which card would be the most economical to use.

But this payment plan was not necessary. Burt accepted that, on his salary, he could not afford a luxury car, or the lifestyle that went with it. Because he needed a car to get to work, he sold his luxury car and got a much cheaper one. Burt acted before he could no longer afford to make payments on the status car, so he ensured that he could still get a loan for the new one. He decided to **consolidate** (put together) the remaining credit card debt (which averaged 16 percent in interest) and took out the personal loan at 10 percent to pay it off. The bank manager was willing to lend him the money once he had lowered his living costs.

Obtaining Credit

You should use a credit card only for expenses that you expect to pay off within a month. For longer-term debts, many other types of consumer credit—loans for a variety of purposes at a variety of interest rates—are available. Usually, the interest rates are lower. The manager at the financial institution decides whether the borrower qualifies for the loan. You have already learned basic facts about mortgage loans in Chapters 10 and 11. The following are some other major varieties of consumer credit.

Personal Loan

If you are a qualified borrower, a financial institution may allow you to take out a personal loan for almost anything: a computer, a holiday, home renovations, or an investment. The financial institution is not concerned with whether your purchase is a good idea, only with whether you can afford the monthly payments, given your sources of income and your level of debt and assets. Personal loans must be repaid in equal monthly payments for the term of the loan—usually between one and five years.

Car Loan

The interest rate for a car loan is often less than the rate for a personal loan. But financial institutions usually restrict these loans to the purchase of new cars. This is because a new car has several features that assist financial calculations:

- a generally agreed value
- marketability at or near the agreed value
- a warranty against serious defects, which would significantly reduce its value (usually three years or 60 000 km).

Thus, the car itself is collateral against the loan. By contrast, the value of older used cars (more than three years old) can vary significantly, depending on where, how, and how much they were driven. For a used car, the bank may insist on the higher "personal loan" rate. So, when deciding between new and used, the customer needs to weigh differing interest rates and performance guarantees against the vehicle's price.

Car loan customers are wise to get pre-authorization from the bank before they go shopping. **Pre-authorization** is the bank's guarantee that it will advance the customer an agreed amount of money; it is based on the customer's income and other debts. Recall that Lawrence got pre-authorization for a mortgage loan. Pre-authorization assures you and the seller that you can afford the purchase. It reduces the risk of signing an agreement for which you cannot raise the funds.

Personal Line of Credit

A **personal line of credit** is a permanent offer of a loan from a financial institution. If you have a personal line of credit, for example, you can write a cheque for more than your chequing account balance and the financial institution will advance you the amount required to make

Biz.Bites

Don't shop for a large purchase alone—take a skeptical, neutral friend. Do not sign anything on the sales floor. Break for a snack with your friend, talk it over, consider other options, and then decide.

up the total. The amount that is advanced becomes a personal loan. Similarly, the personal line of credit would ensure that funds were advanced to meet an automatic monthly payment. The interest on these loans is lower than on credit cards, but only customers with very good credit ratings are eligible for this type of loan.

Installment Plan

An **installment plan** is a loan granted either by or through a retailer for an expensive purchase such as a TV. Or a fuel gas company, for example, may offer financing for energy-saving renovations that will be paid for on the fuel bill. The fuel company already knows whether the customer is reliable. The item is delivered or installed immediately, and the loan is paid off monthly thereafter. To qualify for these types of loans, the customer must choose a product offered by or through the retailer or provider.

Interest rates for installment plans match retail credit card rates or home renovation loan rates. But sometimes the creditor offers lower rates to get business. Items may even be sold on "interest free" installment plans—in other words, the retailer pays the interest costs of the loan. "Interest-free" offers usually require the installment loan to be paid within one year.

Are installment plans good or bad for the customer? It depends on the alternatives. An installment plan for fuel-saving renovations might be smarter than trying to save the money while paying higher fuel costs. However, with TVs, the company may be trying to clear outdated or unpopular stock by offering bargain financing. Another problem is that, lured by an offer of "no money down," you may buy a more expensive item than you can afford.

Dealing with Credit You Cannot Afford

Failure to Make Payments

When a customer does not make payments on credit cards or personal loans, after a few reminders by phone or mail, the financial institution may use a collection agency. A **collection agency** is a company hired to collect overdue accounts from customers. The agency may resort to annoying, persistent, embarrassing calls and letters to get action.

Collection agencies must operate according to rules established by law:

- They may contact you at home or at work to try to collect a debt but only between 7:00 am and 10:00 pm.
- They cannot call you or your family so often that the number of calls could be considered harassment.
- Collection agencies can only discuss the details of your debt with you and the creditor.
- Collection agencies cannot contact your friends, neighbours, family, or employer except to have the employer verify employment, or get your address or phone number.

When customers do not pay regularly on an installment plan or car loan, the purchase may be *repossessed* (taken back) and the customer's credit rating will be damaged. A bank may take money from bank accounts to pay outstanding debts. Wages can also be **garnisheed**— money is removed from the pay cheque at the same time as income tax and mandatory government deductions.

Personal Bankruptcy

The customer who simply cannot pay debts faces personal bankruptcy. This disastrous outcome is happening to increasing numbers of Canadians who use credit unwisely. The conditions for **bankruptcy** are that the person must

- owe at least $1 000
- be unable to meet regular payments
- owe more than his or her assets are worth.

Personal bankruptcy is devastating—you must sell all assets other than clothing, furniture, and personal items. You cannot get credit for seven years. Fortunately, the use of a budget and financial plan make bankruptcy a very unlikely event.

Figure 12-7 Do you think that credit problems could cause stress in real life (as opposed to the life of a cartoon character)? What kinds of stress?

Check Your Understanding

Knowledge/Understanding

1 Suggest two ways you can establish a credit rating.

2 What does co-signing for a loan mean? Would you co-sign a loan for someone? Explain your decision.

Thinking/Inquiry

Skills
Appendix

analysing media

3 No Money Down! No Payments Till Next Year! Do these claims in ads sound too good to be true? Obtain flyers offering these incentives and *read the fine print* regarding the terms and conditions. What did you learn? Could the merchandise end up costing more than a straightforward credit purchase? If the offer is good only on "selected merchandise," could there be hidden pitfalls? Explain.

Communication

4 Debate the following statement: Society would be a better place if financial institutions stopped people from getting into high credit card debt before they reach a crisis.

Application

Skills
Appendix

brainstorming

5 Must a good time be an expensive time? Assume an unexpected expense has cut deeply into your savings. Explain how you would handle the following situations:

- You promised to treat a friend to a birthday dinner and movie. You can spend $20.00. Research reduced-price nights and two-for-one deals and present the best local deal to a group or the class.
- You need to buy holiday gifts for five family members, including an elderly man, a middle-aged woman, a teen (girl or boy), a seven-year-old girl or boy, and a baby. You can spend $50.00. (*Note:* You can offer services instead of money, as long as they have a financial value.) List what you would do and why.

Calculating the Cost of Credit

As you know, when banks lend money, they calculate the interest rate using a number of factors:

- credit risk
- inflation
- term
- profit for the bank

As a result, interest rates can range from a low of 5 percent per year for a mortgage to 16 percent per year or more for a personal loan.

Burt's car loan, at 10 percent, is costing him a lot. The status car cost $42 085, which included taxes, air conditioning, and delivery, Take a look at Figure 12-8 to see just how this breaks out.

Burt's current car loan:

Facts	Figures
Sticker price of car 4 years ago	$35 900.00
Add in taxes, delivery costs, etc.	$42 085.00
Monthly payment	$905.08
Term	5 years
Down payment	$2000.00
Annual interest rate	10%
Gross cost of car including interest costs	$56 304.90
Trade-in value after term (5 years)	$12 137.79
Net cost of car	$44 167.11

Figure 12-8

Bear in mind that Burt will also spend over $5 000 a year to operate the vehicle, including fuel, insurance, fees, and repairs not covered by warranty.

If Burt had researched and negotiated different loan conditions, would he be better off? Figure 12-10 takes a look at available options.

Different loan conditions would have reduced Burt's indebtedness, but he still could not really afford a status car. After he had drawn up a financial plan, Burt sold his status car and bought a Honda Civic coupe. The trade-in price for the four-year-old car, which is four years old, was less than $16 000. This almost covered the cost of the two-door Civic, including all taxes. Burt was smart enough to search for a two-year-old car, still on warranty, with very low mileage.

Burt, Lawrence, and Bobby had a steak barbecue to celebrate Burt's car-loan and credit-card freedom day. Burt cut up two of his three cards. "Sure, I miss the luxuries," he said, "but I don't miss the sleepless nights. Last year, my heart was racing more often from opening my bills than from driving a beautiful car."

Car Loan Options Available to Burt

If Bert changed loan conditions:	Sticker price of car – 4 years ago	Add-in taxes, delivery. costs, etc	Monthly payment	Term	Down payment	Annual interest rate	Gross Cost of vehicle including interest costs	Trade in at end of term	Net cost of vehicle (Gross cost minus trade-in)
Change term to 4 years	$35 900.00	$42 085.00	$1 080.40	4 years	2 000.00	10%	$53 858.98	$15 577.01	$38 281.97
Change term to 3 years	$35 900.00	$42 085.00	$1 374.52	3 years	$2 000.00	10%	$51 482.64	$19 604.99	$31 877.65
Change term to 3 years and negotiate 8% interest rate	$35 900.00	$42 085.00	$1 334.87	3 years	$2 000.00	8%	$50 055.19	$19 604.99	$30 450.20
Change term to 3 years and negotiate 8% interest rate and increase down payment to $8 000.00	$35 900.00	$42 085.00	$1 146.85	3 years	$8 000.00	8%	$49 286.54	$19 604.99	$29 681.55

Figure 12-9

If Burt had researched and planned his car purchase more carefully, the overall cost at the end of the loan term would have changed greatly.

Once he had sorted out his car problems, Burt arranged to pay off the credit card companies. Remember that the bank manager had given him a personal loan to consolidate them. Why is that an advantage? You'll recall from Figure 12-6 that Burt had amassed a whopping $17 000 balance on his three credit cards. The balance compounded daily, with an average yearly interest rate of 16 percent. But the $17 000 personal loan has only a 10 percent interest rate. Also, the loan will compound monthly, whereas the charge card balances compounded daily. Have a look at Figure 12-10 to see how much difference this consolidation will make to Burt.

Consumer credit is not good or bad in itself any more than the interest rate is good or bad in itself. The smart personal financial manager develops a good credit rating, and then treats credit as a financial instrument to be used—or set aside—as part of a plan for building wealth.

Saving on Interest Debt

Figure 12-10 With the same monthly payment, Burt will pay off his consolidated loan sooner and with less interest than he could pay off the credit cards. How much will Burt save in interest?

$17,000.00 Debt	Monthly Payment	Total Interest	Total Interest & Principal	Time to Pay Off
Charge Cards 16%	$450.00	$6 802.00	$23 802.00	4 years and 5 months
Consolidated Loan 10%	$450.00	$3 503.97	$20 503.97	3 years and 10 months

Knowledge/Understanding

1 Identify two factors that determine the final cost of borrowing $5000.

Thinking/Inquiry

2 Kim Seong's father will buy her a computer system for up to $1500 on credit. He has asked her to research financing options. Byte Shoppe wants $1200 for a suitable system. Kim has identified the following options:

a) Bank loan at 9% interest compounded monthly for one year.

b) Zed Computer Store's installment plan—a zero-interest loan for one year, repayable in 12 equal monthly installments. However, Kim must pay $1365 for an identical system.

c) Byte Shoppe's once-a-year Midnite Madness sale happens tonight. At 10:00 p.m., Kim and her father can get the same system for $1150. Because of the rush, her father can finance the purchase only by getting a Byte Shoppe credit card at 22% interest, compounded daily. He can afford to pay off the cost as follows: $250 before the due date; $400 on the next monthly statement, and $500 on the one thereafter. Which offer results in the lowest overall cost to Kim's father? Ignore taxes and delivery when computing your answer.

Communication

3 Prepare a chart that Kim can use to demonstrate to her father which option costs least. Include figures for all three options.

Application

4 Assume that after the sale the Byte Shoppe agrees to hold an unsold computer system for Kim for two weeks, for a firm price of $1150. This gives Kim's father time to obtain a credit card sponsored by a financial institution. Research the best rate available to him. Can you find a rate lower than the personal loan rate?

Skills
Appendix

researching

Your high school education is funded by local property taxes and provincial grants. Once you graduate from high school, you must finance further education yourself. The first big credit decision many Ontario students make is how to finance postsecondary education. Your school's guidance office provides many resources on this subject. Consider the following options:

Financial assistance as a gift (not a loan). First, research any assistance you need not repay:

This includes scholarships (financial reward for academic achievement), bursaries (award based on need), and grants (money awarded by government under a specific program). Also find out whether a union or religious or cultural organization of which your parent or guardian is a member offers financial assistance to students.

Ontario Student Assistance Plan (OSAP). OSAP is a loan program sponsored by the Ontario government. If you must borrow to get postsecondary education, the government pays the interest on your loan while you are studying. You do not start to pay back the principal or interest until six months after you graduate. The payment-free period gives you time to find a job.

However, you must ask, will my degree, diploma, or certificate lead to a job? By law, universities, community colleges, and vocational schools that participate in OSAP must tell you how many students graduated, how many graduates got jobs, and how many defaulted on loans. This information is available through the Ontario Student Assistance Plan.

Registered Education Savings Plan (RESP). An RESP is a tax shelter, like the RRSP you have learned about in this unit. An eligible adult can invest money for your education before taxes are calculated. This is the most economical way that an adult who has a taxable income can assist you. A manager at a financial institution can help to arrange an RESP.

Personal savings. While personal savings will not likely pay the whole cost of your education, they can help you deal with unexpected problems. For example, suppose a payment from a funding source is delayed. Personal savings let you pay your bills. You can focus on your education, not on urgent financial worries.

Research university co-op programs. To earn while you learn, a co-op program may be your wisest choice. Your education will take a year or two longer, but you gain valuable work experience—and may get a job with a co-op employer. Over 35 000 Ontario postsecondary students participated in co-op programs in 2001.

ACTIVITIES

1 List five sources of income for postsecondary students in Ontario.
2 Explain how the student can benefit from the requirement that a program eligible for OSAP must say how many graduating students got jobs.
3 John's guardian is worried about John going into debt for postsecondary education. What if he can't get a job in today's economy? Using facts you have learned about employment, education, and credit, give your own view.
4 Find the Web site for Schoolfinder and make a point form list of the types of information aimed at a student who is investigating postsecondary education.

Chapter Review

Points to Remember

- An advantage of consumer credit is that it can be used to purchase assets with a high financial value. A disadvantage is that consumers may finance expenses they cannot afford.

- Some assets appreciate in value, and others depreciate in value.

- For future success, it is important to get and keep a good credit rating.

- Interest is charged on credit card purchases only if the balance is not paid by a certain date.

- Credit counselling agencies assist consumers who cannot manage their debt.

- Pre-authorization means a bank agrees in advance to lend the customer a specific sum of money.

- An installment plan is a loan, offered by a business, that allows customers to purchase an item and pay part of the cost on a regular basis over a specific period of time.

- A car loan is generally available for new cars. A personal loan is available for used cars and for a variety of other purposes.

- A consumer may save money on interest charges by consolidating debts into one loan with a lower interest rate.

Activities

Knowledge/Understanding

1 What four factors affect the way banks determine the interest rate at which they will lend to an individual? Which of these factors does the Bank of Canada affect?

2 Explain specific steps a young person can take to establish a good credit rating.

3 What three factors lower the net cost of a car loan?

4 Which types of loans have the lowest and highest interest rates? Why?

Thinking/Inquiry

1 Could you live using credit only (no cash)? As you go through a day, list the financial transactions that you could have put on a credit card. Also, list those that required cash. Treat debit card transactions as cash transactions. What types of transactions require cash? What types permit credit? If possible, compare notes with other students.

Skills
Appendix

researching,
working in groups

2 Working in a small group, investigate the student loan offers of Canada's six chartered banks. Note important features of each type of loan, including interest rate and rules about when and how the money is paid back. As a group, vote on which you think is the best package.

Communication

1 Write and present a short monologue called "A Day on Credit." Explain how a typical day in your life would change if you could not use cash or a debit card. Assume that you are legally entitled to a credit card. How would you adapt? Some research will be needed. After you walk your audience through your all-credit day, tell them what aspect of cash you would miss the most.

Skills
Appendix

oral presentations

2 Working with a group, prepare a flip chart presentation on the key features of student loans. Base your presentation on what your group learned while investigating these loans in Thinking/Inquiry Activity 2.

Application

1 You saw from Figure 12-10 that changing the loan conditions affected the net cost of Burt's car. This principle applies to mortgages as well. The chart below shows Lawrence's present mortgage costs and the costs he would face if interest rates were higher.

Interest on $176 000.00 mortgage. (This interest rate is fixed for five years, compounding semi-annually.	Monthly payment	Paid off each year, in addition to monthly payment each year	Interest paid over life of 5-year mortgage. Assume 25 years to pay off whole amount
@ 6.25%	$1 170.00	$5 000.00	$74 297.00
@ 10.00%	$1 378.00	$5 000.00	$117 760.00
@ 12.00%	$1 589.13	$5 000.00	$138 772.00

Note the difference in monthly payments between the 6.25% and 12.00%. Looking back at Lawrence's budget in Figure 11-18, calculate the effect on his savings. If he had a 12.00% mortgage, could he pay off $5 000 a year on the principal? (Assume no other expenses change.) Would a 12% mortgage rate affect his credit when he went to the bank for the renovation loan? Explain. (*Note:* Canada Mortgage and Housing Corporation does not recommend more than a 32% ratio of mortgage, taxes, and heating to one's total income. And no more than 40% total debt.)

2 Looking back at Lawrence's budget (Figure 11-15,), answer the following questions. Assume that Lawrence heats his home with natural gas.

- Does Lawrence really need the income from the basement apartment? That is, what difference does it make to his total debt service ratio? Is it a critical difference?
- When Lawrence has paid off the capital improvement loan for the basement apartment, how will the ratio change? Will not having that debt make a significant difference?
- Assume Lawrence can buy and operate a truck for $800.00 per month. Can he do it, within the current budget situation? Explain, using ratios, and assuming that $340.00 of the expense is debt.

3 For the following question, assume that Lawrence is allowed to raise Burt's rent by 4% per year. Can Lawrence afford the truck after the renovation loan is paid off in three years' time? Explain.

UNIT 4 Entrepreneurship

Overall Expectations

By the end of this unit, you will

- identify characteristics and skills associated with successful entrepreneurs

- evaluate the roles and contributions of entrepreneurs

- analyse the importance of invention and innovation in entrepreneurship

An entrepreneur is a business person who is willing to take the risk of starting a new enterprise, often based on a new idea or invention. There is considerable financial risk involved because not all new ideas work out. You will learn about the characteristics of successful entrepreneurs in Chapter 13. Entrepreneurship has a long history in Canada, so you will also learn about famous Canadians who have impacted our business community with their new ideas, products, and services.

The entrepreneur usually starts by discovering an opportunity, an unfilled need, or an unserved market. He or she often sees opportunity where others see only a problem or inconvenience. In order to develop the opportunity into a business, however, the entrepreneur must get funding. To get funding, he or she must convince others that the business will be profitable. In Chapter 14, you will learn how entrepreneurs find opportunities and develop them into businesses.

The development of new technologies has meant a hugely increased role for inventors and innovators in Canada. But often new developments come at the expense of making old technologies and businesses obsolete. In Chapter 15, you will learn what happens when someone invents a new product, process or service, or introduces a new idea into the business marketplace. You will also explore the relationship between inventors, who develop a new product or service, and entrepreneurs, who develop a business around it.

13 Characteristics and Skills of Entrepreneurs

KEY TERMS

entrepreneur
dot-com company
aptitude
initiative
risk-tolerance
confidence
creativity
mission statement
integrity

Specific Expectations

After studying this chapter, you will be able to

- **describe the characteristics and skills often associated with successful entrepreneurs**

- **explain how these characteristics and skills can be applied to any kind of entrepreneurial endeavour**

- **describe the lives and accomplishments of a variety of Canadian entrepreneurs**

- **analyze your own entrepreneurial strengths and interests**

Entrepreneurs can be in their teens or in their 70s, male or female, formally educated or self-educated. They come from many countries and backgrounds. But they have some characteristics and skills in common. Entrepreneurs recognize business opportunities more quickly than other people. They see potential business opportunities in problems and are not afraid to take risks, to make decisions, or to work hard. They are problem-solvers who communicate well and who inspire others to follow their lead.

As you will see in this chapter, you too can become an entrepreneur. Many of the skills shared by successful entrepreneurs can be learned and developed at home, at school, at work, and in the community.

Prokop-O'Brien

Jeen O'Brien, Stephan Szczesniak, Christina Prokop, and Jeff Lowe are the partners in Prokop-O'Brien. These four, all still in their 20s, are bringing together their talents and skills to write, perform, and produce jingles for commercials on radio and television, at Web sites, and in video games.

Jeen, who writes her own music, has been singing with a band since the age of 15. She has a powerful, rich voice which she has been training for years. Jeen has appeared on television, had music CDs and videos made, and has played in clubs wherever there was an opportunity to perform and have her music heard.

Stephan started playing the drums when he was 8. He too has played in bands, and he has toured with country music artists. Stephan went to the Etobicoke School of the Arts and then on to Humber College. He is the music arranger. He works with a song to make it feel right, creating bridges between the verse and the chorus, establishing the tempo and the colour of the different instruments that will be used.

Christina began her business career as a model, working in different locales around the world. By the time she was 20, she decided that her modelling career was over. She was getting too old. So, she came back to Canada and joined the film industry. She works with the producers of commercials. She takes care of the details of a commercial shoot, working with clients and the creative people who are making the commercials, coordinating the details of the project and keeping track of the financial details so that everyone stays on budget.

Jeff has been playing the guitar since he was 10 years old. He and Stephan have performed together with various bands over the years. Jeff also provides music for films. He is the one of the four who most clearly combines his artistic gifts with a sound knowledge of business and how it works. He knows the people who would hire Prokop-O'Brien, and he knows how to talk to those people in a convincing manner.

So, how will Prokop-O'Brien solve problems for clients and differentiate themselves from the competition? They will offer music that will be more creative than the usual commercial music and that will appeal to the large demographic group from teenagers up to 40-year-olds. They are, as they say, real musicians, people who love music. Music isn't just a job to them. It's their passion! Their clients will have that talent and passion working for them in the commercials created by Prokop-O'Brien.

Jeen O'Brien

Stephan Szczesniak

Christina Prokop and Jeff Lowe

Figure 13-1 Jeen, Stephan, Christina, and Jeff are launching Prokop-O'Brien, a new entrepreneurial enterprise. Their motto will be "Art for the sake of advertising."

The group knows that they have a lot to learn and will need a lot of help as they get started. But they have some strong support systems in place. Stephan's father, Tom Szczesniak, and his partner, Ray Parker, will help. The two men are musicians who have been writing and producing music for 35 years for companies like Nelvana. You've probably heard Tom and Ray's songs in Beetle Juice and Babar films. The two mentors have the sound equipment as well as the experience, and the four young entrepreneurs will have access to both as they start out. Stephan points out that this is a tremendous advantage, because the equipment is far too expensive for a new company to invest in and the experience would take years to acquire.

Jeen, Stephan, Christina, and Jeff meet often to work out their business plan, to select the music for their demo CD, and to make decisions together. They are determined to keep their business grounded in the real world. Jeen, who will be the primary writer, knows this will be a challenge for her. She says she recognizes that she will need to write to satisfy what the client wants, rather than "writing from the heart."

The four partners are in the process of putting together their demo CD. Jeff and Christina have the business connections, so they will take the demo around to prospective clients. Once they have a couple of clients and are earning some money, then they will invest in their own equipment. They'll still have their mentors, Tom and Ray, to help. The young people know that the experience of the older artists will be invaluable to them.

As you read this chapter on the roles and characteristics of entrepreneurs, keep Prokop-O'Brien in mind. How do their skills, talents, and characteristics fit the profile of an entrepreneur? How have they used their strengths and interests to start their new business venture?

What Is an Entrepreneur?

Entrepreneurs have always been with us. Back when people were hunters and gatherers, following herds of animals for food and picking whatever plants they found, someone thought of doing things differently. Some ancient entrepreneur decided to plant crops and raise domestic animals.

An **entrepreneur** is a person who organizes, manages, and assumes the risks of starting and operating an enterprise. Entrepreneurs provide new goods or services that will meet people's needs and wants, or solve their problems. Many entrepreneurs start businesses to make a profit. Others are motivated by different goals, such as helping the people in their communities. This form of entrepreneurship might involve starting a charitable organization like a food bank to solve the problem of hunger.

Figure 13-2 Mark Cullen comes from a family of entrepreneurs. He is the president of Weall and Cullen Nurseries Ltd. Mark's sister, Susan, runs Cullen Gardens and Miniature Village in Whitby, Ontario.

Why Become an Entrepreneur?

Some people seem to be born with an entrepreneurial spirit. As children they figured out how to sell the most chocolate bars for school fund-raisers. In high school, they started a window-cleaning business and hired others to work with them. They seem to be able to solve a problem before other people even recognize there is one. They want independence as they earn an income, and they aren't afraid of hard work or being different. They have the characteristics and skills to run a successful enterprise.

Leaps in technology have made it easier for young people with talent and skills to develop ideas and start their own businesses. Teenagers and 20-year-olds have started dot-com companies. A **dot-com company** does business on the Internet or helps other companies offer products or services over the Internet. With minimal investment and a good computer, these young entrepreneurs build successful companies. Not all of them survive in the long-term, but the trend of younger people taking on the entrepreneurial challenge has been featured in numerous media stories in the past five years.

At the same time, technology has advanced to the point that start-up business costs, especially those for a home office, are relatively affordable. Many people who may not have considered starting their own businesses now think about entrepreneurship.

New Directions

Frequently, a sudden change in circumstances motivates, or even forces, people to start businesses in order to earn an income that will provide for their wants and needs.

With the recession that started in 1989 and continued into the early 1990s, many people were laid off. People who thought they had job security until retirement were suddenly out of work. Since so many companies had cut jobs, no one was hiring. Rather than continue to job-search, some people chose to start their own business.

Many people who have immigrated to Canada–such as Frank Stronach of Magna International and Peter Munk of Barrick Gold Corp.–have used their experience and skills, along with their personal drive and ambition, to start their own very successful business ventures. Dissatisfaction with current employment can motivate some people to start their own businesses.

Some groups have found opportunities for advancement in employment difficult. Women, for example, have had difficulty in getting promoted to the highest levels of corporate management, although this is less the case today. Women still are one of the fastest growing groups of entrepreneurs. One third of self-employed Canadians are women.

Sometimes the opportunity to start an entrepreneurial venture is related to geography. For example, Patrick Akpalialuk is the founder of Northstar Networks in Nunavut. Northstar manufactures and services computers in Canada's newest territory. Patrick turned the challenge of being far from major computer suppliers into a business advantage. He provides the people in his community with one-stop computer shopping and servicing.

Figure 13-3 In 2000, Patrick Akpalialuk won the Young Entrepreneur Award for Nunavut from the Business Development Bank of Canada. As part of his award, Patrick will have a leading senior business person from Nunavut to help him with his business for a year.

Characteristics of Successful Entrepreneurs

Imagine an entrepreneur who didn't like to take risks. Or consider what would happen to someone who gets terrific ideas but can't persevere. Successful entrepreneurs need a variety of characteristics, including risk-tolerance and perseverance.

Although not every entrepreneur has every one of the following character traits, most entrepreneurs will have most of these characteristics in common. While you're reading, think about whether you share some of the same aptitudes and characteristics.

Aptitude

Most people have a wide range of **aptitudes**–natural talents, tendencies, or capacities. Entrepreneurs apply their aptitudes to their business ventures. Some aptitudes that could be useful in an entrepreneurial venture are the following:

- Artistic–Entrepreneurs can use their artistic talents in many different ways. For example, they may be recording artists, producers of movies or television shows, creators of video games, or Web designers.
- Perceptive–Some people just seem to be more perceptive than the rest of us when it comes to understanding other people's intentions, ideas, or emotions. Perceptive entrepreneurs can define the real problem that people are having in satisfying their needs and wants.
- Logical–Other people are able to apply reason quickly to solve consumer and business problems.
- Mechanical–People with this aptitude can understand how machines and mechanisms work and how they could be improved.
- Spatial–People with this aptitude–for example architects and interior designers–can use space in an attractive or economical manner.
- Physical–Great athletes often have superior physical abilities. They have strength, endurance, co-ordination, and the ability to excel at sports.
- Intellectual–People with this aptitude have a desire to seek out knowledge, to plan ahead, and to come up with original ideas and combinations of ideas.

What are your aptitudes and talents? Perhaps you can draw cartoons, ski exceptionally well, or teach ballet to children. These talents just seem to be part of who you are. With practice, hard work, and education, you can take a basic talent and turn it into an entrepreneurial enterprise.

Vision

Entrepreneurs can visualize their end results or goals. They have a **vision** of their success, and they constantly work toward making it real. They make business decisions with this end in mind and don't get sidetracked. Often, they have written our their vision, either formally in a mission statement, or informally, perhaps in a personal journal. A **mission statement** presents the aims, objectives, and general principles that a company focuses on. Entrepreneurs refer back to this statement often. The vision can evolve as the business grows, but remains clear and attainable to the successful entrepreneur.

Risk-tolerance

Risk tolerance is the degree to which you can comfortably accept taking chances. Entrepreneurs need to have a pretty high tolerance of risks. This doesn't mean that they are gamblers, but they do take calculated risks. For them, the opportunity of success outweighs the possibility of failure. And even if they do fail, entrepreneurs are likely to try again.

Figure 13-4

Entrepreneur Heather Reisman turned a small book shop into a flourishing modern bookstore with an online component and later bought out Chapters, a larger chain of stores.

For example, Heather Reisman, the founder of Indigo Books, Music & More, has a high risk tolerance. She heads up the merged Chapters and Indigo companies in a tough business environment and a fragile industry. But, then, Heather is not afraid of tough situations.

In 1996, she left her job as president of Cott Corporation, the soft drink manufacturer, and decided to take the risk of starting her own book-selling company. She was warned that she couldn't compete against Chapters. Chapters was the major bookstore in Canada at the time. The risk of taking on this giant was considerable. However, Heather judged that consumers wanted something different from their bookstore. And Indigo was different, offering coffee and music as well as books in both its physical stores and its virtual store on the Internet. Heather Reisman's risk paid off.

Confidence

Those who have **confidence** believe in their own abilities. Because they are sure of themselves, it is easier for others to believe in them. Even if they fail, they know they will succeed the next time. This is a key characteristic of entrepreneurs. Their confidence can help them work through setbacks and sell ideas to potential customers and investors. Sometimes this can be the confidence to know when to ask for help. A confident person can say "I don't understand" or "I need help" without feeling embarrassed.

Creativity

Creativity is the ability to create things, usually in an imaginative way. Artists are creative. As you saw in the Business Profile at the start of this chapter, the four partners of Prokop-O'Brien are all creative artists in their own fields. Whether the **creativity** appears as an invention, an innovation, or as marketing or problem solving, the successful entrepreneur is an "idea" person. Entrepreneurs see opportunities everywhere. Just walking down the street, they see gaps between needs and wants. Usually, they have many more ideas than they can ever implement.

Figure 13-5 Sarah McLachlan's Lilith Fair took the idea of a rock concert and merged it with a festival. In this photo, Sarah, Eden A.K.A. and Melanie Doane (from left to right) sing together at the Toronto stop of the 1998 Lilith Fair.

Sarah McLachlan, for example, used her singing and songwriting along with her understanding of the music industry, especially the lack of opportunities for women performers and bands. She created Lilith Fair, which showcased talented women performers in a unique festival atmosphere. Lilith Fair success has boosted Sarah McLachlan's profile internationally and expanded her audience.

Perseverance

Have you ever been so determined to succeed at something that you just kept trying until you got it right? That's a sign of **perseverance**.

Creating and running a business is hard work. It often means long hours, disappointments, and setbacks. Perseverance is the determination that pushes the entrepreneur to keep going, keep trying. This trait, which was introduced in Chapter 4 as a key requirement of a successful business, is necessary for a successful entrepreneur. Often, a new business can take two or more years to become profitable. A successful entrepreneur is prepared to continue selling his or her ideas through the tough times.

Figure 13-6 Miriam Goldberger of Wildflower Farms, whom you met in the Chapter 10 Business Profile displays many of the characteristics of the successful entrepreneur. She has the initiative and perseverance to see her dream through to reality.

Initiative

When an entrepreneur sees an opportunity, he or she takes the initiative. **Initiative** is the readiness and willingness to start a new enterprise. Entrepreneurs are self-motivated and quite willing to take on this leadership role and make themselves personally responsible for the success or failure of an operation.

For example, at the age of 17, Corey Hill was already showing initiative. She was the only Aboriginal person—and the only woman—in her welding class at the Guelph, Ont. technical college she attended. She successfully learned that trade. Then, after several years as a welder with the local gas company, she decided that she wanted to open the first health spa and fitness centre in Ohsweken, near Brantford, Ontario. Her spa, Choosing To Live Healthy, features a building of her own design which she built with the help of the local business development office, her father, and people from her community.

Figure 13-7 Feel Goods Cars turn antique Dauphine automobiles into clean-running electric cars. But it's their commitment to their customers and their own integrity that makes them so special.

Integrity

Integrity is the personal commitment to keep your promises, to do what you say you're going to do and when you say you're going to do it.

An entrepreneur with integrity creates confidence in customers and investors. When someone follows through on promises, customers keep coming back, and may even tell friends about the business. Personal integrity can help entrepreneurs maintain their commitment to their vision. Offering customers superior workmanship on products and providing good service may take a little longer, but the entrepreneur knows that his or her reputation depends on that high quality. Entrepreneurs with integrity are likely to be more successful than those who do not have integrity. Honest producers of goods and services tend to foster the loyalty of both their customers and their investors.

Feel Good Cars is one example of a business with integrity. The Canadian company converts Dauphine cars from the 1960s into completely pollution-free electric cars. In 2000, just as the cars were ready for production, someone discovered that the batteries used to power the vehicles were faulty. The faulty batteries could have burst in a front-end collision, and sprayed hazardous battery acid over the driver and passengers. Feel Good Cars quickly researched alternatives. The replacement batteries that the company found were more expensive, but Feel Good Cars used them because they were safer. Safety was non-negotiable. And the company didn't even raise the price on its cars.

Passion

Entrepreneurs are passionate about their ideas, their company, and their vision. Talk to any entrepreneur for five minutes about her company and you'll hear excitement in her voice. This passion helps entrepreneurs overcome the long hours, the disappointments, and the various challenges they will face.

Entrepreneurs love what they do. Often, their ideas arise from within, from something they love, like a hobby, or invention. As you saw in the Business Profile on Prokop-O'Brien, sometimes a group of people who have the same passion can join together to form an entrepreneurial enterprise. Jeen, Stephan, Christina, and Jeff are using their interest and experience in their arts of music and film to seize a business opportunity. Their enthusiasm for their idea keeps them moving forward.

What are you passionate about? A pastime, hobby, or sport? How could you turn your hobby into a business?

Check Your Understanding

Knowledge/Understanding

1 In your own words, define entrepreneurship.
2 Create a checklist that briefly defines the characteristics of a successful entrepreneur.

Thinking/Inquiry

3 Research a newspaper or magazine article on an entrepreneur. Identify and record how many of the entrepreneurial characteristics, from your checklist, that they have.
4 Throughout *Exploring Business for the 21st Century*, there are many stories, examples, and profiles of entrepreneurs—both in the chapter text and in the chapter features. Select two of these entrepreneurs and create a comparison chart to show how they have used their aptitudes successfully in their businesses.

Communication

5 Working in small groups, select two characteristics of entrepreneurs and develop a brief skit demonstrating those characteristics. Ask your classmates to identify the characteristics that your group is acting out.

Skills
Appendix

researching

Skills
Appendix

working in groups

Imagine yourself in the position of an entrepreneur struggling to make his or her idea or business a success. Select a famous entrepreneur like Bill Gates or Heather Reisman, for example. Write a page from his or her diary describing the day's problems and decisions. Be sure to demonstrate some entrepreneurial characteristics in your diary entry.

Entrepreneural Skills

Entrepreneurs need to have a wide variety of skills to run a successful business, including the skills listed in the Conference Board of Canada's Key Employability Skills (page 76-77). There are, however, some skills that are especially important for entrepreneurs: problem-solving, communication, planning, decision-making, and leadership skills.

Problem-solving

All of us have to deal with problems and find solutions to them. The successful entrepreneur sees opportunities in these problems where many of the rest of us only see difficulties. Sometimes the best new ideas come from the need to solve a problem.

Bombardier, as you saw in Chapter 4, was hit hard by the energy crisis in the 1970s. With gas prices soaring, consumers stopped buying the company's snowmobiles; they were just too expensive to run. So, how did a company that built gas-consuming vehicles handle the situation? Laurent Beaudoin of Bombardier solved the problem in an innovative way by diversifying the company's product line. He started the change in the company's focus by making vehicles for mass transit. Once that venture was successful, the company moved on to producing regional airplanes. Now, Bombardier is one of the world's top producers of subway cars and small and mid-sized jet airplanes.

Ted Rogers of Rogers Communication Inc. is also a problem-solver. Since 1962, he has recognized business opportunities in the challenges of changing communication technology. For example, when consumers' interest in the Internet grew, Rogers anticipated a decline in the popularity of television. Rather than fight the new media, he decided to work

Connecting Business with *Cartoon*

Lynn Johnston

Figure 13-7 "Most cartoonists start the way I did: doodling on anything as soon as I was able to hold a pen. . . I've always loved to draw. I always knew I would be a cartoonist, I never expected to make my LIVING as one!" (Lynn Johnstone)

In 1972 when Lynn Johnstone discovered that she was expecting a baby, she left her job as a medical artist at McMaster University. At her doctor's request, Lynn drew 80 cartoons spoofing the experience of being pregnant. The doctor displayed the cartoons in his office. They were a great success and were soon published in her first book, *David, We're Pregnant!*

With a new baby to take care of, Lynn became a freelance artist, working from home. She had trained for her career by studying art at the Vancouver School of Art and at Art College, before coming to live in Ontario. As a freelancer, she designed cereal boxes, billboards, leaflets, posters, flyers, and book illustrations. This was a difficult time, but very educational.

Two more well-received efforts brought Johnston to the attention of Universal Press Syndicate, which wrote to her in 1978 and asked if she was interested in doing a daily comic strip. She sent off 20 examples of "The Johnstons"—a series based on her own family—and later signed a 20-year contract.

Lynn's comic strip is unique because it deals with everyday, down-to-earth situations. "What sets Lynn's strip apart from the others," says Elizabeth Andersen, Johnston's editor at Universal Press Syndicate, "is that her characters and readers are not spared mid-life crises, financial hardships or confrontations with prejudice, child abuse and death."

Lynn Johnston's For Better or for Worse comics now appears in over 2000 newspapers in Canada, the United States and 23 other countries. They are translated into eight languages. Twenty-three books are currently in print. Along the way, Lynn Johnston became the first woman recipient of the "Reuben" (the comics world's "Oscar"), was named to the Order of Canada in 1992, and landed a Gemini for one of her seven animated television programs.

ACTIVITIES

1 Draw a comic strip or write a short story on turning an artistic talent into an entrepreneurial business.

2 Working with a partner, discuss why Lynn Johnston's cartoons are so popular. Relate her popularity to meeting consumer's needs and wants.

with it and launched Rogers@Home, a high-speed Internet provider service that operates through the cable lines. Rogers already had experience with the method of transmission laid because of its cable television service.

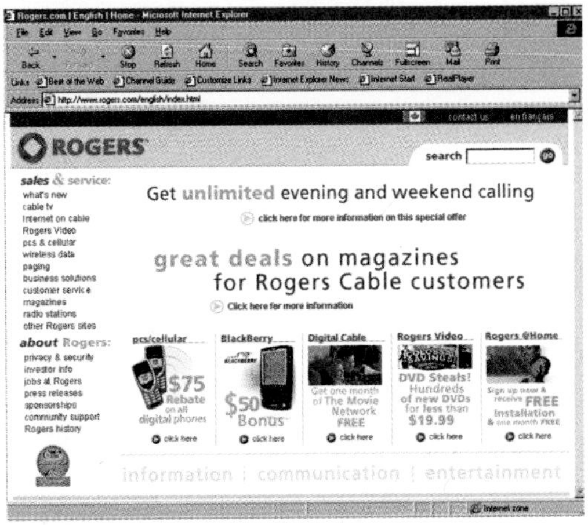

Communication

No matter how creative, talented, and confident you are, if you can't communicate to others that your ideas are worth their consideration, you won't be successful. Entrepreneurs have to be able to communicate clearly with customers, suppliers, banks, investors, and employees.

Figure 13-8 The Rogers @ Home web site shows how really *multi-media* Ted Rodgers' company is.

Entrepreneurs must answer e-mail, write letters and reports, and supervise the design of brochures or Web sites. They must read and review information. And, perhaps most importantly, they must listen. After they have read, observed, talked, viewed, or listened, they must analyze the information and their reactions. for material they can apply to their business.

Even if busy entrepreneurs hire others to handle most of these tasks, they still must communicate with the people they hire to ensure the work is done properly.

How are your communication skills? Are you able to explain your ideas in a way that people understand? Are you able to actively listen to someone else's ideas, asking appropriate questions to make sure you really know what they mean?

Writing

Writing well is critical to an entrepreneur. If, as an employee, you write clear and polite responses to customer-complaint emails, your writing will reflect well on your company. The customer may not remember your name, but he or she will be impressed with your company.

But if you are an entrepreneur and you write the same kind of clear and polite responses to complaints from customers, both you and your company are likely to be remembered favourably. Being able to write clearly, accurately, and persuasively can help you keep your customers. Good writing skills will also help you write stronger proposals, more efficient reports, and clearer press releases.

Web Connect

www.school.mcgrawhill.ca/resources/
How well do you communicate? Is faulty grammar
stopping you from expressing yourself clearly?
There are some useful online tools to help
you test both your communication
and grammar skills.

Reading

Being able to read quickly, accurately, and with a high level of recall is extremely useful in this age of information. With daily newspapers, weekly and monthly magazines and the Internet—the world's largest library right at your fingertips—you can get buried in information and quickly overwhelmed. In a way, an entrepreneur must be researching every day. Good reading skills can mean the difference between reacting in time to trends, or scrambling to catch up.

Speaking

Many people fear public speaking. Fortunately, you can learn to overcome these fears by learning speaking skills and techniques to turn your nervous energy into enthusiasm.

Often, potential investors, business customers, or even banks require business owners to make a presentation on their product or service. A presentation is a formal speech in which you "sell" your idea to your audience. Slightly different than a regular speech in which you simply share information, the presentation is designed to persuade listeners. Using sophisticated software programs, such as Microsoft PowerPoint, slide projectors, flip charts, or overhead projectors, the entrepreneur will try to convince his or her audience that the product or service is valuable and necessary. Making a compelling presentation means making a sale or impressing banks or investors. Entrepreneurs who learn this skill have a greater chance of success.

Listening

Good listeners have the ability to understand the intentions, ideas, or emotions that others express. An entrepreneur has to be able to listen carefully to find out what the customer really needs and wants.

For example, as a good listener, you may be able to turn an angry customer into one with a renewed commitment to your company. When a customer calls to complain, a wise entrepreneur sees this as an opportunity. Here is a real customer who took the time to provide you with feedback. This is valuable information.

If you listen in a respectful way, customers will recognize your sincere interest and willingness to correct the problem. They will end the call with a sense of accomplishment and a belief in your company's integrity. You will keep your customer and gather valuable insights.

Viewing and Representing

Entrepreneurs today also have to have sound viewing and representing skills. In a world that is full of media images—on television, on the Internet, on billboards, in newspapers and magazines—business people have to understand the impact such images have on consumers. In order to appreciate the effect that their own marketing and advertising campaigns will have on potential customers, entrepreneurs have to be able to analyse their own and their competitors' media images.

They also need to know how to make their own visual and media texts convincing for their target audience. While entrepreneurs may not actually be the ones who create the advertisement or the packaging, they do have to know what purpose the advertisement or package is to serve and how best to achieve that purpose. They have to be able to visualize the end result and identify the steps needed to achieve that result. They have to be able to keep their focus on that purpose and audience as they go through the brainstorming, planning, and drafting stages of media works.

Web Connect

www.school.mcgrawhill.ca/resources/

Media awareness covers a wide range of topics that are important to the entrepreneur, for example, news reporting, advertising, the protection of personal privacy, and online marketing directed at children. Learn more about these topics at the Media Awareness Web site.

Planning

Having a great idea is only the first step to becoming an entrepreneur. The difference between success and failure can be your ability to plan.

The advantages of planning are two fold. Planning allows you to prepare for the future. If you know you will need to replace expensive equipment in three years, you can begin saving now, rather than going into debt to purchase the replacement, or having the equipment break down because it has worn out.

Planning also means you are planning for growth. Thinking ahead about the changes your company needs to make to continue growing means it will grow with fewer surprises. Massive unexpected growth can leave entrepreneurs scrambling for equipment, staff, and time. Sometimes companies that grow rapidly without planning, collapse soon afterwards. They couldn't sustain the growth. We will have more to say about business and financial planning in Chapter 14.

Decision-making

Decision-making is another essential skill for the entrepreneur. Entrepreneurs.who put things off can miss opportunities, wasting time and money. An entrepreneur must

- look carefully at the advantages and disadvantages of each possible decision, weighing the short- and long-term risks
- consider a broad range of ideas from different sources, gathering and analysing information
- survey the market and talk to customers

The need to be right keeps some people from making a decision. Despite the possibility of making a mistake, the decision has to be made. If it turns out to have been a poor decision, a wise entrepreneur will learn from the mistake and move forward.

Leadership

Leadership is the ability to lead others. Leaders inspire others to follow their example. They don't have to do everything, or know everything, but they have to know what they want and who they, themselves, are.

Good leaders set an example by having superior works habits and acting with integrity. People are more likely to follow someone they respect.

Asking people for advice, praising ideas, and encouraging contributions are excellent leadership tactics. The more others feel they are valued, the more they seek ways to help and the more ideas they will contribute to the company. When things go wrong, strong leaders take full responsibility, but when they go well, attribute successes to the efforts of their team.

Figure 13-9 Leadership leads to success in all walks of life. Hockey great Wayne Gretsky shows leadership on and off the ice.

Check Your Understanding

Knowledge/Understanding

1 Create a checklist that briefly defines the skills of a successful entrepreneur
2 With a partner, brainstorm some of the situations you have been in where you displayed some of the entrepreneurial skills described in this chapter.

Thinking/Inquiry

3 Identify someone whom you think has strong leadership skills. What makes them a good leader?
4 In a small group, discuss the characteristics and skills that are common to all successful business people. What is different about the entrepreneur? Work together to reach a consensus on this question and then present your conclusion to the rest of the groups in your class.

Skills
Appendix

critical thinking

Communication

5 Let's test your communication and listening skills. Three students from your class will be seated in a triangular position so that they cannot see one another. Each student has an identical set of twenty pieces of coloured paper of various shapes and sizes. The team leader has to describe to the other two people how to build the structure that he or she is creating out of the pieces of paper. The two people who are building may not speak at all, nor can they turn and look at the speaker. They must listen to every instruction and interpret it as best as they can. The rest of the class observes and records what they are learning about listening and communication skills.

Skills
Appendix

writing reports

Application

6 Identify a short or long term goal that you would like to accomplish. It might be to enter into a career, excel at a competition, or find a specific part-time job. Write a brief report explaining how you can use each of the entrepreneurial skills to reach your goal.

Who Wants to Be an Entrepreneur?

Do you think operating your own business sounds great, but are wondering where to start? You have many choices. You may already have an idea, but just don't realize it!

As we discussed earlier, entrepreneurs are passionate about their businesses. So what are you passionate about? Do you love animals? Are you good at fixing computers? Maybe you can play the guitar. Starting off with something you already love to do and are pretty good at is often the best way to find the inspiration for your business idea.

Think about your hobbies and then look for a unique way you can use that as a business idea. Remember, it has to be something that people will need and/or want, or you won't be running a business; it will still be a hobby. Let's say you love animals, especially dogs. You have a dog and so do many of the people on your street. A dog-walking service might be something people need, especially in nasty weather.

Lynn Young had always loved dogs. She took great pride in obedience training her dog, Becky. As a new mom, Lynn was looking for a way to spend more time at home. She put together her knowledge of dog-training and new parenting skills to create Dogma, an obedience training program for dogs with a specialty in preparing the family dog for a new baby.

Jot down a few of your hobbies and talents, or things you just like doing. Then, watch for opportunities and inspiration around your community. You'll be surprised what ideas will come to you.

Self-assessment

Do you have what it takes to be an entrepreneur? How about to be a successful entrepreneur?

Before you launch yourself as an entrepreneur, you need to be able to assess your skills and characteristics honestly to see which areas you need to work on. For example,

- Would you be prepared to take the risks needed to start a new business? Do you like to take the initiative? Could you handle the stress involved in starting up a new venture?
- Are you confident about your own abilities and skills? Do you know which skills you'd need to work on or get help with? Have you started building up those skills?
- Can you identify the root causes of problems? Do you enjoy solving problems? Do you consider most problems to be an opportunity?
- Can you evaluate new opportunities coolly and calmly without letting your enthusiasm run away with you?
- Can you make decisions, even if there is a risk of failure?
- Do you usually stay committed to a project even when you run into difficulties?
- Are you willing to work long hours for little reward, at least at the start of your venture?
- Can you plan ahead? Do you get things done on time? Do you usually finish what you start?
- Do you have the knowledge you need—about the market, competitors, production and other processes? Are you willing to continue learning as long as you live?
- Can you lead other people? Can you take responsibility? Can people trust what you say?

How Can You Get the Skills You Need?

Now that you've assessed some of the characteristics and skills you have and those you might need to work on, how do you get the training you need? There are many ways to find out the things you need to know.

Taking Courses

Even if you don't know exactly what business you want to start, or whether entrepreneurship will work for you, taking some courses related to this field will help you, no matter what career path you choose.

For example, accounting courses are a good choice. No matter what business is right for you, there will be money involved. Knowing how to manage finances will help you realize your dreams. Getting the know-how early means getting there even faster. If you decide to let someone else handle your bookkeeping, you're still ultimately responsible. A basic understanding of accounting principles, lets you ask the right questions and understand the answers.

Web Connect

www.school.mcgrawhill.ca/resources/

More and more schools and organizations are offering courses online. Write a list of some skills you want to develop or improve, and then investigate some of these online resources.

Going to college or university or apprenticing to learn more about your business idea, or just to learn about the world and train your mind to think analytically and creatively, is a great start. Knowledge, even when it seems totally unrelated, is never wasted. Martha Stewart who produces the popular television show "Martha Stewart Live" worked in the financial industry before becoming a caterer. Now, she runs a vast multimedia empire. She tapped into all her past experience to create her business and make it successful.

Courses may also be available through Human Resources Canada, your local library, or Parks and Recreation services. Many organizations, such as The Conference Board of Canada and Planet Entrepreneur, offer conferences and seminars on a wide range of business-related topics. Many are specifically targeted to younger entrepreneurs.

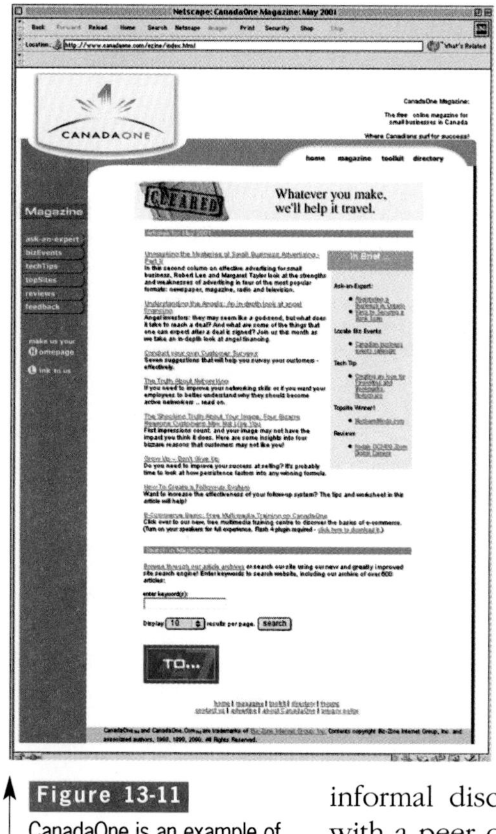

Figure 13-11 CanadaOne is an example of an online magazine specifically for entrepreneurs.

Researching and Reading

A vast network of information on how to start a business and how to keep it running smoothly is also available. It can be found on the Internet and in various media. Many daily newspapers have business sections. Newspapers, like *The Globe and Mail's* Report on Business section, magazines, such as *Profit and Realm*, and television programs, such as *Venture*, provide in-depth coverage. They discuss trends and government decisions that could affect businesses.

Organizations and Programs

Learning from others with the same interests is a rewarding way to gain the experience needed to succeed as an entrepreneur.

Many organizations are devoted to developing small business skills through workshops, seminars, informal discussions, and mentoring programs. You may be paired with a peer or adult with more experience whom you can call on for support and counsel. You might ask the person to let you intern as a volunteer so you gain real-world experience.

A mentor is someone who has business knowledge and experience and who offers support and practical help. Mentoring is so important to new entrepreneurs that the Business Development Bank of Canada (BDC) offers it as a prize for their Young Entrepreneurs Awards competition. BDC provides small businesses in Canada with information, financial and management services, and business loans.

The 4-H Club of Canada offers leadership training, and Toastmasters International offers great tips and seminars on public speaking.

The Canadian Youth Business Foundation offers an online mentoring program. According to their Web site, you can either learn from your own experience, or from someone else's. You can do it yourself, but learning from someone who's been there makes it easier to avoid the pitfalls.

Other organizations are also offering advice, training, awards, financing, and other services helpful to the budding entrepreneur.

The Association of Collegiate Entrepreneurs (ACE) is a national not-for-profit organization dedicated to helping young entrepreneurial Canadians succeed in the new economy.

Junior Achievement is an international nonprofit organization dedicated to educating and inspiring young people about business. It helps people discover leadership and entrepreneurial skills so they can achieve their highest potential as citizens in the global community.

Check Your Understanding

Knowledge/Understanding

1 How could taking courses help prepare you to become an entrepreneur?
2 What are some of the organizations and programs that are available to young entrepreneurs?

Thinking/Inquiry

3 Investigate some of the business courses and programs that are available for new business ventures in your community. Research one of these courses or programs further, and prepare the script for a brief television news clip on how it could be useful to young entrepreneurs.

Skills
Appendix

researching

Communication

4 To assess your risk tolerance, create a chart listing five circumstances in which you decided to take a risk. For each circumstance, state the outcome of your decision. What was the worst thing that could have happened? What was the best thing that could have happened? What were the consequences of your decision?

Application

5 Use the self-assessment list on page 364 to assess your entrepreneurial strengths. First work with a partner to answer the questions. Offer examples of times when you showed these characteristics in your daily life at home, at school, at work, and in your community. Then write a plan describing how you could further develop one of your entrepreneurial characteristics or skills.

In August, 2000, Mara Cole had an avalanche in her front room—a fitting climax to a summer spent helping her kids build a mountain of goodwill for other people.

She and her three sons—Evan, 9, Darren, 6, and Griffen, 3—were waving good-bye yesterday to the last of 1000 back-to-school "kidpacks" they'd put together for the Daily Bread Food Bank to distribute to needy children.

"I'm tired. It'll be great to have my house back," said Mara Cole.

The backpacks, filled with everything from socks and toothbrushes to school supplies and snacks, were Evan's and Darren's idea after their mom challenged them to come up with an idea to help other people.

"They thought about it and they said, 'We wanna help kids. Kids need tonnes of stuff.' I said, 'How many backpacks do you want to do?" They said 1000 and I laughed. But not for long."

The boys wrote a letter to companies such as Wal-mart and Nike, and in their letter they said,

"We think we are very lucky because we have a lot of nice things and we never have to worry about things . . . We really like going back to school because we get all kinds of new stuff.

Some kids don't. Our goal is to get 1000 special backpacks for kids, filled with things they need to be happy when they go back to school . . .we need your help . . ."

They got it. Wal-Mart donated backpacks and other companies gave the stuff to go in them. Each is worth about $60.

"I had no concept of what we were getting into until 86 big boxes of Pokémon pencil tines showed up," Cole said. "They just filled the place."

Handing out backpacks isn't something the Daily Bread usually does, said Jim Russell, who heads the food bank's community relations program. "This is different, for sure, but there's such pressure on poor families at the start of the school year. What these kids have done is pretty amazing. I'm impressed."

Mara Cole hopes to get more kids involved next year and register the scheme as a charity. "Then we can issue tax receipts. Some companies have a policy that they don't give to non-registered groups. Most of them gave anyway but not nearly as much as if we were a charity."

Source: Adapted from "Packing Goodwill," by Bill Taylor, *The Toronto Star*, August 9, 2000, page B1.

ACTIVITIES

1 What problem did the three Cole brothers identify in their community? What steps did they take to solve that problem and respond to the needs of their community?

2 Which of the characteristics of entrepreneurs do the Cole brothers have?

3 In groups, brainstorm some of the needs in your own community. First work together to identify the problems. Then suggest some possible practical solutions to those problems. After your brainstorming session, work with your group to list the steps that you could take to implement one of your solutions.

Chapter Review

Points to Remember

- Entrepreneurs sometimes have natural talents or aptitudes that they are able to use to their advantage in their entrepreneurial venture.

- Some of the characteristics usually associated with entrepreneurs include vision, risk-tolerance, confidence, creativity, and integrity.

- Entrepreneurial skills include problem-solving, communication, planning, and leadership skills.

- Self-assessment is a good beginning step for a potential entrepreneur to take.

- There are many ways to get the skills you need, by taking courses, researching, and joining organizations.

Activities

Knowledge/Understanding

1 List two things that you have done that displayed entrepreneurial characteristics and skills. Describe the incident and list the characteristics and skills.

2 Select three entrepreneurial characteristics and or skills that you possess and explain how you might use them in a present or future entrepreneurial endeavour.

Thinking/Inquiry

1 Write a brief explanation on what entrepreneurs can learn from setbacks or failures. How do you think failure helps entrepreneurs?

2 Identify two entrepreneurial skills that you would like to improve or work on. Conduct research to discover what opportunities are available in your community to help you improve these skills.

3 Do this activity in small groups. Your goal will be get a piece of paper in or as close to a basket as possible. The objective of the game is to gather as many points as possible for your team. The closest point to the basket is a one-point wager, the next closest point is two-point wager and the farthest point is a threepoint wager. Each member of

your team will get a chance to participate. Each team member must decide on how many points to wager prior to tossing the paper towards the basket. If a team member misses the basket the amount of the wager is deducted from the team's score. After the game brainstorm as a class. Think about how your individual and group experiences in this activity relates to the skills and characteristics of Entrepreneurs.

Communication

1 Interview an entrepreneur and use the checklists you developed to identify which of the entrepreneurial characteristics and skills that they possess.
2 Examine the definition of an entrepreneur. Think of people who you admire who fit this definition. Prepare an interview script in which you inquire how they became successful and the role that their entrepreneurial skills and characteristics played in their success.

Application

1 With a partner identify an entrepreneurial idea that would benefit your school or community. Write a business letter to your school principal or relevant community organization describing the idea. You must ensure the letter is professionally written and convincing.

Roles and Contributions of Entrepreneurs

KEY TERMS
market research
networking
information interviews
questionnaire
business plan

Specific Expectations

After studying this chapter, you will be able to

• **describe how entrepreneurs discover opportunities in people's needs, wants, and problems**

• **identify a variety of goods and services produced by entrepreneurs in your community or a nearby community**

• **investigate opportunities for entrepreneurship within your school or community, using a variety of techniques and methods, and evaluate these opportunities**

• **identify the human and financial resources necessary to create a venture based on one or more opportunities and ideas discovered within your school or community**

How often have you heard someone say "Now why didn't I think of that?" in response to a new business idea? Or perhaps you have even thought it yourself. Once the entrepreneurial idea, service, or product is out in the marketplace, it often seems to be obvious and even simple. But how do entrepreneurs find such opportunities? How do they know whether or not their bright ideas will work? Look around in your school and community. Many entrepreneurs find business opportunities close to home. Once you have your idea, figure out the resources you'll need to make your venture a success.

Ray Kroc and McDonald's

Ray Kroc, the entrepreneur who built McDonald's Corporation into the largest restaurant company in the world, started out in 1922 selling paper cups for Lily Tulip Cup Co. Without his ability to discover business opportunities in people's needs and wants, he might have continued in that job to the end of his working days.

As he travelled around the U.S. selling first those paper cups and then the Prince milkshake multimixer, Kroc saw problems in many of the restaurants that he visited. Some were disorganized, and the service was often slow. The food products in others weren't dependable. One day the food was all right, but the next day it was awful. Some restaurants weren't clean enough and were actually operating under unsanitary conditions. Kroc concluded that these restaurants just didn't offer customers value for their money. There had to be a better way to satisfy fast-food restaurant patrons' needs and wants.

One of Kroc's better multimixer customers was a restaurant in California owned by Dick and Mac McDonald. These two brothers provided their many customers with fast service—they had perfected a hamburger assembly line. They also had a limited menu and charged the lowest possible price for their products. Kroc was so impressed that he persuaded the McDonalds to let him be their agent to open other McDonald's restaurants as franchises around the U.S. He eventually bought out the two brothers.

Kroc knew that he had to compete against other fast food restaurants. But McDonald's restaurants were different from their competitors. Kroc focused on what he believed consumers wanted: quality, service, cleanliness, and value. Quality, for Kroc, meant that whether customers bought their McDonald's hamburgers in California or in Canada, they got the same food, down to the exact weight of the meat and the precise amount of ketchup and pickles.

The service at McDonald's was fast and friendly, so that customers wasted no

Figure 14-1 This was one of the first McDonald's restaurants. How can you tell?

time waiting for their "fast" food. Kroc built an assembly and delivery system that was used in every restaurant in the chain. Cleanliness was also very important to Kroc because he believed that customers demanded it. As for value, McDonald's would keep its prices as low as possible within its limited menu. The results of his efforts were visible in the rapid growth of the chain in the U.S. and in Canada.

Kroc's marketing and advertising strategies contributed to his success. Those golden arches became an easily recognizable symbol for McDonald's. The Ronald McDonald clown quickly became known to millions of North American children. Ronald was targeted at children, and soon going to McDonald's became a cultural event for millions of children and their families.

Kroc also made good use of human resources in his franchised restaurants. In the early days, the franchise fees were so low that he took home less money that many of his franchisees. He treated his franchisees more like partners than just customers who had to buy his products. Initially, he didn't manage his financial resources quite as well. He was so intent on selling new franchises and helping them get established that the company's profits were poor. However, all that changed when he set up the McDonald's Franchise Realty Corporation which bought or leased land in areas that he believed would be developed. McDonald's then rented the land to franchisees at a markup over the original cost.

Kroc and McDonald's also contributed to the communities served by his restaurants. The Ronald McDonald House charities offers a home-away-from-home for families with seriously-ill children who are receiving treatment at nearby hospitals. There are Ronald McDonald Houses in Ontario in Hamilton, London, Ottawa, and Toronto. The families make a small donation to the house if they are able to do so, or they pay nothing at all.

The first McDonald's in Canada was opened in 1967 in Richmond BC. Today there are 1100 McDonald's restaurants in Canada, serving approximately 3 million customers a day and employing 70 000 people—including a number of teenagers in their first jobs. George Cohon, McDonald's Canada's Senior Chairman, who has been with McDonald's Canada for 30 years, was responsible for opening the first McDonald's in Russia.

As you read this chapter keep in mind Ray Kroc's entrepreneurial story. Think about the ways that entrepreneurs achieve success by solving consumer's needs and wants. Are there problems in your community? What are those problems? Could any of them provide a basis for an entrepreneurial business?

Discovering Opportunities

Entrepreneurs play an important and valuable role in our communities. They provide business solutions to our needs and wants. Often, they go a step farther and give back to the community through service and charitable donations. But how do entrepreneurs discover the opportunities that are the basis of their business ventures?

Entrepreneurial opportunities often begin with someone recognizing a problem that consumers are having satisfying their needs and wants. Entrepreneurs are able to succeed in business because they can first accurately identify such problems and then set about solving them. There is more to this than just providing the product, of course. Marketing is often all about persuading consumers that they have the need or want and that a particular product will fill it.

Timing is extremely important for an entrepreneurial venture to be successful. Often the success of a venture will depend on how quickly an entrepreneur is able to determine a market niche and fill it. Ideas spread quickly. If an entrepreneur has an idea, she or he must move quickly before the opportunity is lost or someone else comes up with the same idea.

Successful entrepreneurs must also be able to spot trends. They need to discover which new products and services will be needed in the future. Which types of products will likely enjoy increased popularity? Like Roy Kroc, they have to ask themselves what consumers want that they don't have. Are there any gaps in goods or services that a new company could fill or at least fill better than existing companies?

For example, one common problem in today's airplanes is that people are confined to their seats for a long time. There's not much to do as you sit in a narrow seat with your seatbelt on. You can read a book or a magazine, snooze, listen to music, or watch the inflight movie–a limited number of choices. The ISES Corporation, which was founded by five Canadian entrepreneurs, came up with a solution to this problem. The company's Airsoft Travel Kit allows airlines to provide their travellers with online information about their destinations, with language and culture guides, and with a suite of games. In February 2000, ISES merged with White Rock Enterprises and became SNAP2. By 2001, the company has contracts with Air France, Delta Air Lines and BOAC.

Figure 14-2 The developers of the Airsoft Travel Kit discovered an opportunity in the restrictions that passengers have to endure in modern aircrafts. What need or want would the Travel Kit fulfil for airline travellers?

Doing What You Enjoy

Some entrepreneurs recognize business opporturnites in something that they love to do. It could be something artistic, such as drawing, or perhaps it's an interest in model trains, or gardening. Whatever the interest or hobby, this entrepreneur is passionate about it. So, how can he or she take this interest and turn it into a business that will serve the wants and needs of the community?

It may seem obvious that someone with a love of model trains should open a store to serve the needs of model-train enthusiasts in the community. However, the would-be entrepreneur would need to do careful research to find out whether there were enough people in the community to support the store. Would enough people buy enough items to pay for the costs of running the business? Enthusiasm and enjoyment may give an entrepreneur a direction to follow. However, the success or failure of the business will be determined by whether it fills consumers' needs and wants and whether it can provide its owner with enough money to live on.

For example, when Dan Ross was still a teenager in Antigonish, Nova Scotia, he started making customized T-shirts to sell to other students. Dan was artistic, and he was happy doing something that he loved. He was gaining confidence as a business person, but, at first, he didn't make any money. It was a while before he learned how to make his business profitable. His advice to young entrepreneurs is that they should go ahead and capitalize on doing what they love best. However, he cautions, "What I've learned is that you simply can't go out there, work yourself into the ground and not make money. Make certain your endeavour is profitable, and everything else will take care of itself."

Figure 14-3 Dan Ross turned his customized T-shirt hobby into a successful screenprinting business. What difference would it make to you if you could make your living doing something that you loved to do?

Opportunities and Communities

Many successful entrepreneurs start out producing a good or service that responds to a need or want in their own communities. Once they find that they can succeed in business in that arena, they go on to investigate the possibility of expanding their businesses to other parts of Canada or to other countries.

Two Canadian companies that have successfully expanded are Sleep Country Canada and Cirque du Soleil.

Sometimes successful entrepreneurs identify opportunities to give back to their community. They may not make direct profits but they contribute to the quality of life of people who are less fortunate. The other positive result is that customers receive a positive impression of the businesses. This public recognition can lead to higher sales.

Sleep Country Canada

Christine Magee found a business opportunity in her community and then developed a unique way to fill that need. Christine is the president and co-founder of Sleep Country Canada Inc. Before they launched their business, research of the market led Christine and her two business partners to conclude that no one was paying attention to the retailing of the mattress/boxspring market. Consumers wanted friendly staff, cheerful stores, home delivery, and the removal of their old mattresses. They also didn't want to have to drive very far to buy a mattress. In response, the three partners created a business plan that would address customers' needs before, during, and after the sale.

At the time they started their company, they purchased the rights to the advertising jingle and trademark of a small successful specialty retailer, Sleep Country USA, which was also designed with a high customer service focus. Sleep Country USA also confirmed Sleep Country Canada's approach and business plan. Like Ray Kroc and the McDonald brothers, Christine modelled her new venture on a business that was already a success.

In 1994, Sleep Country Canada opened four stores on the same day in the Vancouver area and launched an aggressive radio and television advertising campaign. Within a year, there were twelve stores in the area, and the advertising jingle—"Why buy a mattress anywhere else?"—had caught on. The Sleep Country Canada brand name became so familiar that only a year after the

Figure 14-4 Christine Magee appears in Sleep Country advertisements. She believes that, as president, she can build confidence in potential customers by giving her company a human face.

launch consumers thought the company had been in business for over five years. By the spring of 2001, Sleep Country Canada had 62 stores across Canada with 400 employees. The National Post awarded the company the Ontario 1998 Entrepreneur of the Year-Retail/Wholesale award and named it one of the top 50 privately-owned companies in Canada in 1997 and in 1998.

Giving Back to the Community

For Christine Magee, entrepreneurial activity is about a lot more than just making money and running a successful business. She has used her enormous entrepreneurial spirit to find innovative ways to help people in communities across Canada.

When Sleep Country Canada began offering to remove those customers' old mattresses, Christine realized that there was an opportunity. Could these old mattresses be used in any way to help members of her community? Sleep Country decided to take these used—but still useful—mattresses, and make them available to charitable organizations, such as shelters for the homeless. Sleep Country's mattresses are helping people in need in many charitable organizations and communities across Canada, including Renascent Centre, Covenant House, Halton Recovery House, Women's Centre of Hamilton-Wentworth, the Red Door Shelter, the Salvation Army, the Scott Mission, Woman in Transition, the YMCA, and the YWCA.

Cirque Du Soleil

In the early 1980s, a group of young street performers in Baie-Saint-Paul, Quebec, pooled their talent and dreams. They called themselves the "Club des Talons Hauts" or "High-Heels Club" because most of them were stilt-walkers. The response from their audiences on the street was enthusiastic. So the Club members organized a festival, where street performers came together to perform and to exchange ideas and techniques. Audiences were again enthusiastic.

That was all Guy Laliberté needed. The young accordionist, stilt-walker, and fire-eater saw an opportunity to develop the street performances into a business that would fill a need in the community: the need for family entertainment and for a sense of wonder. He decided to bring all this talent together under one roof, or rather one circus tent, and call it Cirque du Soleil.

Biz.Bites

"Those who are able to walk on stilts can roam the earth unstopped by mountains or rivers. They are able to imagine flying and therefore to reach the Isles of the Immortals."
P'ao-Pou Tseu

Guy realized that many people enjoy the circus. By concentrating on performers, rather than animal acts, and by creating specialty shows, each with its own style, music and costuming, he created a unique circus experience. He thought that people of all cultures would keep coming back to see their shows, and they were right.

Cirque du Soleil's growth has been phenomenal. What began as a small group of travelling performers is now an organization with over 2100 employees worldwide. The company performs all over the world and has several international branch offices. It has four shows in permanent locations and three touring productions. In addition to its live performances on three continents, Cirque has also been featured in an IMAX® film, *Journey of Man*. In the year 2000, close to 6 million people attended their shows worldwide.

Figure 14-5 Guy Laliberté, founder of Cirque du Soleil.

Giving Back to the Community

Cirque du Soleil also serves communities by reaching out to youth at risk through its Cirque du Monde program. Cirque du Monde offers young people an introduction to the discipline and skills needed by Cirque du Soleil's performers. The young participants in the program receive a positive personal experience, which can serve as a catalyst in building self-esteem and a sense of identity. In 2001, circus workshops for young people in difficulty were held in 34 communities in the Netherlands, Senegal, Ivory Coast, Cameroon, South Africa, Mongolia, Singapore, Australia, Canada, the United States, Mexico, Brazil, China, and Chile.

The performers of Cirque du Soleil can readily identify with the situation that these youth face, because the circus life can also a wandering, marginal one. The creators of Cirque du Soleil were themselves young, self-taught artists whose only stage was the street. By helping troubled youth, Cirque du Soleil gives back to the community, and is also training possible future performers.

Knowledge/Understanding

1 Identify the various ways that entrepreneurs discover business opportunities.

Thinking/Inquiry

2 List five of your hobbies or interests. Create an entrepreneurial web of the different types of business opportunities that you might create from a hobby to serve the needs and wants in your community.

Communication

3 In small groups brainstorm some common problems consumers have in filling their needs and wants. List new products or services that provide solutions to these problems. Share your ideas with the class.

Application

4 Investigate a business in your community and identify ways that it might give back to the community. Be sure to identify how your ideas would help create opportunities to solve a community problem. Write a business letter to the business sharing the ideas that you developed.

Skills
Appendix

working in groups

Skills
Appendix

problem solving

What Opportunities Exist in Your Community?

Opportunities for entrepreneurship are all around us in our communities. Consumer needs and wants are constantly changing. As a potential entrepreneur, you need to be always on the lookout for the need or want that isn't being filled.

Your age doesn't have to be a barrier. According to Jackie Vaughan of *Mercury News*, teenagers and young adults have a track record of starting some very successful businesses. When he was 19, Tom Monaghan borrowed $500 to start Domino's Pizza. Estee Lauder first sold skin cream at school when she was 16. Fred DeLuca opened the

Connecting Business with *Sports* ·······························

Odd Noggins' Rules of the Road

Sarah Jane Baxter had just graduated from hospitality studies at Toronto's Ryerson Polytechnic when she realized she had a great business idea: making accessories for bicycle helmets. Baxter, 29, proved she has the instincts of an entrepreneur. In her story we've identified 10 sharp moves she's made that other startups would do well to follow.

1. **Spot the opportunity around you.** As an avid cyclist, Baxter was frustrated with bike helmets' bland, boring lines. She painted a face on her helmet, added teeth cut from a takeout-food container and flashing red lights for eyes. When her customized headgear won raves from other cyclists, she realized other people might want similar headgear—and a business was born.

2. **Bring in the experts.** Baxter consulted a lawyer to determine how to start a business and protect her idea. In a free consultation arranged through the provincial law society, she learned how to trademark her product name, Odd Noggins, in Canada and the U.S.A.

3. **Keep your options open.** Baxter used the generic SJB Enterprises Inc. name for her company rather than "Odd Noggins." She had other ideas for entrepreneurial product lines and didn't want to be associated with just one product.

4. **Be prepared to work.** As Baxter sewed her first several hundred Odd Noggins kits (buzz-saw blades, Viking horns and shark fins made of vinyl), she worked in restaurants to pay her bills. She visited bicycle

Figure 14-6 Noogees webpage spotlights several of Sarah Jane Baxter's various helmet accessories.

stores "begging them to carry my product." But her effort paid off: once three stores started carrying Odd Noggins, cyclists across Toronto started asking for them.

5. **Learn when to hand off to suppliers.** The blisters on her hands from cutting out all her designs prompted Baxter to find someone else to do the work. Finally she contracted to a T-shirt company near Windsor, Ontario.

6. **Look for value-added deals.** Baxter faced a similar problem finding someone to package her product. It was monotonous work, but she wanted workers who would take pride in it. Eventually she turned to a workshop for people with disabilities in Guelph, Ontario. "It took a little bit of work to get across what I wanted, but it's working out well," she says. "They were really excited about this kind of work, too."

7. **Expand strategically.** Baxter has worked consistently to expand. She used trade shows to find sales representatives across Canada and in the U.S.A. She has pushed her product into other sports, from rollerblading to rafting. And this year she introduced a new line, Noogees, featuring more playful designs for children who find Odd Noggins too aggressive.

8. **Think big.** Baxter sent designs to companies like Disney and Warner Bros. and landed a deal to produce 5,000 kits of Shamu, Sea World's killer whale, for Busch Entertainment. With licensing, she notes, "all of a sudden you're in a different league."

9. **Lever relationships.** The best businesses share other people's resources. To fund development of Noogees and gain more industry experience, Baxter recently took on partner Michael Sharpe, a bicycle-trailer manufacturer. She has also forged ties with safety associations, which let their logos be printed on her product because her designs encourage kids to wear helmets.

10. **Have a fallback.** Baxter has a patent pending on a series of reflective dog collars and harnesses, to help motorists spot pets at night. It's an idea she wants to explore, but first she's committed to Odd Noggins: "I'm trying to make this a living and a career."

Source: Adapted from "Odd Noggins" by Rick Spence, PROFIT Magazine.

ACTIVITIES

1 What do you think is the best decision Sarah Jane Baxter made when starting her business? Explain why.

2 How could Sarah's rules of the road be adapted to apply to school situations.

first Subway sandwich shop when he was 17. And Bill Gates started his first software company–Traf-O-Data–when he was 15.

You can also develop your business and leadership skills by being a volunteer entrepreneur. Entrepreneurship is not just about making money. Perhaps you enjoy soccer and would like to try coaching small children who are just learning the sport. Or you may be a computer wizard. Many young people know much more about computers than most adults. Is there a community centre where you could start a program to help seniors learn how to use email or how to search the Internet?

Working people lead increasingly busy lives. What about providing services in your community for some of these harried people? Online shopping and delivery, such as the example of GroceryGateway.com that we looked at in Chapter 1, is one such service business. But there are other service opportunities that a young entrepreneur might take advantage of. Lawn-care and snow-removal, dog-walking, house-cleaning, and a multitude of other services can be designed to help busy people get everything done that they need to.

Environmental issues are high on most people's list of concerns today. New government environmental regulations are providing opportunities for entrepreneurs. Is there some way you could help solve an environmental or recyling problem in your community?

How to Develop Opportunities

Now that you are aware of possible opportunities in your community, you may get 10 ideas a day for new businesses. However, you will need to research these ideas, weed out the ones that have less potential, and focus on those that have the best chance of success and long-term growth. The following research tools will help you examine these opportunities in terms of consumers' needs and wants. What you learn will help you decide whether your entrepreneurial idea is an opportunity worth researching further.

Market Research
Market Research is one of the most important tools of the entrepreneur. It is a way to find new ideas and to analyse them before spending time and money.

Research Sources

Financial Post	10%
Time	7% (13 % of allophones)
Canadian Business	7% (12% on anglophones)
Profit	5%
Commerce	5%
Business Week	4%
The Economist	4% (11% of francophones)
Maclean's	4%

Figure 14-7 A survey by the Business Development Bank of Canada revealed that entrepreneurs read mainly newspapers and business magazines. The publications listed here were in addition to the daily newspaper, which 89% of respondents said they read each day.

Market research is very important for starting up and maintaining a successful business. As you learned in Chapter 7, market research helps you focus on the demographics of your target audience, the social and cultural changes that are occurring, and the competition for your product. Interviewing and questionnaires can be very useful.

For example, for the entrepreneur who is turning a hobby into a business, research can supply a wealth of information about other hobbyists. What else do they like to do? What magazines do they read? Where do they live? If you are planning to set up a model train store, finding out, for example, that a large percentage of model-train enthusiasts live in downtown Winnipeg, will help you chooses your store location. Discovering the magazines or television shows they like to watch means you can run your television commercials or advertisements where they are likely to see them. The more you know about your potential customers, the better you will be able to serve their needs and wants and the better chance you will have at being successful.

Reading

Whether you are looking for the perfect idea for a new company, or growing an existing company, reading is one of the best ways to stay up-to-date. You will find information on trends, new technology, consumer habits, up-coming government changes and any other factors that might affect the needs and wants of Canadian consumers. Books, magazines, newsletters, and the Internet are sources of statistics, advice, and stories of what did or didn't work for other business people. The more you know about the world around you, the more ideas you'll have.

Networking

Sometimes the best way to find opportunities is simply to let people know that you're looking. **Networking** is the process of meeting people in a semi-formal or informal environment and telling them what you need in a conversational way. If you already have an idea, this can be a great way to get informal feedback. If you are looking for an idea, sometimes asking people the simple question, "What product or service would make your life easier?" can provide some interesting results.

Examples of networking opportunities are all around us. Sometimes they can be business functions, like awards dinners, chamber of commerce meetings, or association meetings. But sometimes they can be very casual, like parties or coffee shops. You could talk to other students or teachers and staff at lunch or during a band or team practice.

A good entrepreneur always has business cards on hand and is ready to talk about the company or idea in an enthusiastic and positive way. Even if you don't have a firm idea yet, having a simple business card to present to new people is a way to show you mean business. When networking for information and ideas, the trick is to describe what you need in an exciting, convincing way in 30 seconds or less. That's usually all the time someone will give you at a first meeting. Then, if they seem interested, you can tell them more. If this is done well, they'll keep your card and the next time they need a product or service like yours or have a terrific idea, they'll remember you and call.

Information Interviews

Information interviews are a more formal way of talking with people. Depending on the kinds of opportunities you are looking for, you may either speak with consumers, or with people in a particular industry.

When you interview business people, you need to book an appointment and have a list of prepared questions so you can use the interviewee's time effectively. A well-conducted information interview can be a pleasant experience for both people. Be prepared to explore concepts that the interviewee brings up. Use phrases such as "tell me more about…" and "what was that like?" for this exploration. Also be prepared to steer the interview back to your prepared questions if the conversation wanders too far off-track.

Remember that having your key questions answered is your goal for the interview. However, if you are respectful of the interviewee's experience and time, you will come away with more than just your basic questions answered. One question that you should include in every interview is, "Who else do you recommend that I speak with?" The reply to this question provides you with your next step, and because you have the recommendation, the next interview will be that much easier to arrange.

Questionnaires

A **questionnaire**, sometimes also called a survey, is a way to get a number of answers and opinions from a selected group of people. These can be peers, classmates, people in your community, or people who read a particular publication or who visit a certain Web site. You can choose from a number of methods. You can use printed surveys and send them by regular mail and e-mail. You can ask questions in person or over the telephone.

A well-written questionnaire can provide you with valuable research information. Because people are busy and their time is valuable, it can be difficult to get enough questionnaires completed and returned. You might get better results if you position the questionnaires as a contest or offer a prize for spending the time to respond. Certainly, offering a reward for providing you with valuable information and research is worth considering. The longer the questionnaire, the bigger the reward or the potential prize should be. Remember that you should always act with integrity. If your questionnaire will take 30 minutes to complete, it is best to be honest. These people are your future customers, so start building a good relationship with them from the beginning.

In order to *enhance our services* to you, we would like to ask a few questions about your interests and usage of the Internet. Please take a moment to respond to the following survey. **Thank you.**

1. What level of Internet user would you classify yourself to be?
☐ A Beginner — new to the web
☐ B Intermediate — e-mail use, browsing, researching
☑ C Advanced — e-mail use, browsing, researching, download plug-ins, buying online

2. What activities do you and other users in your household do on the Web? *(select all that apply)*
☐ E-mail ☐ Banking
☐ Research ☐ Managing Investments
☐ Travel Planning ☐ Audio, video, software downloads
☐ Shopping *(comparison)* ☐ Playing games
☐ Shopping *(actual online purchases)* ☐ Chat rooms

3. What topics are you interested in? *(select all that apply)*
☐ News ☐ Travel
☐ Sports ☐ Careers
☐ Health ☐ Computer & Internet
☐ Investments ☐ Government & Organizations
☐ Business ☐ Entertainment
☐ Parenting tips

4. HTML emails display graphics & images such as pictures, logos and bolded text. If your email software allows, would you like to receive HTML emails from us?
☐ Yes
☐ No

5. Which is your preferred language to receive our communications?
☐ English
☐ French

At Bell, our longstanding commitment to safeguarding your right to privacy is the reason for our reputation as a leader in the protection of customer privacy. To view our full policy on Customer Privacy please visit: ***http://www.bell.ca./en/legal/security.asp***

Figure 14-8 Bell Sympatico sends out a questionnaire to each new customer to find out more about their wants and needs. That way, they make sure the company is continuing to fulfill its customers wants and needs.

Review Results

Once you have thoroughly explored your ideas, you should have a clear idea of whether your idea meets a consumer need or want. If the answer isn't clear, it's time to do more research, or revise your questionnaire. Perhaps you're asking the wrong questions. But until you get strong feedback that potential customers will use your good or service, spending a huge quantity of time and resources pursuing it may not be wise. You also want to be sure that you can earn the money you need from your idea.

At this time you may want to ask yourself some simple questions.
- Have I communicated my idea clearly?
- If I refine my idea, will it answer a need or want more thoroughly?
- Have I been thorough with my research?
- Have I asked the right market about my idea—could it be marketed to another consumer group more effectively?

Once you've asked yourself these questions and answered them honestly, it's time to try again. Revise, refine, adapt—if you're passionate about your business, all this effort will be worth it. You will also be able to build on all the thinking you have done.

Frank O'Dea is very good at evaluating business opportunities. Frank has started many successful businesses including The Second Cup Coffee Company, Pro-Shred Security and The Simple Alternative Funeral Homes. He has a simple business philosophy—if you really want to do it, you can.

An "idea" entrepreneur, Frank O'Dea creates companies based on ideas and vision and through smart research and marketing. Frank analyses consumer wants and needs and creates products and services to fill the gaps. As you can see from the very different kinds of companies listed above. Frank O'Dea doesn't limit himself to only one kind of business. He is limited only by what the consumer will want.

He is currently developing a new international central registry for medical records and spends a great deal of time on not-for-profit projects. "Everything I am today is a result of what I thought yesterday. I had to think it in order to get here. And I have to keep thinking about what it is I want to be in the future. If I have some general idea of where I'm going, I'll probably get there."

Figure 14-9 "Remember only one thing: be loyal to your vision. " Frank O'Dea , Second Cup Coffee Company

Human and Financial Resources

Once you have your idea and have done your research, what's next? You'll need resources, both human and financial. For many entrepreneurial businesses, the only human resource is you, the owner. In Chapter 13, we discussed the skills necessary for a successful entrepreneur: problem solving, communication, planning, decision-making, leadership. But you may need technical skills, for example, in Web design or computer programming. You may already have some or can learn them, or you find them by hiring an expert.

Web Connect

www.school.mcgrawhill.ca/resources/
Scott Adam's Dilbert Web site provides space for people to publish their entrepreneurial ideas and have them rated.

Financial resources are also critical. You may have done all your homework, but unless you have money, you can't start. For a store, you'll need a rent deposit, money to buy the products you'll sell, advertising and marketing money to tell people you're in business and much more. If you work from your own home, this might not be an enormous investment at all, but if you're starting a factory, the costs will be high.

Once you have a workable idea, you want to be able to use your resources—including your time—well. Writing a business plan is a good way to help yourself make good decisions about your resources.

Human Resources

Entrepreneurs have a tough job. They may have skills and characteristics to draw on to create their vision, but they have to do so much more. They may know everything there is about model trains, for example, but know nothing about running a store, doing tax returns, advertising and marketing and the many other things that businesses need to survive and grow.

Wise entrepreneurs are able to accurately assess their own talents and skills, acknowledge the gaps and seek help to fill in those weak spots. Sometimes the gap is simply the need for another pair of hands to do the work. Successful entrepreneurs don't wait until they miss deadlines, or exhaust themselves before getting the help they need to run their business. Hopefully, the growth stages of the business have been set down in the business plan and the times to start seeking assistance have been identified in advance.

Entrepreneurs have a variety of choices on how to obtain human resources. They can create strategic alliances. By working with another company, an entrepreneur can share his or her knowledge about one aspect of business, while receiving information on an aspect where he or she is weaker. The company can be in a similar industry, or something completely unrelated.

Another option is to hire a supplier. Accountants, consultants, financial advisors, computer specialists, lawyers—there are many other small businesses run by other entrepreneurs with expertise in specific areas. It is often better to pay a little money for expert advice and save yourself a lot of time and trouble later.

Employees are also a consideration. Sometimes there just aren't enough hours in the day to do all the work that's necessary. Even if you have unlimited time, you may still need someone with different skills than what you have as an entrepreneur. Knowing when to hire staff is the sign of a wise entrepreneur.

Financial Resources

There are many ways to obtain financing for your business. Personal savings, loans from family, loans from banks, finance companies, and venture capitalists. A venture capitalist is an individual or company that invest in new businesses in exchange for partial ownership.

Many other financing opportunities exist for young entrepreneurs. New government initiatives, HRDC Canada, the Business Development Bank of Canada, and young entrepreneurs awards programs all provide start-up financing for qualified applicants. The source for your financing should be covered in your business plan.

Figure 14-10 Sources of small and medium-sized Enterprises' (SMES) External Financing

- Half of SMEs report that they currently borrow from a financial institution for business financing (50%).

- Supplier credit is the second most utilized source (48%).

- Credit cards are the third most common source (46%).

- Equipment and vehicle leasing is fourth (28%).

Many companies use multiple sources of financing. In 1998 only 10 percent used a single source. Personal savings were utilized by 45 percent of SMEs.

But not only your business finances should be considered here. While you're busy spending all your time and money starting this new venture, how will you pay yourself? Most businesses take quite a long time to bring in enough money to provide an adequate income. Having enough money to meet your needs should also be included in your plan.

You may wish to review Unit 3 on Personal Finance to help you assess you financial needs. In particular, you will want to consider those things that are specific to entrepreneurs. For example, company benefits, such as disability insurance, and pensions, are available only to employees. Entrepreneurs must contribute to private plans, or, they must hire a benefits company to provide these services for themselves and any employees they might have. Contributing to these plans, investing, saving for the future and possible "rainy days" means a more successful future. When the rainy days come, you'll be prepared. Or if you get sick or hurt, you'll have insurance to cover you as you recover. Your retirement will also need to be considered.

Biz.Bites

Approximately 95% of all bank business-borrowing customers are small and medium-sized (SMEs) businesses.

Business Plan

As we have discussed in Chapter 13, planning is important to entrepreneurs. No matter what your business idea is, a well thought out business plan is what helps turn that idea into a reality. A business plan is a description of how you will use your business ideas to achieve your business goals. A business plan is an important tool. A good business plan will

- make your business objectives clear and give you goals to shoot for
- give you a better understanding of the industry and business you are getting into
- show the potential strengths and weaknesses of your business
- give prospective investors the means to determine whether your company is a suitable investment
- give you a chronology of events and financial milestones against which you can compare your actual results

Sometimes, businesses hire consultants to write a business plan for them, but entrepreneurs often write them themselves. It's a useful exercise to help you focus your thoughts on the practical aspects of creating a successful business.

Also, once an entrepreneur is busy selling his or her goods or service, he or she can get distracted from reaching the business's goals. Entrepreneurs can sometimes suffer from "not being able to see the forest for the trees." They become so focussed on the details of sales and marketing, that they don't watch the direction in which the company is moving, or even celebrate their successes. Have you ever been concentrating so hard on your spelling in an essay project that you don't quite answer the question correctly? Spelling is still an important part of an essay, but you need to focus on the big picture—answering the question—before worrying about the details. When the goals are written down, the entrepreneur can review them and recall the big picture. The **benchmarks** you have set remind you to celebrate your achievements regularly. They also remind you where you still need to go. A benchmark might be the gross sales you want to make by a certain date or the number of potential clients you want to call each day.

Before starting to write a business plan, you should ask yourself the following questions:

- Have I identified my goals?
- Am I ready to make immediate, short and long term projections?
- Do I need more information before I start writing?
- Do I need to consult with any other people before I start writing?

The Lanky Renovator

Justin Bowditch always had an entrepreneurial spirit, but he felt like he had always been waiting for just the right idea. When he bought a cottage and began the renovations, he knew he was on to something. Friends and neighbours began asking for his help with their renovations and Lanky Renovator was born soon after. But before Justin leapt into his business venture and quit his comfortable full-time banking job, he spent some time drafting a formal business plan.

His business plan outlined his assets, his tools, his experience, cash in the bank, and pickup truck, the money he would require for marketing, registering his business and hiring occasional workers and specialty skills, like painters. He also made sure he set goals for his business, tangible benchmarks along the way where he could assess the progress of his business, celebrate his successes and reevaluate if things weren't going the way he thought. Justin attributes much of his current success to having spent the time to plan in the beginning.

Figure 14-11 Justin puts his talents for renovations to work for himself in his aptly-named company, Lanky Renovator.

Business Plan Guidelines

Good business plans should be based on the following guidelines:

- A business plan should focus on the product or service and its markets.
- Sales estimates should be realistic. You should be precise, and back up your projections by citing the market's past, present, and projected growth rates.
- The plan should be flexible in order to incorporate the changes that will inevitably occur in the business environment.
- Challenges should also be addressed. No one expects starting a business to be easy. In other words, be honest with yourself and others.
- The presentation of a business plan is important, but the plan itself does not have to be elaborate or expensive in order to be effective.
- A business plan also provides an opportunity for you to express your belief in a venture. To do this effectively, your writing style must express both the substance of your proposal and your enthusiasm for the idea.

Although formats can vary, a business plan usually contains the following sections:

- Introduction
- Summary
- Company Background (or entrepreneur's skills and previous experience)

- Product or Service
- Market and Marketing Plan
- Manufacturing Plans (if applicable)
- Financial Data
- Investment Required
- Strategic Plan and Timetable
- Appendix (statistics, interviews, questionnaires used to research your idea and the market)

You can find helpful business plan outlines in many books and on Web sites for businesses organizations.

A good plan will keep guiding you if you keep it up to date. On a regular basis, perhaps monthly at first, compare your results to your goals. Revise any goals that need to be more realistic. Check your action plans for reaching goals. You may realize that a strategy, such as an advertising plan, is not working. Then you can adjust your plan and try another approach.

Web Connect

www.school.mcgrawhill.ca/resources/
The Royal Bank's Big Idea business plan template provides detailed instructions and sample business plans to help you design your own a business plan.

Check Your Understanding

Knowledge/Understanding

1 Explain how you can use the following methods to locate entrepreneurial opportunities in your community.
   a) reserach
   b) networking
   c) information intervews
   d) questionnaires

2 Assuming you were to start your own part-time or summer business, identify the types of human and financial resources you might require. How will you go about getting them?

Thinking/Inquiry

3 In order to gather ideas for finding a summer or part-time job, you will conduct an information interview with an entrepreneur who could potentially hire you. Create a list of at least seven questions that you might ask in an information interview.

4 Research the financial resources that are available to start your own business by visiting or using the Web sites of a local bank or financial institution. Gather the information that you are required to provide to the financial institution in order to get a small business loan.

Skills
A p p e n d i x

researching

Communication

5 Select a business idea that you brainstormed in small groups (see communication questions in last section). Develop a questionnaire or a survey to evaluate the potential for your business opportunity.

Skills
A p p e n d i x

working in groups

Application

6 Create an outline of the kind of information that you would include in a business plan. Be sure to indicate what methods of gathering information you will use to develop your business plan (ie. Information interviews, research, questionnaires, networking).

The North Simcoe Business Development Centre serves an area which includes Midland, Penetanguishene, Christian Island, and the Townships of Tay, Tiny, Georgian Bay and Springwater.

The North Simcoe Business Development Centre (NSBDC) was created by local people to improve employment opportunities in the communities of their region. NSBDC focuses on filling five needs in the local communities of its region:

- supporting the development of a common vision for regional identity
- promoting training and education that are relevant to today's needs for both young people and adults
- maintaining and growing existing business and industry
- supporting the development of tourism opportunities
- encouraging and supporting support entrepreneurs in niche and small enterprises

The demographic mix in the region is made up of English, French, and Native communities, with a population of approximately 42 000.

Since it began in 1985, NSBDC has helped over 1000 small businesses either to start up or to expand. This creates new jobs for people living in the area or helps people keep the jobs that they already have.

For example, five years ago, the organization started a comprehensive Small Business Week Program which focused on the different business sectors that are active in its area. To address a shortage of places for tourists to stay, NSBDC set up tours of the existing Bed & Breakfast (B & Bs) establishments. B & Bs are run by local entrepre-

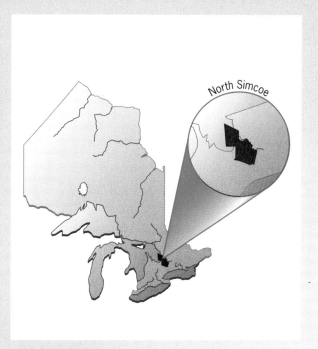

Figure 14-12 Map of Ontario showing the region covered by the North Simcoe Business Development Centre.

neurs who offer guests a room in their homes and provide them with breakfast the next morning. NSBDC hoped to raise the profile of these businesses and to encourage other people in the region to think about starting up their own B & Bs. The organization also decided to help another group of local entrepreneurs at the same time by displaying the work of one or more local artists and artisans at each of the homes.

Five years after the project was initiated, the area B & B's have formed an association to develop marketing materials, joint tour packages, and advertising materials. More tourists are staying at all of the B & B's that participate in the tour.

Many of the participants in the tour can directly relate increased wedding, family reunion, and school reunion traffic to their being part of the tour. There has also been a marked increase in the number of new B & Bs. In fact, a number of people who were guests on early tours, have now started their own B & Bs.

Other local tourism operations have developed packages with a number of the B & B operators, and hotels are now referring their overflow guests. Overall, a bond of mutual respect, cooperation and trust has developed among a group of people who once saw themselves as competitors. They have now carved out unique niches for themselves and work well together in a co-operative environment.

This project is just one example of the assistance given to a local community by the NSBDC. It also provides loans and guidance to new entrepreneurs who want to start up businesses in their area. To be able to get financing, people must
- prepare a full business plan
- demonstrate that they are committed to managing the business well
- have collateral for the loan
- show that jobs will be either created or maintained by the venture.

If the new entrepreneurs need help preparing a business plan or figuring out how to do market research, the Centre provides both counselling and library resources to help them get started.

The North Simcoe Business Development Centre is one of a number of Ontario development corporations that offer services to help Ontario's rural and northern communities expand their economies. The corporations are in turn supported by Industry Canada and the Federal Economic Development Initiative in Northern Ontario. These two federal bodies help provincial community corporations with funding, advice, and support.

ACTIVITIES

1 How does the North Simcoe Business Development Centre help entrepreneurs take advantage of business opportunities in its region?

2 Why does the Centre have requirements for people who want to borrow money? How would these requirements help to ensure a healthy business environment for everyone in the community?

3 With a partner, brainstorm a number of business opportunities in your area. Select one and investigate how you could get federal, provincial, and regional support for your venture.

Chapter Review

Points to Remember

- Entrepreneurs discover opportunities in people's needs, wants, and problems.

- Entrepreneurship is about recognizing opportunities to give back to the community as well as earnings a profit.

- Every community offers opportunities for different kinds of new business ventures.

- You can improve your chances for success by using market research, networking, questionnaires.

- Entrepreneurs also need to plan carefully how to use their human and financial resources.

Activities

Knowledge/Understanding

1 Briefly describe how three of the entrepreneurs you read about in this chapter discovered opportunities in peoples needs, wants, and problems.
2 Identify fifteen goods and services produced by entrepreneurs in your community.

Thinking/Inquiry

1 Create a personal web of your business network. Develop a list of friends and family and identify how these people might help you find a part-time job or create a business opportunity.
2 Develop a panel discussion about strategic alliances that entrepreneurs in your community might develop in order to provide more human resources to their own businesses.

Skills
Appendix

building an argument

Communication

1 Sit in a circle and ask each student to identify a part-time job or business that they would like to develop or find. The first student who has someone in their network that can help them tosses a ball of yarn to the student and identifies how he or she knows someone in their network who might be able to assist in the job search or business development. A web is created showing the power of networking.

Interview an entrepreneur in your community. Create a list of interview questions that identify the following key ideas.

- How did the entrepreneur discover an opportunity and get started in the business venture?
- What are the goods or services produced by the entrepreneur?
- What were the techniques and methods that the entrepreneur used to evelute the potential for the success of the business venture?
- What human and financial resources where necessary in order to start their business.

2 In pairs, identify problems that occur in your school or community. Work in small groups to identify entrepreneurial solutions to these problems. Do these solutions create opportunities for entrepreneurship in your school or community?

Application

1 Using the Business Plan Guidelines develop a business plan for one of your most promising new business ideas. Be sure to evaluate your idea using the questions on page 390 of the text.

2 Working in small groups you will act as business consultants. Locate an Entrepreneurial Activity in your school or community that would that would welcome your groups assistance. Evaluate the entrepreneurial activity and create a business plan to improve the success of the activity. Report your groups findings to the class. And share your findings with the people organizing the Entrepreneurial activity.

Skills
Appendix
working in groups

Internet Extension

1 Research youth entrepreneurship Web sites to find out how some beginner entrepreneurs are learning how to handle human and financial resources.

15 Inventors and Innovators

inventor

patent

innovator

research and
development

invention

convergence

Specific Expectations

After studying this chapter, you will be able to

- **contrast the role of an inventor with that of an innovator and an entrepreneur**

- **describe a variety of Canadian inventions and innovations, and identify characteristics and skills of some Canadian inventors**

- **demonstrate how innovation has affected a variety of products over time**

- **describe how innovation and invention lead to the development and application of new technologies**

Now that we've explored the characteristics and skills of entrepreneurs and how they find opportunities in the needs and wants of their communities, what about the inventor and the innovator? Canadians have a long history of invention and innovation, providing the world with new technologies, products and services to fulfill our wants and needs. But how do inventors and innovators compare to the entrepreneur? And how are they different from each other? In this chapter, we will examine the characteristics of inventors and innovators and their impact on the Canadian community. We will also examine how they have developed and applied new technologies.

An Inventive Partnership

What started out as a presentation on a Ph.D. research project by a Prince Edward Islander, turned into a high-tech device recognized worldwide for it's innovative and useful technology.

Nancy, with her husband and fellow engineer Chris Mathis, started their company, Mathis Instruments Ltd. in 1995 from an idea she had researched for her thesis at the University of New Brunswick in Fredericton. Nancy had developed a device, which they named the TC Probe™, to test for flaws in materials. They were encouraged to further develop this device, seek patent protection and proceed into commercialization. Chris and Nancy were committed to the quality and value of this product and have worked tirelessly in the pursuit of their goal.

What's so special about Nancy's invention? Go ahead and touch a piece of metal with one hand and a piece of wood with the other. The metal feels colder to the touch, right? Both materials are in fact the same temperature – room temperature. What you've just discovered is relative thermal conductivity. Metal has a higher transfer ability, or thermal conductivity, than wood, letting the heat from your hand leave faster. The TC Probe™ works in very much the same way as your hand. The technology is essentially an automated hand that supplies and detects heat flow on the same side of a material to determine thermal properties. This thermal testing instrument tests for flaws of a variety of materials for a variety of purposes all non-destructively.

The industries already using this unique device include aerospace, automotive, electronics, medical, appliances, food processing, pharmaceutical and textiles, and it can test such materials as insulation, foams, glass, pastes, polymers, adhesives and ceramics. The TC Probe™ is unique in its ability to provide fast results while needing access to only one side of the test material. Therefore, it provides many different industries the opportunity to do thermal property testing of their materials and products without waiting for time-consuming laboratory results and even while the

Figure 15-1 & 15-2 Nancy and Chris Mathis intend to continue to develop solutions to manufacturers quality control problems and to increase worldwide distribution of their products.

materials are installed. For example, delicate instruments in the Space Shuttle could be tested in place without being damaged. That saves time and money, both valuable to high-tech industries.

The practicality of the instrument has earned Mathis a place alongside some of the 20th century's most revolutionary inventions including automated tellers, fax machines, Polaroid's Polacolour film and the halogen lamp. Recognition of their invention came from receiving a 1999 R&D 100 Award given in acknowledgement of the significant advance represented by the TC Probe™. Other awards for Mathis include winner of the "1999 Export Achievement Award" for New Brunswick, and a ranking as one of "Canada's Hottest Startups" presented by Profit Magazine. Chris and Nancy have also been listed as Honored Professionals in the Nation Wide Register's "Who's Who" in Executive & Businesses.

Mathis Instruments Ltd. looks forward to further growth and increasing their distribution channels worldwide. They continue to push the technological envelope to find new applications for non-destructive testing equipment and adapting their current technology. A key mandate is to establish Mathis Instruments as a quality producer of new and highly innovative testing products.

Their business partnership has allowed both Chris and Nancy to focus on those things at which they best excel; Nancy is involved in the research and development and Chris is responsible for marketing and product development. It is a successful partnership and a successful business. The Mathis' are great believers in sharing with others in the business community the knowledge and experience they've gained through research and collaboration. Because they both have the confidence to rely on the strengths of each other and the confidence in their technology, their business venture is thriving. Chris' business planning skills allowed the business a solid foundation on which to grow. Nancy's risk-tolerance as an inventor and her perseverance to create a non-destructive testing device are also key entrepreneurial characteristics. Their mutual support also provides a strong partnership both in and out of the business. Working as a scientific and entrepreneurial team, they have managed to put Mathis Instruments Ltd. on the world stage of product development and manufacturing.

As you read more about inventors and innovators in this chapter, remember the qualities and characteristics displayed by Nancy and Chris Mathis. What similarities do they have with the other inventors and innovators in this chapter?

The Role of Inventors and Innovators

Inventors and innovators, like entrepreneurs, come from different backgrounds. They can be of any ethnicity and come from any country. They may be young or old, men or women. What inventors and innovators have in common with entrepreneurs is their creativity and passion. Inventors and innovators are inspired by the things around them. Their creative ideas come to them through their everyday lives. Perhaps the inventor sees a technology that doesn't work well. He thinks of something that would perform better. Or an innovator will see an existing product, and think that with some changes, the product could better fill consumers' needs and wants.

You have already been introduced to a number of Canadian inventors and innovators in this text. Take a few minutes to re-read the Business Profile on Armand Bombardier in Chapter 4. At 15, Armand invented his first snowmobile. Not long after, he launched his career as an entrepreneur. Many years later, Laurant Beaudoin rescued Bombardier by innovating its product line and developing it into a global transportation company.

It is difficult to imagine our world without the contributions of inventors, innovators, and entrepreneurs. Consider the computer, for example. Throughout history, people have been trying to find quick ways to do mathematical calculations. Early digital computers or calculators were invented by Blaise Pascal in the 1600s. These calculators were mechanical machines that used interlocking toothed wheels, similar to the gears in a clock. During the 1930s and 1940s, Alan Turing, a British mathemetician, developed the new "computer science" and a theory of how a computer could work.

In 1944, a large digital computer was built in the U.S.A. This early computer was more than 15 metres long. Two years later at the University of Pennsylvania, the first electronic computer was created, using vacuum tubes. It could multiply 300 numbers each second. When transistors replaced vacuum tubes, computers got smaller. Up until this point, computers were so enormous that what we refer to today as "bugs" in the system, were actual bugs, insects, that found their way inside the computers and caused electric shorts. Further advancement has allowed today's computers to be even smaller, faster, and smarter to the point that even some insignificant appliances have more computing power than those early computers of the 1940s.

Biz.Bites

Not all inventions work. In the 1950s and 1960s, researchers in the U.S.A. tried hydraulic, or water-powered, computers. According to Dr. Bert Hall, professor of the History of Science at the University of Toronto, "They were stupifyingly slow. Water molecules have weight; electrons don't. There was just no way to make them fast enough."

Canadian Inventions

1833 - screw propeller
1838 - newsprint
1846 - kerosene
1857 - submarine telegraph cable
1859 - steam foghorn
1874 - first patented lightbulb
1876 - telephone
1878 - Standard Time
1891 - basketball
1900 - wireless radio
1908 - hydrofoil
1909 - five-pin bowling
1913 - zipper
1922 - insulin
1922 - snowmobile

Canadian Inventions

1922 - variable-pitch propeller

1925 - snowblower

1927 - television

1931 - pablum

1931 - plexiglass

1934 - television camera

1937 - electron microscope

1940 - paint roller

1950 - cardiac pacemaker

1958 - Avro Arrow's first test flight

1960 - goalie mask

1968 - IMAX film

1971 - disintegrating plastic

1972 - computerized braille

1976 - Mcintosh apple

1980 - Trivial Pursuit

Figure 15-3 These are just a few of the inventions that Canadians have contributed to the world.

The people who invented the computer, the innovators who refined it, and the entrepreneurs who marketed it and sold it to us have changed our lives and our world.

Three Little Farmers

Inventions and innovations don't always involve complex technology. Ole, Aksek, and Anders Ivo in Listowel, Ontario, are innovators and entrepreneurs. After reading a book about soap and soapmaking, Ole was so inspired that he decided to learn how to make his own soap. He enlisted the help of his brothers and soon they were developing their own bars of soap.

What is unique about the Ivo brothers is their ages. Ole is nine, Aksel is seven, and Anders is six. Their company, Three Little Farmers, is thriving. They now produce 60 varieties of soap with ingredients like vitamin E, aloe vera, fruit juices, and herbs. Now that the company is doing so well, the rest of the Ivo family is helping out.

Inventors' Characteristics and Skills

Inventors create new devices or processes by assembling previously unrelated elements in a new way. Inventors are motivated by the urge to solve problems that they have identified. They may differ from scientists who are often motivated more by curiosity and the need to know the "why" of things. The scientist may want to know what it's like on Mars. The inventor will figure out how to get there.

An inventor may also develop new technology, a new process, or product that is so different from the original that it requires a new name. It is clearly separate and distinct from the item that inspired it. For example, radio inspired the invention of television. Both transmit sound and television, is in a way, merely a radio that also transmits pictures. But no one could confuse the two now. Television is very different from radio and further advanced in scope.

Figure 15-4 Ole, Aksek, and Anders Ivo are partners in The Three Little Farmers.

For inventors, finding a solution to a particular problem is exciting and challenging. Inventors are generally creative people who maintain a childlike curiosity throughout their lives. They also have to be patient, persistent, and meticulous observers.

Inventors are also risk-takers. Any activity that has the potential to fail involves risk. Through trial and error and experimentation, inventors perfect their creations. Oftentimes, inventors learn more from their mistakes than from their successes. After many failures, Thomas Edison commented on yet another failed light bulb, "Oh but I have not failed once. Now I know 500 ways of how not to make a light bulb."

James Gosling and Java Script

Canadian James Gosling invented Java Script in 1994 as an employee of Sun Labs, the research division of Sun Microsystems. Today he is a vice-president and research fellow at the company. Gosling's invention was simple and elegant. Java technology-based software works just about everywhere—from the smallest devices to supercomputers. Java technology components don't care what kind of computer, phone, TV, or operating system they run on. They just work, on any kind of compatible device that supports the Java platform. Java technology was widely regarded as revolutionary, because it was designed to let computers and devices communicate with one another much more easily than ever before.

When explaining the process of inventing Java, James Gosling says, "We subscribed to 'Hammer Technology': taking a bunch of existing stuff and hammering it together. Learning by doing."

As an inventor who was not an entrepreneur, Gosling could indulge his curiosity and his desire to find solutions for problems without having to worry about marketing and selling his inventions. He also had the financial resources of his employer, Sun Microsystems, to help. The company supported him financially through the trial and error process, leaving him free to concentrate on inventing.

A major breakthrough in book publishing: aromatic books.

Figure 15-5 Not all inventions and innovations are wanted or needed by consumers. Your invention may seem like a terrific idea, but if there isn't a market for it, it won't succeed.

Figure 15-6 James Gosling, the inventor of Java script, is now a vice president of Sun Labs.

Innovators' Characteristics and Skills

Web Connect

www.school.mcgrawhill.ca/resources/

Visit James Gosling's home page to read about some spectacular inventions that failed.

In their work, innovators do not usually start from scratch, as inventors do. Innovators take a pre-existing good or service and change it in a way that makes it more suited to the current needs and wants of the market. Some concentrate on a working out a process; others focus more on finding the opportunities and resources needed to make an adaptation a profitable business venture.

Innovators develop ideas or inventions from others and either make them work or work better. For example, an inventor might create the wheel; an innovator would come up with a wheelbarrow. Innovators may also be entrepreneurs, or they may work for companies developing and improving existing products. They come up with improvements in all areas of life.

Biz.Bites

Our innovators have given novelty, variety, and colour to our lives with their great practical gifts, and the world would be an exceedingly boring and grey place without their vitality." - Roy Mayer

Ron Foxcroft and the Fox 40 Whistle

Rox Foxcroft, a Canadian professional basketball referee, came up with a better whistle that helped him launch a profitable new business. With three decades of experience at events such as gold medal Olympic competitions, the Pan American Games, and the NCAA, he knows the importance of a reliable whistle. But referees could not always count on them. Sometimes the little round ball that helped create sound inside the whistle would get stuck.

In 1987, as he walked across the floor of the gymnasium to referee a Pan-American basketball game, Foxcroft clutched one of only two operating prototypes of his innovative Fox 40 whistle. Would the new whistle work? He had been in dangerous situations at other games when a whistle didn't work. In 1984, he needed a police escort out of a gymnasium in Brazil. His regular whistle had failed to blow at a critical moment in a pre-Olympic basketball game.

Figure 15-7 Ron Foxcroft innovated a known product to solve a problem.

But his Fox 40 whistle did work, so well that it startled everyone in the gym. When the games were over, Foxcroft had orders for 20 000 whistles, and commitments for the financing to move into full production. With no moving parts to malfunction, Fox 40 whistles feature ultrasonic welding, precision injection molding, and harmonically tuned air chambers. The harder you blow, the louder the sound.

Over 100 million Fox 40 whistles have been sold in over 126 countries to international sports federations and conferences, and to members of the military, police, search-and-rescue, and coast guard.

As the owner of Fluke Transport, Ron Foxcroft was already a seasoned entrepreneur. The Fox 40 whistle innovation provided him with yet another entrepreneurial opportunity, but this time he was the innovator. With two companies to run and several others in the works, he is very successful.

His confidence and ability to tolerate risk are apparent. Taking one of two prototypes to a "live" test at the Pan-American games was an enormous risk. Not only was he risking the future of his innovation and the reputation of his new company, but he was also risking his personal safety.

Figure 15-8 What might be the consequences of failure of a whistle under these circumstances?

Check Your Understanding

Knowledge/Understanding

1 In your own words, explain the difference between inventions and innovations.

2 What can inventors and innovators learn from failures?

Thinking/Inquiry

3 From Figure 15-4 above, choose a Canadian invention, or find another Canadian invention that interests you. Using the Internet, or the library, research and write a brief report on who the inventor was and how the idea evolved. Be sure to include the contribution this invention has made to the community. The contribution could be to the consumer, or to other businesses.

Skills
Appendix

researching

Communication

4 With a partner, choose a famous inventor and role-play the invention process. One person will play the inventor, the other will play a journalist. Prepare a list of questions ahead of time and research as much as possible about the inventor's life and contributions. Possible inventors you could choose include: Alexander Graham Bell, Thomas Edison, Sir Sanford Fleming, Stephanie Louise Kwolek, Leonardo da Vinci, Louis Pasteur.

Application

5 In groups, choose a current product you can buy today. Brainstorm ways in which it could be innovated or improved. Remember to keep in mind the wants and needs of the consumer. Improvements must be things that the consumer wants and needs, not simply changes.

Skills
Appendix

working in groups
brainstorming

Comparing the Roles of Inventors, Innovators, and Entrepreneurs

There are many similarities among the inventor, the innovator, and the entrepreneur. In fact, sometimes one person can play all three roles. But when it comes to business, there are often differences. As we have seen, the innovator or the inventor can sometimes be an employee putting his or her skills and talents to work for a corporation, the government, or perhaps a business operated by an entrepreneur. Or the innovator or inventor may have the aptitude, characteristics, and skills to also be an entrepreneur.

The inventor and the entrepreneur share a number of characteristics such as perseverance and an interest in practical solutions. However, the inventor may not have the ability or the financial resources to be an entrepreneur. In many cases, just the creative process of inventing is fulfilling enough. Building a company to produce and market the invention may not be a goal.

The innovator is slightly different. Because the innovation process is more like tinkering with existing products to improve them, innovators' interest and excitement is often more driven to providing their innovation to the world. Many innovators are entrepreneurs who develop and change a product to respond to the needs and wants of consumers.

Connecting Business with *Invention*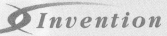

Mapping Cyberspace

Tim Bray, a pioneer of on-line search engines and co-inventor of the Internet programming language XML, is now working to change the face of the World Wide Web by making maps of cyberspace. His Vancouver-based company Antarcti.ca Systems Inc. creates 2-D and 3-D maps for navigating on-line networks. "In the real world, once you've found a place, you know where it is. It's easy to communicate to other people how to get there. The premise of our company is to take networks and make them more like real places," he says.

As co-founder of Open Text Corp. in Waterloo, Ontario, Bray created one of the Web's first search engines in the early 1990s. But he says you can only go so far in cyberspace with a tool that searches Web sites for keywords. "Right now

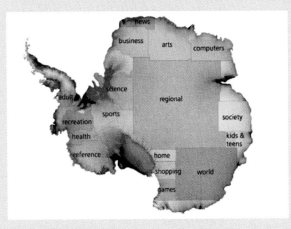

Figure 15-10   Antarcti.ca

search engines do a good job of finding individual items. They don't do a good job of giving you a feel for the general shape of what's out there, how much stuff is available and what the important things are."

He believes that the mapping software that he and his company have developed has the potential to change the way people use the Internet as radically as the introduction of Windows or Macintosh-based graphical interfaces changed personal computer use over the last decade.

Antarcti.ca has created a map of the World Wide Web, which is available for public use. The map is superimposed on an outline of Antarctica, dividing the land mass into different sized regions representing various categories of on-line content, such as business, arts, sports, entertainment, and shopping. Visitors can navigate by clicking on regions and zooming in to see more detailed maps showing sub-categories and the location of individual sites, in much the same way as an electronic map presents increasingly detailed views of regions, cities and neighbourhoods.

Figure 15-9   The invention of fibre optics allowed us to have more telephone calls with better quality sound than ever before.

Mr. Bray says he chose the uninhabited continent as a location because he wanted to create the impression of a real place without having people confused by associations with places in the populated world. He says Antarctica resonates also because early maps of the world represented it as an unknown land, much like the uncharted Internet.

Once the basic structure of a network has been determined, Antarcti.ca accumulates additional information with the help of a robot, a piece of software that visits each site and extracts data such as the name and category of the site, the number of pages it has, the number of graphical images per page, the number of other sites that link to it, the number of broken links the site contains, and the speed at which it can access.

This information about the sites is used to differentiate one from another on the map, so that a Web surfer can see at a glance how big a site is, what kind of services and information it offers, how well connected it is and how easy it is to navigate.

When viewed using its most detailed 3-D maps, Antarcti.ca's "street level view" of the network shows individual sites as buildings of different sizes, shapes and colours. This makes it possible for people to give each other directions to Web sites, even when they do not know the precise address by saying, for example, "It's in Business-Financial Services-Financial Consulting, and it's a green building a couple of clicks left of Deutsche Bank," Mr. Bray explains.

People navigating through Antarcti.ca's maps can meet one another in much the same way as they might if they were wandering around in a real place, Mr. Bray says. "Whenever you go to one of our sites, you can click on chat. And if anybody else happens to be there at the same time, you can chat with them and, presumably, you have an automatic, instantly created community of interests."

Internet industry analyst Peter O'Kelly says Antarcti.ca's visual maps could make networks more accessible and useful for many people, and provide a solution to companies grappling with the problem of managing Web content.

"It is conducive to collaboration, because everybody sees the same thing. If we search for the same concepts on their site and look around we might be able to see each other and be able to collaborate in context," says Mr. O'Kelly, a senior analyst at Boston, Mass.-based Patricia Seybold Group.

Although he is mapping the hitherto uncharted expanses of cyberspace, Mr. Bray says he is not trying to tame the wilderness. "The Web is unmanageable and that is one of its virtues. Nothing centrally planned could ever have achieved this amount of dynamic vivacity. We're not trying to bring order to the Web or enterprise intranets. We don't want to stifle creativity. We're just trying to draw pictures."

Source: adapted with permission from "Antarcti.ca plumbs World Wide Web to map cyberspace," by Kevin Marron Thursday, 1/18/2001. *The Globe and Mail.*

ACTIVITIES

1 Is Tim Bray's mapping idea an innovation or an invention?
2 What makes Tim Bray an entrepreneur?
3 What need or want is Tim Bray's creation fulfilling for consumers?
4 Imagine that you might invest in Antartic.ca. Using the Internet, find three reasons why Antartic.ca might be a good investment.

The Inventor/Entrepreneur

Those inventors, who are not entrepreneurs are often employees of large companies that can afford to have people run lengthy and expensive experiments. These departments are called **research and development** or R & D. These inventors develop new products, medicines, technology—whatever the company is interested in. When the invention is completed, the company owns the rights to it. Like James Gosling of Sun Labs, the inventor will get credit for his or her contribution, but the rights to the patent and the sales of the invention belong to the sponsoring corporation.

A **patent** is a legal registering process that ensures exclusive rights to make, use, or sell an invention for a specific number of years.

Some inventors start their own business to market their invention to the community. This gives them control over their invention and over the way it is produced and marketed to the consumer. This option also provides them with the opportunity to get feedback from the community and improve and modify their invention, or even innovate and expand, which they may not be able to do as employees.

Inventors of the Light Bulb

Sometimes a number of people share in the invention of a new product, but it is the person who is able to bring the product to market who gets the credit. Take the case of the light bulb. Thomas Edison was perhaps the last inventor to perfect the light bulb. Canadians Henry Woodward and Matthew Evans patented the light bulb in 1875. Although there was a market for their invention, the inventors were not able to secure enough money to develop and market their invention.

Thomas Edison, however, who had been working on the same idea, bought the rights to their patent. Capital was not a problem for Edison: he had the backing of a group of industrial interests with $50 000 to invest–a sizeable sum at the time. So, although Edison was not the original inventor of the lightbulb, nor the first to patent it, because he had secured the finances to commercialize this invention, he was able to make it successful.

Edison successfully demonstrated the light bulb in 1879, which was a year after he read an article in *Scientific American* by an inventor, Joseph Swan, who had received a British patent for the light bulb in 1878.

As both an inventor and an entrepreneur, Thomas Edison exhibited many of the characteristics discussed in Chapter 13. His ability to accept the risk of failure using trial and error testing proves his perseverance, risk-tolerance, and confidence. This confidence must have been obvious to the many investors in Edison's inventions.

But it was his financial planning skills that set him above his Canadian competitors. So, more than a hundred years later, Thomas Edison is remembered as being the inventor of the lightbulb, not because he was the most intelligent inventor, but because he was able to finance the commercialization of the lightbulb.

Edison went even farther than that. He owned the electric company that supplied electricity to power his lightbulbs, creating an instant market and need for his new invention. This story bears many similarities to the Clearnet story in Chapter 2. By licencing radio spectrum before there was a demand and then developing the cellular phone technology to use it, Clearnet was able to ensure a clear market advantage. Their risk, like Edison's paid off. Reread the Clearnet Business Profile in Chapter 2 and note the similarities between it and Edison's business venture.

The Innovator/Entrepreneur

Figure 15-11 An Air Hogs Sky Shark.

In a sense, all entrepreneurs are innovators; they take an idea that comes from a consumer need or want and turn it into a business. Usually the ideas are twists or updates on an existing idea, but the innovator refines it to better suit the needs and wants of the consumer.

Anton Rabie and Ronnen Harary evolved Spin Master Toys from a part-time business they ran while attending the University of Western Ontario to the international toy company it is today. Their first product, the Earth Buddy, generated sales of more than $500 000 in 1994. Similar to the Chia Pets, which grow sprouts like green fur, the Earth Buddy, which grows grass on its head, is quirkier and weird rather than cute.

Another success story involved the Air Hogs Sky Shark, a toy airplane that can fly more than 100 metres using compressed-air. The Sky Shark was listed as one of the top-three sellers in North American toy departments during the Christmas season in 1998. For that year, Spin Master's sales topped $45 million.

Rabie and Harary's products are really just twists on existing toys. After all, Chia pets and toy airplanes have been around for years. But it was their innovation of these toys into something new and appealed to the wants of the market and launched them into the successful company they now are.

Rabie and Harary have the creativity and passion that are critical skills in entrepreneurship, especially in the toy business. Their business partnership provides them the mutual support and confidence to rely on the skills and characteristics of their partner.

Web Connect

www.school.mcgrawhill.ca/resources/

Learn more about other young inventors and innovators and about how they protect their creative ideas through copyright and patent protection.

Innovation and pre-existing products

Innovation is most often linked with technology, but is not limited to it. For example, pizza is an invention, but pizza home delivery is an innovation in service. Many innovations can be made to a good or service or a period of time to match the changing markets. Sometimes these changes can be dramatic, like the Fox 40 whistle, but they can also be subtle. An example of a more subtle innovation would be Apple Computers new iMac line. Although the technology wasn't dramatically different from the familiar Apple Macintosh computers, the bold new design and colours revolutionized this industry. (See photograph on page 58.)

Today, it can sometimes be difficult to remember that the technology that we now take for granted had very humble beginnings. For example, we may have trouble remembering what it was like without the telephone when we are so accustomed to telephone, the Internet, and cellular technology. But it started out with an invention that was innovated over time until it reached the level of sophistication we now know.

Samuel Morse, an American painter and inventor fascinated by electricity, laid out his first plans for a telegraph machine on a trip in 1832. In 1835, he created a model telegraph and finally developed a complex system of dashes and dots designed to easily transmit language and numbers over wires. The code for letters and numbers–Morse Code–emerged as the international communication system, allowing the transmission of ideas and information around the world.

Biz.Bites

"The Internet's pace of adoption eclipses all other technologies that preceded it. Radio was in existence 38 years before 50 million people tuned in; TV took 13 years to reach that benchmark. Sixteen years after the first PC kit came out, 50 million people were using one. Once it was opened to the general public, the Internet crossed that line in four years." Quote from the US Department report "The Emerging Digital Economy."

Morse worked with his colleague Alfred Vail, who helped him perfect his invention. His machine worked by clicking dashes and dots to create or break an electric current between the machine's battery and its receiver. By 1843, Morse received government funding for his invention and constructed a mini-telegraph system along a railroad line between Washington, D.C. and Baltimore, Maryland. On May 24, 1844, the first telegraph message was transmitted: "What hath God wrought!"

The universal distress signal "SOS" was developed and used because the Morse code signal, which is made up of a series of dots and dashes (. . . - - - . . .), could be easily transmitted and easily understood.

Development of the Telephone

Morse's invention of the telegraph inspired another invention, the telephone.

Alexander Graham Bell invented the telephone in 1875. At the time, it was not seen as the revolutionary communications tool we now know it to be. The Biz Bite from Western Union in Chapter 4 (page 100) about the telephone provides a good example of how it was received originally. Now, however, we could hardly imagine our lives without this technology.

Alexander Graham Bell's mother lost her hearing when Bell was 12 years old and his father was well-known as an expert in correct speech. Iit isn't surprising, then, that Bell was fascinated by sounds and communications. In fact, later, Bell went on the found a school for teachers for the hearing-impaired. In 1866, Bell carried out a series of experiments to determine how vowel sounds are produced. He was assisted by Thomas A. Watson, a friend from a nearby electrical shop. On June 2, 1875, Bell was at one end of the line and Watson worked on the reeds of the telegraph in another room when Bell heard the sound of a plucked reed coming to him over the wire.

The next day, after much tinkering, the instrument transmitted the sound of Bell's voice to Watson. The instrument transmitted recognizable voice sound, not words. Bell and Watson experimented all summer and in September, 1875, Bell began to write the specifications for his first telephone patent.

The telephone has undergone tremendous change since Alexander Graham Bell's

Figure 15-12 This telegraph was made and used in the 1860s to communicate messages across great distances. How would this invention have changed the business world and competition?

original invention. Constant innovation to this technology refined it to the point where many other offshoot technologies were possible.

When the telephone became available to the general public, it had to be hand-cranked to get a signal. Then an operator would manually plug your line into the right spot to reach the person you were calling Now, this process is done through complex electronic switching devices. You pick up the phone, dial the number and you're automatically connected to your friend across the street, or across town or across the world.

In 1955, the laying of transatlantic telephone cables began to connect North America and Europe. Through this gigantic extension cord, people on different continents could call their friends and families directly.

Through a collaboration between NASA and the Bell System, Telstar, the world's first international communications satellite, was launched in 1962. Satellites in orbit around the earth are now used for long-distance service. With satellite technology, you can call your best friend in Hong Kong in seconds or less.

Then fibre optic cables, which carry greater numbers of telephone calls than satellite links could, were used. CorningGlass researchers Robert Maurer, Donald Keck and Peter Schultz invented fibre optic wire or "Optical Waveguide Fibers" in 1970. It was capable of carrying 65 000 times more information than the copper wire that was being used. Electrical telephone signals are fed into tiny lasers, which produce pulses of light in response to incoming signals and are bounced down the inside of extremely thin glass fibres.

Biz.Bites

"Who could have foreseen what the telephone bells have done to ring out the old ways and to ring in the new; to ring out delay and isolation and to ring in the efficiency and friendliness of a truly united people?" Herbert Casson (1910)

Figure 15-14 Often, in the course of human history, the invention of one technology will lead to innovations and new inventions as businesses develop new ways to meet consumers, needs and wants.

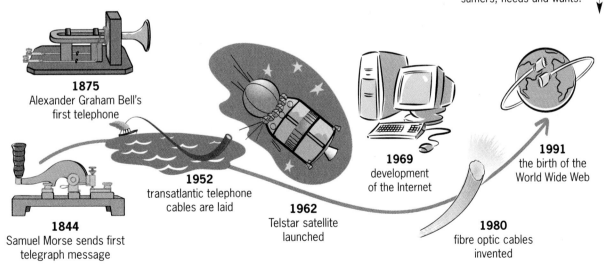

1875
Alexander Graham Bell's
first telephone

1844
Samuel Morse sends first
telegraph message

1952
transatlantic telephone
cables are laid

1962
Telstar satellite
launched

1969
development
of the Internet

1980
fibre optic cables
invented

1991
the birth of the
World Wide Web

A further innovation was the cellular phone. Each cellular telephone unit also has its own central transmitter-receiver, permitting it to receive seamless transmission as they enter and exit from a cell.

And now, we have the Internet. Innovation has made the Internet accessible technology for young and old, for communication, information exchange, and even shopping.

The Internet is not technically an innovation of the telephone. Rather it is based on computer technology, which has now converged with telephone technology, both using fibre optics to send data. **Convergence** is the coming together of two separate technologies into one. For example, now you can watch television on your computer, play music and make long-distance calls. The three technologies have all come together into one.

Check Your Understanding

Knowledge

1 Create a chart that identifies the roles of a) an innovator, b) an inventor, c) an entrepreneur. Describe how their roles are similar and how they are different.

2 Define convergence and predict three examples of products that might converge in the future. Explain why you believe they might converge.

Thinking/Inquiry

3 Research a product that has been selling in the consumer market for over 10 years. Prepare a one-page report describing how innovation has affected the product over time. Discuss how the features and benefits of the product have been improved through innovation?

Communication

4 In role as a Canadian inventor, write a short newspaper article about an invention that you created. Be sure to include a headline and an illustration. Include the personal characteristics and skills that helped you develop your ideas.

Application

5 Work with a partner to develop a list of 15 commonly used products in the home, office or school. Working together, come up with an innovative feature for at least four of these products. Select your best idea and demonstrate your innovation by either a) creating a model or prototype of the new product, or b) sketching a sample design for the product. Share your model or sketches with the class.

Skills
Appendix

writing reports

Skills
Appendix

brainstorming

The Colombian physician-biochemist, Manuel Elkin Patarroyo, has dedicated years of his life to inventing a synthetic malaria vaccine. In 1986, after years of trial-and-error studies and laboratory testing, the vaccine—called SPf66—produced results on the 66th trial. In 1998, SPf66 went into mass production with the support of the Colombian government.

Malaria is a disease caused by a parasite that is carried by mosquitoes. It claims one life every 30 seconds, about 3 million deaths each year. Malaria kills more people worldwide than any other disease, and the disease affects 40 percent of the world's population. It occurs most often in hot, humid tropical regions, where the vast majority of people in the developing world live.

Large pharmaceutical companies are sometimes hesitant to invest significant resources in research into vaccines that offer little promise of financial return. Vaccines take years and years of costly research and testing to develop. And if research into a vaccine for malaria had been successful at one of these companies, the people affected by the disease would not have been able to afford it. Even a cost as low as $5 per dose would be an overwhelming expense to a family in Colombia where the GDP per capita in 1999 was $6200.

Dr. Patarroyo has a unique perspective on the development of vaccines and patents and financial returns. He refused an offer of US$60 million for the patent to his malaria vaccine. Instead, he donated the patent to the World Health Organization so it would be available to anyone who needed it anywhere in the world for between 20 and 40 cents per dose. In his view, researchers and inventors have a moral responsibility to work for the welfare of all humanity. "The vaccine should be made available to governments so that

Figure 15-15 Dr. Manuel Elkin Patarroyo.

they can organize massive vaccination campaigns. It should not be sold and I do not want to earn money from it. That is why I offered it to WHO for nothing, because in my opinion WHO is the most suitable organization to distribute it in the countries where it is needed."

Dr. Patarroyo is also delighted that, following his lead, more and more Colombian school children are interested in becoming scientists. To him this is success. As he says, "What other success could I claim better than that one?" He has brought to his country's children an enthusiasm for becoming scientists and helping other people throughout the world.

ACTIVITIES

1 What decisions did Dr Patarroyo make that have influenced the school children of Colombia to become more interested in science? Why does he consider this to be his greatest sucess?

Chapter Review

Points to Remember

- Inventors and innovators both contribute to business by developing products with economic potential.

- Inventors create new devices and processes from previous unassembled elements. Many enjoy the process of discovery.

- Innovators adapt existing products to suit current needs and wants. Most innovators have a strong interest in developing practical products that could be sold.

- Innovators tend to be entrepreneurs and, in some senses, all entrepreneurs are innovators because they turn ideas into businesses.

- A pre-existing product can go through so many innovations that later versions hardly resemble the original.

Activities

Knowledge/Understanding

1 From the stories of innovators and inventors in this chapter, draw up a set of common characteristics that they share.

Thinking/Inquiry

1 Track how innovation in a specific product has affected the supply and demand for that product. How do consumers react to a new invention or to an innovation in a known product?
2 How have Nancy and Chris Mathis, of Mathis Instruments, demonstrated that they are inventors and innovators? What similarities do they have with the other inventors and innovators in this chapter? What characteristics do they share?

Communication

1 Investigate the career of one innovator who is also an entrepreneur. Trace the progress of his or her career and see how entrepreneurial characteristics and skills have contributed to his or her success. Prepare a radio news report on the results of your findings.

Skills
Appendix

brainstorming

2 Figure 15-14 shows the development and changes in one type of communication technology. Select another technology that has been developed over the last 100 years and create an illustrated flow chart to show the development of that technology.

Application

1 With a small group, brainstorm some existing products that you might consider innovating further. What are some of the problems in current products that could be improved by further changes?

a) Consider your market for your new products. How would they be an improvement over existing products?

b) Then, working independently, draw up a plan for the production and marketing of your product. What problems would you have to overcome in order to successfully launch the new product?

c) Go back to your group and present your plans. Discuss any further changes that you would have to make in order to be able to sell your product to consumers.

Skills
Appendix

working in groups
brainstorming

Internet Extension

1 The Internet and the World Wide Web have contributed to new inventions and innovations in many fields. Research some of these new products, services, and technologies and speculate on the changes that will occur in the future.

Skills
Appendix

researching

UNIT 5 International Business

Overall Expectations

By the end of this unit, you will

- describe how nations become interdependent through international business

- analyse the impact of trade on the Canadian economy

- describe Canada's key international economic relationships

In Unit 1, you learned that business depends on you, the consumer. You also learned that business affects the economic, social, and environmental health of your local community.

In Unit 2, you learned how business works—its day-to-day operations within a market and environment, including its relationship with employees.

In Unit 3, you learned how Canadians use the money they earn from employment, usually in businesses, to further their own goals and dreams.

In Unit 4, you learned how entrepreneurs start businesses, and how inventors and innovators start industries. New businesses and industries are important sources of new jobs.

In this unit, to understand more fully how business has become a global affair. Historically, countries have always traded with each other to exchange goods. Today, nations still depend on each other to exchange goods and services. And thanks to the technological revolution, many businesses are treating the whole world as their customer base.

In Chapter 16, you will learn how international trade works. You will learn about imports and exports, and explore the reasons why countries need to trade goods and services. You will also analyze all the factors that affect international trade, such as the ability of consumers to buy goods, the value of currency, regulations for transporting goods, language and cultural factors, and how nations try to regulate trade.

In Chapter 17, you will examine Canada's role in international trade in more detail. You will review the trade agreements Canada has with other nations, and you will start to appreciate how "free trade" affects you, the consumer.

The globalization of business also has its detractors, though. In this chapter, you will have the opportunity develop your own view on free trade. Who benefits? Who suffers? You decide.

CHAPTER 16
Global Interdependence

Specific Expectations

After studying this chapter, you will be able to

- identify the differences between the concepts of imports and exports

- explain why goods and services are traded among nations

- analyze factors that affect the flow of goods and services among nations

In the next two chapters, you will be reading a great deal about the changing global economy, and about the effect of international business opportunities on nations as well as on people. You will also be reading about the barriers to doing international business, and the downside of globalization. Global trade has many implications, not just for trade, but for the economies of individual countries. You will be presented with the challenge of determining if these developments are good or bad—for Canada and for other nations.

In this chapter, you will learn about importing and exporting, and how countries produce goods for export. You will also read about the basics of international trade, and the factors that affect it.

ATI Technologies Inc.

ATI Technologies Inc. dreams in colour and three dimensions. The company was founded in 1985 by Kwok Yuen (K.Y.) Ho. KY, as he likes to be called, has built ATI into the world's largest computer graphics company and Canada's third-largest trading company. ATI is a highly successful Canadian transnational firm. In 2000, its revenues were $137 billion U.S.

In 1996, ATI released the world's first 3-D graphic card for the personal computer. Graphic cards present images in three dimensions: height, width, and depth. The cards make the images on computers much more like those on TV. The better the card, the clearer and richer the image on your computer monitor. Who was responsible for ATI's success? Only an international workforce operating in eight different countries.

Log on to the ATI Web site, and you will find ATI "dream jobs," as the company calls them, all over the world. On one day, here were some of the jobs listed.

In Chennai City, India, they need hardware engineers for one of their subsidiaries, ATI Research Silicon Valley, Inc. Applicants must also have good people management skills. In Munich, Germany, they need sales and marketing support staff for the European market.

Employees in these jobs will be working closely with staff in other ATI offices in London, Paris, Madrid, and Dublin. In Orlando, Florida, they need a senior software engineer immediately, someone who can design and develop graphics software, and who wants to work in the area of multimedia technology. In Toronto, Canada, there are some brand new opening in human resources, finance, and technical marketing.

Figure 16-1 K.Y. Ho is the founder of ATI Technologies.

And so it goes. Why does it take all these people in all these locations to develop, manufacture, and market graphics technology? It doesn't. But when your product is high-tech, and when your market is worldwide, operating at a global level can increase efficiency and dramatically increase your profits.

It helps if you have a wonderful product. ATI did not invent 3-D, which was already available in the early 1990s for very expensive computer systems. But by refining the 3-D chip so that it produced more realistic results and could be used with different computer operating systems, ATI pushed demand over the top. Now architects want 3-D for design, geographers want it for mapping, medical schools want it for modeling the human body, and consumers of all ages want it in their video games.

All of these people can get the technology at an affordable price. That's because ATI carried out every facet of its operations in strategic locations. In India, the new high-tech centre of Southeast Asia, it created a subsidiary for research and development. In Dublin, Ireland, a gateway to Europe and North America, it created a massive distribution centre. In Europe and North America, it created separate sales and marketing offices. In other words, it chose the best people in the best locations to work on different phrases of the production flow. Later in this chapter, you will learn how important this is to a company's strategic plan, and how technology and free trade have encouraged this trend.

Next time you are surfing the Internet, try logging on to ATI Technology's Web site, and see where it takes you. Probably almost anywhere.

The Global Marketplace

Tennessee native Terry Wallick buys and trades license plates from around the world. He has lots of Canadian plates in his collection—one of his plates depicts the Yukon gold rush and sells for $40.00. His personal home page lets you link up to even more collectors and traders, such as Gregorz Labe (or "Yellky"), who lives in Poland and trades Canadian, American, and European plates.

In many ways, businesses such as Terry's and Yellky's remind us how the world has become a global marketplace. Now Wild Rose Country (Alberta) gets exposure in Warsaw. Collectors and buyers from around the world come together on the Internet to exchange goods. In an instant, cultural barriers seem to tumble.

According to one international trade organization, the International Monetary Fund (IMF), "Global markets offer greater opportunity for people to tap into more and larger

Figure 16-2 The world ... in license plates.

markets around the world. It means that they can have access to more capital flows, technology, cheaper imports, and larger export markets." On a small scale, this means that Terry Wallick's license plate business functions much better when he reaches customers around the world. For a country such as Canada, the implications are even more dramatic. It means the difference between 30 million customers within its borders and 6 billion potential customers around the world.

Figure 16-3 International trade has an effect on both the exporting and importing countries. How would the production and export of running shoes from a foreign country to Canada affect Canadian businesses and consumers?

Why Nations Trade with Each Other

To understand international business, you have to understand why countries depend on trade. Historically, nations have traded with each other because of the need to exchange goods and services. You probably know that some countries specialize in producing certain goods. For example, Saudi Arabia produces oil, Columbia and Brazil produce coffee, Switzerland produces watches, and Japan produces electronics. Since no country can produce all its own goods and services, trade is the obvious solution.

Canada's GDP by Sector

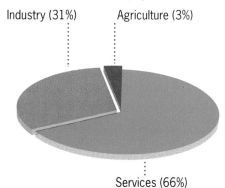

Industry (31%)   Agriculture (3%)

Services (66%)

Figure 16-4 In the 1940s, 60 percent of Canada's workforce worked in the goods sector—natural resources, manufacturing and construction. This pie graph illustrates how much things have changed. It represents the breakdown today.

The Role of Natural Resources

Some countries are rich in **natural resources**. Colombia and Brazil, for example, have just the right climate conditions for growing coffee. Saudi Arabia has huge oil deposits. Canada is rich in natural resources—its first exports were fish and furs. Canada also produces forest products, and agricultural products such as wheat.

Centuries ago, Canada's entire economy was based on its natural resources. With time, it has moved into the manufacturing and service areas and has become less dependent on its resource base. Most recently, Canada has become a world leader in information technology.

The Role of Strategic Planning

Some countries lack a natural resource base and make up for it in planning or expertise. Japan has emerged as the star of the electronics field because of a carefully managed program of economic recovery following World War Two. At the end of the war, many Japanese centres of industry had been destroyed by bombing. But with the help of the United States, along with the Japanese commitment to fund research and to establish emerging industries, Japan became a major economic player. By the 1980s, it had the people, the expertise, and the infrastructure to produce and export some of the most in-demand goods, including televisions and VCRs, radios, stereo systems, cameras, and video cameras. An **infrastructure** is a system that makes an organization or a nation run. It includes roads, postal service, telephone wiring, and so forth. Today Japan is a world leader in computer technology and robotics because it followed a well-thought out strategic plan.

Exports and Imports

Countries export the goods they produce and don't need. Successful exports are goods that a nation can produce easily, and that other nations need and desire. **Exporting** is the selling and shipping of finished products or raw materials (such as lumber) to other nations.

Exports are important to countries that have a small population base. In spite of its relatively small population, Canada produces a huge quantity of grains, automobiles, auto parts, lumber, manufactured goods, minerals, newsprint, and metals. Since Canada can't use all these products, exporting brings in a substantial amount of revenue. Canada ranks seventh among the top ten exporting nations of the world, and its exports account for more than $417 billion in revenue.

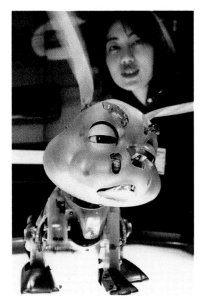

Figure 16-5 Japan is a world leader in the area of robotics.

Canadian Exports and Imports 2000

EXPORTS	(BILLIONS)	IMPORTS	(BILLIONS)
Agricultural and fishing products	$27.6	Agricultural and fishing products	$18.6
Energy products	$52.5	Energy products	$17.8
Forestry products	$41.4	Forestry products	$3.0
Industrial goods and materials	$64.6	Industrial goods and materials	$70.4
Machinery and equipment	$105.6	Machinery and equipment	$122.7
Automotive products	$96.2	Automotive products	$77.4
Other consumer goods	$14.7	Other consumer goods	$40.0
Special transactions trade	$8.0	Special transactions trade	$6.5
Unallocated adjustments	$7.0	Unallocated adjustments	$6.6
Total	**$417.6**	**Total**	**$363.1**

Source: Statistics Canada, CANSIM, Matrix 3685 and 3651.

Figure 16-6 Canadian imports and exports in 2000. Examine the totals for each and draw a conclusion.

www.school.mcgrawhill.ca/resources/
Compare Canadian import and export figures over the last four years at the Statistics Canada Web site. Which imports and exports have increased and which have decreased? What might have caused these changes?

Nations import items that they cannot produce themselves. **Importing** is the buying of raw materials or products from other nations in order to use them at home. Canada, for example, is unable to grow citrus fruit, cotton, and fruits and vegetables during winter, so we import them. Japan, on the other hand, has to import lumber. In recent years, the terms importing and exporting have also come to refer to services that are bought and sold.

The Comparative Advantage

The theory of **comparative advantage** states that some countries are better equipped to make and sell particular goods or services. Think of it this way. You know what subjects you excel at and which ones you have to work at. The theory states that you would be better off specializing in the subject you excel at because you can master it efficiently. If studying produced goods instead of marks, your best business decision would be to stick with your best subject instead of the one that requires you to study for hours a day.

Comparative advantage, sometimes known as competitive advantage, is based on the factors that affect a country's ability to trade. Maybe the country has an abundance of natural resources, or maybe it has developed the best infrastructure to specialize in certain products. Canada, for example, has a comparative advantage when it comes to producing grain and pulp and paper because of its resource base. Over time, Japan has developed a comparative advantage in electronics. (The longer a country specializes in a field, the easier it is to figure out how to make production even more efficient and less costly.) On the other hand most Western countries import their rice from East Asia and Southeast Asia because it would be much more difficult to grow rice at home. The theory of comparative advantage also states that nations should import the materials or products they cannot produce easily.

Knowledge/Understanding

1 List three reasons why countries trade internationally.

2 Explain, in your own words, the concept of comparative advantage.

Thinking/Inquiry

3 What effect does international trade have on you? How have imports from countries around the world helped you fill your needs and wants? Create a chart showing at least 6 imported products, the country they came from, and whether or not they filled a need or a want.

Skills
Appendix

problem solving

Communication

4 Look back at Figure 16-6. First figure out the percentages for each of the categories in the chart (both exports and imports). Then create two pie charts to demonstrate the breakdown in the percentages. Write a caption for each of your charts in which you draw a general conclusion for your audience about Canadian imports and exports in 2000.

Application

5 Work with a partner to research one successful Canadian export company. Investigate the role of natural resources and/or strategic planning in the company's success. Create a flowchart to demonstrate your findings.

Skills
Appendix

researching

International Trade: How It Works

Nations are always concerned with how much they have to import, and how much they can export. Does it matter if the total value of exports exceeds the total value of imports?

Say you specialize in producing student agendas but you need to buy other goods such as pens and notebooks because you don't produce them. What happens if you sell $50 worth of agendas and need to buy $25 worth of pens and notebooks? You have $25 left over to buy your supplies. But what happens if you purchase $25 worth of pens and notebooks and sell no agendas? You are now in a bad financial position—exactly the position all nations wish to avoid.

Connecting Business with *Pets*

Marianne Bertrand and Muttluks

In January 1994, when she received a gift of ineffective dog boots for her Basset hounds, Marianne Bertrand set out to build a better mouse trap-or, in her case, a better dog boot. She called them Muttluks. The name comes from the original Inuit sealskin boots known as "mukluks." The Inuit mukluk, tried and proven under Arctic conditions for hundreds of years, has a legendary reputation as durable, warm, and water resistant. All of which qualities Marianne decided that her Muttluks would also have.

Encouragement for the Muttluks concept came quickly when her first one hundred and thirty sets sold out in less than a week. They were bought by local Toronto area pet stores who also recognized the need for quality canine paw wear. Muttluks was incorporated in September 1994.

When Marianne started getting calls from U.S. consumers and pet stores interested in her leather doggy boots, she was thrilled-and worried. "One of the most difficult issues when you start exporting is there's a higher risk, if things go wrong, of not getting paid," she says. Soon after she started exporting, she called the Export Development Corp. (EDC) to buy insurance.

"What we cover are commercial and political risks," says Jen Empey, underwriting manager with the EDC emerging exporters team. These risks could mean anything from a client canceling a contract to a country undergoing political upheaval or war. The federal Crown corporation also conducts credit checks.

When Bertrand gets a nibble from a potential client, the EDC checks it out and delivers a verdict, usually within 24 hours. "If there's a problem," notes Empey, "we consult with our client to come up with a plan of action." The credit checks allow

Figure 16-7 Marianne Bertrand and two of her satisfied customers.

Bertrand to be more flexible about payment terms, which helps Muttluks compete with bigger suppliers.The EDC charges a $500 start-up fee, then exacts 1.5 to 2 percent from gross monthly sales. In months when there are no sales, there is no fee. Export insurance has fueled Muttluks's growth: 30 percent of sales spring from export, and Bertrand expects that to rise to 60 to 70 percent by year-end. She's also considering her next move-into Europe. "I'm taking on larger clients now," she says. "Because of the EDC, I have peace of mind."

[Source: Adapted with permission from "How to make sure the buck stops here," by Hilary Davidson, Chatelaine, September, 1999.]

ACTIVITIES

1   Why did Marianne Bertrand decide to call her dog boots Muttluks? Why was this a smart marketing move?

2   Muttluks Inc. was born when Marianne decided to solve a problem in an existing product. How did she use her innovative and entrepreneurial problem-solving skills as the basis for her export business?

3   Investigate the Export Development Corp., further and write a paragraph explaining one other way in which they help Canadian exporters.

When governments evaluate their economic policies and the economic performance of their countries, they rely on two measures, the balance of trade and the balance of payments. The **balance of trade** is the comparison between the total value of imports (the pens and notebooks) and the total value of exports (the agendas). If the value of exports is greater than the value of imports, there is a favourable balance of trade, also called a trade surplus. Using our student agendas example, this means that students bought so many agendas that their total worth added up to more money than the amount you needed to spend on pens and notebooks. Similarly, it means that other nations bought more from Canada than Canada needed to buy from other nations. In an unfavourable balance of trade, also called a trade deficit, the value of imports is greater than the value of exports.

TOTAL $ EXPORTS >
TOTAL $ IMPORTS =
TRADE SURPLUS

Figure 16-8 How many agendas do I need to export?

Leading Exporters and Importers in World Trade, 1999

Rank	Exporters	Share of World Trade	Rank	Importers	Share of World Trade
1	United States	12.4%	1	United States	18.0%
2	Germany	9.6%	2	Germany	8.0%
3	Japan	7.5%	3	United Kingdom	5.4%
4	France	5.3%	4	Japan	5.3%
5	United Kingdom	4.8%	5	France	4.9%
6	Canada	4.2%	6	Canada	3.7%
7	Italy	4.1%	7	Italy	3.7%
8	Netherlands	3.6%	8	Netherlands	3.2%
9	China	3.5%	9	Hong Kong	3.1%
10	Belgium	3.1%	10	China	2.8%

The World Trade Organization ranks these 10 countries as the major exporters and importers in the world. Note that the U.S. and Canada have the same ranking for both exports and imports. What does this mean for the balance of trade for these countries?

Figure 16-9 This chart shows that Canada's exports have continued to exceed its imports since 1995.

Source: The World Trade Organization, International Trade Statistics 2000.

If the Canadian economy exports more than it imports, the country is better off and so are the lives of all Canadians. Canada has had a favourable balance of trade since 1981. As a result, Canada is a relatively prosperous country, even with its small population.

Exporting and importing are not the only factors that contribute to a nation's revenue. There are many ways of participating in the global marketplace. For example, Canadians travel around the world and people from around the world visit Canada. Some Canadians invest in Germany and receive income, while some Britons invest in Canadian companies and receive interest and dividends. Canada provides foreign aid to developing nations, and Canada receives foreign direct investment. In other words, money is flowing into Canada and out of Canada all the time. A nation's **balance of payments** is the total flow of money going into the country minus the total flow of money leaving the country. This sum is known as the balance of payments.

Connecting with the Global Marketplace

CANADA
Product is researched

USA AND INDIA
Product is designed and engineered

Malaysia
Product is assembled

Germany and Hong Kong
Product is marketed in Europe and Asia

Ireland
Product is distributed worldwide

Figure 16-10 Possible production flow of a transnational company.

Exporting goods is one way of reaching out to the global marketplace. However, there are other ways. Sometimes Canadian companies license foreign companies to manufacture their product or use their trademark. Or they can establish a **foreign subsidiary**—a company that operates in the foreign country but is owned by the parent company. Franchises are another way to reach international markets. As you learned in Chapter 2 a franchise is the right to use a business's name and sell its products in a given location. Choice Hotels Canada and Country Style Donuts are examples of Canadian companies that go international through franchises. Establishing an overseas presence can involve direct investment in another country. Such investment is often welcome, as it creates new jobs and new wealth in the recipient country.

In the last decade, some companies have tapped the global marketplace in a new way. Such companies, known as **transnational** companies, use raw materials and labour from many different countries to make their products. They might design their product in one country, use the raw materials from another, manufacture or assemble the product in a third country, and then sell it to people around the world. These companies maximize the competitive advantage by letting each country contribute in the most efficient way. The creation of transnational companies such as ATI Technologies Inc. featured in this chapter's Business Profile, has meant that the nations of the world are interdependent in a whole new way, and that business is the driving force.

Check Your Understanding

Knowledge/Understanding

1 Explain, in your own words, the difference between balance of payments and balance of trade.

Thinking/Inquiry

2 Research one company that has a foreign subsidiary in Canada. What are the advantages and disadvantages to Canadians of this company operating in Canada? Prepare an argument for and an argument against this company's presence in your country.

Skills
Appendix

building arguments

Communication

3 Review Figure 16-9. Why do so many of these countries rank within the top 10 countries in the world for both exports and imports? What is the total percentage of the world's importing and exporting that is done by these 10 countries? Write a three-paragraph essay explaining the factors that would have contributed to these countries' ranking. Be sure to offer evidence for your conclusions.

Skills
Appendix

writing reports

Application

4 Prepare a graph comparing the balance of payments and the balance of trade of three countries from three different continents. In the caption for your graph, suggest reasons for the differences among the three countries. Consider a solution that will meet the concerns of governments, retail stores, and consumers. Once you have drafted a solution, form small groups and compare your suggestions. Develop a group response and share it with the class.

Factors Affecting International Trade

International trade doesn't just happen—it ebbs and flows in response to events occurring around the world. Did you know that you affect the progress of international trade, mostly through your buying choices? In this section, we will look at factors that affect the flow of goods and services between nations.

Consumer Needs and Incomes

On the most basic level, international trade takes place when there is a ready market for goods or services in another nation. For example, there is a market in Canada for fresh produce (fruits and vegetables) from the United States and Mexico. First, Canada cannot produce fruits and vegetables in the winter. Second, Canadian consumers want to eat fruits and vegetables throughout the year because these foods are delicious and part of a healthy diet. Finally, some Canadians are able to pay for imported fruits and vegetables during the winter months. While individual consumers may decide not to buy expensive fruits and vegetables, Canadians are happy to be able to buy these foods.

Trade also depends on trends and innovation. In the developed world, computers, computer software, digital cameras, and cell phones have not only become customer favourites—they have transformed the way people live and work. As a result, nations that excel in the production of electronics and computer hardware and software currently have a ready market to buy their exports.

Occasionally consumers will spend a great deal of money on something they really can't "afford." In 1990, for example, a McDonald's restaurant opened in Moscow's Pushkin Square in Russia. It broke McDonald's opening day records for customers served—more than 30 000 men, women, and children. To this day, the Pushkin Square McDonald's continues to be the busiest

Figure 16-11 A hamburger is still a luxury in Russia, but many people are willing to pay the high prices.

McDonald's restaurant in the world. Yet at the time it opened, the cost of a "Big Mac" was approximately two weeks' salary of the average Muscovite. Today, a trip to McDonald's is still beyond the means of most Russians, yet the restaurant continues to flourish.

Culture and Language Differences

Understanding a foreign market and communicating with people in another country is another key factor in successful international trade. If you have lived or traveled in other parts of the world, you may have some sense of the difficulties involved. Every nation has its preferences—biases, customs, likes, and dislikes. Understanding them is as necessary to reaching a foreign market, as is understanding the language.

To do business with a country, it is also necessary not to give offence. Canadians and Americans doing business in Asia have often been criticized for being too open or casual, for example, for calling people by their first names. In Asia, this kind of familiarity may be interpreted as rudeness. North American companies have also discovered that they usually cannot send female executives to negotiate business transactions in Asian or Islamic countries. Similarly, when the Japanese automobile manufacturer, Honda opened manufacturing operations in Alliston, Ontario, it discovered that Canadian workers were very different from Japanese workers. The Canadians were more outspoken, more independent, and less deferential than their Japanese counterparts.

Religious observances can also have an impact on business operations. In Islamic countries, the dawn-to-dusk fasting during the period of Ramadan affects how business gets done.

Accounting for cultural and language differences is bound to cost money. Let's say you decided to export your agendas to Poland. In addition to brushing up on proper etiquette in Poland, you would need to

• determine the buying habits of Polish customers and their need for agendas (who will buy, when, where, and why)

- translate the contents of your agendas into Polish, paying close attention to any cultural significance of holidays. (For example, would you have remembered that Thanksgiving, a uniquely North American holiday, would not be celebrated by Poles?)
- translate all your advertising and packaging information into Polish
- establish a Polish distribution system
- acquire knowledge of Polish customs and documentation regulations
- pay for all these services if you do not handle the tasks yourself

Transportation

Transportation costs are an important consideration in the import-export business. Goods must be distributed by air, truck, or rail to their destinations. Transportation charges can be significant. Distribution businesses and networks have grown up to accommodate international trade. However, some developing nations have inefficient transportation or storage or handling systems. Food exports are sometimes ruined because they cannot be handled properly before they reach customers.

When a nation imports goods, the cost of shipment must be added to the cost of the goods themselves. Eventually, this cost gets passed on to the consumer.

Local Laws and Regulations

International business is affected by local laws. Therefore, anyone wishing to do business in Canada must become acquainted with our laws at the federal, provincial, and municipal level. These laws cover such issues as labour relations, patents, and taxes, just to name a few. Local regulations differ from country to country. For example, if you decide to export your agendas to a number of nations, you will need to understand the regulations of each one. Moreover, you may not always receive adequate answers to your questions because of local bureaucracy or language difficulties. Sometimes business people get local sponsors in foreign countries to interpret the local regulations and to intervene on their behalf. Such services also add to the cost of doing business abroad.

Figure 16-13 The value of currency changes all the time, as every traveler knows.

The Value of Currency

Currency is a nation's money. Most nations have their own currency, though Europe now has a common European currency—the Euro, which was introduced on January 1, 1999. The value of a country's currency is a reflection of its financial health. If its economy is unstable, its currency "falls" relative to the value of other currencies. The standard currency against which all other currencies are measured is the U.S. dollar.

When you go on a trip and convert your Canadian currency to another currency, for example, U.S. dollars or British pounds, your transaction is determined by the **foreign exchange rate**. This rate rules how much of another nation's currency your own currency will buy. The foreign exchange rate is a critical factor in international trade because it can dramatically affect the cost of exports and imports. After all, when nations buy products from another country, they have to pay the bill in that nation's currency.

So how can the foreign exchange rate affect trade? Let's say that in Week 1 you decide to import your much-needed pens and notebooks from Italy at a time when 1400 Italian lire equals $1 Canadian dollar. You like the products so much that you decide to buy more. The following week, you discover that the value of the Canadian dollar has dropped. Now it is worth only 1200 Italian lire. What will happen? The products will cost you more in Week 2 because your Canadian dollar will buy fewer lire. You get exactly the same product, but you pay more.

The relative values of currencies are affected on a daily basis by their prices on world money markets. For this reason, the price of a product can rise without notice if a particular currency is stronger on world markets than the Canadian dollar. The next day or week, the situation might be reversed as the dollar gains strength against another currency. When transactions involve millions of dollars, the foreign exchange rate can be a significant factor in trading.

Italian Lira

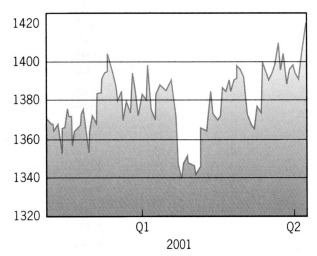

Figure 16-14

Changes in the Italian Lira from 1 Jan 2001 to 20 April 2001, relative to the Canadian dollar.

www.school.mcgrawhill.ca/resources/
Check out some of the Canadian bank foreign exchange calculators to see how much it would cost you to do business in a foreign currency today.

Protectionism

When countries protect their domestic economy by keeping out foreign-made goods, they are engaging in **protectionism**. Protectionism involves using both tariff and non-tariff barriers, and is used to achieve a favourable balance of trade.

Tariff barriers

Consumers enjoy choosing from an array of imported goods, but domestic manufacturers may not be as happy about the competition. In order to protect domestic manufacturing, countries place a tax, called a tarrif on in-coming goods. A **tariff barrier** slows the entry of foreign goods by making them more expensive than domestic products. There will still be a market for the import, but not as large as if the tariff did not exist.

When nations negotiate trade agreements with other countries, import duties (tariffs) are always important. The trend toward globalization has resulted in some tariff barriers being lowered or dropped altogether. Agreements between and among nations to create free-trade zones, industries without tariffs, have been negotiated. You will examine some of these agreements in the next chapter.

Non-Tariff Barriers

There are also **non-tariff barriers** to imported goods. A non-tariff barrier restricts trade, but does not involve a tax.

One non-tariff barrier is the import **quota**. This is a limit on the number of products in a category that can come into a country. It is a way of keeping foreign goods out of Canada in order to protect Canadian industries. An **embargo**, on the other hand, ends trading with another nation. It is a complete halt to the transfer of goods, and it is often used as a form of political or social protest. Canada placed an embargo on all goods, from South Africa for many years when South Africa refused to change its policy of apartheid.

Health and safety standards are another non-tariff barrier. If a particular food product does not meet Canadian standards, it cannot enter the country. Similarly, Canada stipulates that children's clothing must be fire-resistant, so clothing without this claim can be stopped at the border.

International Trade Organizations

International trade organizations play a huge role in facilitating trade around the world. These groups work to help nations agree on how to conduct trade. One of the earliest trade agreements, GATT (General Agreement on Tariffs and Trade), brought together major trading nations in 1947. The participants agreed that tariff and non-tariff barriers to trade should be gradually eliminated. Another early organization was the IMF (International Monetary Fund) which was formed to rebuild the world economy following World War II. Today the IMF still loans money to nations facing economic problems and helps to keep the exchange rate stable.

Sometimes, trade organizations work toward free trade. Canada participates in a number of free trade agreements, which you will read about in the next chapter. An example of an international trade organization working for free trade is APEC (Asia-Pacific Economic Cooperation). Canada was a founding member in 1989, and it is working to create a Pacific free trade agreement.

Figure 16-15 Canadians gather in protest over Indonesian president Suharto at the 1997 APEC summit in Vancouver.

These organizations have supporters and detractors. Some people say these organizations have helped to stabilize the global economy and bring prosperity to many nations. Others say that their assistance comes at a price. For example, the IMF loans money to nations but also tells nations how to slash their budgets—sometimes by ordering them to cut their social programs. Other critics have said that GATT policies and free trade in general can ruin domestic industries by letting businesses take advantage of cheap labour in the developing world. Finally, organizations such as APEC have come under fire because some member countries have a poor human rights record. Canada's challenge is to determine how to participate in the global economy while not ignoring the importance of democracy and human rights.

Web Connect

www.school.mcgrawhill.ca/resources/
Investigate current issues involving some of the International Trade Organizations. What effect do these issues have on the lives and standard of living of Canadians?

Check Your Understanding

Knowledge/Understanding

1 Explain how the value of country's currency has an affect on its international trade?

2 What is the difference between tariff and non-tariff barriers? Why do countries use such barriers

Thinking/Inquiry

3 Select one imported product that you use on a regular basis. Write a paragraph explaining why this product is imported rather than manufactured or produced in Canada.

Communication

4 Find an article in your daily newspaper relating to the factors affecting international trade in one country. Analyse the article carefully and prepare a cause and effect graphic organizer which shows how the factors have caused the outcome.

Application

5 Working with two or three other students, discuss why and how Canada's cultural mix of peoples from all over the world is an advantage to Canada and to Canadians when it comes to international trade. Prepare a group presentation in which you explain how having people from many cultures who speak many languages benefits Canadian business.

Skills
Appendix

analysing media

On a recent Friday afternoon, Qin Wenli discovered she had missed the company bus she normally takes from her place of work to her home in Beijing's western suburbs.

She was annoyed. Now it would take her nearly two hours to get home using public transit. But her face suddenly cleared. She was not going to go home angry. She would go shopping instead.

Shopping in China today is far different from what it was a decade ago. In the past, shopping in outdoor markets and neighbourhood stores was a leisurely activity. Most products, from yogurt to face cream to bamboo-flavored toothpaste, were domestic brands. Costs were totalled on an abacus. Shoppers made daily trips to the market and carried their purchases home in cloth mesh bags balanced on the handlebars of their bicycles.

But with China surging ahead economically over the past decade, many small stores and outdoor markets have given way to large modern department stores and supermarkets. "Shopping is much better now," says Beijing resident Deng Tianmei. "We like it because we can go to one store and get everything we need in one place. It's more convenient than going to small shops like before, and the quality is guaranteed. In the past, in small shops, often the quality of goods wasn't so good."

Everything is available and usually reasonably priced. Attracted by the huge Chinese market, foreign retailers have been streaming into China. The world's top three retailers—America's Wal-Mart, France's Carrefour, and Germany's Metro—are all making plans for expansion in many of China's bigger cities. Competition in China's retail industry has become increasingly fierce.

Figure 16-16 These young women are shopping in one of the new department stores in Beijing. What effects do you think such Western-style stores have had on the lives of the people of Beijing? How has it changed their cultural environment?

"We love going to the stores now," enthuses Deng Tianmei. "They're larger and cleaner. Everybody likes them." But while just about everything is under one roof, so is just about everyone in the neighbourhood. It's a rush hour year-round in Beijing's stores.

Changes in working and living conditions contribute to the crush. Offices are more Westernized and business-like, with stricter working hours. It's no longer as simple as it once was to slip out and buy food for that night's meal or to bargain for clothes. And more people live farther away from their work in the new suburban housing developments, and they face long commutes.

So more and more busy Beijingers, like their counterparts in the West, have to squeeze in their shopping on the weekend or after work.

Some grocery stores sell everything imaginable: jellyfish threads, edible fungus, sugared pineapple slices, Kraft yogurt, Nescafe, fresh tofu, live fish, and ginseng. But it is the meat department that is most daunting to a Western shopper. Every part of a cow, pig, lamb, or chicken is available. Today, butchers cut up the meat behind glassed-in counters. Ten years ago, everything was in the open. It wasn't unusual to see pork carcasses stacked on the street.

Extremely popular among Beijing shoppers is the Carrefour department store on Baishiqiao Road, which has a basement-level food section that resembles a Loblaw's superstore, complete with an on-site bakery. Every section is crammed with customers.

Entire families—grandparents, parents, toddlers, nannies, and various other relatives—can be seen wandering the aisles looking at the latest TV's from Panasonic, Sony video cameras, vacuum cleaners, microwave ovens, small household appliances, scooters, sports equipment, and endless aisles of clothing and shoes. For the Westerner, shopping can be exhausting. One has the feeling of being in a rugby match, fending off shopping carts, plastic baskets, and elbows.

At the checkout counters, bar-code scanners have replaced abacuses, and Chinese shoppers no longer carry their own bags to take their purchases home. Instead, everything is put into plastic bags, which contribute to China's never-ending environmental problems. Known as "white pollution," the bags are evidence that not all change is progress. They can be seen floating across the parks and soccer fields, snagged on trees, even covering entire villages in the countryside.

So was Qin Wenli successful on her unexpected shopping excursion after missing her bus? She models a beautiful cherry red jacket with delicate embroidery at the collar and a three-quarter length black skirt.

"I didn't intend to buy anything—just look," she says. "But I tried it on. And, well, it was a bargain. It was only 360 kuai."

Not bad for $70 Canadian.

ACTIVITIES

1   What traditions in China have been lost under the influence of Western-style shopping?
2   What might be some negative effects of Western-style shopping in China?
3   Did the Beijing residents interviewed for this article welcome the new Western stores and trends? Why? Explain your answer.

Chapter Review

Points to Remember

- International trade provides opportunities for nations and individuals.

- Nations trade with each other to get goods they do not have and to sell goods they can easily produce.

- Some countries have a comparative advantage because they are better equipped that others to make and sell particular goods or services.

- Many ways exist of connecting with global markets.

- Numerous factors affect international trade.

- Countries can protect their economies by using tariff and non-tariff barriers to control trade.

- International trade organizations work to make global trade easier.

Activities

Knowledge/Understanding

1 How do consumer needs and incomes affect international trade?

2 Explain how international trade is affected by changing currency values.

3 Identify the ways in which culture affects business activity and Canada's international economic relationships.

4 In 1970 our exports were $16 820 million. In 1999 they were $76 158 million. Calculate the percentage increase.

Thinking/Inquiry

1 While some economists feel that we should eliminate all barriers to trade in order to be globally competitive in the new millennium, others disagree. Protectionists believe Canadian industries must be protected from cheap imports or the Canadian economy will cease to exist. Discuss both points of view in small groups. Create a chart comparing the points of view.

Skills
Appendix

building arguments

2 This table shows the total amount of trade Canada had with each region in 1999.

a) Create the table below using a computer spreadsheet program.

b) Total the exports and imports. Which is larger?

c) Calculate as a percentage of the total imports, the imports from each region.

d) Create a bar graph to illustrate the imports from each region.

Region	Exports (Millions of dollars)	Imports (Millions of dollars)
United States	111 380	87 894
Asia-Pacific	16 235	19 534
Western Pacific	14 459	19 626
Latin America & Caribbean	1 321	600
Middle East	1 434	1 157
Africa	1 086	1 125

Communication

1 With a partner prepare a bulletin board display that shows the goods and services that Canadian businesses export.

2 With a partner choose a country you are interested in. Research what it is like to do business there and compare your findings with doing business in Canada. Examine factors such as standard of living, weather, politics, education, housing, economy, and any others that affect the way in which business is conducted. Share your findings with the class.

3 In small groups brainstorm a list of goods and services that Canada could export to another country. Select the good or service your group believes has the most potential. Prepare a proposal to present to your bank to get funding for your new venture.

Application

1 Think of a product you would like to develop and market to people on your planet-Xobni. Now imagine that you must assemble a team of imaginary people to help you achieve your goal. These employees hail from neighbouring planets and have different skill sets. Some of their planets have natural resources that could be used in production. One planet still allows slavery, in contravention of the Planetary Code. Create a list of steps for

- creating your product
- marketing your product
- distributing your product
- selling your product

Now assign each step, or phase, of the production flow to one or two members of your imaginary team, based on their knowledge and skill, location, and other factors that might be important. After you have developed your plan, share it with the rest of your class. What did you learn from this exercise? Did you behave in an ethical manner? Explain.

Internet Extension

1   Various sites on the Internet offer suggestions and guidelines for Canadians who are doing business in other countries. Investigate some of these sites to see how you might prepare yourself for exporting Canadian goods to other countries.

2   Imagine that you have just invented or innovated a product that you are sure people everywhere will want to buy. Work with a partner. First decide what your product will be. Then draw up a plan for exporting your product internationally. Use guidelines provided on the Internet to keep you from making the kind of false moves that could lead to disaster.

17

Canada, the Global Player

KEY TERMS

G8

trading partner

Free Trade Association (FTA)

trade bloc

North American Free Trade Association (NAFTA)

Free Trade Area of the Americas

European Union (EU)

Asia-Pacific Region

Specific Expectations

After studying this chapter, you will be able to

- summarize the impact of trade on employment and job creation in Canada

- analyze the impact of trade on the quality and quantity of products available

- identify Canada's major trading partners

- describe how a company's profit and growth can be affected by its international business activity and participation in the markets of other nations

- identify ways in which culture affects business activity and Canada's international economic relationships

In the previous chapter, you learned the basics of international trade. In Chapter 17, you will hear more about Canada's role as a world trader. Canada is a major trading country and a leading exporter of goods. Trade generates revenue for Canada, and directly affects your quality of life.

In this chapter, you will learn how trade enhances the lives of Canadians, and why international trade is so important to the Canadian economy. You will also learn about Canada's major trading partners and the agreements Canada and other countries are making to open up trade even more. Free trade and globalization have their critics, though, and you will hear from these voices as well. Throughout the chapter, you will be invited to weigh the competing interests in the new global economy.

Viceroy Homes Work Around the World

Viceroy homes is a Canadian firm that has been an innovator in pre-fabricated homes. Since the 1950s, the "pre-fab" label had meant something less than beautiful. Viceroy Homes of Port Hope, Ontario, ended that idea. In the last 40 years, it has built 35 000 homes, incorporating desirable design features such as an open floor plan, vaulted ceilings, turrets, and "superwindows," which keep the weather out and let all the light in. The homes arrive at the customer's building site in pieces, and are assembled according to instructions.

Today, Viceroy has manufacturing facilities in Ontario and British Columbia, and is "the largest supplier of Canadian housing technology to a growing export market," according to company literature. In 1999, it won Canada's "Exporter of the Year" award, presented by Canada's International Trade Minister, Pierre S. Pettigrew.

Viceroy has worked to make its products desirable in an international market, where housing needs and building codes vary around the world. This means that its homes can be sold in many locations by adapting them to meet local requirements. In addition, the company promises to meet consumers' needs in a "cost-effective" fashion and give them support and instruction.

Buyers can choose from four basic designs and have them customized to almost any degree. After customers select a design, Viceroy draws the floor plan. Next the plan is approved and the home delivered to

Figure 17-1 Billed as "Canada's Housing for the World," Viceroy Homes is now the largest manufacturer of pre-cut homes in North America. Working with builders and developers overseas, the company sells many of its homes to customers in other locations—some as far away as Asia and South America.

the customer's site in a pre-packaged form. This package contains all the materials needed to complete the exterior of the home—framing, doors, windows, roofing, and siding. The interior is partially completed, and buyers hire local workers to finish the home.

The cost of a Viceroy home, combined with the cost of local labour, is usually far below the cost of housing in many areas of the world. Such innovative partnering of Canadian know-how with local business is one reason why Viceroy is attracting notice.

Currently, Japan is one of Viceroy's best markets. Between the first and last quarters of 2000, shipments of Viceroy Homes to Japan increased by 52 percent. In that period, sales within Canada increased by 24 percent, and sales to the U.S. increased by 5 percent. Viceroy's total sales for the last nine months of 2000 were $69.5 million compared to $51.9 million for the same period one year earlier.

How has Viceroy identified a consumer need and met that need in an original way? Will pre-cut homes increase in popularity in the future? Why do you think so?

The Impact of Trade on Canadians

In Chapter 16, you learned that the market inside Canada is much smaller than the huge market outside Canada. Canada's population is about 30 million, whereas the population of the world is 6 billion, and growing by 90 million people every year.

It seems to make sense for Canada to be a global trader. Canada logs 20 million import/export transactions every day, according to Statistics Canada. It is one of the world's leading trading nations, as well as the leading exporter of the **Group of Eight** or **G8** industrialized economies. The G8 is an association of the world's most powerful trading countries, including Britain, France, Germany, Italy, Canada, the United States, Japan, and Russia. Canada also participates in the global marketplace through franchises or foreign subsidiaries. However, people disagree on whether free trade is entirely good for Canada. Some people maintain that it opens up opportunities, while others say that importing so many foreign-made goods threatens job security at home.

Figure 17-2 Exporting businesses are always looking for new markets in addition to satisfying the demands of their current customer base.

The impact of international trade is always felt at home. It affects employment as well as the types of products a country's citizens can buy. In general, trade enhances people's lives. For example, when Canada exports the products in which it has a comparative advantage, it receives revenue for them. The more revenue exporting generates, the more money the government has to spend on programs that will improve the lives of Canadians. Similarly, when Canada imports the products it cannot produce easily or produce at all, Canadians have a much wider range of products to choose from. If Canada chose not to trade, there would be a loss of consumer choice and a decline in the standard of living.

Employment

Through international trade, Canadian workers have opportunities in a huge variety of industries—local companies, Canadian businesses abroad, and foreign companies operating in Canada. The exporting business alone

SHORT 1 2 FULL
SEALER
TEMP 3 4
END CONV 5 H/L

Figure 17-3 The Toyota plant in Cambridge, Ontario, led all car manufactuers in assembly productivity in 1998.

employs 3 million Canadians. Foreign investment in Canada also creates new jobs. For example, when the Japanese firm Toyota opened an assembly plant in Cambridge, Ontario, in 1998, it created more than 2000 new jobs.

Canadian businesses benefit from international trade by selling their production knowledge around the world. If Canadian firms were restricted to Canadian markets, production quantities would be greatly reduced, as would employment and benefits. Canadians are employed by businesses in Canada, whether these companies are entirely owned by Canadians or not. When Canadian business is globally competitive, Canadians benefit in several ways.

- Canadians have jobs because of the increase in exported goods and services.
- They have opportunities to invest in companies that are involved in international trade and to receive income in the form of capital gains and dividends.
- Canadian entrepreneurs have the opportunity to increase profits by marketing their products all over the world.
- New Canadians can open importing businesses and sell a wide variety of products from their countries of origin.

Some people feel that Canadian business should be protected from outside competition. These critics say that unrestricted trade, which allows transnational companies to take advantage of a low-wage workforce in another country, threatens jobs in Canada. Manufacturing jobs and jobs involving unskilled labour are most likely to be threatened in an era of free trade. However, automation also threatens these kinds of jobs. Both globalization and automation have changed the nature of employment, and both have forced Canadians to look seriously at the issue of education and training for a new kind of workforce. These problems will not be resolved easily, certainly not by halting the progress of trade or technology.

Some people say that Canadian branches of foreign firms do not serve the best interests of Canadians. The senior management in these firms answers to the parent company, so the major decision-making takes place outside Canada. More impor-

Web Connect

www.school.mcgrawhill.ca/resources/
Investigate current events involving Canada and her trading partners in G8 countries. What are some of the global-trade issues being reported and discussed in the newspapers around the world?

tantly, the company profits leave Canada, and benefit only those in the country of origin. They say that, while it is true that these corporations pay taxes and create employment in Canada, the jobs are often low paying. However, raising tariff barriers is not a perfect solution. It always causes other countries to do the same, and it reduces the volume of Canadian exports.

Choice of Products

Figure 17-4 The IKEA® name is known in Canada and around the world.

In Chapter 16, you learned that Canada has to import many winter fruits and vegetables because our climate doesn't allow us to grow these products during the long winter season. However, fruits and vegetables are only some of the items you would have to go without if Canada did not import products.

For example, many Canadians recognize the brand name IKEA® and understand the concept of ready-to-assemble furniture. IKEA® began in a small farming village in Sweden in 1922 and has grown through the years to become a major Swedish exporter which sells its products in 29 countries around the world. IKEA® sells good-quality, low-priced furniture. Many of its products are sold in ready-to-assemble components that are packed flat so that customers can transport the furniture in a car or van. The IKEA® story shows how international trade expands consumer knowledge, product choice, and opportunity to buy.

Figure 17-5 Nintendo 64 was launched in Japan in 1996. It was the world's first true 64-bit home video game system. Nintendo Co., Ltd., of Kyoto, Japan, is also the creator of Pokémon, known by children around the world.

Canada imports a wide array of products that you and your family members might miss if they were not available, for example

- office machines and equipment—computers, faxes, and photocopiers
- electronic equipment and custom video technology such as Nintendo 64 and Sony PlayStation
- cosmetics and perfumes; watches and jewelry; clothing, shoes and accessories; furniture and rugs; and dishes and tableware
- books, magazines, tapes, and CDs
- specialty foods and beverages from around the world, including world-famous chocolate and cheeses.

Check a product that you use frequently to see where it was made. Then think what your life would be like without it.

Check Your Understanding

Knowledge/Understanding

1 Why does Canada need to engage in foreign trade?

2 How does international trade affect employment and job creation in Canada?

3 How does international trade affect the choice of products Canadians can buy?

Thinking/Inquiry

4 Keisha and Salim are discussing Canada's participation in the global economy. Keisha says that Canada's extensive foreign trade is, on the whole, good for Canadians. Salim says that because Canada is a highly developed manufacturing economy, we could produce domestically much of what we now import. He says that with the technology of climate control, we could even produce fruits and vegetables year round. Create two organizers, one to show the advantages of foreign trade and globalization, and the other to show the advantages of producing goods and services in Canada.

Communication

Skills
Appendix

building an argument

5 Is trade protectionism good for domestic producers? First, discuss this issue in small groups. Then, choose class members to support each side of the issue and present your arguments as a debate. Have the rest of the class act as the judges of the debate.

Application

Skills
Appendix

working in groups

6 In a small group, investigate the use of foreign and domestically produced goods and services in your home and everyday life. Have each person in your group list the goods and services used in their homes under the following headings: Food, Clothing, Transportation, Electronics, Furniture, and Entertainment. For each category, identify the origin of the item as foreign or domestic. Show your findings in a bar graph or pie chart. Share your finding with the class.

Career Connect — *Becoming an Exporter*

Have you always wanted to start your own export business? You don't need a formal degree to become an exporter, but understanding two or more languages, respecting cultural differences, following government regulations, and working hard are all necessary qualities.

Here, William Lasley, owner of a retail/wholesale craft manufacturing business, answers the question, "How do I know if I'm ready to start an export business?"

You should examine a few issues before jumping into the global marketplace.

Products Are your products exportable? It is much easier to export candles than large furniture. Team Canada's Step-by-Step Guide to Exporting can help you determine if your product is marketable outside Canada.

Commitment Exporting, although profitable, will require more thought and work than conventional forms of marketing. You should talk to your associates before deciding to export. Regulations abound and take time to digest.

Production capacity As with any wholesale marketing, you need to be able to produce enough goods to satisfy your buyers' needs. Most import buyers will want to know how large your production capacity is before placing an order.

Financial resources Do you have the funds to attend the large international trade shows? Traveling expenses, booth fees, and literature can add up, and you may not get orders right away. However, this is where the buyers are.

Respect for culture It will help if you have the time to learn about the customs of your customers. For instance, a quilt-producer I met has changed a line of couch-throws to a smaller design for some of her buyers in Japan where the couches are smaller than they are in North America. Language is another issue. When you get something translated into another language, be very careful to get the translation done by someone who is reputable. I've heard too many horror stories of folks who have had translations that were incomplete, inaccurate, or even vulgar! (An offended customer is a lost sale, and that's not funny at all.)

You must also identify your customers.

Population Heavily populated countries will contain more possible buyers of your products.

Industrialization It doesn't do much good to have a very heavy population if no one has a paying job. Therefore, industrialized countries are another plus.

Disposable income If everyone in a country has a sub-minimum salary, there won't be much money left to spend on goodies. Make sure you target a market with a high amount of disposable income, especially if you are dealing in non-essential goods.

Still want to get into the exporting market? Don't worry. All of this sounds a little overwhelming at first. It did to me too! If you just take the time to get prepared, it can be a very profitable experience.

Source: Adapted from William's Lasley's online tutorials, artsandcrafts .guide@about.com.

ACTIVITIES

1   What aspects of the export business were unfamiliar to you before you read this feature? Would you start your own export business? Why or why not?

Canada's Trading Partners

International trade is extremely important to Canada's economy. In fact, almost half the goods produced in Canada are exported. For example, coal is exported to Korea and grain is exported to Greece. Canada has nearly 200 international trading partners, but the bulk of its trade is with the United States, the United Kingdom, the European Union, and Asian countries.

Canada-US Trade

Canada does most of its foreign trade with the U.S. Cars, trucks, and parts make up 25-30 percent of Canada's exports to that market. This is a direct result of the 1965 Canada-United States Auto Pact, which was designed to stimulate the auto industry in both countries. The agreement equalized Canadian-U.S. interests by insisting that U.S. firms operating in Canada assemble one car for every car they sold in Canada. As a direct result of the Auto Pact, the Canadian auto-making industry became a billion dollar industry.

The Auto Pact was repealed on February 19, 2001. According to Industry Canada, the loss of the Auto Pact will not have a serious impact on automobile production or jobs in Canada. Industry Canada believes that Canada's automobile manufacturing companies are now internationally competitive and can succeed without the Auto Pact.

Natural resources have also been a huge part of Canadian exports, including pulp and paper products, lumber, agriculture, fish products, energy products, and minerals. Canada is rapidly developing industries in the areas of biogenetics, telecommunications, computers, air and rail transport, and materials technology.

Bombardier, Nortel Networks, and SPAR Aerospace are some examples of globally successful Canadian firms that specialize in technology.

With international trade comes the need to negotiate agreements with major trading partners. **Trading partners** are two or more countries that do business with each other in

Figure 17-6 Canada's automobile industry is internationally competitive. What effect do you think that the repeal of the Auto Pact will have on the Canadian economy?

exports and imports. In Chapter 16, we examined how tariff barriers were used to protect domestic industries. Canada and other countries, however, have found it necessary to reduce or eliminate many tariff barriers in order to increase their access to international markets.

The Canada-US Free Trade Agreement (FTA)

The U.S. is Canada's largest two-way trading partner. In 1990, 70 percent of Canada's exports were made to the U.S. By the year 2000, this figure had risen to 80 percent as a result of the **Free Trade Agreemen**t (FTA), enacted in 1989. Under the terms of the Free Trade Agreement, all tariffs on the sale of goods between Canada and the U.S. were removed by 1999. In other words, the two countries could trade with each other without restrictions. Together, they made up a **trade bloc**, or trade zone. The FTA also made it easier for Canadians and Americans to invest in or buy businesses across the border.

Not everyone agrees on the final impact of the Canada-U.S. Free Trade Agreement. Some people believe that the FTA benefits the Canadian economy, while others think it harms the economy. The FTA has exposed Canadian industries to greater competition from American companies, forcing them to become more competitive. Supporters of the FTA think this is essential if Canada is to be globally competitive now that the world has effectively become one market. They point out that Canadian producers now have access to larger markets. The population of the U.S., for example, is approximately 10 times that of Canada.

Second, Canadian consumers are now able to buy cheaper American goods. American products are often less expensive because manufacturing and distribution costs are lower in the U.S. than they are in Canada. Third, the FTA has increased entrepreneurial activity in Canada by opening up a huge new market. As Figure 17-7 shows, two-way trade between Canada and the U.S. grew by 46 percent between 1994 and 1999, under the FTA and NAFTA.

Opponents say that the FTA has forced Canadian manufacturers to close or downsize and has led to unemployment. They note that it has given the U.S. guaranteed access to Canadian oil and gas resources, in effect, preventing Canada from having its own energy policy. They believe that American foreign

Biz.Bites

In 1999, the U.S. sold $167 billion worth of goods to Canada, a 7 percent increase over the previous year. Canadians bought U.S. merchandise worth about $5,446 per person. The U.S. bought $201 billion worth of Canadian goods, approximately $736 for every American.

Figure 17-7 U.S. Trade with Canada Exports and Imports, Goods, Services and Income 1988-1999, in billions of U.S. dollars.

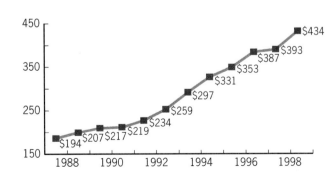

U.S. Trade with Canada Exports and Imports, Goods, Services and Income 1988-1998, in billions of U.S. dollars

investment in Canada will increase and that the Canadian marketplace will be flooded with American-made goods, possibly leading to a loss of Canadian identity and culture. They even suggest that without some kind of protectionism, Canada will become more and more American because American culture is so dominant.

The North American Free Trade Agreement (NAFTA)

In 1990, Mexico and the U.S. began discussing a free trade agreement similar to the Canada-U.S. Free Trade Agreement. In 1991, Canada joined the discussions. On January 1, 1994, the **North American Free Trade Agreement** (NAFTA) took effect. Because Mexico had implemented an economic reform program in 1987, many analysts viewed that country as a market with tremendous growth potential. Mexico's population was young and, despite the poverty that affected much of the country, a growing middle class had been demanding goods and services that Canadians take for granted. The trade agreement with Mexico was regarded as an opportunity to increase Canadian exports as demand for such products grew. As with the Canada-U.S. Free Trade Agreement, some believed that NAFTA would benefit the Canadian economy, while others feared the results.

Today, those favouring NAFTA say that Canadian producers benefit from the new market. They claim that Canadian consumers benefit from cheaper products made available through low-cost Mexican labour. And supporters forecast that as Mexico's economy expands, its need for technology-based equipment produced in Canada will increase. Finally, they note that the Mexican economy is attractive to investors interested in emerging markets. In the years following the ratification of NAFTA, finance and high-tech Canadian companies have successfully entered the Mexican economy.

People opposed to NAFTA are concerned that Canadian manufacturers have moved south to take advantage of lower wages and operating costs in Mexico. Another major issue for them is the lack of labour and environmental regulations in Mexico. While few regulations can keep manufacturing costs low, the

Figure 17-8 More than 1 million Mexicans work in about 3800 foreign-owned manufacturing and assembly plants in northern Mexico. While wages can be higher than those earned by most Mexicans, the cost of living in a border-town is very high—about 30% higher than in southern Mexico.

result is often violation of human rights or destruction of the environment. Canadian workers, by contrast, are protected by human rights legislation and environmental regulations. Finally, opponents say that foreign control of Canadian manufacturing will certainly rise as American and Mexican investors purchase Canadian companies.

In 2001, three economic institutes issued a report on the impact of NAFTA on job loss and job creation in Canada, the United States, and Mexico. The report concluded that in Canada and the U.S., NAFTA had eliminated more jobs than it had created, and had resulted in falling wages or wage freezes. The report also noted that total employment in Mexico had risen by 1.2 percent, but that foreign-owned plants in Mexico were relocating to areas where environmental standards were the most lax and wages were the lowest.

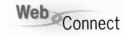

Web Connect

www.school.mcgrawhill.ca/resources/

Visit the Web sites of people on the different sides of some of these trade issues. Analyse the methods of persuasion that they use to convince you to agree with their viewpoint.

The Free Trade Area of the Americas (FTAA)

Canada and the U.S. have adopted the strategy of making the Western Hemisphere into one huge trading bloc. The U.S. could dominate this bloc because its economic power is so much greater than Canada's. In 1997, for example, the U.S. stalled the process of allowing Chile to enter NAFTA, so Canada went ahead and signed its own free trade deal with Chile—the Canada-Chile Free Trade Agreement (CCFTA). While Canada and the U.S. have a valued business relationship, such disputes have discouraged Canada from being overly dependent on its southern neighbour.

In April 2001, the leaders of 34 nations from North and South America (all but Cuba) met in Quebec City, Canada, for the Summit of the Americas. Here they worked to complete the first draft of the Free Trade Area of the Americas (FTAA). The idea for this agreement had been launched in 1994, when the western nations first met to plan a strategy for greater cooperation and freer trade. This trade bloc is huge, representing a market of more than 700 million people.

Biz.Bites

In 2001, the U.S. refused to allow Canada to export its softwood lumber under the terms of NAFTA. Canada had been waiting for the chance to sell its lumber to U.S. markets ever since the Softwood Lumber Pact expired on March 31, 2001. At issue is the U.S. softwood lumber industry.

Figure 17-9 The "People's Summit" staged its own events at the Summit of the Americas, held in Quebec City in 2001. About 60 000 people marched to protest globalization and the conditions of workers in Mexico under free trade. Unions and non-governmental organizations were well-represented.

The European Union

Europe is Canada's second-largest trading partner after the U.S. In 1992, two existing trading blocs in Europe joined to form an even larger trading bloc. The European Communities (EC) and the European Free Trade Agreement (EFTA) bloc of nations joined to form the **European Union** (EU). The European Union consists of a vast market of 370 million people, with free movement of people, goods, services, and capital. Fifteen European countries are members, and the EU is about to expand again, this time into Eastern Europe.

Currently, the EU is an economic union, but it does have political and social objectives, including the introduction of European citizenship and the development of EU law. In 1999, 11 of the 15 members voted to phase out their own currencies and to use the Euro as the common currency of the European Union. Members hope that the Euro will be strong enough to replace the U.S. dollar as the currency of choice on world markets. Canada is anxious to maintain good relations with the EU because this market includes some of the world's wealthiest customers.

Figure 17-10 One side of the Euro coin is common to all countries of the European Union. The other side represents the country where the coin is issued.

The Asia-Pacific Region

Figure 17-11

These buildings are on the North Side of False Creek in Vancouver. Many of them were built on former Expo '86 land by Li Ka-Shing, a very wealthy resident of Hong Kong.

The **Asia-Pacific Region** is much larger than the European market. The powerhouse of the region is still Japan, although this country is slowly being overtaken by China. Some other countries in this region are South Korea, Singapore, Malaysia, Thailand, Indonesia, the Philippines, and India. Although they have no formal agreement, they are working toward cooperation in trade matters.

Today, Canada's trade with Asian nations accounts for only about 8 percent of its total trade. Three percent of this figure represents trade with Japan. As trade matters now stand, Canada imports much more from these countries than it exports to them. British Columbia, however, has occasionally traded more with the Asia-Pacific region than it has with the United States. Because of its location, the province has strong ties with Asia. In the 1990s, Japanese and Hong Kong investment in British Columbia grew substantially. Many people regard British Columbia as Canada's gateway to Asia.

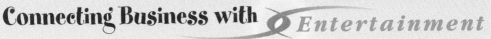

Connecting Business with *Entertainment*

IMAX® and Cirque du Soleil™ Journey of Man

When the film *Cirque du Soleil™ Journey of Man* opened in 26 countries around the world in December 1999, it was truly an all-Canadian moment. Not only did the film feature the Montreal-based circus troupe Cirque du Soleil, it was no ordinary movie. It was a 3-D IMAX® movie, a Canadian innovation.

IMAX® technology uses a giant screen to project images that extend beyond a viewer's peripheral vision (what people see out of sides of their eyes). It also features wrap-around sound. First developed in the 1960s by a trio of Canadian filmmakers – Graeme Ferguson, Roman Kroitor, and Robert Kerr. The first IMAX® film was shown at Expo 67 in Montreal. Three years later, the first multi-screen film was shown at Expo 70, in Osaka, Japan. The first permanent IMAX® projection system was constructed at Ontario Place's Cinesphere in 1971. In 1997, Imax® Corporation received a unique Oscar Award for scientific and technical achievement by the Academy of Motion Picture Arts and Sciences.

IMAX® Corporation is headquartered in Mississauga, Canada, and its theatres are scattered around the world. The company estimates that more than 600 million people have enjoyed The IMAX Experience® --something so special, it carries a registered trademark. In 2000, the company's revenues were approximately $200 million.

Cirque du Soleil™ Journey of Man represented a business partnership as well as a creative one. As you read in Chapter 14, Cirque du Soleil is an international enterprise, with a head office in Montreal and regional headquarters in the Americas, Asia-Pacific, Europe and Las Vegas. Its subsidiary, Cirque du Soleil Images, is a multi-media division dedicated to the creation of original materials in tel-

Figure 17-12 The Cirque du Soleil and IMAX®—a Canadian partnership seen around the world.

evision, video, film and music. *Journey of Man* is Cirque du Soleil's second feature film, and its first IMAX® film.

Work on the film, which explores the stages of human development from birth to maturity, began in 1998. It was quickly apparent that IMAX® technology showcases the troupe's acrobatic talents in a brand new way. Every spin, roll, and bungee jump is designed to make viewers feel they are perched on the artists' shoulders. As the story unfolds, each stage of human development is introduced by a Cirque du Soleil performance in varied locations around the world (only one constructed set was used for the film's opening sequence). Amazingly, many of the artists involved in the film gave their usual performances each night and performed in the film during the day.

To ensure that the final film would be dazzling, the directors and the performers left nothing to chance. For one sequence, they used a private home in San Mateo, California, drained the pool of water, scrubbed it clean and filled it with water dyed black, giving the surface a deep, reflective quality. In Barbados, an underwater ballet sequence had to be shot with the IMAX® Solido camera encased in a metal bubble. The camera was suspended from a crane and then dropped in the water. Because the camera could only hold enough film to shoot for three minutes, the performers had to shoot the scene many times.

It was worth it, though, when Time Magazine noted: "Here are humans achieving the impossible, beautifully, in a film worthy of being displayed on a screen eight stories high."

Cirque du Soleil™ Journey of Man is distributed world wide by Sony Pictures Classics in 3D and 2D. The film is currently playing in large format theatres around the world.

In the meantime, Imax Corporation is interested in pursuing a variety of partnerships. Its next corporate move will be bringing the IMAX ® brand to consumer products such as consumer electronics, photography and optics, as well as to consumer and business services.

Letting fans around the world bring home a piece of the IMAX® magic? Seems like one of the smartest partnerships going.

Figure 17-13 The acrobatic skills of Cirque du Soleil performers and the technological skills of the Imax filmmakers makes for a powerful artistic partnership.

ACTIVITIES

1 How did the business partnerships described in this feature benefit both parties?

2 How does the use of technology demonstate the innovative nature of the Imax company? Why might this technology be risky in a business sense?

3 Write a research report on the production of *The Journey of Man* at the Cirque du Soleil's Web site. What does the Web site itself indicate about the company?

The Asia-Pacific region accounts for approximately 60 percent of the world's population, 50 percent of global production, and 40 percent of consumption. Canadian producers, who sell nearly 80 percent of their products to the United States, are poised to move outside North America and explore these growing world markets.

The Business of Canadian Culture

By virtue of its linguistic and cultural diversity, Canada seems ready for globalization. It beckons the rest of the world with its attractive urban regions, comparatively advanced science and technology, and social safety net. Yet Canada is a small nation living next to a giant one. Historically, Canada has always tried to protect its identity from being overshadowed by the United States. In an era of free trade, there is still one area of Canadian life that the Canadian government and the citizens of Canada wish to protect—Canadian culture.

A recent government report, *Canadian Culture in a Global World*, notes that:

Culture is the heart of a nation. As countries become more economically integrated, nations need strong domestic cultures and cultural expression to maintain their sovereignty and sense of identity. Indeed some have argued that the worldwide impact of globalization is manifesting itself in the reaffirmation of local cultures.

Through a combination of regulations, including rules on foreign investment, the Canadian government ensures that Canadian culture can continue to grow. An examination of some statistics reveals how necessary these regulations are. Even with Canadian regulations, foreign firms and products account for

- 45 percent of book sales in Canada
- 81 percent of English-language consumer magazines on Canadian newsstands and over 63 percent of magazine circulation revenue
- 79 percent (over $910 million) of the retail sales of tapes, CDs, concerts, merchandise and sheet music
- 85 percent ($165 million) of the revenues from film distribution in Canada
- between 94 and 97 percent of screen time in Canadian theatres. The situation is most extreme in the film industry where the Hollywood studios have historically treated Canada as part of the US market.

Figure 17-14 How many non-Canadian magazines do you read?

The Canadian government scrutinizes all foreign investment in a cultural industry. In addition, Canada's policy states that new businesses in the cultural industries must be Canadian-controlled. Finally, a Canadian-controlled business can only be acquired by a foreign company under very special circumstances.

Foreign investment in broadcasting has increased under government guidelines introduced in 1996. Until then, no firm applying to the CRTC (Canadian Radio and Television Commission) for a broadcasting license in Canada could have more than 20 percent foreign investment. In 1996, the rules changed so that up to 46.7 percent of a company can be foreign-owned. The purpose of this increase was to give Canadians more access to foreign capital so they could remain competitive and keep up with the technological changes in broadcasting.

Check Your Understanding

Knowledge/Understanding

1 What are the advantages and disadvantages of the North American Free Trade Agreement to Canadians and Canadian business?
2 Why has it become necessary for countries to organize huge trading blocs that establish free trade zones?

Thinking/Inquiry

3 Jason is reading about the protests surrounding the Summit of the Americas held in Quebec City. "What's the big problem?" he asks Laura. "A free trade zone of the Americas would be a tremendous opportunity for Canadian business." Research this issue and prepare a role play of the discussion between Jason and Laura.

Application

4 Use the Internet and library to research the imports and exports Canada has with each of her major trading partners. Show this information graphically. Is Canada a net importer or exporter of goods and services?

Undoubtedly, you own at least a small piece of Honduras, or some other gold-producing country. Many people do, although they may not know it. You may also be unaware that international mining companies sometimes cause environmental problems.

The newly formed *Associacion de Organismos No Gubernamentales* (ASONOG) is a new anti-mining campaign in Honduras. It has spent more than a year investigating the recent arrival of gold mining companies from Canada and the United States in Honduras. In just two years, 1996 – 1997, the Honduran mining department has issued mining concessions totaling 5.2 million hectares— more than 30 percent of Honduras' territory—to foreign companies.

ASONOG's first public meeting attracted 75 people representing 15 communities close to eight different mines. At issue was the Honduran General Mining Law, passed in December 1998, just four weeks after Hurricane Mitch. The new law reduced company taxes and allowed mining firms to petition for the removal of communities located near mineral deposits.

The meeting noted that some abuses have yet to be resolved through the courts. One Canadian firm (since auctioned off to a new company) has been accused of making illegal discharges of waste into a nearby river, using cyanide within 22 metres of occupied homes, and causing the death of farm animals. An American firm faces civil and criminal charges for usurping water from nearby communities and for cutting down a forest without permission.

The ASONOG anti-mining campaign "Honduras is worth more than gold" has several objectives. They are

- prohibiting the use of cyanide in mining operations
- prohibiting the expropriation of campesino and indigenous lands
- strengthening mining and environmental laws

Those in favour of expanding mining operations say that Honduras is a poor country that should attract venture capital at all cost. Certainly the new mining regulations encourage investment. The General Mining Law offers companies lifelong concessions, low taxes, unlimited access to water, and legal rights to expropriate campesino and indigenous lands— all with few environmental restrictions.

In December 2000, the International Monetary Fund (IMF) pressured Honduras to reduce taxes even further, by eliminating export tax on mining products. Land use fees are as low as $1500 a year for a large mine, and there is a nominal 1 percent municipal tax.

ACTIVITIES

1 There are two sides to every issue, and the anti-mining campaign in Honduras has a clear agenda. Describe its views in three sentences. Now describe an opposing view. Who might hold this view? Why?

Chapter Review

Points to Remember

- International trade has economic advantages and disadvantages for Canadians.

- International trade gives Canadian access to a wide array of imported goods.

- International business creates new jobs, but may also eliminate certain jobs for Canadians.

- Canada's major trading partners are the United States, Mexico, the European Union, and Asia.

- Free trade agreements create large trading blocs by lowering trade barriers and reducing regulations.

- Some Canadians support free trade because of its economic benefits. Others oppose it because businesses can operate in countries with fewer labour laws and standards.

Activities

Knowledge/Understanding

1   What were the traditional areas of the Canadian economy?

2   What new areas are being developed for international trade by Canadian companies?

3   What is the main purpose of the North American Free Trade Agreement?

4   List the advantages and disadvantages to NAFTA for Canada and Canadians.

5   How have the countries of Western Europe responded to the growing trend of establishing huge trading blocs?

6   What remains the largest untapped market for Canadian international trade?

Thinking/Inquiry

1   What do you think are the most difficult obstacles facing a business that wants to expand into another country? Explain.

2 How has trade affected the quality of goods and services produced by Canadian companies?

   a) Select one of the companies used as examples in *Exploring Business for the 21st Century*. Use the Web Links feature at the McGraw-Hill Ryerson Web site to find out more about these different companies.
   b) Research the impact that imports and exports have on the company and its products.
   c) Write a report explaining this cause and effect situation.

Communication

1 During the call-in portion of a television current affairs show, a caller suggests that there should be no protection of Canadian culture. She suggests that Canadians want American television, music, movies, and magazines, so what, exactly, are we protecting? She goes on to say that free trade agreements have forced other industries to become globally competitive, and that the entertainment industry should be no different. Prepare a panel debate on the issue of preserving Canadian culture and the Canadian entertainment industry. Present your panel discussion for the class.

Skills
Appendix

building an argument

Application

1 Due to price increases from suppliers, a small manufacturer has seen the cost of raw materials rise by 25 percent in the last two years. Costs used to be $100 000 to produce 120 000 units, with a selling price of $3.35 per unit. In addition, other expenses ran consistently at about $100 000 per year. Because the demand for this product is highly elastic and because tariffs have been removed due to NAFTA, prices cannot be raised. Calculate the difference in profit in this business before the costs rose and after the costs rose.

Skills
Appendix

problem solving

2 Use various sources of information, such as television news reports, newspapers, business magazines, and the Internet, to research the status of Canadian business after the implementation of the Canada-United States Free Trade Agreement (FTA) and the North American Free Trade Agreement (NAFTA). Has it had the effect, both good and bad, that people predicted it would have? Write a newspaper article outlining your findings.

Skills
Appendix

research,
writing reports

Analysing Media Skill Helper

Media refers to all the forms of mass communication that you experience every day. Media work describes many types of media production—movies, billboards, books, magazine advertisements, and CD inserts, for example. *Media works* both reflect and influence culture. That is why it is important to critically analyse the messages, and how and why they are produced.

Canadian John Pugente developed the "Key Concepts of Media Literacy" to provide a basis for understanding and analysing media messages. Here are some of his concepts and questions that you can use to analyse media.

1 All media works represent a point of view on reality but they are not reality. They were created by a business or organization for a specific purpose.

Question: What purpose does this media work serve? What is it trying to persuade me of?

2 To a great extent, you learn to interpret the world through the media works that you experience.

Question: What version of reality does this media work represent? How does its message influence my behaviour, attitude, or values?

3 Your own experiences and attitudes also influence the way you view media works.

Question: What is my response? Why am I reacting this way?

4 Many media messages have a commercial purpose.

Question: Who will make money if I believe this message? How is it designed to appeal to me?

5 Media texts contain explicit and implicit messages about values.

Question: What message about values is buried in this media work? Do I agree? Am I being manipulated?

6 Media works have social and political implications.

Question: Are people stereotyped? Do the stereotypes influence the way I interpret people?

7 The form and content of a media text are closely related.

Question: What media conventions are used in this work? What effect is created?

8 Each medium has a unique artistic form.

Question: What elements went into the planning, drafting, and production of this media work?

Brainstorming Skill Helper

What is brainstorming?
It is a strategy to help you generate and investigate new ideas about a topic or solutions to a problem or questions that you need to investigate further

When is brainstorming used?
It is used to collect new ideas, to allow you to use your creative thinking skills, and to think of possible solutions to problems. You can brainstorm on your own or, very productively, with a group of people.

The Do's and Don'ts of a brainstorming session

Do
- Accept all ideas while brainstorming. There are no right or wrong answers or ideas.
- Encourage spontaneous ideas about the subject. Get the creative juices flowing.
- Try to get as many ideas on the subject as you can at this point. Anything even remotely connected to the subject will do fine.
- You can "hitchhike" a new idea onto one that has been suggested already or use one idea as a "springboard" for a new idea.
- Encourage fresh and innovative ideas.
- Listen carefully to the ideas of others.
- Use your own knowledge and experience to contribute to the group session.
- Offer ideas from your own perspective, using the talents and skills that you are best at.
- Designate a member of the group to write down the ideas as they come up. If possible have your recorder write on a blackboard or flip chart so that everyone can see the ideas that have been suggested.

Don't
- Make judgements during a brainstorming session.
- Criticize the ideas of fellow students or co-workers.
- Hold back your own ideas even if you think they are far-fetched. Take the risk and put your idea out there for others to consider.

After the Brainstorming Session
- At the end of the session, evaluate what you have according to the purpose for your brainstorming session.
- Eliminate ideas that won't work for your purposes.
- Select the best ideas for further study, investigation, discussion, or future brainstorming sessions.
- Consider the combination of all of the ideas. Group similar types of ideas together (categorize them) to see how the different groupings would work.

Building an Argument Skill Helper

Guidelines

- Before you begin, make sure you can state your argument clearly in one sentence. Keep working on the sentence until it is as clear as you can make it. Remember that if it is not clear to you, it will not be clear to the people you are trying to convince.
- Assemble all the evidence you can find that supports your argument. If you are going to use facts, quotations, or statistics, make sure that you have understood and reported them correctly.
- Select the three or four best pieces of evidence that support your argument. Do not try to list every possible piece of evidence. Weak evidence will hurt your case.
- Read evidence that goes against your argument so that you know what challenges you face. Don't underestimate this evidence. Think of reasonable responses that you can make.
- Make sure that your basic response to each counter-argument can be stated in one sentence that you can clearly understand.
- Practice your arguments with a friend who will tell you honestly if he or she thinks your arguments are effective. Use the ones that are most effective.
- If you are giving your argument orally, pay attention to your tone of voice, posture, and facial expression, as well as your words. Don't read from your notes; look at your audience and at anyone who is asking you a question.
- If you are giving your argument in a written form, proofread for spelling, grammar, punctuation and usage.

Checklist

- ❏ Can I state my argument in one sentence?
- ❏ Have I assembled enough evidence for my argument? Do I understand it?
- ❏ Have I chosen the best evidence?
- ❏ Have I looked at the evidence that is against my argument and thought of responses?
- ❏ Can I state my basic response in one sentence that is easy to understand?
- ❏ Have I practised my arguments and discovered which ones are most effective?
- ❏ Am I learning to pay attention to my tone of voice, posture, and facial expression, as well as my words. Do I look at my audience?
- ❏ Have I proofread my written material for spelling, grammar, punctuation and usage?

Critical Thinking Skill Helper

Critical thinking can help you work through any situation that is problematic. Having this skill will help you decide what to believe and how to act. When you are trying to make a reasoned judgement, critical thinking allows you to look at possible alternatives and choose the one that is best for you. When you think critically, you analyse, evaluate, and solve problems.

Guidelines

- Do you have enough background information about the subject? Do you need to do further research of some kind to be sure that you have enough information?
- Is your evidence valid? Is it real evidence or is it opinion? Is your evidence objective and factual? Have you got enough evidence to make a reasoned judgement?
- Are your sources reliable? Is there any evidence of bias in your sources or in your conclusion? Are you being fair to everyone involved?
- Have you decided on the criteria that you're going to use to make your judgement and choose among the possible alternatives?
- Will you or your fellow workers actually be able to follow through on your conclusion?
- Will it actually help the situation you're in?
- Have you considered other points of view?
- Are you keeping an open mind to the alternatives to your idea? Can you see the point of view of others who have different ideas and have reached different conclusions?
- Are you willing to familiarize yourself with the different issues and points of view?
- Would a graphic organizer (concept web, cause and effect diagram, flow chart, decision making model) help you visualize, organize` and relate the different aspects of your situation and the problem you're trying to resolve?
- Would talking the situation through with a partner help? Or maybe even a role play?
- Can you accept and respond fairly to people who question your ideas?
- Can you examine your usual way of thinking and are you willing to change when there is convincing evidence to do so?
- Do you examine the short- and long-term consequences of your own and others' actions and words?

Decision-Making Skill Helper

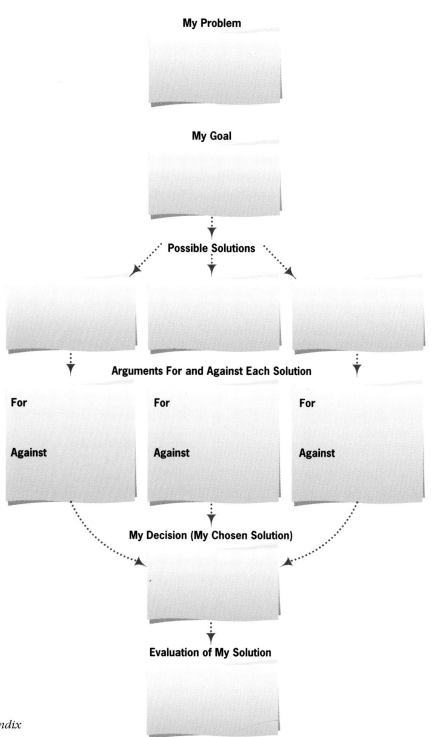

My Problem

My Goal

Possible Solutions

Arguments For and Against Each Solution

For

Against

For

Against

For

Against

My Decision (My Chosen Solution)

Evaluation of My Solution

Oral Presentations Skill Helper

Checklist

Before presenting, have I

- ❏ chosen my topic and made sure that it covers my school or work assignment
- ❏ drawn up a plan that fits my topic, my purpose, and my audience
- ❏ done any research I need to gather more information to support my argument
- ❏ organized my material into an effective opening, body, and conclusion
- ❏ practised my presentation

While presenting, do I

- ❏ use an effective and interesting opening that will explain my main message
- ❏ organize my ideas clearly and logically and use transitions and repetition to keep my audience on track
- ❏ stay focused on my main message, my purpose and my audience all through the presentation
- ❏ support my main message with appropriate evidence using factual details and relevant examples
- ❏ use clear and correct language that suits the purpose and audience of my presentation
- ❏ use a delivery style that is appropriate to my topic, purpose, and audience
- ❏ watch for reactions from my audience and adapt my content and delivery to meet audience needs
- ❏ use visual and audio aids effectively
- ❏ speak loudly enough and slowly enough so that everyone can hear me
- ❏ talk to everyone in the audience and make eye contact
- ❏ use body language and gestures appropriately
- ❏ listen carefully to questions from the audience and answer them respectfully and effectively

Problem-Solving Skill Helper

7 Steps for Problem-solving

1 Clearly identify the problem.

What is the problem? Why is it a problem? For whom is it a problem? What do I know about similar types of problems? What caused them and how were they solved?

2 Collect information about the problem.

Ask people for their point of view. Collect opinions, facts, and evidence, and then evaluate the different points of view. What do the different people who are affected by the problem say are its causes? What evidence do they offer to justify their opinions? What do they suggest is a solution?

3 Identify the main cause or source of the problem.

What is the source of the problem? Is the source what most people think it is, or is it something else? What seems to be the most important cause of the problem? Is it a problem about relationships among people? Could I use my knowledge of technology or science or mathematics to solve this problem? What are the different parts of the problem?

4 Explore possible solutions.

What are some possible solutions to this problem? Can I use or adapt any of the solutions suggested by other people? Is there some new way (that nobody else has suggested) to solve the problem? Are there different angles that I can use to look at the problem? What tools could I use to solve the problem, for example, science, technology, and/or mathematics? Should I do further research into any of these subjects to investigate more possibilities?

5 Evaluate solutions and decide on one.

What are the pros and cons of each of the possible solutions? What would be the short- and long-term effects of each one? Which is the most practical and workable solution in this situation?

6 Put the solution into practice.

How shall I put the solution into effect? What steps should I follow? Should I try it out on a small group of people first?

7 Evaluate the solution once it has been put into practice.

How shall I keep track of the solution to see if it works? Does it work? How could it be improved? How might I put the improvements into practice?

Researching Skill Helper

Guidelines

- Make sure you can state the subject of your research in a single word, phrase, or sentence. Do not start gathering information until you are sure what you are looking for.
- Determine what you already know about the subject. What have you learned in school, from personal reading, from media, and from your own experience?
- Be sure you understand clearly how you will present your findings. Will you need to provide charts? An oral presentation? Audiovisual aids? Footnotes and bibliography? What is the deadline?
- Ensure that you have read carefully and understand clearly all requirements for length, listing of sources, and in the case of an oral presentation, number of minutes allotted.
- Establish how you will find the information that you do not now have. Library? Internet resources? Interview? Be sure to allow yourself time to accomplish these tasks.
- Keep your topic in mind to ensure that you do not spend a lot of time collecting information you will not need. Keep track of where you found your information.
- Go over your work to make sure you have found everything you need to write your report. Review the information to make sure that it is reliable, accurate, and up-to-date.
- Summarize what you have learned in your conclusion.

Checklist

- ❏ Am I sure of the subject of my research? Can I state it clearly in a single word, phrase or sentence?
- ❏ Have I included what I have learned in school, from personal reading, from media, and from my own experience?
- ❏ Have I established which components my presentation must include?
- ❏ Have I read clearly and do I understand all the requirements for the way my research will be presented and when?
- ❏ Do I know how I am going to find the information I do not now have? Have I allowed enough time?
- ❏ Am I sticking to my topic while researching? Have I recorded my source for everything?
- ❏ Have I found everything I need to write my report? Have I reviewed my information to make sure that it is reliable, accurate, and up-to-date?
- ❏ Have I written a conclusion that summarizes what I have learned?

Working in Groups Skill Helper

You've heard the old saying that "two heads are better than one." In reality, this is only true when two—or more—people work effectively together. Groups who know how to work together effectively to accomplish a goal are far more effective than one person alone. But groups that do not know how to work together effectively can be *less* effective than one person alone.

Guidelines

- Make sure that every member of the group understands the purpose for which the group is meeting.
- Begin by brainstorming the best way to accomplish that purpose. Don't leave it to one person to decide everything.
- Assign members of the group to specific tasks to ensure that the purpose is accomplished. These might include a discussion leader, a recorder, and a monitor who ensures that everyone gets a chance to be heard.
- Agree that everyone will speak respectfully to everyone else, even if they disagree.
- Allow honest discussion, even if it means hearing some things that you would rather not hear.
- If you are deciding on a plan of action, make sure that everyone's opinion is heard and considered before a vote is taken or a consensus is reached.
- If there is serious disagreement about the goal or plan, ensure that a consensus is reached and that everyone agrees to go along with the final decision.
- Make sure that everyone who helped in a project is given credit for what they did.

Checklist

- ❑ Did we make sure that every member of the group understands the purpose for which the group is meeting?
- ❑ Did we begin by brainstorming the best way to accomplish that purpose?
- ❑ Did we assign members of the group to specific tasks to ensure that the purpose is accomplished?
- ❑ Did we all speak respectfully to each other, even when we disagreed?
- ❑ Did we allow honest discussion, even when we didn't necessarily want to hear a different view?
- ❑ Did we make sure that everyone's opinion was heard and considered before a vote was taken or a consensus was reached?
- ❑ Did we ensure that everyone agreed to go along with the final decision?
- ❑ Did we make sure that everyone who helped in a project was given credit for what they did?

Writing Reports

What is a report?

A report is an account of what you have learned about a subject. It's a place for facts, not opinions. A report should be objective. It should have a clear subject, a firm purpose, and a focus on your audience.

How do I plan a report?

- Know what your purpose is. Write out a statement of that purpose. Why are you writing the report? What do you want your readers to do with the material in your report?
- Know who your audience is. What do they already know about your subject? What will they expect your report to do for them?
- Focus your subject clearly and let your readers know the limits of your subject. Is everything in your report related to your subject?
- Research your subject. Do you have enough facts? Do you need outside resources? What kind of resources will be of the most help to you?

How do I write the report?

- Organize your material so that it presents a clear argument with a solid conclusion. Keep your readers on track so that they know where you are going.
- Know what your main idea is and the evidence you will need to support your main idea. Write a clear introduction and then support it with clear evidence.
- Try out different organizing tools—comparison, cause-and effect, description or analysis. Would a graphic organizer help you organize your ideas?
- Write a first draft. Then revise and edit that draft until your report is clear and focused on your purpose and audience.

What is the format for a report?

- Open with a clear statement of the purpose for your report. Summarize that purpose and your main idea at the beginning.
- Give your readers any background that they will need to have.
- Discuss your findings in the middle part of your report.
- Finish your report with a clear conclusion and perhaps recommend some action to be taken by your reader.

Glossary

accounting the system used by an organization to keep a record of all the money that comes in and goes out.

accounts payable the money that the business owes to other businesses that supply it with goods or services.

accounts receivable money for which a company has billed its customers, but has not yet received payment.

advertising any paid use by an identified sponsor to inform a target market about a product, service, idea, or organization.

affirmative action the process of improving employment practices so that they are fair to people who may have been discriminated against in the past.

AIDA an acronym for four steps of the basic selling approach (*attract* attention; hold *interest*; arouse *desire*; take *action* to close the sale).

annual fee a yearly charge.

appreciate to go up in value.

aptitude natural talents, tendencies, or capacities.

Asia-Pacific Region the market consisting of Asian countries along the Pacific Rim and in South-East Asia.

assessment evaluation.

assets anything a company or person owns that has a dollar value.

baby boom generation the large group of people born between 1947 – 1965.

balance of payment the total flow of money into a country minus the total flow of money leaving the country.

balance of trade comparison between a country's total value of imports and the total value of its exports.

balance sheet a financial statement that shows the company's assets, liabilities, and net worth on a given date.

bankruptcy a legal situation in which a company (or individual) declares that it cannot pay its debts and must sell assets and suffer some penalties.

benefits the financial and psychological value of a job apart from income. Financially, it includes insurance and health insurance.

blue chip successful and profitable companies.

bonds a certificate offered by a company or government promising to repay money borrowed and to pay it back with interest on a certain date.

bonus extra amount of money paid to employees, usually once a year.

brand name the name that identifies the goods or services of one business.

budget a plan of how to spend money.

business the production and sale of goods or services to consumers.

business cycle the movement from prosperity to inflation to recession to depression and then to recovery.

business-to-business the exchange of goods and services between businesses.

business plan an important tool that describes how you will use your business ideas to achieve your business goals.

Canada Savings Bond (CSB) a certificate issued by the federal government promising to repay an amount of money at a given time and at a given rate of interest. CSBs may be purchased by individuals.

capital money available for investment purposes such as starting a business and keeping it running.

capital improvement upgrading of a tangible property.

channel of distribution the path a product takes from the manufacturer to the final consumer.

collection agency a company hired to collect overdue accounts from customers.

common shares the units investors purchase to buy part of a company and have a claim on its profits. Dividends are paid on common shares after those for preferred shares. Also known as stocks. Common shares give investors a vote at the annual meeting.

communication the ability to explain ideas and ask appropriate questions.

comparative advantage a theory that states that some countries are better equipped than others to make and sell particular goods or services.

compensation payment and benefits when used in relation to employees, can includes wages and benefits.

competition a situation in which two people or companies try to achieve the same end.

complementary goods goods that are used with one another.

compounding period a set length of time in which an account is credited with interest.

confidence belief in own abilities.

consolidate put together.

consumer someone who purchases goods and services to meet needs and wants.

consumer credit money borrowed for mortgages and personal loans and when using credit cards.

consumer protection a situation in which the federal and provincial governments try to protect consumers by making sure that the buying and selling of goods and services is fair.

controlling ensuring that company performance is going as planned.

convergence a process in which two or more separate technologies come together to form a new one or to perform new functions, and which the old technologies could not do on their own.

co-operative businesses owned and operated by a group of people with a strong common interest.

corporation a legal business entity that exists independently of its owners.

co-sign another person signs a borrowing agreement and promises to pay debt if the borrower cannot do so.

creativity a quality of developing ideas and expressing them in some tangible form.

credit bureau a company that gathers and provides information on credit history.

credit history the history of paying back debts.

credit rating the reputation for paying back money owing.

crown corporation a legal business entity that exists independently of its owners. Crown indicates that it is owned by federal, provincial, or municipal governments. It usually provides a special service to the public.

debentures a sealed bond issued by a corporation, usually to get a long-term fixed-interest loan.

decision-making taking action.

deductions the money an employer takes from an employee's salary to cover taxes and benefits.

default a failure to pay.

deflation a business situation in which costs and prices fall.

demand the desire for goods and services. It represents the consumer side of the market.

demography the study of statistics relating to populations or communities.

depreciate to drop in value.

depression a period in the business cycle when economic activity is very low and unemployment is very high.

development a long process of upgrading an employee's ability to perform.

direct competition the rivalry that exists when two or more businesses produce similar goods or services.

direct mail promotional material such as advertising pamphlets, brochures, leaflets and flyers that are delivered in the mail.

discretionary income the amount of money left after all compulsory deductions are taken from gross income and after required expenditures, such as taxes, are paid for. This money is available for a person to spend as they wish.

discrimination unfair treatment on the basis of a characteristic such as race, sex, national or ethnic origin, age, marital status, or disability.

disposable income the amount of money left from gross income after compulsory deductions have been taken.

dot-com company a company that does business on the internet or helps other companies offer products or services over the internet.

Dow Jones Industrial Average the oldest and most famous measure of stock performance.

down payment a sum of money paid at the time of a purchase, usually on a large purchase such as a house. (It lessens the amount the purchaser must borrow to pay the total cost.)

e-business short-form for "electronic business," business that is conducted over the Internet.

economy made up of contributions from business, labour, and the government. The wealth and resources of a community.

embargo a total restriction on trading with another country, can be placed on all goods or on some categories of goods.

emotional quotient degree of emotional health and expressed in self-awareness, altruism, personal motivation, empathy, and ability to love and be loved.

employability skills skills you must have to succeed in business. Skills are abilities that can be acquired by repetition.

employment working for a company or organization.

entrepreneur a person who organizes, manages, and assumes the risk of starting and operating an enterprise.

entrepreneurship the activity of people who bring together all the factors to start a business.

equal opportunity the right to freedom from discrimination in areas such as employment.

equilibrium the point where the forces of supply and the forces of demand are balanced.

ethics standards of conduct that society believes people should follow.

European Union a bloc of 15 European countries in primarily an economic partnership.

The Union does also have political and social objectives.

expenses the amount of money an organization or individual spends to run an operation. In business, it includes wages to employees, cost of supplies, taxes, and payments on loans.

exporting the selling and shipping of raw materials or finished products to other nations.

extranet a network of computers a company has with selected suppliers that allows the company to share information with selected suppliers or with other businesses.

factors of production items required to produce goods and services including land, capital, labour, information, and entrepreneurship.

false advertising saying a product will do something when it will not.

finance the managing of money.

financial institutions companies and organizations that are permitted to hold savings deposits, offer loans and mortgages, issue credit ratings, exchange currency and offer stocks and bonds for sale.

financial instruments a tool used by financial institutions to provide services. They include investments such as savings accounts, GICs, bonds, stocks, mutual funds.

financial management process of deciding how to use money.

financial plan forecast of how much money is needed to achieve a given financial goal.

financial statements formal documents that use a standard format to provide the key information about a company's financial position.

fiscal year an accounting year for an organization is a period of 12 consecutive months, at the end of which the business produces is annual financial statements.

flexibility ability to change goals and adapt plans.

foreign exchange rate a rate that rules how much of another country's currency your country's currency will buy.

foreign subsidiary a company from one country operating in another country.

franchise a type of business in which a person buys the right to use a business name and to sell a product or service. The purchaser must follow the franchise owner's rules in operating the company.

Free Trade Agreement (FTA) a treaty between Canada and the United States that took effect in 1989 and by 1999 removed all tariffs on the sale of goods to each other.

Free Trade Area of the Americas (FTAA) the group of North and South American countries (all of them except for Cuba) that are trying to develop freer trade and more cooperation among themselves.

front-line employees the employees who work directly with customers, taking orders, helping them find what they want, responding to complaints, and helping solve problems.

fundamental accounting equation an equation that accounting is based on where the two sides must balance.

future value amount that will be earned because of the interest that is added to the original amount saved.

G8 the Group of Eight, an association of the world's most powerful trading countries. Canada is a member.

garnisheed money removed from a pay cheque.

generally accepted accounting principles (GAAPs) the guidelines developed by professional accountants for the way accounting records and financial statements are prepared.

globalization doing business internationally.

good any tangible item or product that you can purchase, possess, and use.

gross domestic product (GDP) the annual total value of final market goods produced and services provided in a country.

gross pay pay or wages before deductions.

guarantee formal promise or assurance, that an obligation will be fulfilled or that goods are of a specified quality and durability.

guaranteed investment certificate (GIC) guarantees a fixed interest rate on a sum of money deposited at the financial institution for a fixed term.

harassment repeatedly annoying someone.

health and safety program a preventative, includes training for workers, regular inspections by professionals in the health and safety field, a process for reacting swiftly to accidents and injuries.

human resources the aspect of business operations that deals with attracting and keeping employees.

illegal pricing a practice that lessens competition and gives consumers less choice than they should have.

importing the buying of raw materials or finished products from other nations in order to use them in the home country.

income also known as revenue, earnings by an individual or business from a variety of sources.

income statement the financial statement that reports a business's income and expenses for a fiscal period.

income tax an amount of money the federal government requires those who earn income (individuals and corporations) to pay to it. It is used to pay for government and government programs.

indirect competition competing with other businesses selling different goods, also known as substitute competition.

inflation refers to a rise, over time, in the price of goods and services.

information knowledge. The development of computers and other technologies has made knowledge an important factor in business because so much can be gathered and shared.

information interviews a formal way of talking with people, in hopes of having all your questions answered.

infrastructure a system that makes a nation or organization run.

initiative ability to take action without the prompting of others.

innovator a person who adapts an existing good or service to improve it or its appeal to current consumers.

installment plan a loan granted by or through a retailer for an expensive purchase that can be repaid at set intervals over a period of time.

integrity the personal commitment to keep promises.

interdependence the dependence between two parties such as consumers and producers

interest rate the rate a financial institution charges for the money it lends.

interest money paid for the use of money.

intranet a network of computers connected within a company.

inventor a person who creates new devices or services by assembling previously unrelated elements in a new way, or who develops a good or service so different from the original that it requires a new name and is clearly separate and distinct.

investment a financial tool in which one puts money for a period of time in exchange for a chance to earn interest.

ISO Standards the benchmarks set by the International Organization for Standardization to help companies develop and maintain widely accepted standards of quality and measurements.

job description a description of the requirements to perform a job and the responsibilities of the job.

labelling the part of packaging that provides the consumer with information, such as product ingredients.

labour includes all mental and physical work that people put into producing goods and services.

labour movement the efforts by workers, often in organized groups such a unions, to protect workers' health, safety, and rights.

land natural resources used to produce goods and services.

law of demand a situation in the market in which the level of demand for a good or service influences prices. High demand tends to lead to higher prices, while low demand often means lower prices.

law of supply a situation in the market in which the price of a good or service influences the level of production. Producers increase the level when the price rises and reduce it if the price drop too low.

leadership ability to inspire others to follow their example in a positive way.

leading setting a direction.

limit the amount of money a financial institution is willing to let a consumer borrow.

limited liability the extent to which shareholders are responsible for a company's debts. It is the same as their financial involvement.

liquid asset assets such as bonds, GICs, and term deposits, that can be quickly turned into cash.

management the planning, organizing, and controlling of all business activities.

manufacturer the company or business that produces goods.

market a place where buyers and sellers come together to do business, the buyers with money to exchange for the goods or services offered by the sellers.

market niche a small segment of a larger market.

market research the gathering and analysing of data to provide a business with information on consumers' needs and wants.

marketing all the business activities used to plan, price, promote, and distribute goods or services to satisfy consumer needs and wants.

marketing mix product, promotion, place, and price.

misleading advertising distorting the truth about the goods being offered.

mortgage loan to buy a house or a business.

motivating encouraging employees to act using positive or negative methods or a mix of both. This is external motivation. Internal motivation or influences comes from within.

mutual fund an investment fund in which the contributions of many individuals are combined and invested by a professional fund manager in a variety of stocks and bonds.

natural resources a material available in nature that has the potential to be of economic value.

needs a good or service that is essential for life and in business describes a factor that motivates individuals to act.

net pay money available to spend after compulsory and voluntary deductions are taken off gross pay.

net worth the difference between what one owns and what one owes.

networking the process of meeting people in a semi-formal or informal environment and telling them what you need in a conversational way.

non-profit corporation a legal business entity that is not organized to make a profit. Purpose is to undertake fundraising, do research, or lobby for a cause in order to help people.

non-tariff barriers a method, other than taxes, of reducing the quantity and value of foreign-made goods that come into the country.

North American Free Trade Agreement (NAFTA) an agreement among Mexico, Canada, and the United States that took effect in 1994 and is similar to the Free Trade Agreement.

objectives goals set by management.

organizing creating the structure and the right systems to implement the plan.

owner's equity amount of money the owner invested when starting the business, plus any accumulated profits or minus any accumulated losses.

packaging the container or wrapper for a product, the design of the container and the information printed on the container.

partnership a form of business organization in which two or more people own and operate the business together. The business is unincorporated.

patent a legal registration process that ensures exclusive rights to make, use, or sell an invention for a specific number of years.

pension income employees receive after they have retired.

per capita a Latin term meaning by each head or person.

performance standards specific, measurable, easy-to-communicate expectations that are used as part of the process in assessing employees' performance.

perseverance the determination to keep going and keep trying.

personal line of credit a permanent offer of a loan from a bank, trust company, or credit union.

personal performance doing more than is needed just to keep the job.

personal selling any one-to-one communication of information that tries to persuade a customer to buy a good, service or idea.

planning first critical step for managers. Involves forecasting the future and begins with research.

portfolio a group of investments usually in reference to those held by one person.

pre-authorization a financial institution's guarantee that it will advance the customer an agreed amount of money, usually for a major purchase.

pre-authorized payments agreeing to allow a company or government to deduct money on a regular basis from your chequing account.

preferred shares the units, or stocks, investors purchase to buy part of a company and have a claim on its profits. Owners are entitled to a fixed dividend that must be paid out of earnings before any dividend is paid to common share-owners. Owners do not have a vote at annual meetings.

principal an original amount before interest charges are added.

private corporation a legal business entity in which shares are not offered to the public.

producer someone who makes goods or provides services.

product recall the call back of a product usually because it poses a health or safety risk.

production the process of converting a business's resources into goods and services.

profit the amount by which the revenue of a business exceeds its expenses.

promotion informs consumers about a product or service and encourages them to buy it.

property tax the amount of tax property owners pay. It is used to cover the cost of municipal services.

prosperity a period in the business cycle of good economic times. Businesses are producing a significant level of wealth.

protectionism the efforts of a country to keep out foreign-made goods.

public corporation does not have restrictions on its number of shareholders.

public relations all the activities by which a business tries to maintain its good reputation and promote good will with the public.

publicity the act of bringing company activities to the attention of the public.

quality control a process for determining which products can be sold and which rejected. It is done by comparing them to pre-set standards.

quality of life includes peoples' material standard of living and a number of social and environmental factors.

questionnaires sometimes called a survey, is a way to get a number of answers and opinions from a selected group of people.

quota a limit on the number of products in a category that can come into a country. It is used to keep foreign-made goods out of the country.

recession a period in the business cycle when the whole economy slows down and business no longer creates as much wealth.

recovery a period in an business cycle when the economy starts to improve.

recruitment the process of attempting to hire an employee or enrol someone in a program.

research and development a department in a company devoted to doing the experiments required to develop new goods or services or adapt existing ones.

retailer one who sells goods or services directly to consumers.

return the amount of money earned on an investment.

revenue the money a business receives from the sale of goods and services.

risk-tolerance the ability to take calculated risks, to decide that the opportunity for success outweighs the possibility of failure.

sales promotion all the activities a business does to stimulate buying.

sales tax an amount of money paid on retail purchases.

saving putting away a portion of income today, in order to have money for the future.

selection the process whereby a company chooses an employee from a group of candidates.

self-actualization self-fulfillment.

services helpful acts performed in exchange for pay.

service charges the fees charged for transactions.

shareholders people who buy stocks in a company and so are part owners of the company.

small business a business that is independently operated, not dominant in its field, and meets certain size limits in terms of employees and annual sales.

social assistance programs that provide income for people unable to work due to illness, layoffs, or age.

social responsibility the duty to care for others whose actions can be affected in a damaging way.

sole proprietorship a form of business owned and operated by one person. It is unincorporated.

standard of living a measurement of the number and quality of goods and services that the members of a country or community enjoy.

stocks the money organizations raise by selling ownership in the company in the form of shares.

stock option shares in a company.

structure the arrangement of positions in a company based on who is responsible for what.

substitute goods a good that can easily be replaced by another.

supply the quantity of goods and services that producers and sellers are willing or able to sell consumers.

systems procedures that will help a company achieve its goals.

target market a group of consumers the business wants to reach.

tariff barriers a tax on goods coming into a country. It is intended to reduce the quantity and value of foreign-made goods that come into the country.

tax credit an amount of money that can be deducted from tax payable.

tax shelter a financial device that keeps money from being counted as income for the purpose of computing income tax.

taxable income net income of an individual or a for-profit organization.

telecommute working from home and sending work through the Internet.

telemarketing alternative to personal selling, using telephone technology including facsimile machines to maintain regular contact with customers.

total income income from all sources.

trade bloc a zone in which trading occurs without restriction between and among countries.

trademark a registered brand name.

trading partner two or more countries who do business with each other in exports and imports.

training a program that improves a person's ability to perform job skills. It is given over a set length of time.

transnational companies companies that use raw materials and labour from many countries to make their products.

transportation costs the costs of moving raw materials and finished products from one location to another.

trend a pattern over time.

TSE 300 the Canadian index that reflects the share price of 300 Canadian companies list on the Toronto Stock Exchange.

unemployment a condition in which people are out of work and actively looking for work.

unlimited liability a condition in which a person is responsible for paying all the debts or liabilities of the business.

vision ability to visualize end results or goals and work toward making them real.

wants a desire for goods or services that are not essential for basic life and in business describe a factor that motivates individuals to act.

warranty provides after-sales service on a product for a specified period of time.

wholesaler one who buys goods and services in order to sell them to other businesses for resale.

worker's compensation payment of benefits to injured workers.

Credits

Photo Credits

p. 2 left, CORBIS/MAGMA PHOTO; p. 2 right, Courtesy of Canadian Tire Corporation; p. 3, © AFP/CORBIS/MAGMA PHOTO; p. 7, Photo appears Courtesy of the Saturn Corporation; p. 10, Courtesy of Marks Work Warehouse; p. 13, FOR BETTER OR FOR WORSE © UPS Reprinted by Permission; p. 14, Eastcott/Momatiuk/VALAN PHOTOS; p. 15, Courtesy of The Body Shop Canada; p. 17, First Light; p. 18, CORBIS/MAGMA; p. 20, Courtesy of Grocery Gateway; p. 23, © AFP/CORBIS/MAGMA PHOTO; p. 24, Summers © Tribune Media Services; p. 29 top, Photo Courtesy of TELUS Mobility Corporate Communications; p. 29 bottom, Photo Courtesy of TELUS Mobility Corporate Communications; p. 34, Copyright © 2001 Universal Press Syndicate; p. 35, Michael Polselli; p. 37, Courtesy of Inco; p. 38, Comstock; p. 39, Courtesy Nortel Networks; p. 41, Printed with permission from Co-op Atlantic; p. 42, Courtesy of Mountain Equipment Co-op; p. 44, Courtesy of Yogen Fruz Canada; p. 46, PhotoDisc; p. 47, © AFP/CORBIS/MAGMA PHOTO; p. 50, Courtesy of the author; p. 52, Avid Technology; p. 53, Eastcott/Momatiuk/VALAN PHOTOS; p. 55, Andrew Vaughan/CP Picture Archive; p. 57, Bebeto Matthews/AP Photo/CP Picture Archive; p. 58, Courtesy of Apple Canada Inc.; p. 63, Courtesy of Canadian Tire Corporation; p. 64, Courtesy of Canadian Tire Corporation; p. 66, © N. Piluke/Ivy Images; p. 68, Courtesy of Maritime Life, photo: Kim Stallknecht; p. 70, Courtesy of Foster Parents Plan; p. 72, TJP Photography; p. 73, United Way/Photo Credit: James Ip; p. 78, Courtesy of Talvest Mutual Funds and Diesel Marketing, Photographer: Ron Felhien; p. 80, Museum of the City of New York/Archive Photos; p. 81, Nick Brancaccio/ Windsor Star/CP Picture Archive; p. 82, Andrew Tolson/ National Post; p. 83, Mike Pinder/Maclean's/CP Picture Archive; p. 84, Mike Blake/Reuters; p. 86, © Vern McGrath/ Valan Photos; p. 87, © Phillip Norton/Valan Photos; p. 89, Jim Rankin/Toronto Star/CP Picture Archive; p. 97, J. Armand Bombardier Museum; p. 97, J. Armand Bombardier Museum; p. 98, J. Armand Bombardier Museum; p. 99, Courtesy Via Rail Canada; p. 101, Glenn Lowson/National Post; p. 102, Courtesy of Ebay; p. 103, Courtesy of Mark McLane/Printer Works; p. 104, Courtesy of Jones Soda; p. 106, Courtesy of Atlantis Submarines; p. 108, Courtesy of Business Development Bank of Canada (BDC); p. 109, Rob Simpson/Valan Photos; p. 110, MAGMA PHOTO; p. 112, Courtesy of FACES; p. 114, Dick Hemingway; p. 117, © Reuters NewMedia Inc./CORBIS/ MAGMA PHOTO; p. 118, © Robert B. McGouey/Ivy Images; p. 121, Web page courtesy of Radical Entertainment, Inc. Design and implementation by Simon Paul and Jon Vandermeer; p. 122, Web page courtesy of Radical Entertainment, Inc. Design and implementation by Simon Paul and Jon Vandermeer; p. 127, Photo courtesy of Christine Lomas; p. 138, North Nahinni Naturalist Lodge Ltd/Business Development Bank of Canada; p. 140, Library of Congress LC-USZ62-95653; p. 142, John Larter/Artizans; p. 145, © Competition Bureau, Industry Canada, www.strategis.gc.ca; p. 148, David Tanaka Photos; p. 151, Colin Corneau for The Toronto Star; p. 152, Colin Corneau for the Toronto Star; p. 134, © Richard Nowitz/Valan Photos; p. 157, The Toronto Star/K. Faught; p. 158, Jobs Canada; p. 159, Wayne Cuddington/Ottawa Citizen/CP Picture Archive; p. 165, FOR BETTER OR FOR WORSE © UPS Reprinted by Permission.; p. 166, © Roger Ressmeyer/ CORBIS/MAGMA PHOTO; p. 172, Stephen Chung; p171, Courtesy of Grand & Toy; p. 173, © Frank Chmura/First Light; p. 186, www.weblife2000.com; p. 186, Blue Cat Design Inc., www.bluecatdesign.com; p. 189, Dick Hemingway; p. 198, © Jeff Greenberg/Valan Photos; p. 199, Benny Sieu/Milwaukee Journal Sentinel/CP Picture Archive; p. 202, Illustrations by Simon Tuckett of Roboshop/IMAGINEX; 202, Illustrations by Simon Tuckett of Roboshop/IMAGINEX; p. 201, Photography by Hunter Freeman/Goodby, Silverstein and Partners; p. 203, Courtesy of Yogen Fruz Canada; p. F7-18, The Toronto Star/V. Talotta; p. 206, Chuck Stoody/CP Picture Archive; p. 208, Courtesy of the Canadian Marketing Association; p. 215, Johh Alexander/Net Gain Communications Consultants; p. 218, Hudson's Bay Company Archives, PAM-P385; p. 232, Used with permission of MYOB Canada Inc.; p. 233, Noel Ford/Cartoon Stock; p. 247, Take Stock Inc.; p. 254, Chuck Stoody/CP Picture Archive; p. 257, FOR BETTER OR FOR WORSE © UPS Reprinted by Permission.; p. 265, Courtesy of Wildflower Farm; p. 318, Edward Regan/Globe and Mail/CP Picture Archive; p. 327, The Image Bank; p. 328, Toronto Eaton Centre, The Cadillac Fairview Corporation Ltd./Ivy Images; p. 9/335, Reprinted with special permission of King Feature Syndicate; p. 349, Courtesy of Mark Cullen; p. 350, Peter Bregg/Maclean's/CP Picture Archive; p. 355, Phil Snel/Maclean's/CP Picture Archive; p. 355, Courtesy of Feel Good Cars; p. 358, FOR BETTER OR FOR WORSE © UPS Reprinted by Permission.; p. 359, Courtesy of Rogers Communication; p. 362, Jeff McIntosh/CP Picture Archive; p. 364, Photo by Mr. Lynn Ball/Ottawa Citizen; p. 366, Courtesy of Canada One, www.canadaone.com; p. 381, Used with permission of Odd Noggins; p. 373, © Sandy Felsenthal/CORBIS/MAGMA PHOTO; p. 375, SNAP2 Corporation; p. 376, Courtesy of Daniel Ross/Ross Screenprint; p. 377, Courtesy of SleepCountry Canada; p. 379, Photo: Francesco Bellomo © Cirque du Soleil Inc.; p. 387, Dick Hemingway; p. 391, Credit?; p. 399, Courtesy of Mathis Instruments Ltd.; p. 402, Photo by Diane Sewell/Stratford Beacon Herald; p. 403, CLOSE TO HOME © John McPherson. Reprinted with permission of UNIVERSAL PRESS SYNDICATE. All rights reserved.; p. 403, Sam Morris/AP Photo/CP Picture Archive; p. 404, Courtesy of Ron Foxcroft, Fox 40 International Inc.; p. 405, Courtesy of Spin Master Toys; p. 410, PhotoDisc; p. 407, Courtesy of Antarti.ca; p. 407, Courtesy of Antarti.ca; p. F15-14, AP Photo/CP Picture Archive; p. 421, Courtesy of Mr. K.Y. Ho and ATI Technologies Inc.; p. 423, © John Slater/ CORBIS/MAGMA PHOTO; p. 423, © Michael S. Yamashita/CORBIS/MAGMA PHOTO; p. 425, © AFP/CORBIS/MAGMA PHOTO; p. 432, © Vittoriano Rastelli/CORBIS; p. 433, MAGMA PHOTO; p. 433, Ivy Images; p. 434, © Jeff Greenberg/Valan Photos; p. 439, Fred Chartrand/CP Picture Archive; p. 445, Courtesy of Viceroy Homes; p. 445, © Paul A. Souders/ CORBIS/MAGMA PHOTO; 447, Courtesy Toyota Canada; p. 448, Dick Hemingway; p. 449, © Reed Kaestner/CORBIS/MAGMA PHOTO; p. 449, © AFP/ CORBIS/MAGMA PHOTO; p. 452, © Annie Griffiths Belt/CORBIS/MAGMA PHOTO; p. 454, Paul Chiasson/CP Picture Archive; p. 455, Daniel Maurer/AP Photo/CP Picture Archive; p. 456, © Kevin R. Morris/CORBIS/MAGMA PHOTO; p. 456, Dick Hemingway; p. 457, Courtesy of IMAX; p. 458, Courtesy of Sony Films

Text Credits

P. 17, Excerpts from Peebles, Tanya, "A Woman's Attitude: How It Affects an Automaker," *Contemporary Women's Issues Collection*, February 1, 1995, Vol 7, pp. 14-16; p. 33, *Understanding Canadian Business*, McGraw-Hill Ryerson Limited, © 2000, p. 169; p. 46, Adapted from Jennifer Hunter, "Kitchen-table tycoons," *The Maclean's Guide to Personal Finance*, January 1, 1999, p. 87; pp. 48-49, Adapted from PBS Technology Timeline 1752-1990, "American Experience"; p. 63, "35 Best Companies to Work For" by Andrea Gordon, *Report on Business*, February 2000; p. 70, *Marketing Magazine*, Vol 103, September 7, 1998, p. 16; p. 76-77, Conference Board of Canada Employability Skills 2000+; p. 80, Excerpt from "True Stories," Young Worker Awareness Program, www.yworker.com, Workplace Safety & Insurance Board; p. 104, Canadian Population by Age, adapted from the Statistics Canada CANSIM Database, http://www.statcan.ca/ english/CANSIM/cansim1.htm, Matrix No 6367; p. 116, StreetCents, Canadian Broadcasting Corporation; p. 132, Statistics Canada; p. 146, Health Canada; p. 139, Statistics Canada; p. 151, Reprinted with permission — *The Toronto Star Syndicate*; p. 179, Adapted from "Do men and women thrive under different management styles?"; p. 161, Adapted from "Bue Chip Help is Hot," by Dana Flavelle, *The Toronto Star*, November 20, 2000, p. E1.; p. 163, "Lifelong learning on the knowledge highway," Office of Learning Technologies, Human Resources Development Canada, http://olt-bta.hrdc-drhc.gc.ca; p. 174, The Conference Board of Canada Employability Kills Toolkit; p. 192, "Ads 101: Wisecracks—and work," by John Heinzl, *The Globe and Mail*, January 12, 2001, p. M1; p. 197, *Understanding Canadian Business*, McGraw-Hill Ryerson Limited, © 2000, p. 549; p. 252, Statistics Canada, 1996 Census Nation Tables; p. 252, Statistics Canada; p. 258, Statistics Canada, Catalogue No. 82F0075XCB; p. 269, Statistics Canada; p. 275, Canada

Index